Religion in America

THE MYSTERY HID

FROM

AGES AND GENERATIONS

Charles Chauncy

ARNO PRESS & THE NEW YORK TIMES

New York 1969

Reprint edition 1969 by Arno Press, Inc.

*

Library of Congress Catalog Card No. 70-83414

*

Reprinted from a copy in
The New York State Library

*

Manufactured in the United States of America

*The Mystery hid from Ages and Generations,
made manifest by the Gospel-Revelation :*

O R ,

THE SALVATION

O F

ALL MEN

THE GRAND THING AIMED AT IN THE
SCHEME OF GOD,

As opened in the New-Teftament Writings, and entrufted
with JESUS CHRIST to bring into Effect.

ERRATUM.

P. 384, line 1, *for* deſtroyed *read* puniſhed.

The Myſtery hid from Ages and Generations, made manifeſt by the Goſpel-Revelation:

OR,

THE SALVATION

OF

ALL MEN

THE GRAND THING AIMED AT IN THE
SCHEME OF GOD,

As opened in the New-Teſtament Writings, and entruſted
with JESUS CHRIST to bring into Effect.

IN THREE CHAPTERS.

The Firſt, exhibiting a GENERAL EXPLANATION of this glo-
riouſly benevolent Plan of GOD.——*The Second,* proving
it to be the TRUTH OF SCRIPTURE, that MANKIND
UNIVERSALLY, in the FINAL ISSUE of this Scheme, ſhall
REIGN IN HAPPY LIFE FOR EVER.——*The Third,* largely
anſwering OBJECTIONS.

By *One who wiſhes well to the whole Human Race.*

Ωσπερ εϐασιλευσεν η αμαρ]ια εν τω θανα]ω ου]ω και η χαρις
βασιλευση δια δικαιοσυνης εις ζωην αιωνιον, δια Ιησου
Χριστου του Κυριου ημων.   Apoſtle *Paul.*

LONDON:
PRINTED FOR CHARLES DILLY, IN THE POULTRY.

M.DCC.LXXXIV.

THE

PREFACE.

THE *whole human race* are considered, in the following work, as made for *happiness*; and it *finally* fixes them in the everlasting enjoyment of it, notwithstanding the *lapse of the one man Adam*, and all the *sin* and *misery* that ever has been, or ever will be, consequent thereupon. The *subject* is certainly interesting and important; and if what I have offered to ascertain its *meaning*, and justify its *truth*, is worthy of regard, there can be no need of an *apology* for its *publication*. This must be left with the reader to determine : Though, whatever his judgment is, I may be allowed to say for myself, that I have gone through a great deal of hard labour in *searching the scrip-*

tures,

tures, that I might be able to put together what is here prefented to his view. I had indeed no idea of the fentiments expreffed in the following pages, till I had been gradually and infenfibly let into them by a long and diligent comparing of *fcripture with fcripture.* What I therefore now offer to the world is not the refult of *my own imagination,* or *wifdom :* Nor was it fetched from any *fcheme of man's invention;* but *folely* from the fountain of revealed truth, the *infpired oracles of God.* Thefe were my *governing rule* in this enquiry ; and I have taken great care, and fpared no pains, that I might underftand them in their *genuine fenfe.* And it appears to me that I have really done fo : Though I am far from expecting, or defiring, that any fhould implicitly take my word for it. Nay, I fhould be heartily forry, if any one fhould be fo unadvifed as to receive what is here delivered, either in whole, or in part, for *facred truth,* till he has thoroughly examined the *texts* that are brought to fupport it as fuch, and is inwardly *convinced* thereupon that

they

they are a real and juft fupport of it. His
faith will then reft upon the word of him
who is *faithful and true*; and he may
pleafe himfelf with the thought, that he
has acted a *reafonable part*, and will certainly meet with the *approbation* of his Maker
and Judge.

I am not infenfible, that, in a performance of this nature, where the *proof* is
of the *moral kind*, and depends upon a
variety of *circumftances* duly adjufted and
fituated with refpect to each other, there
will be always room left for *difference* of
fentiment in different perfons, according
to the *difference* there may be in their temper of mind, manner of education, condition in life, freedom in the exercife of their
faculties, attachment to names, religious
fyftems, and the like. It would not therefore be a matter of wonder to me, if what
is herewith emitted, fhould be *very differently* received by thofe into whofe hands
it may fall. Many will, doubtlefs, efteem

it *dangerous grofs herefy*. And fome, it may be, without previous examination, upon feeing only the *title-page*, will at once pronounce me a *perverter of the Gofpel*, and fix my *final ftate*; though an *Apoftle* has faid, " Who art thou that judgeft another man's " fervant? To his own mafter he ftandeth " or falleth." I am not at all concerned about either the *opinion*, or *doom*, of *this kind* of perfons. And, to fpeak the plain truth, I do not think, whatever a man's character may be in other refpects, that he is duly prepared to pafs fentence upon the prefent work, if he has not *often* read over the New Teftament, and in the *language* in which it was originally wrote, and with a *fpecial view* to take in an idea of the *fcheme of falvation*, as it is there fet forth in its *native purity* and *fimplicity*; and fhould any, while confcious to themfelves that they have not done this, be free in cafting reproach upon it, I fhould not envy them the honour they would hereby procure to themfelves. Thofe only, as I imagine, are proper judges in this debate, who

who have made the *facred writings in gene-*
ral, and the *apoftolic writings in particular,*
efpecially the *writings* of the apoftle Paul,
their careful and diligent ftudy, and this for
fome confiderable time. There are a number, and I would hope it daily increafes, of
whom this may be faid with exact truth.
From *fuch* I expect no ill treatment. They
will, doubtlefs, difcern in this work a great
many marks of weaknefs and imperfection ;
and may, probably, be able to point out to
me wherein, through inattention, or want
of better fkill, I have put a wrong fenfe
upon this or that particular text. It would
indeed be very extraordinary, if I fhould
not, in thefe ways, or others ftill more
faulty, have mifunderftood fome or other
of thofe numerous fcriptures I have endeavoured to explain : Though I am not confcious to myfelf that I have; and can honeftly declare, that I have not *knowingly*
forced any one of them to fpeak a fenfe it
did not contain. And this is efpecially the
truth with refpect to thofe texts which are
the

the *principal support* of the scheme of thought
here advanced : In which I am clearly satisfied, I have exhibited *the truth as it is in
Jesus*; though I presume not to say dog-
matically even here, that I have not been
misled, either by the weakness of my faculties, or an insufficient attention in the
exercise of them; or by the undue sway
of some undiscerned prejudice in favour of
sentiments peculiarly agreeable to my natural benevolence of temper. And should it
be the truth, that I have really been misled,
it would be a kindness (I should esteem it
such) in some Christian friend of better
abilities, greater integrity, and more learning, than I can boast of, to set me right.
I can truly say, it would be a pleasure
to me to·be favoured with the candid
endeavours of such a friend. If I know
myself, I am still open to conviction. I
was at first brought into this train of
thought by being willing, in opposition to
previous sentiments and strong biasses, to
follow the light wherever it should lead
me.

me. And as I am yet poffeffed of the fame difpofition of mind, I would hope, if I am in an error, I am not fo inverately fixed in it, but that fuitable means of conviction may be effectual to reduce me. If any fhould think fit to *rail* at, rather than *argue* with me, they may be affured before-hand, their conduct will have no other influence than to excite my pity towards them : But if they will be at the pains to apply to my underftanding in a fober and Chriftian way, I fhall think myfelf obliged to let them know, that I have either changed my mind, or can give a good reafon why I have not done fo.

I fhould not be juft to what I account *diftinguifhed merit*, if I did not take this opportunity publicly to acknowledge my obligations to the writings of the late reverend Dr. *John Taylor* of *Norwich*. Had it not been for his *Scripture Doctrine of Original Sin*, and his *Paraphrafe and Notes upon the Epiftle to the Romans*, with the previous

vious *Key to the Apostolic Writings* in general; I should never, I believe, have been able to have composed this work. I do not mean, by what I now say, to insinuate to the world, as though this excellent writer was of the opinion, that *all men shall finally be saved*; for I know he had quite other sentiments of the matter: But what I would suggest is, that it was his *example* and *recommendation* that put me upon studying the *scriptures* in that *free, impartial,* and *diligent* manner, which led me into these sentiments. And further, it was, in a great measure, from the *light* reflected on the sacred writings by his learned labours, that I was enabled to proceed in my enquiries, till they issued in what now appears to the reader. I have often, as occasions were offered for it, enlivened and strengthened this performance by using his words; and have taken care to give him the honour of what I could not have expressed so well myself. And though I widely *differ* from him in the in-

3   terpretation

terpretation of fome very important texts, yet even here I am beholden to him; and fhould not, perhaps, have been qualified to have gone into this *difference* of fentiment, had it not been for the light and inftruction I had firft received from him. Of this the reader may fee a flagrant inftance in what I have offered upon Rom. v. from the 12th to the end. My illuftration of that paffage very much differs from Dr. *Taylor*'s; and yet, I could not have wrote *mine*, if I had not enjoyed the advantage of reading *his*. But though my fentiments difagree with his, and in points too of very confiderable im- portance; yet the opinion I have of his cha- rity, candour, and greatnefs of mind, will not fuffer me to fufpect, that, had he been now living, he would have thought the worfe of me merely upon this account: Efpe- cially, as he has advifed his readers ' freely ' to ufe their own judgment, without re- ' garding his;' that is, unlefs they fhould perceive it to be grounded on good evi- dence. He has himfelf exemplified this

advice

advice in his own conduct towards **Mr.** *Locke*; falling in with his judgment, when he apprehended he had juft reafon to do fo: Otherwife diffenting from it, and with all freedom, as led thereto by the light of truth. And this is the way in which we fhould always read the writings of others, efpecially upon the *fcriptures*, however high an opinion we may entertain of their integrity, capacity, or learning. We fhall then ufe them as *helps*, as we reafonably may, in order to underftand the true meaning of *revelation*; founding our *faith*, not on what *they fay*, but on what we are enabled by their affiftance to be fatisfied is the *word and will of God.*

Had it been a matter of importance for any to know the author of the following work, I fhould not have fent it into the world without my name: But as this can neither add to, nor take from, the real force of any of the arguments upon which I have refted the caufe I am engaged in,

I am

I am quite willing to lie buried in obfcu-
rity; and this, if even good judges fhould
entertain a better opinion of my labours than
I can reafonably fuppofe they deferve.

I hope none of my readers will make
an *ill ufe* of the doctrine here fet forth as
a *facred truth*. It is capable, I own, of being abufed; and fo is every other truth,
whether *natural* or *revealed*. If any fhould
pervert its proper defign, and genuine tendency, taking occafion from it to *continue
in fin*, the fault will be their own. The
hope of the gofpel, as illuftrated in thefe fheets,
is powerfully adapted to excite our moft
earneft endeavours that we may *enter into
life* without paffing through the *fecond death:*
But if we will be fo difingenuous as to *turn
the grace of God into wantonnefs*, we can
juftly lay the blame no where but upon
ourfelves, fhould we be made to fuffer for
our folly, God only knows *how long*, and
to how *awful a degree*, in the *ftate that is
beyond the grave.*

5   I fin-

I fincerely refign the following effect of much pains to the difpofals of Providence; wifhing, on the one hand, that it may meet with no acceptance in the world, if it tends to *deceive unwary fouls,* and *turn them afide from the fimplicity of the gofpel;* and, on the other hand, that it may univerfally gain admittance into the hearts of men, in fpite of all oppofition, if it fhould be the *truth of fcripture-revelation,* as I have no doubt but it really is.

THE AUTHOR.

PROOFS

THE

PROOFS

OF

UNIVERSAL SALVATION.

INTRODUCTION.

AS the Firſt Cauſe of all things is infinitely benevolent, 'tis not eaſy to conceive, that he
ſhould bring mankind into exiſtence, unleſs he intended to make them finally happy. And if this
was his intention, it cannot well be ſuppoſed, as he
is infinitely intelligent and wiſe, that he ſhould be
unable to projeƈt, or carry into execution, a ſcheme
that would be effeƈtual to ſecure, ſooner or later,
the certain accompliſhment of it. Should it be
ſuggeſted, Free agents, as men are allowed to be,
muſt be left to their own choice, in conſequence

whereof

whereof blame can be reflected juftly no where but upon themfelves, if, when happinefs is put into their own power, they chufe to purfue thofe courfes which will end in mifery: The anfwer is obvious, Their Creator, being perfectly benevolent, would be difpofed to prevent their making, or, at leaft, their finally perfifting in, fuch wrong choices; and, being infinitely intelligent and wife, would ufe fuitable, and yet effectual, methods, in order to attain this end. Should it be faid further, Such free agents as men are may oppofe all the methods that can be ufed with them, in confiftency with liberty, and perfift in wrong purfuits, in confequence of wrong determinations, to the rendering themfelves finally unhappy: The reply is, This is fooner faid than proved. Who will undertake to make it evident, that infinite wifdom, excited by infinite benevolence, is incapable of devifing expedients, whereby moral agents, without any violence offered to their liberty, may certainly be led, if not at firft, yet after various repeated trials, into fuch determinations, and confequent actions, as would finally prepare them for happinefs? It would be hard to fuppofe, that infinite wifdom fhould finally be outdone by the obftinacy and folly of any free agents whatfoever. If this might really be the cafe, how can it be thought, with refpect to fuch free agents, that they fhould ever have been produced by an infinitely benevolent caufe? If the only good God knew (as he muft have known, if he is infinitely intelligent),

gent), that fome free agents would make themfelves unhappy, notwithftanding the utmoft ef-
forts of his wifdom to prevent it, why did he
create them? To give them exiftence, knowing,
at the fame time, that they would render themfelves finally miferable, by abufing their moral
powers, in oppofition to all that he could do to
prevent it, is fcarcely reconcileable with fupremely and abfolutely perfect benevolence ; which, in
this cafe, one would be ready to think, muft have
withheld the gift of exiftence.

But however uncertain the final ftate of men
may be, upon the principles of mere reafon, the
matter is fufficiently cleared up in the revelations
of fcripture. For we are here informed, not only
that men were originally made for happinefs, but
that they fhall certainly attain to the enjoyment of
it, in the final iffue of things. The falvation of
the whole human kind is indeed the great thing
aimed at, in the fcheme, the bible has opened to
our view, as now in profecution, by the benevolent Deity, under the management of that glorious perfonage, Jefus Chrift ; who, we are there
affured, will go on profecuting this defign, till all
the individuals of the human race that ever had,
now have, or ever will have, exiftence, fhall be
fixed in the poffeffion of compleat and everlafting
happinefs.

This, I am fenfible, is very contrary to the
common opinion, which fuppofes that the greateft
part of mankind will be finally miferable, notwith-

ftanding

ſtanding the appointment of Jeſus Chriſt to the office of a Saviour, and all that God has either yet done, or will hereafter do, under his miniſtration, in order to prevent it. Nay, it is the opinion of ſome, that the elect (a very ſmall number comparatively conſidered) are the only ones, the benevolent Deity has concerned himſelf for, ſo as effectually to ſecure their ſalvation; having left all others, whom he might as well have ſaved, had he ſo pleaſed, to bring upon themſelves remedileſs and eternal ruin, for the praiſe of the glory of his juſtice.

Theſe ſuppoſed doctrines of revelation have ſo long been received for important truths, not by the vulgar only, but by perſons venerable for their learning and piety, whoſe buſineſs it has been to enquire into things of this nature, that it may ſeem to many an affectation of novelty, if not an argument of ſomething worſe, ſo much as to call them in queſtion. Multitudes, having been taught, from their early childhood, the doctrine of eternal torments, and, what is commonly connected with it, the final miſery of the greateſt part of mankind, are become inſenſibly and ſtrangely prepoſſeſſed in favor of theſe tenets, however ſhocking to unprejudiced minds; inſomuch that it would be no wonder, if they ſhould determine, at once, without examination, that an eſſay intended to prove, that the ſcheme of redemption concerns the human race univerſally, and will, in its final reſult, inſtate them all, without diſtinction or

limitation,

limitation, in perfect bleffedness, muft needs be an heretical undertaking, the very propofal of which ought to be rejected, as carrying along with it its own confutation.

But yet, there are fome, it may be hoped, who are not fo far under the government of prejudice, but that they can fufpend their cenfures, at leaft, till they have deliberately read what may be offered from the books themfelves, containing the revelations of God, in fupport of the hypothefis, that all men fhall finally be happy. And, fhould it be found capable of being fully confirmed by folid proofs, from thefe books, none who regard their authority, as facred, fhould withhold their affent. To be fure, they ought not to do fo, as being influenced thereto by an undue attachment to their fpiritual leaders, however renowned for knowledge, or judgment, or exemplary virtue: For they are certainly fallible, and may therefore be miftaken.

And this, I am deeply fenfible, is the truth with refpect to myfelf. I know I am liable to err, in common with other men. Nay, I pretend not but I may have been betrayed, in the prefent cafe, into an apprehenfion of that as true, which is really falfe, through the undue prevalence of fome undifcerned wrong bias or other. For which reafon, inftead of finding fault with any, into whofe hands thefe papers may fall, for reading them with caution, I would ferioufly advife them to do fo ; left they fhould be deceived with the mere

appearance

appearance of truth: Only, they ought to take care that they do not fo mix prejudice and jealoufy with their caution, as to prevent a fair and impartial enquiry. All I defire is, that, if the proofs here offered fhould appear to any, upon a thorough examination, to be juftly conclufive, they would honeftly yield to conviction. If they fhould perceive no ftrength in them, or not ftrength fufficient to fupport the caufe that is refted on them, I think, they would act commendably, and becoming their character as men and chriftians, if they fhould ftill adhere to their former fentiments. Every man muft judge for himfelf: though, if his judgment is wifely and reafonably formed, it will be the effect of apparent evidence, upon an honeft and full enquiry.

That I may proceed, in the illuftration of this fubject, without perplexity, I fhall begin with mentioning a few things, in a preliminary way, tending to prevent a mifconception of my meaning, when I affirm, that *all men fhall be finally happy.* It will then be natural to exhibit the proper arguments in fupport of this affirmation: Which, having confirmed by direct proofs, I fhall endeavour further to ftrengthen by particularly going over, and invalidating the contrary evidence.

CHAPTER I.

Containing Preliminary Explanations.

AS I am defirous of avoiding confufion of me-thod, and would, at the fame time, guard, as much as may be, againft the undue operation of prejudice in thofe who may think it worth their while to read the following effay, it may not be amifs to begin with a few particulars, tending to prevent a mifconftruction of my meaning, in the propofition I have advanced, and fhall endeavour prefently to prove, namely, that *all men, according to the fcripture-fcheme, fhall finally and certainly be happy.* And they are thefe that follow:

I. I would not be underftood to mean hereby, that all men will be admitted to the enjoyment of happinefs in the ftate that next fucceeds the pre-fent. This would be a direct contradiction to the general tenour of the fcriptures. Nay, it fhould feem, from feveral paffages in the New Tefta-ment, as though the greater part of mankind would mifs of happinefs in the ftate that follows next upon this. To this purpofe is that of our Sa-viour, " (*a*) Strait is the gate, and narrow the way,

(*a*) Matt. vii. 4.

" which

" which leadeth unto life ; and *few* there be that
" find it." And, when one came to him with that
queſtion, " *(b)* Lord, are there *few* that be ſaved ?"
he plainly concedes that it was ſo, by the reply
which he makes in the following verſe, " Strive
" to enter in at the ſtrait gate ; for *many*, I ſay unto
" you, will ſeek to enter in, and *ſhall not be able.*"
And it is obſervable, the concluſion of two of his
parables is ſummed up in theſe emphatical words,
" *(c)* For many are called, and few are choſen."
To theſe and ſuch like texts it may be owing,
that the ſalvation of comparatively but a few of
the human race has been received as an undoubted
doctrine of the bible. And I ſee not, I confeſs,
but that ſuch texts would be a full confirmation of
this doctrine, if it were a truth (as has been
generally ſuppoſed) that the next is the final ſtate
of men. But if this, inſtead of a truth, ſhould
turn out a falſe notion, grounded on miſtaken ap-
prehenſions of the genuine ſenſe of ſcripture, the
above declarations, importing that many ſhall not
be ſaved in the next ſtate, are no inconſiſtencies
with the affirmation we have laid down to be
proved. And that it is a miſtake, and a very groſs
one too, greatly tending to the diſcomfort of mankind, as well as giving occaſion for unworthy reflections on the Deity ; I ſay, that it is a miſtake
to ſuppoſe the next ſtate a final one, we ſhall en-

deavour to evince, in its proper place; where it will be feen, that the fcripture is fo far from afferting this, that it very plainly and frequently infinuates the contrary, and cannot indeed be underftood, as to the main thing it has in view, upon any other fuppofition.

II. Though I affirm, that all men will finally be happy, yet I deny not but that many of them will be miferable in the next ftate of exiftence, and to a great degree, and for a long time, in proportion to the moral depravity they have contracted in this. There is no reafonable room for debate here. It is not only plain from the threatenings of God in general, compared with the known characters of men, but from feveral parables fpoken by our Saviour, as well as from the frequent reprefentations that are made of the great, and (as it is commonly called) laft judgment, that many, in confequence of their prefent ill-conduct, will have their next exiftence in the place of "weeping, " and wailing, and gnafhing of teeth." Moft interpreters, I am aware, fuppofe this to be a place of everlafting torment. And they ftrengthen themfelves in fuch a thought, by certain phrafes, which frequently occur in the facred pages; imagining they carry in them this fenfe, and cannot well be underftood in any other. And if this is the real fenfe of fcripture, I readily own, the hypothefis here advanced is incapable of proof. But that the fcripture ought not to be interpreted in this

fenfe,

senfe, we shall take care to make clearly evident afterwards.

In the mean time, it ought to be particularly remembered, and confidered, that the future mifery, though not everlafting, according to the prefent fyftem, may yet be awfully heightened in degree, and protracted in continuance; which I the rather mention, left any should foolishly take occafion, from the doctrine here advanced, to encourage themfelves in their evil ways. Let not any fay, if we shall finally be faved, we may then live as we lift. For, according to the fcheme we are illuftrating, there will be no falvation for thofe, in the next ftate, who habitually indulge to luft in this; but they muft be unavoidably miferable, notwithftanding the infinite benevolence of the Deity, and to a great degree of feverity, God only knows how long, in proportion to the number and greatnefs of their vices. And this ought, in all reafon, to be a powerful motive to reftrain men from making themfelves vile: Though it be a truth, that, in the final refult of things, they shall be happy.—But of this, as it is a matter of vaft importance, I shall fpeak diftinctly and largely in the fequel.

III. I would not be underftood, when I fay, that all men shall be finally happy, to infinuate as though this would ever be their lot, till they are all cured of their moral depravity, and formed to a meetnefs for heaven, by being brought back to

a virtuous

a virtuous temper of mind. Men, who are intelligent and moral agents, cannot be rationally
happy, but in the regular exercise of their intel-
lectual and moral powers. While in a degenerate
ſtate, they muſt be miſerable. 'Tis impoſſible in
the nature of things it ſhould be otherwiſe. And
if ever they are delivered from their miſery, it
muſt be by effecting a change in their moral character. It is not, perhaps, in the power of an all-
wiſe intelligent being, however benevolent, to
make reaſonable creatures happy in any other
way. If therefore the next ſtate (conformably to
the common mode of thinking) is a ſtate of puniſhment, not intended for the cure of the patients
themſelves, but to ſatisfy the juſtice of God, and
give warning to others, 'tis impoſſible all men
ſhould be finally ſaved : whereas, if the next ſtate
is a ſtate of diſcipline, deſigned for the amend-
ment of the ſufferers themſelves, as well as the
good of others, and wiſely adapted as a mean to
this end, they may be recovered, and formed to
a meetneſs for immortality and honor. Or, ſhould
any have ſo ſunk their natures in this, as not to
be capable of a recovery in the next ſtate ; a
ſtate beyond that may be again a ſtate of diſcipline, wherein miſery will be inflicted with a ſalu-
tary view : Upon which ſuppoſition, their recovery
will be ſtill poſſible ; they may, in the end, become the capable ſubjects of happineſs. And that
this will be the operation of the ſcheme of God,
with reference to the whole human kind, as it is

ſet

set forth in the scriptures (the effect whereof will finally be the accomplishment of their salvation) we shall see more reason to believe, in the progress of this attempt, than we may, at present, be ready to imagine.

IV. Upon the whole therefore, what I mean to prove, in the following essay, is, that the scheme of revelation has the happiness of all mankind lying at bottom, as its great and ultimate end; that it gradually tends to this end; and will not fail of its accomplishment, when fully compleated. Some, in consequence of its operation, as conducted by the Son of God, will be disposed and enabled, in this present state, to make such improvements in virtue, the only rational preparative for happiness, as that they shall enter upon the enjoyment of it in the next state. Others, who have proved incurable under the means which have been used with them in this state, instead of being happy in the next, will be awfully miserable; not to continue so finally, but that they may be convinced of their folly, and recovered to a virtuous frame of mind: And this, as I suppose, will be the effect of the future torments upon many; the consequence whereof will be their salvation, they being thus fitted for it. And there may be yet other states, before the scheme of God may be perfected, and mankind universally cured of their moral disorders, and in this way qualified for, and finally instated in, eternal happiness. But whether,

whether there are any other fuch ftates befides the next, or not; or however many ftates fome of the individuals of the human fpecies may pafs through, and of however long continuance they may be ;—the whole is intended to fubferve the grand defign of univerfal happinefs, and will finally terminate in it : Infomuch that the Son of God, and Saviour of men, will not deliver up his truft into the hands of the Father, who committed it to him, till he has fully difcharged his obligations in virtue of it ; having finally fixed all men in heaven, when God will be all in all.

This, in general, I take to be the fcheme of revelation, with reference to the human kind. And it exhibits the Deity in fo amiable and interefting a light, and reflects fo much glory on the mediatorial undertaking of Jefus Chrift, that every man, one would think, fhould, beforehand, be difpofed to wifh it might be well fupported from the fcriptures. Can the thought be difpleafing to any fon of Adam, that the whole human race fhall finally have entrance miniftered to them into the kingdom of heaven, to partake there of joys that flow for ever from God's right hand ? Where is the man fo deftitute of benevolence, fo bereft of humanity, as not to bid God-fpeed to an attempt, intended to eftablifh it as a revealed truth, that this, before the fcene of providence is finally fhut up, fhall be the portion of all men, of whatever nation, character, colour, ftation, or condition ? It cannot be fuppofed, that any fhould be fo filled with envy, or foured by rancour, hatred,

or

or malice, as not to hope, that fo benevolent a plan may be found, upon the ftricteft enquiry, to be a true one.

Some generally received doctrines, it is confeffed, muft be given up, if this is admitted to be the fcheme of God, with reference to mankind. And it is high time they fhould be renounced, and others embraced in their room, that are more honorable to the Father of mercies, and comfortable to the creatures whom his hands have formed. I doubt not, it has been a perplexing difficulty to moft perfons (I am fure, it has been fuch to me), how to reconcile the doctrine, which dooms fo great a number of the human race to eternal flames, with the effential, abfolutely perfect, goodnefs of the Deity. And, perhaps, they contain ideas utterly irreconcileable with each other. To be fure, their confiftency has never yet been fo clearly pointed out, but that a horror of darknefs ftill remains, that is fadly diftreffing to many a confiderate tender heart. Whereas, there is no difficulty of this fort attending the prefent fcheme. All objections to the infinite benevolence of God vanifh at once; and this attribute of the divine nature fhines even more confpicuous, as viewed in the light of revelation, than in the light of mere reafon. Nor is there any fcheme that fo illuftrioufly fets forth the powerful efficacy, and extenfive advantage, of the mediation of Jefus Chrift. If mankind univerfally are the object of his concern; if he died for them all; if he is afcended up to heaven for them all; if he is there acting

on

on their behalf, and managing all things, in the kingdom of grace, with a view to their falvation, and will not give up his miniftry, in this kingdom, till he has actually accomplifhed this great defign, and inftated the whole human kind in eternal glory ;—what more noble idea can we form of his undertaking for us ? 'Tis now carried to its utmoft height, and appears to be a defign eminently worthy of God's contriving, and of Chrift's executing, and that lays a juft foundation for the everlafting admiration and adoration of all angels, and of all men : Whereas, upon the common fcheme, the extent of God's benevolence is comparatively fmall, as well as the advantage of Chrift's mediation. For notwithftanding all that has yet been done, or ever will be done, the greateft part of mankind will continue God's enemies, and the devil's flaves ; corrupt in their difpofitions, and " veffels of wrath fitted for eternal de-" ftruction." Is there any room for debate, which of thefe fchemes reflects moft honor on God, and Jefus Chrift, and is moft beneficial to men ? If any are prepoffeffed in favor of doctrines, they have been taught, even from children, to revere as divine truths, it may be hoped, they will fo far lay afide prejudice as fairly and impartially to hear what may be faid in proof of this ; as the good of mankind in common, as well as the honour of God, and of his Son Jefus Chrift, are clofely connected with it.

CHAP.

CHAPTER II.

Exhibiting the Proofs of the main Point in Debate.

THE way being thus prepared, I now come to make it evident, *that mankind univer-sally, according to the scriptures, shall, in the final result of things, be happy.* And I am in no strait here for want of forcible arguments, as those may be ready to imagine, who have been accustomed to read the Bible under a strong bias in favor of contrary principles. This was the manner, I freely own, in which I formerly read the sacred scriptures : Nor could I, for a while, without considerable difficulty, consult them upon the present point unrestrained from previously imbibed sentiments. It was with care and pains that I brought myself so far to suspect the truth of common doctrines, as to be able, with tolerable freedom of mind, to enquire whether this had a just foundation in the word of God, or not. But when I had once disengaged myself from the influence of former notions, so as to be able to look into the scriptures, with a readiness to receive

whatever

whatever they ſhould teach for truth, it was truly ſurpriſing to me, to find in them ſuch evident traces of the doctrine I am now going to prove to be a revealed one. And indeed the difficulty, in this part of my ſubject, is not ſo much to find good evidence, as to collect it together from the various parts of the Bible, and range it in ſuch order, as that the reader may eaſily have a clear and diſtinct view of it, and be able, without perplexity, to judge upon it, in its full and united force.

The ſeveral texts, containing this evidence, I ſhall bring to view under five or ſix propoſitions : Only deſiring that the produced texts may be conſidered, not apart from each other, but in connection. What I rely on as proof, in the preſent argument, is, the reſult of all theſe texts, not conſidered ſingly, but in one conjunct view : Though, perhaps, moſt of the texts, taken ſeparately, will appear to have conſiderable force, and ſome of them to be ſtrongly concluſive even of themſelves alone.

PROPOSITION I.

" From the time that ſin entered into the world " by the firſt man Adam, *Jeſus Chriſt* is the per- " ſon *through whom*, and *upon whoſe account*, happi- " neſs is attainable by any of the human race."

I am ready to think, the λογος, who, if we may believe the ſcripture, certainly exiſted before the

C

creation

creation of this world, would have been employed in the government of it, and of mankind in particular, in order to their being formed to a meetness for the final fruition of God, in glory, if Adam had not finned. But be this as it will, 'tis undoubtedly true, that, since the entrance of sin and misery into the world, he is the glorious personage, through whose mediatory intervention, the displays of God's goodness are made to the sons of men, and that in particular, which will fix any of them in final and eternal happiness. Hence he is represented, as far back as the days of Adam, " as the seed of the woman, who should " bruise the serpent's head *(a)*." Hence he is spoken of, in the times of Abraham, as one " in whom all " nations," yea, " all families, of the earth, should be " blessed *(b)*." Hence those types and figures, under the Mosaic dispensation, which derived their principal value from the reference they had to that sacrifice of himself, which, in the fullness of time, he was to offer up to God to put away sin. Hence the prophetic descriptions, scattered all over the writings of the Old Testament, pointing out his office and character, as the Saviour and King of men. And hence, in fine, those numerous passages in the Apostolic writings, which ascribe it to his mediatory undertaking for men, that they are prepared for, and finally crowned with, eternal life ; in consequence whereof, the redeem-

(a) Gen. iii. 15.   *(b)* Gen. xii. 3.

ed

ed are brought in, ſinging that hymn of praiſe to
him, Rev. i. 5, 6, " Unto him that loved us, and
" waſhed us from our ſins in his own blood, and
" hath made us kings and prieſts to God, and his fa-
" ther; to him be glory and dominion for ever and
" ever. Amen."—But I need not enlarge here. This
is a point that will not be diſputed, at leaſt, by
thoſe with whom I am now concerned.

PROPOSITION II.

" The *obedience* of *Chriſt*, and eminently his
" obedience to *death*, when he had aſſumed our
" fleſh, in the fullneſs of time, is the *ground* or
" *reaſon* upon which it hath pleaſed God to make
" happineſs attainable by any of the race of
" Adam."

Hence we are ſaid to be " reconciled to God by
" the death of his ſon *(c)* ;" to " have redemption
" through his blood, the forgiveneſs of ſins *(d)* ;"
to be " redeemed from the curſe of the law," by
" his being made a curſe for us *(e)* ;" to be "made
" righteous through his obedience *(f)* ;" and to obtain " the juſtification of life through his righteouſ-
" neſs *(g)*." And hence, in a word, eternal life,
which is the ſum of all ſpiritual and heavenly
bleſſings, is ſaid to be " the gift of God through
" our Lord Jeſus Chriſt *(h)*."

(c) Rom. v. 10.   *(d)* Eph. i. 7.   *(e)* Gal. iii. 13.
(f) Rom. v. 19.   *(g)* Rom. v. 18.   *(h)* Rom. vi. 21.

It

It would be too great a digreſſion, and beyond the deſign of this preſent work, to ſtop here to fix the precise ſenſe in which the obedience and death of Chriſt may be conſidered as the reaſon of God's making the grant of final happineſs in the goſpel. It will be ſufficient, to, our preſent purpoſe, to ſay only in general, that it was with a view to the obedience and death of Chriſt, *upon this account, upon this ground, for this reaſon,* that God was pleaſed to make the goſpel promiſe of a glorious immortality to the miſerable ſons of men. And in this, thus generally expreſſed, there is an agreement on all ſides, each explaining the matter according to their own ſchemes.

PROPOSITION III.

" Chriſt died, not for a ſelect number of men
" only, but for mankind *univerſally,* and *without*
" *exception* or *limitation.*"

The ſacred writers are ſingularly emphatical in expreſſing this truth. They could not indeed have been more full and peremptory in declaring it, had they intended to guard againſt men's ſtraining their words to another meaning. They ſpeak not only of Chriſt's " dying for " us *(i),*" " for our ſins *(k),*" "for ſinners *(l),*" " for the ungodly *(m),*" "for the unjuſt *(n)* ;" but

(i) 1 Theſ. v. 10.   (k) 1 Cor. xv. 3.   (l) Rom. v. 8.
(m) Rom. v. 6.   (n) 1 Pet. iii. 18.

affirm,

affirm, in yet more extenfive terms, that he died
" for the world *(o)*," " for the whole world *(p)* ;"
yea, that they might not be mifunderftood, they
fay, that God, " laid on him the iniquities of us
" all *(q)*," that he " gave his life a ranfom for
" all *(r)* ;" yea, that he " tafted death for every
" man *(f)*." And, as though it were on purpofe
to prevent a mifconception of this extenfive defign of his death, he commiffioned his apoftles,
and fent them forth to " preach repentance, and re-
" miffion of fins, through his name, to all na-
" tions *(t)* ;" yea, " to every" reafonable "creature
" under heaven *(u)* :" which he could not have
done, in confiftency with wifdom, or fincerity,
or mercy, if, in virtue of his death, the forgivenefs of fins, and eternal life, had not been attainable by all the fons of men.

I know there are fome, who, notwithftanding all
thefe texts, fo ftrongly expreffive of the univer-
fality of Chrift's death, are fixed in the opinion,
that he died only for the elect, that is, a few comparatively of the human race. But it would, in
my apprehenfion, be a mifpending of time and labour to argue with men, fo blinded with prejudicate
notions, as thofe very evidently muft be, who can
ferioufly go about to contrive fhifts to evade the
meaning of fuch language as the fcripture has
ufed upon this head. They might as eafily elude

(o) John i. 29.—iii. 16, 17.   *(p)* 1 John ii. 2.
(q) Ifa. liii. 6.   *(r)* 1 Tim. ii. 6.   *(f)* Heb. ii. 9.
(t) Mat. xxviii. 19.   *(u)* Mark xvi. 15.

the

the ſenſe of any other words, this truth could have been delivered in.——But it is not my purpoſe to inſiſt here ; not having come as yet to that which is peculiar to the preſent ſyſtem.

Only, before I proceed, I would make this general remark, that, if Chriſt died for all, the ſcheme we are eſtabliſhing perfectly falls in with the great deſign of his death.   And 'tis far more reaſonable to believe, that the whole human kind, in conſequence of his death, will finally be ſaved, than that the greater part of them ſhould periſh. More honor is hereby reflected on God ; greater virtue is attributed to the blood of Chriſt ſhed on the croſs ; and, inſtead of dying in vain, as to any real good that will finally be the event, with reſpect to the greateſt part of mankind, he will be made to die to the beſt and nobleſt purpoſe, even the eternal happineſs of a whole world of intelligent and moral beings.

PROPOSITION IV.

" It is the purpoſe of God, according to his " good pleaſure, that mankind *univerſally*, in con" ſequence of the death of his Son Jeſus Chriſt, " ſhall *certainly* and *finally be ſaved*."——The texts that aſcertain this, are thoſe that follow :

The firſt is Rom. v. 12, to the end. I ſhall, that I may convey my ſenſe of this ſcripture in the faireſt and eaſieſt way, in the firſt place ſet

it

it down with a paraphraſe, containing what I take to be its true meaning; I ſhall then juſtify the paraphraſe by critical notes; and finally apply the notes and paraphraſe to the main point in view.

TEXT.	PARAPHRASE.
12. *Wherefore, as by one man ſin entered into the world, and death by ſin, and ſo death paſſed upon all men, for that all have ſinned.*	*For this cauſe* or *reaſon* (1) we have received reconciliation by Jeſus Chriſt, namely, becauſe as ſin entered into the world by the one man Adam, and death by his ſin in eating of the forbidden tree, and thus (2), by this ſin of his, death hath come upon all men, *whereupon, upon which, in conſequence of which,* they have all ſinned (3):—[That all have ſinned, and yet that " death " paſſed upon all," by means of the ſin of the one man Adam, as I obſerved in the foregoing verſe, and would briefly prove before I proceed to finiſh the compariſon I there began, is exceeding evident;
13. *For until the law ſin was in the world; but ſin is not imputed where there is no law.*	*for* all along, from the time of Adam's lapſe to the giving the law by Moſes, ſin was in the world (4): But whatever ſin may, in its own

nature,

Text.

Paraphrase.

nature, be ſuppoſed to de-
ſerve, it is not reaſonable to
ſuppoſe, that it ſhould be univerſally reckoned to death,
when no law is in being that
makes death the ſpecial penalty of tranſgreſſion : And

14. *Nevertheleſs,* yet, death reigned thus uni-
death reigned from verſally through the whole
Adam to Moſes, even period of time between Adam
over thoſe that had and Moſes, and over thoſe
not ſinned after the too (5) who did not violate,
ſimilitude of Adam's as they might have done, a
tranſgreſſion, who is poſitive command of God,
the figure of him that " after the ſimilitude of A-
was to come. " dam's tranſgreſſion," between whom and " him that
" was to come," namely,
the *Meſſiah,* there is a likeneſs (6) as to the damage occaſioned by the one, and the
gift beſtowed through the

15. *But not as the* other : Not that the damage
offence, ſo alſo is the occaſioned by the lapſe of the
free gift. For if, one man Adam, and the ad-
through the offence vantage ariſing from the free
of one, many be dead; gift through the one man
much more the grace Jeſus Chriſt, exactly corre-
of God, and the gift ſpond to each other ; for if
by grace, which is by the *many,* that is, *all men,* are
one ſubjected

TEXT.

one man, Jeſus Chriſt, hath abounded unto many.

16. *And not as it was by one that ſinned, ſo is the gift: for the judgment was by one to condemnation ; but the free gift is of many offences unto juſtification.*

PARAPHRASE.

ſubjected to death through the lapſe of the one man Adam, the grace of God, and the gift by this grace of his (7), which grace is beſtowed through the one man Jeſus Chriſt (8), hath *much more abounded* unto the *ſame many*, or *all men*. And not as the damage (to repeat what I obſerved in the beginning of the former verſe, that I may be more explicit in opening myſelf upon a matter of ſuch importance ; I ſay, not as the damage (9) through the " one man that " ſinned," that is in the one inſtance in which he was tried (10), ſo is the gift through the one man Jeſus Chriſt : For the judicial ſentence took riſe (11) from the lapſe of the one man, and proceeded to condemnation, condemnation ſubjecting mankind to mortality, and *thereupon* to ſin alſo ; but the gift takes riſe from the *many ſins* which men commit in the courſe

TEXT.   PARAPHRASE.

courfe of their lives, and proceeds, in oppofition to the
power and demerit of them
all, fo as finally to terminate
in juftification, juftification
including in it their deliverance from fin as well as
death, their being made
righteous as well as reigning
in life.   And it is quite reafonable to think thus of the
17. *For if by one*   matter; *for* if, by the lapfe
man's offence, death   of the one man, death, in all
reigned by one; much   its confequences (12), reign-
more they which re-   ed through this one man over
ceive abundance of   all men; *much more* fhall thefe
grace, and of the gift   *all men,* who are the *recipi-*
of righteoufnefs, fhall   *ents* (13) of the abounding
reign in life by one,   of the grace of God, and of
Jefus Chrift.   the gift that fhall make them
righteous (14), finally reign
in life through the one man
Jefus Chrift.]   I fay therefore (15) (to refume now,
and purfue, the comparifon I
began in the 12th verfe) as it
18. *Therefore as*   was by the lapfe of the one
by the offence of one,   man Adam (16) that the ju-
judgment came upon   dicial act, " duft thou art,
all men to condemna-   " and unto duft thou fhalt
tion; even fo by the   " return,"
righ-

TEXT.

righteoufnefs of one, the free gift came upon all men unto juftification of life.

19. *For as by one man's difobedience many were made fin-ners; fo by the obedi-ence of one fhall many be made righteous.*

PARAPHRASE.

" return," came upon *all men* (17) fubjecting them to death; even fo by the righte-oufnefs of the one man Jefus Chrift, the oppofite advan-tageous gift is come upon the *fame all men,* which de-livers them from death to reign in life for ever (18). And this may be admitted without difficulty; *for,* to proceed in the comparifon, as by the difobedience of the one man Adam, *the many,* or *all men,* in *confequence* of a divine conftitution, fubject-ing them to a frail mortal ftate, occafioned by this dif-obedience of his, *became fin-ners* (19); even fo by the obedience of the one man Jefus Chrift, the *fame many,* or *all men,* in *confequence* of an oppofite conftitution, grounded on this obedience of his, fhall *become righteous perfons* (20), and as fuch be fubjectively qualified for the juftification of life, or, what

means

TEXT.

PARAPHRASE.

means the fame thing, an eternal reign in happy life.

Now (21), the introduction of the law among the Jews is fo far from being an objection, as fome perhaps may be ready to think, against what I have been faying, in the above verfes, that it perfectly coincides with the defign of it: to which purpofe let it be obferved, the law was introduced among the Jews, a fmall part of mankind; that fin, upon fuppofition of its being committed, might abound, be increafed, heightened, in its malignity and guilt (22): But then it ought to be remembered, that the *grace* I have been fpeaking of *abounds much beyond* the utmoft increafed malignity, or guilt, of fin, by means of the law (23): Infomuch that it may be juftly concluded, and fairly faid, as fin hath *univerfally* reigned by death; fo fhall grace

20. *Moreover, the law entered that the offence might abound: but where fin abounded, grace did much more abound.*

21. *That as fin hath reigned unto death;*

TEXT.	PARAPHRASE.
death; even ſo might grace reign through righteouſneſs unto e-ternal life, by Jeſus Chriſt our Lord.	grace reign *as univerſally,* and *triumphantly,* through righteouſneſs, *unto eternal life* (24), by Jeſus Chriſt our Lord.

NOTES *in ſupport of the above* PARAPHRASE.

(1) *For this cauſe* or *reaſon.*] The Engliſh phraſe that moſt exactly anſwers the true import of the Greek one, διⱥ τουτο, is, as I apprehend, *for this cauſe* or *reaſon.* There is always an argumentative connection between the difcourſe that goes before, and that follows after, this demonſtrative pronoun ; and its proper uſe is, to point out the reaſon, cauſe, or ground, of this connection. Only, it ought to be particularly minded, the cauſe or reaſon of this connection is fometimes to be found in what goes before διⱥ τουτο, and fometimes in what follows after it. It is uſed here in the latter ſenſe. The words that follow διⱥ τουτο, viz. " As by one man ſin entered into the world," &c. are brought in as the proof or illuſtration of ſome foregoing words ; and the deſign of this pronoun is to point out the rational connection there is between them. The only difficulty is to ſay pre-ciſely what theſe foregoing words are. It ſeems evident to me, they are the immediately preceding ones, ver. 11, " by whom [that is, Jeſus Chriſt] we " have received the [above ſpoken of] reconcili-
" ation."

" ation." Accordingly, the defign of δια τουτο in this 12th verfe, and αρα ουν in the 18th verfe, is to introduce a proof of the credibility, the fitnefs, or reafonablenefs, of what the apoftle had faid in the 11th verfe, namely, that " we have *received reconci-* " *liation*," and have received it by *Jefus Chrift*. The thought intended to be conveyed by thefe particles, I fuppofe, is this; that fince fin and death entered into the world, and have reigned over all men, without any wilful fault of theirs, but purely by the difobedience of one man; *for this caufe* or *reafon*, it feemed agreeable to the infinite wifdom and grace of God, that this damage fhould be repaired, and mankind refcued from the ftate of fin and death, to which they had been thus reduced, in a way analogous hereto, viz. by the obedience or righteoufnefs of one man. As if the apoftle had faid, ' I obferved ' juft now, that by *Jefus Chrift* we have *reconci-* ' *liation* with God; and it is *for this reafon* that ' the free gift, by the righteoufnefs of one, is ' come upon all men to juftification, namely, ' becaufe it was in fuch a way, viz. by the ' offence of one, that judgment came upon all ' men to condemnation.' And I imagine the apoftle's primary view in ufing thefe connect-ing particles was to fhew, that as the change from a ftate of righteoufnefs and life to a ftate of fin and death was certainly introduced by one man (as he has proved, ver. 13, 14); it is equally credible, that a change back again, from this ftate

of

of fin and death to the contrary ftate of righteoufnefs and life, fhould likewife be made by one
man ; the ftrefs being plainly laid upon this,
that *each* of thefe *changes*, great as they were, and
univerfal in their confequences, was effected by
one fingle perfon.

It will perhaps be here faid, it has indeed often
been faid, that the apoftle, in the foregoing 11th
verfe, is fpeaking of *believers*, and the reconciliation
they have received; for which reafon, the advantage by Chrift, treated of in the following paragraph, and introduced with διⱥ τουτο, ought to be
confidered as *their appropriate privilege.* Dr.
Doddridge attributes it to non-attention to this
thought, that many commentators have given a
wrong fenfe to this paffage of fcripture. His
words are thefe, [Note *(e)* on this chapter.] 'As
' this 12th verfe is an inference from the 11th, it
' feems evident that believers only are fpoken of;
' for it is plain, from comparing the 9th, 10th,
' and 11th verfes with the firft, that it is only they
' who are juftified by faith, who have peace with
' God, and who joy in Chrift as having received
' the reconciliation. And this obvious remark
' clears the following paffage of difficulties, which
' would be exceeding great, if it were to be con-
' fidered without regard to this connection, and
' which have in fact mifled many commentators,
' who, for want of attending to it, have plunged
' themfelves, and their readers, into great per-
' plexity, and given a fenfe to the paragraph of

9   ' which

' which it is by no means capable.' It is to me
very furprizing, that a gentleman of Dr. Doddridge's clear difcernment fhould be able to fatisfy himfelf of the truth of his own interpretation,
upon the force of this remark. It fhould feem as
evident as words can well make it, that the apoftle
is running a comparifon between Adam and Chrift,
as the refpective oppofite fources of death and life
to mankind *univerfally*. When he fays, ver. 15.
" If through the offence of one *many* be dead,
" much more hath the grace of God abounded
" unto *many*;" what a ftrange interpretation muft
it be, to underftand by the firft *many*, *all mankind*;
and by the fecond, *believers only*, that is, a very
few of mankind ? efpecially, if it be remembered,
that the apoftle is here profeffedly fhowing *how
much* the advantage lay on Chrift's fide of the
comparifon. But when he fays, in the 18th verfe,
" As by the offence of one judgment is come
" upon *all men* [εις παντας ανθρωπους] unto con-
" demnation ; even fo by the righteoufnefs of one
" the free gift came upon all men [εις παντας ανθρω-
" πους] unto juftification of life," it can be no other
than a flat contradiction to the exprefs words of the
apoftle himfelf to fay, that, in the latter part of this
comparifon, not *all men* are meant, but *believers only*,
that is, a few of them. If any can bring themfelves
to embrace a fenfe of this paffage, that is attended
with fo grofs an abfurdity, I fee not but they are prepared to make the fcripture fpeak what they pleafe.
—But to return to the pretended ground of this interpretation,

terpretation, the apoftle's fpeaking of believers only, in the 11th verfe, when he fays, " by whom " we have received the reconciliation." And in order to fet this matter, becaufe a very important one, in a clear point of light, I muft defire the reader to bear with me, while I lay before his view the general defign and connection of the apoftle's difcourfe, from the beginning of the epiftle to the 12th verfe of this 5th chapter.

Let it then be obferved, after fuitably introducing the epiftle, he makes it his main bufinefs, till he comes to the 20th verfe of the 3d chapter, to prove, that both Jews and Gentiles, that is, mankind univerfally, were under fin; infomuch that " every mouth was ftopped, and the whole world " become guilty before God." Upon this proof, from the 20th verfe of the 3d chapter to the end of it, he opens and eftablifhes the gofpel method of juftification, namely, that by faith through Chrift, in oppofition to a claim founded on works done in obedience to ftrict rigid law. He then, in the 4th chapter, illuftrates this method of the finner's juftification by the example of Abraham, whofe " faith was counted to him for righteoufnefs," that is, was as available with God, in the great affair of his juftification, as though it had been a perfect righteoufnefs: Which example of juftification was written, ver. 23, 24, " not for his fake alone, but for us alfo," us Jews and Gentiles, " to whom " faith fhall be imputed," to the fame merciful

D purpofe,

purpofe, " if we believe on him that raifed up Jefus " our Lord from the dead ;" upon which thofe ob- fervable words, in the 25th verfe are added, " who " was delivered for our offences," the offences of us Jews and Gentiles, of us the whole world, who had become guilty before God, and were therefore incapable of being juftified upon the foot of mere law, " and was raifed again for our juftification," that we might be brought back to a capacity of being juftified, that we might be put into the gofpel method of juftification by faith reckoned for righteoufnefs. He now proceeds, in the former part of the 5th chapter, to mention the great advantages connected with, and confequent upon, this method of juftification he had opened and eftablifhed ; introducing the juftified by faith, the perfons he fpeaks of in the firft verfe, as boafting, or glorying, and upon juft reafons, in three things efpecially. 1. They *gloried*, or *boafted*, [fo the word is in the original, Καυχησις, a noun from the fame verb, is the word ufed, chap. iii. 27, when the apoftle demands " where " is boafting then ?"] " in hope of the glory of " God," ver. 2. Mankind univerfally, and not be- lievers only, are fo far reconciled, changed in their ftate, through Chrift, as that they are made capable of obtaining this glory ; [this the apoftle had proved before, as we have feen above ; and further proves afterwards, as we fhall fee pre- fently] though believers only, fuch as are juftified

by

by faith, can, in the fenfe here meant, boaft, in
hope of this glory. 2. They boafted, or gloried
in their fufferings, ver. 3. And why? Becaufe
they knew, ver. 3, 4, 5, " that tribulation," duly
improved, would " work patience; and patience
" experience; and experience an increafe of
" hope;" fuch hope " as would not make them
afhamed." And why did they know this? Becaufe,
ver. 5, a fenfe of " God's love was poured into
" their hearts by the Holy Ghoft." And, having
here mentioned the love of God, he goes on, in
the 6th, 7th, and 8th verfes, to fet forth the exceeding greatnefs of it, from this confideration in
particular, that it was [mind this] while we were
without ftrength, in a weak helplefs ftate, incapable of delivering ourfelves from fin and death,
ungodly, and *finners*, that Chrift died for us.
Surely, by *us*, he does not here mean the juftified
by faith only, of whom he had before been fpeaking, but finners in common, the Jews and Gentiles,
of whom he had faid, chap. iii. that they were all
under fin; yea, " all the world," which he there
declares to have " become guilty before God."
And as though he had it in exprefs view to lead us
into this conftruction, he fays, ver. 6, " when we
" were without ftrength Chrift died." For whom?
Mind here, he does not fay *for us*, nor for us
while *we were ungodly*; but, in general, *for the
ungodly*, υπερ ασεβων (a); which plainly points out
the

(a) It may be obferved here, Dr. Doddridge himfelf, in
his

the fenfe of the perfonal pronouns *we* and *us*, till
we arrive to the 11th verfe, extending them to finners in common.   And, in truth, the doctrine of
juftification, as fet forth in this epiftle, can have no
other juft foundation in true reafon than this, that
Chrift has died for finners univerfally ; which is
the plain doctrine of the whole New Teftament.
The apoftle, having thus magnified the love of
God from the character of the perfons for whom
he fent his fon to die, goes on, in the 9th verfe, to
teach us what to argue herefrom, " *much more* then
" being *now* juftified by his blood, we fhall be faved
" from wrath through him." By the *we* here, we
muft by no means underftand believers, only as
they are included in the weak, ungodly, and finners,
for whom Chrift died ; that is, all who were incapable of juftification upon the foot of mere law,

his note upon this word *ungodly*, oppofes Mr. Locke, who underftands by it *Gentiles*, as he does alfo by the words, *weak,
finners, enemies, &c.* faying, " They are undoubtedly included,
" but it feems very inconfiftent (and I join with him in
" faying fo) with the whole ftrain of the apoftle's argument,
" in the foregoing chapters, to confine it to them.   Compare
" chap. iii. 9, 20, 22, 23. iv. 5. I therefore all along
" explain fuch paffages in the *moft extenfive terms*; and
" think nothing in the whole New Teftament more plain,
" than that the gofpel fuppofes *every human creature*, to
" whom it is addreffed, to be in a ftate of guilt and condem-
" nation, and incapable of being accepted with God any
" otherwife than through the grace and mercy it proclaims.
" Compare John iii. 16, 36, &c. and efpecially 1 John i. 10,
" than which no affertion can be more pofitive and exprefs."

as

as having " become guilty before God," chap. iii.
19, 20, 21. For theſe all *now*, under the goſpel,
ſtand juſtified in fact by the blood of Chriſt; that
is to ſay, they are by his death put into ſuch a
ſtate, as that they may have faith imputed
to them for righteouſneſs, and ſo are capable, in
this way, of obtaining eternal life. It is a groſs
miſtake to think, that the apoſtle, in this verſe, is
ſpeaking of that juſtification he had, in the firſt
verſe of the chapter, connected with faith; and
for this deciſive reaſon, becauſe, if we underſtand
him in this ſenſe, we ſhall abſolutely deſtroy the
force of the argument he here uſes; for as ſalvation from wrath is one thing eſſentially included
in that juſtification which is the reſult of true
faith, it would be ridiculous to argue, " *much more*
" being juſtified," meaning hereby this juſtification,
" we ſhall be ſaved from wrath." Beſides, the particle νυν, *now*, connected with the juſtification here
treated of, is emphatical; making it clear, that
the apoſtle is not to be underſtood of juſtification at the great day, but of juſtification that
had at that preſent time been compleated. It was
now, in the then goſpel day, that the perſons here
ſpoken of ſtood juſtified by the blood of Chriſt,
ſo juſtified as that their ſalvation was rendered
poſſible; they were, in one word, ſo juſtified as
to be freed from the condemnation they had been
ſubjected to through the lapſe of the one man
Adam; as the apoſtle has explained this matter at
large, from the 12th verſe to the end of the chap-

ter,

ter *(b)*. And, in this view of the words, the
apoſtle might, with the greateſt reaſon, as well as
force, argue, " *much more* being juſtified, we ſhall
" be ſaved from wrath." And, perhaps, upon
trial, it will be found, that there is neither reaſon nor
force in his argument, upon the common interpretation. He goes on, in the next, or 10th verſe,
to illuſtrate the pertinency and ſtrength of the
above argument. " For if, when we were enemies,
" we were reconciled to God by the death of his
" Son; *much more* being reconciled we ſhall be
" ſaved by his life." By the *we* here, we muſt
underſtand the ſame perſons ſpoken of in the
former verſe, that is, not believers, only as they
are included in the ungodly and ſinners for whom
Chriſt died. And 'tis obſervable, it was *while*
they were *enemies*, that is, enemies by being *un-*
godly and *ſinners*, that they were reconciled. The
words expreſsly declare this. Now, in what poſſible
ſenſe, conſiſtently with the ſcope of the new-

(b) It appears to me indiſputably clear, that a double
juſtification is ſpoken of by the apoſtle Paul. The one means
the ſame thing with abſolution at the day of judgment, and
is always connected with a character, commonly faith. The
other is, not that which Dr. Taylor contends for, a viſible
ſtanding in the kingdom of God, in oppoſition to heatheniſm;
but the advantageous ſtate mankind univerſally and abſolutely are put into, through Jeſus Chriſt, in oppoſition to the
diſadvantageous one they were ſubjected to through the lapſe
of Adam. I might largely explain and confirm this double
juſtification; but it would take up too much room for a
note.

teſtament

teftament writings, can perfons, *while enemies,* by being *ungodly* and *finners,* be faid to be reconciled to God, but in the fenfe in which we explained their being juftified in the preceding verfe? 'Tis certain the *juftification* in that verfe, and the *reconciliation* in this, mean the fame thing, though fignified by different allufions. And plainly, the gofpel knows of no juftification or reconciliation for finners, *while finners,* but their change of ftate in regard of their condemnation through the one man's lapfe, or its being made poffible for them, of the grace of God, through the death of Chrift, to obtain falvation upon the foot of faith reckoned for righteoufnefs, notwithftanding the fin of Adam, and all their own perfonal fins added thereto. [Critically read what is faid, fome pages onwards, in illuftration of Col. i. 20; where all the texts in the New Teftament, containing the words *reconcile, reconciled, reconciliation,* are particularly confidered.] And, in this point of light, the apoftle's reafoning, in this verfe, is ftrongly conclufive; for if it was, while we were all enemies, by being finners and ungodly, (believers themfelves as well as others) that " we were reconciled to God," brought back to a ftate of peace and friendfhip with him fo far as to be rendered capable of eternal life, notwithftanding the condemnation we were under through the lapfe of Adam, and our own perfonal fins, " by the death of his Son: *much more* being " thus reconciled, we fhall be faved by his life;" there can be no imaginable reafon to doubt, fince

God

God has taken ſuch an extraordinary ſtep as this, whether he will go on till he has accompliſhed his kind intentions towards us in our final ſalvation. And, I would add here, 'tis.eaſy to ſee how this arguing of the apoſtle, though thus generally extended, is yet to the purpoſe of proving, that the believer's.hope ſhall not make him aſhamed ; for as believers, conſidered as ſinners in common with the reſt of Adam's poſterity, were abſolutely juſtified, and reconciled to God, *while they were ſinners,* in the ſenſe above explained, the apoſtle's reaſoning is ſtrictly concluſive with reſpect to this point : though if it was not, it would not diſprove what we have offered, becauſe the apoſtle, from the 6th verſe to the end of the 10th, is upon the head of illuſtrating the love of God, which he took occaſion to do, from having mentioned it in the 5th verſe. 3. Believers *boaſted,* or *gloried,* [the ſame word, in the original, is uſed here, as in the foregoing inſtances of glorying] in God, that is, as their covenant God, and father, through our Lord Jeſus Chriſt. And now come in the words " by " whom we have now received the reconcili- " ation *(c)* ;" that is, the change of ſtate ſpoken of in the preceding verſe. It may be worthy of

---

(c) Mr. Taylor ſays, in his note upon this verſe, " I can- " not imagine what ſhould induce our tranſlators to render " καταλλαγην by *atonement,* when they render the verb " καταλλασσω by *reconcile* in the foregoing verſe, and in all " other places; and καταλλαγη in all other places by *recon-* " *ciliation.*" Dr. Doddridge has a like note upon this verſe.

our remark here, 'tis, common with the apoftle
Paul to join a verbal noun with λαμϐανω, inftead
of ufing the verb itfelf. For inftance, to
" receive condemnation," Rom. xiii. 2, is the
fame thing as to be condemned ; to " receive a
" reward," 1 Cor. iii. 14, as to be rewarded ;
to " receive edifying," 1 Cor. xiv. 5, as to be
edified ; to " receive trial," Heb. xi. 36, as to
experiment: fo to " receive reconciliation" is the
fame thing as to be reconciled. In what fenfe
now, is it here faid of believers, that by Jefus
Chrift they have been reconciled ? Evidently in
the fame fenfe in which the apoftle had faid, in
the foregoing verfe, " when we were enemies we
" were reconciled." The reconciliation intended,
is that change of ftate, which believers, while
they were finners, in common with the reft of
mankind, were brought into by the death of
Chrift ; as has been above explained. This the
word νυν, *now*, confirms. For it was eminently
now, that is, in the gofpel day, in the times
of Chrift, and by his death, that they and all
mankind were put into this ftate of reconciliation.
The meaning of the apoftle therefore plainly and
briefly is, " We believers glory or boaft in God, of
our intereft in, and relation to him as our covenant God, through Jefus Chrift ; by whom we
were fo changed in our ftate, *while enemies*, by
being finners and ungodly, in common with the
reft of mankind, as to be made capable of this
privilege, yea, and of final juftification, upon the
foot

foot of faith reckoned for righteouſneſs." This, I doubt not, is the true ſenſe of the apoſtle in theſe words: and as it is a noble ſenſe, ſo it perfectly coincides with the former part of this chapter, and the whole foregoing epiſtle, as well as the paragraph we have begun to illuſtrate. And, perhaps, it will appear, before we have done, that it is the only ſenſe that will make out a conſiſtency in the apoſtle's diſcourſe.

(2) *And thus,* καὶ οὑτως.] It is the opinion of ſome, and of no ſmall note neither, that οὑτως here anſwers to ὡσπερ in the beginning of the verſe. Accordingly, they make the ſenſe of the apoſtle to be this: " As by one man ſin and death entered into the world, *even ſo, ſo alſo,* hath death paſſed upon all men." But if the apoſtle had intended, that the particles οὑτως, and ὡσπερ, in this 12th verſe, ſhould anſwer to each other ſo as to compleat his ſenſe, he would have wrote οὑτως καὶ, and not καὶ οὑτως; for the καὶ, thus placed before οὑτως, is plainly copulative, joining the words that follow οὑτως with thoſe that went before it, as in the paraphraſe. There is the more weight in this criticiſm, becauſe the οὑτω anſwering ὡς, in the 18th verſe, has the καὶ placed after, not before, it. The καὶ has the ſame place in the 19th verſe, where it anſwers to ὡσπερ; and yet again, in the 21ſt verſe. To which I may add, that, throughout the New Teſtament, when οὑτω or οὑτως are correlates to ὡσπερ, the καὶ, when uſed, as it moſt commonly is, is invariably placed after, never before, οὑτω or οὑτως. Not

a ſingle

a fingle inftance to the contrary can be produced. Befides, as there is fo evidently a comparifon carried on, through this whole paragraph, between the one man Adam and the one man Jefus Chrift, it is far more natural, as well as reafonable, to underftand this 12th verfe as beginning this comparifon, and containing its former part only. The 13th, 14th, 15th, 16th, and 17th verfes will then obvioufly fall in by way of parenthefis, and the comparifon be again taken up, and compleated, in the 18th and 19th verfes. If the reader fhould defire further fatisfaction upon this point, he may meet with it in Locke, Taylor, and Doddridge, *in loc.*

(3) *Whereupon all have finned.*] 'Tis to me very furprifing, that this eafy natural conftruction of εφ ω παντες ημαρτον has never yet (that I know of) been hit upon. It makes out a perfectly good connection with the apoftle's reafoning in this epiftle, even from the firft chapter, the main fcope of which evidently is, to prepare the way for his doctrine of *juftification* upon the foot of *grace through Jefus Chrift*, by proving that *mankind univerfally have finned*, and confequently cannot be juftified upon a claim founded on *mere law.* Nor can it be faid, with juftice, that it gives the prepofition επι a wrong fenfe; for it takes it in the very fenfe in which it is moft commonly ufed throughout the New Teftament, when joined, as here, with a dative cafe. I have now by me more than threefcore examples, felected from

thefe

theſe writings only, beſides others ; in which it has preciſely the ſame force I have given it in this paſſage ; that is to ſay, it ſtands in them all to denote the *occaſional cauſe* of the things ſpoken of, or that *by which, through which, upon which, in conſequence of which*, they were as they are in thoſe places repreſented. It ſhall ſuffice at preſent to mention only two or three inſtances by way of ſpecimen. Thus, in Luke, v. 5, επι, joined with τω ρηματι σου, means *upon*, or *in conſequence of.* The tranſlation, in our Bibles, *at thy word*, perfectly agrees herewith ; for the particle *at*, as here uſed, has preciſely the ſame force with *upon*, or *in conſequence of.* So in 1 Cor. viii. 11, where επι is joined with τη ση γνωσει, it has the ſame ſenſe. The common verſion is, " *through thy* " *knowledge* ſhall thy weak brother periſh :" but it comes to one and the ſame thing, whether επι be here tranſlated *through, by, upon*, or *in conſequence of* ; for it certainly has the force of an occaſional cauſe. In like manner, this ſame prepoſition, joined with παση τη μνεια υμων, is juſtly rendered in our Bibles, Philip. i. 3, " upon every remembrance of you." 'Tis true, I don't make the article ω, in my way of conſtruction, to agree either with ανθρωπος, or θανατος, the only foregoing ſubſtantives. But this is an objection of no weight, becauſe it may as well have for antecedent the whole foregoing ſentence. And thus the very phraſe, εφ ω, is uſed, and by the apoſtle Paul too, in 2 Cor. v. 4, " For we that are in this tabernacle do groan,
" being

" being burdened," [εφ ω ου θελομεν] "*upon which*"
[groaning and being burdened] " we do not defire
" to be unclothed; but to be clothed upon, that
" mortality might be fwallowed up of life." In like
manner, if the preceding words, in the text under
confideration, namely, " and thus, in this way,
" death hath paffed upon all men," be taken for
antecedent to ω, and the prepofition επι, joined
with it, be conftrued *upon which*, an eafy fenfe
will be given to the words which next follow, *all
have finned*, and, at the fame time, a very important
one ; yea, the very one in which the apoftle had
ufed thefe words before. He means by the expreffion, in this place, " all have finned," precifely the fame thing as when he faid, chap. iii. 9,
all are under fin; and again, ver. 19, *all the
world are become guilty before God* ; and yet again,
ver. 23, *all have finned*. Only, in the text we are
upon, according to the fenfe I have given of his
words, he lets us into the true *occafional fource* of
this univerfal defection, by carrying our view back
to Adam, through whofe lapfe a weak, frail,
mortal nature has been tranfmitted to us, *upon
which*, *in confequence of which*, we have all finned
ourfelves, in our own perfons, as we muft do, if
we are juftly, or even intelligibly, chargeable with
being finners at all. And there is the more reafon
to give in to this conftruction, becaufe the apoftle
Paul, in all his epiftles, efpecially in this epiftle,
particularly in the 7th chapter, confiders our
bodies, in their prefent *frail, mortal ftate*, as the

true

true source, by means of their appetites, of that dominion which fin has over us.—But I have only hinted the reasons, upon which I ground the above construction of εφ ω παντες ημαρτον; because I have greatly enlarged upon them in the work, I had occasion just now to refer to, as designed for a still further illustration of this.

(4) *For from Adam to Moses sin was in the world.*] The apostle, in the comparison he had begun in the former verse, having mentioned two disadvantages consequential upon Adam's lapse, viz. death's having passed upon all men, and their having all sinned, makes a pause before he proceeds to finish it; introducing, by way of parenthesis, a summary proof of what he had thus said. It is with this view he brings in the 13th and 14th verses, in which he endeavours to shew, that all have sinned, and yet that it was through the one man Adam that death hath passed upon them. " *For,*" says he, " until the law sin was in the " world." The plain meaning is, that mankind made it evident that they were sinners, through the whole space that intervened between Adam and Moses. The Jews could not be insensible of this, as the sacred history acquainted them with the enormous wickedness of the world, during this interval of time. But, lest they should argue from hence, that men were subjected to death for their own sins, the apostle goes on to prove the contrary, by shewing that they were thus subjected on account of the lapse of the one man Adam.

His

His reafoning is to this purpofe : ' Sin is not imputed when there is no law.'   What he means is,
not that men can't be guilty of fin, when they
are not under a promulgate law like that of
Mofes ; for he had faid, in the foregoing words,
that they had in fact finned before the giving of
fuch a law : But what he intends is, that fin is
not reckoned, brought to account, ought not to
be looked upon as being taxed with the forfeiture
of life, [fee Locke's note *in loc.*] when there is no
law in being with death as its affixed fanction.
" *Nevertheless*," fays he, " death reigned from
" Adam to Mofes," that is, through the whole interval between the lapfe and the giving of the law.
The confequence from whence is, that the true
caufe of this univerfal fubjection to death muft be
fetched from the law given to Adam in Paradife,
" In the day thou eateft thereof thou fhalt furely
" die ;" for there was no other law that fet a
price upon fin, taxing it with the lofs of life.

If any fhould here afk, Why does the apoftle go
back to the time before the giving of the law by
Mofes, to prove that mankind died in Adam ?
the proper anfwer is, After the giving of the law
by Mofes, death, in a great number of cafes, was
the penalty with which tranfgreffion was threatened.   For which reafon, had he not fhewn that
death reigned in the world, and univerfally too,
before there was any law in being which threat-
ened fin with death, his account of the reign of
death, through the lapfe of the one man Adam,

2   might

might have been objected to: Whereas, 'tis now unanswerably clear and strong.

(5) *And over those too.*] I suppose the apostle might now have in his thoughts the patriarchs Abraham, Noah, and others, who died, in common with the rest of the world, though they sinned not after the similitude of Adam's transgression, as they might have done, having received a positive command from God for the trial of their obedience. The καὶ, upon this supposition, besides having its common and most natural meaning, will be emphatical, giving an additional force to the apostle's reasoning; as it seems to me it plainly does in the paraphrase. And I know not but the apostle might intend to take in the case of infants also; though, not being so clear in this, I did not mention them in the paraphrase.

(6) *There is a likeness.*] The apostle, having mentioned our first father Adam, takes occasion to speak of him as the figure, or type [τυπος] of him, that is, the *Messiah*, that was to come. What he intends to denote hereby, is, " that there was something with reference to Christ, which was to bear a correspondence, or to answer to something with reference to Adam." [See Taylor *in loc.* who has, as I think, set this matter in a very clear and strong point of light:] Only, as this correspondence was not exact, the advantage by Christ *exceeding*, *going beyond*, the disadvantage by Adam; he proceeds, in the 15th, 16th, and 17th verses,

to

to point out the difference between thefe two grand counterparts in the fcheme of God, with re-fpect to mankind, before he refumes the com-parifon he had begun in the 12th verfe. And what he fays, upon this head, in thefe three verfes, is *that alone* which enables us to underftand the *true force* and *full meaning* of his reafoning in the 18th and 19th verfes; which I defire may be par-ticularly noticed: And the rather, becaufe the *true meaning* of thefe verfes, as I imagine, has not been underftood by expofitors. See note (15.)

(7) *The grace of God, and the gift by grace.*] By this η χαρις του θεου, και η δωρεα εν χαριτι, the apoftle intends the advantage (whatever that be) on the part of Chrift, which *exceeds, reaches beyond,* the dif-advantage on Adam's part of the comparifon. Thefe phrafes mean precifely the fame thing with το δε χαρισμα, ver. 16, and η χαρις και η δωρεα της δικαιωσυνης, ver. 17; and anfwer exactly to the το χαρισμα, ver. 15, and the το δωρημα, ver. 16, which are oppofed to the difadvantage by Adam's lapfe, fpoken of in thofe verfes; which ought to be par-ticularly attended to.

(8) *Which is beftowed through the one man Jefus Chrift.*] Dr. Taylor conftrues the words, η δωρεα εν χαριτι τη του ενος ανθρωπου Ιησου Χριστου, thus; *the gift by grace, which* (grace) *is of the one man Jefus Chrift.* Here, fays he, ' The grace, favor, ' benevolence, of our Lord Jefus Chrift, his ' good-will to mankind, is made the ground of ' the gift of God, or the donation of benefits in

E   ' the

' the gospel, as well as his obedience to God,
' ver. 19th.' Raphelius (who is herein followed
by Wolfius) grounds this gift on the grace or favor
which the one man Jesus Christ has with God.
His words are these, ' εν χαριτι τη του ενος ανθρωπου
' Ιησου Χριστου, i. e. Ex gratia, *in qua* Deus ha-
' bet *unum istum hominem Jesum Christum*, five
' ex amore, *quo Deus eum amplectitur.* Nam χαρις
' τινος non tantum active, sed etiam passivè acci-
' pitur. Ut χαρις του Ιησου sit gratia Jesu, in qua
' apud Deum Patrem est. Sic et Latini dicunt, in
' gratiam alicujus quid facere, pro amore erga
' illum, five illius causa, propter illum.' In further justification of this sense, he produces two
or three similar passages out of Polybius. Vide
Raphel. Annot. Philolog. vol. ii. page 256. But
it does not appear to me, that either of these great
men have hit upon the true sense of the apostle.
The sacred books of the New Testament, do no
where speak of the gift of salvation as grounded
upon, or originating in, either the benevolence of
the one man Jesus Christ, or his being a person in
favor with God. 'Tis true, the grace of Christ,
that is, his *benevolence* towards men, is often
celebrated in the New Testament, particularly
in Acts xv. 11. Rom. xvi. 24. 2 Cor. viii. 9.
Matt. xx. 28, the texts cited by Dr. Taylor in
justification of his sense of the passage. 'Tis true
also, the favor of Christ with God, the " Father's
" being well pleased with him," is spoken of as a
thing witnessed to by a voice from heaven. But

still,

ftill, the *benevolence* of *God*, not of Chrift; and his benevolence *towards men*, not towards Chrift, is the true and only fource of gofpel falvation. And this is always the language of the fcripture upon this head *(a)*. The way, indeed, through which this benevolence, or grace, of God is communicated, is the obedience, death, or blood, of the " one man Jefus Chrift ;" and thus the facred writings invariably fpeak upon the matter *(b)*. I have accordingly interpreted the paffage under confideration, as though it had been wrote, δωρεα εν χαριτι τη δια του ενος, &c. And I the rather fuppofe the prepofition δια is here underftood, and ought to be fupplied, becaufe is is expreffed in the 17th verfe, where the apoftle, fpeaking of this very gift, and of its abounding too, declares it to be δια του ενος Ιησου Χριστου, *through the one man Jefus Chrift.*

(9) *And not as the damage,* &c.] The apoftle, in the foregoing verfe, had affirmed only in general, that the gift *reached beyond* the offence, without faying in what fpecial refpect. In this verfe, he proceeds to fay particularly wherein, or in what fpecial refpect, the gift *abounded* beyond the lapfe. I fuppofe therefore, that the words, ουχ ως δι ενος αμαρτησαντος, το δωρημα, are nothing more

(a) John iii. 16.—Rom. v. 5.—Eph. ii. 4, 9, 10.—2 Thef. ii. 16.—1 John iii. 1.—iv. 9, 10, 11, 16, 19.

(b) Rom. iii. 24.—v. 9, 10, 18, 19.—vi. 21.—Eph. i. 6, 7.—Col. i. 6.—2 Tim. i. 9, 10.

than

than a repetition of the ουχ ως το παραπτωμα, ουτω και το χαρισμα, in the foregoing verfe ; and that they are introduced by the copulative και, *and*, to lead us into this conftruction. As if the apoftle had faid—I obferved, in the foregoing verfe, that the offence and gift did not exactly correfpond to each other; *and* I fay again, that I may take occafion to explain myfelf more particularly upon this point, 'the damage through the one man that finned, and the gift through Chrift, do not perfectly correfpond to each other;' *for*, and fo on.

(10) *Through the one man that finned, in the one,* &c.] Mr. Locke here changes αμαρτησαντος into αμαρτηματος ; but, as I imagine, without any juft reafon for it. ' For if ενος, *one*, in this verfe, be to ' be taken for the perfon of Adam, and not for ' the one fin of his eating the forbidden fruit, there ' will be nothing to anfwer πολλων παραπτωματων, ' *many offences*; and fo the comparifon the apoftle ' is upon will be loft.' And 'tis certain, the apoftle's comparifon will be loft, unlefs there be fomething to anfwer the *many offences*, here brought in by way of oppofition. But, in order to find this fomething, there is not the leaft neceffity of chang-ing αμαρτησαντος into αμαρτηματος, in contradiction to all the copies and verfions, two or three only excepted. It is to me a little ftrange, that fo critical an obferver fhould not perceive, that δι ενος αμαρτησαντος, as it ftands in this paragraph,

means

means precisely the same thing with τω του ενος παραπτωματι, in ver. 15, which same phrase is again repeated in the 17th verse: Nor indeed can it be interpreted in any other sense, consistently with what the apostle has observed over and over again, namely, that it was by *one sin*, the *single offence*, of the one man Adam, that his posterity have suffered such damage. Besides, it is to be remarked, the phrase, εκ πολλων παραπτωματων, plainly has reference to the immediately foregoing words, το μεν κριμα εξ ενος, with παραπτωματος understood: Nor was there any need of its being expressed, as it might so easily and naturally be supplied from the following εκ πολλων παραπτωματων, with which it is grammatically, as well as in point of argument, connected. Though, I would add here, το μεν κριμα εξ ενος, with παραπτωματος understood, ought not to be construed, *the judgment was from one offence*; but, *the single offence of the one man.* See the reason for this construction in note (16) on verse 18th.

(11) *For the judicial sentence took rise.*] The words paraphrased, from the particle *For*, are, in the original, το μεν γαρ κριμα εξ ενος εις κατακριμα, το δε χαρισμα εκ πολλων παραπτωματων εις δικαιωμα. Literally translated they stand thus, 'For the 'judgment was *from* one offence *unto* condemna-'tion, but the gift is *from* many offences *unto* justi-'fication.' Their true meaning, as I imagine, is exhibited in the paraphrase. The intelligent reader will readily perceive, that I have had a parti-

E 3   cular

cular eye to the force of the prepofition εξ or εκ and
εις. And if he will be at the pains to confult what
Dr. Taylor has faid upon thefe words, in his note
upon that phrafe, "*from* faith *to* faith," Rom. i. 17,
he will fcarce fail of being convinced, that they
are here, at leaft, interpreted according to their
juft import. The only thing that needs further
illuftration, is the fenfe I have given to the words
κατακριμα and δικαιωμα. To fet this matter therefore in a proper light, let it be obferved ;—when
the apoftle fays, " the judgment was from one of-
" fence unto *condemnation,*" by this condemnation he means the whole damage Adam's pofterity were fubjected to through his one offence ;
not mortality only, but all that was confequent
thereupon. He is certainly fpeaking of the whole
damage arifing from the one offence of the one
man. The grand point he has in view, makes
it neceffary to underftand him in this fenfe : Nor
will his arguing, upon any other interpretation, be
conclufive. And if by this condemnation, we underftand the whole damage occafioned by the one
offence of Adam, it will be found to be more
than fimple death. For, in the 12th verfe, the
apoftle had fpoken of this one offence of Adam's
as the occafional fource of fin as well as death.
Mortality, and *thereupon* a *liablenefs to fin,* fuch
a liablenefs as that, feparate from grace, or gofpel, men would fin, were the two difadvantages
he had mentioned as occafioned by Adam's one
offence. Thefe, therefore, muft both be included

in

in the condemnation here argued from, as this
word, κατακριμα, *condemnation*, is evidently used
to signify the whole damage of the lapse. Now
the word δικαιωμα, in the last clause of this verse,
is opposed to κατακριμα in the foregoing clause
of it; and as κατακριμα signifies *condemnation*, so
must δικαιωμα signify *justification*; and, to make
out the opposition, *justification* in a sense that
will fully answer to the preceding *condemnation*.
Consequently, as the *condemnation* respects men's
sinning as well as dying; the *opposite justification*
must include in it their deliverance from sin as well
as death, their being made righteous as well as
reigning in life, conformably to the paraphrase.
And perhaps the word δικαιωμα is the most proper one to convey the idea of *justification* in this
sense. Mr. Locke has largely examined the meaning of this term. He supposes it signifies ' that
' rule, which, if comply'd with, justified, or render-
' ed perfect, the person, or thing, it referred to;'
supporting this sense of the word by critically
viewing the places where it is used in the New
Testament. See his note upon Rom. ii. 26. If
this great man has given the just import of this
word, as it appears to me that he has in the general, the apostle, by saying, that the gift to mankind is εις δικαιωμα, plainly means, that it is a gift
that will terminate in their being brought to such
a conformity to the rule of right, as that they
shall, through Christ, reign in life for ever; which
sense of the phrase exhibits, as it ought to do,

a mean-a meaning that is oppofite to the meaning of εις καταχριμα in the preceding claufe, as that phrafe has been explained, and neceffarily muft be explained, in order to make out a confiftency in the apoftle's argument. The fum of the matter is, the abounding of the gift by Chrift, beyond the damage of the lapfe by Adam, which is the point the apoftle has in view, he illuftrates thus :—The fentence terminating in a condemnation, which fubjected mankind to mortality, and thereupon to an unhappy liablenefs to fin, took rife from the one offence of Adam only : But the gift by Chrift, on the contrary, takes rife not only from this one offence of Adam, but the *many offences* which mankind, in confequence of that one fin, commit in their own perfons, and finally terminates, in oppofition to the power and demerit of them all, in their conformity to the rule of righteoufnefs, and their being accordingly reftored, not fimply to life, but to reign in it for ever. Critically compare this note with the notes on the 18th and 19th verfes, where it will be feen, that this reigning in life, in the way of being previoufly made righteous perfons, is feparately and diftinctly treated of, and this as the counter-parts to the two grand difadvantages, which have been occafioned by the one lapfe.

(12) *Death in all its confequences.*] So, I think, *death* ought to be underftood here ; anfwering to the *condemnation* fpoken of in the foregoing verfe, and taking in the whole damage of the lapfe.

(13) *Much*

(13) *Much more shall these all men, who are the recipients,* &c.] The sense I have given πολλω μαλλον οι—λαμβανοντες appears to me absolutely necessary, in order to make out a consistent con- nection between this, and the two foregoing verses. Dr. Taylor, in support of a different sense, distinguishes *the grace and gift through Christ* into that which answers exactly to the damage through the lapse, and that which exceeds, abounds beyond, it. The former he extends to mankind universally, the latter he confines to those only who *receive,* that is, *improve,* gospel means and privileges. He gives us his sense of this gift and grace, as to its abounding part, page 287, 288, of his work upon Romans, where he speaks of it as that which is to be received, that is, improved, by those who shall reign in eternal life; and makes this the criterion that distinguishes it from that part of the grace which answers to the offence, and gives restoration to life to all men, whether they do, or do not, receive, or improve, it. For so, says he, ' the apostle saith expressly, *they who* ' receive *the abounding of grace, and of the gift* ' *of righteousness, shall reign in life.* Reigning in ' life is the consequence of receiving the grace ' and gift. Therefore receiving the grace, is a ' necessary qualification, on our part, for reigning ' in life: But the necessary qualification, on our ' part, for reigning in life, according to the whole ' tenor of the gospel, is believing and improving ' all the present privileges, advantages, blessings, ' promises,

' promises, means, ordinances, of the gospel.
' Therefore [*receive*] must here have the same sense
' as in Matt. xiii. 20.—John i. 12.—iii. 11, 32, 33.
' —v. 43.—xii. 48.—xiii. 20.—xiv. 17.—xvii. 8.
' And the *abounding of grace, and the gift of*
' *justification*, must include all the blessings and
' privileges of the gospel, which it is our present
' duty to receive and improve, in order to our
' being qualified to reign in eternal life.   And if
' so ; then this is the sense of the *grace of God*,
' and of the *gift by grace*, which hath *abounded*
' *unto the many*, ver. 15 ; namely, it includes all
' gospel privileges and blessings.'

But however high an opinion I have of the critical skill of this learned and judicious commen-
tator, I must beg leave to think, his discourse here
is quite beside the design of the apostle ; who is
not treating, any where in this paragraph, of gospel privileges, means, or advantages, as *improve-*
able in order to a reign in eternal life: nor are
gospel privileges what he intends by the abounding of the grace and gift he is speaking of in the
15th, 16th, and 17th verses.   The grand point in
view, in these three verses, is to show, that the
advantage arising from the gift and grace through
Christ *abounds to all men beyond* the disadvantage
that is come upon them through the lapse of
Adam.   And, in the 16th verse, he directly, and
ex professo, makes the *abounding advantage* of this
gift to consist in its terminating in the justification
of all men, that is, their reigning in life as righteous

teous perfons ; and this, notwithftanding all the
fins they are perfonally guilty of in the courfe of
their lives, and confequently notwithftanding all
their *finful mifimprovements* even of the gofpel, and
all its means and privileges. The truth is, the
apoftle introduces the 15th, 16th, and 17th verfes,
with an exprefs view to give notice, before he
purfued the comparifon he had begun in the 12th
verfe, that there was a *diffimilitude* between the
damage through Adam, and the gift or grace
through Chrift. And wherein does he make this
diffimilitude to confift ? Evidently in. this, and in
this only, that the gift *exceeded, overflowed, ftretch-
ed beyond,* the damage. Wherein ? Why, the damage took rife from *one offence only,* terminating
in the *condemnation of all men* ; whereas, the gift
takes rife from *many offences,* not only the one
lapfe, but even all the fins, which, in confequence
hereof, mankind univerfally commit in their own
perfons, and terminates, notwithftanding them all,
in oppofition to them all, in their finally reigning
in life as righteous perfons. This is the thought
the apoftle intended to convey ; which will more
fully appear by attending to the order and connection of thefe three intervening important verfes.
Let it then be critically obferved,

In the 15th verfe, the apoftle declares more
generally, that the gift by grace hath *abounded* to
the *fame many,* or all men, who had fuftained damage by the lapfe of the one man Adam ; and
with like certainty too, for the fame peremptory
language

language is ufed in both branches of the verfe. It is as ftrongly affirmed, on Chrift's fide of the comparifon, *the gift hath abounded,* as, on Adam's fide, *through the offence, many are dead.* In the 16th verfe, the apoftle proceeds to fay more particularly wherein the *abounding* of the gift confifted, namely in this, that the judgment took rife from *one offence only,* and terminated in *condemnation,* that is, the whole damage of the lapfe ; whereas the gift takes rife from *many offences,* and as certainly terminates, notwithftanding them all, in *juftification,* that is, a glorious reign in life conformably to a rule of righteoufnefs. With refpect to whom ? Indifputably mankind univerfally. The antithefis will otherwife be loft. For mankind univerfally are the object of condemnation ; the fame mankind therefore muft be the object of the oppofite juftification. Befides, mankind univerfally are *the many* [οι πολλοι] in the foregoing 15th verfe, who are exprefsly mentioned as the perfons unto whom the gift by grace hath *abounded.* For which reafon, this 16th verfe cannot be connected with the 15th upon any interpretation but this, which makes *all men* the perfons who fhall finally be juftified, that is, reign in life as righteous perfons, notwithftanding all the fins they may have perfonally committed. The apoftle having, in thefe two verfes, firft generally afferted, and then particularly defcribed, the *abounding* advantage of the gift *beyond* the damage, goes on, and adds, in the 17th verfe, " For if by one man's offence
" death

" death reigned by one ; much more they which
" receive the *abounding* of grace, and of the gift
" of righteouſneſs, ſhall reign in life by one, Jeſus
" Chriſt." It is obvious, upon a curſory reading
only of this verſe in connection, that it is brought
in to ſhow the fitneſs, the reaſonableneſs, the credibility, of what had been delivered in the two
foregoing verſes, more eſpecially the 16th, with
reference to the *abounding* of the gift through
Chriſt *beyond* the damage through Adam's lapſe.
Conſequently, to make the apoſtle's arguing to
the purpoſe, *reigning in life,* in this 17th verſe,
muſt mean preciſely the ſame thing with *juſtifica-*
tion in the 16th verſe ; and not only ſo, but *man-*
kind univerſally muſt be conſidered as *the recipients*
of, [οι την περισσειαν της χαριτος—λαμβανοντες] *the*
perſons who receive the abounding of the grace and
gift, to their reigning in life. For, in both the
foregoing verſes, with which this is inſeparably
joined by a connecting γαρ, or *for, mankind uni-*
verſally are the object of the gift through Chriſt
in all its *abounding* glory, as well as of the damage
through Adam ; and ſo muſt they be here too,
to give the apoſtle's reaſoning due weight and
ſtrength.

If, by *thoſe* who receive the abounding of the
grace and gift, we underſtand, with Dr. Taylor,
not *mankind univerſally,* but thoſe only, who, in his
ſenſe, receive the grace and gift, that is, *improve*
the goſpel, and its privileges, this 17th verſe, which
is purpoſely introduced to illuſtrate the reaſonable-
nefs

nefs of the thought advanced in the two foregoing
verfes, cannot be connected with them in point
of argument, as it ought to be, and indeed muft
be, to give the γαϱ, or *for*, its juft force, or proper emphafis. The fhort of the matter is, the
apoftle is not treating, either in this paragraph
in general, or in this 17th verfe in particular, of
men's *improving*, or *not improving*, the advantages,
privileges, means and ordinances of the gofpel; but
what he aims at is to fhow, that as mankind univerfally are fubjected to damage through the lapfe
of the one man Adam; fo they fhall as univerfally
be delivered from it through the gift by the one
man Jefus Chrift, and with *fuper-abounding advantage.* And herein (to ufe the words of Dr. Taylor) lies the connection and finews of the apoftle's
whole argument, which ought to be well obferved.
By *thofe* therefore who " *receive* the abounding of
" the grace, and of the gift of righteoufnefs," to
their reigning in life, are meant, not the *improvers*,
but fimply the *receivers* of this grace and gift.
The words, οι λαμβανοντες, plainly intend nothing
more than to point out the *object* of this " abound-
" ing of the grace of God through Chrift," or to
fpecify the perfons upon whom it is beftowed;
who are *mankind univerfally*, as has been faid : Nor
otherwife will the apoftle's arguing be either coherent, or conclufive.

I fhall clofe this note, though long already,
with what a learned friend was pleafed to fend me,
when he returned thefe papers, which I had put

into

into his hands, in manufcript, for critical examination. He fays, ' As λαμβανοντες is a very impor-
' tant word in this paragraph, I have looked into
' every text in the New Teftament where it is
' ufed, and I find that, in general, it fignifies to
' *take,* or *receive* ; though, according to the diffe-
' rent circumftances of the cafe, it is moft properly
' rendered by different Englifh words. It is ufed
' with refpect both to *perfons*, and *things* ; fometimes
' in a bad fenfe, but moft frequently in a good
' one.

' I. It is ufed with refpect to *perfons.* 1. Some-
' times in a bad fenfe ; fignifying *to take hold of*
' *with force and violence*, Matt. xxi. 35, 39. Mark
' xii. 3, 8. 2. Very often it is ufed in a good fenfe,
' to *receive with kindnefs as a friend*, or to *treat a*
' *perfon agreeably to the character he pretends to.*
' 3. It is applied figuratively to the paffions ; the
' feizing of perfons with amazement, fear, &c.

' II. It is ufed with refpect to *things.* 1. Once
' in a bad fenfe, Matt. v. 40, to *take away from*
' *another without his confent.* 2. But moft com-
' monly in a good fenfe, to *take of another with his*
' *confent* ; which is properly to *receive.* It alfo has
' a larger fignification ; to *take up*, to *take hold of*,
' to *catch*, to *obtain*, to *attain.* To *receive a tefti-*
' *mony*, an expreffion common in John's gofpel,
' means to receive it as true ; except once, viz.
' John v. 39, where it is to be underftood in the
' ufual acceptation of λαμβανω, that is, of *having a*
' *teftimony given to one.* In the fame fenfe we are
' to

' to underſtand *receiving words*, John xii. 48.
' Theſe are all the ſenſes which I can find λαμβανω
' has in the New Teſtament.

' Dr. Taylor, Dr. Doddridge, and others, led
' hereto, as they thought, by the whole tenor of
' the goſpel, underſtand λαμβανοντες, in Rom. v. 17,
' to mean improving the preſent advantages, &c.
' of the goſpel ; and in ſupport of this they cite a
' number of texts ; all of them, as it ſeems to me,
' foreign to the purpoſe. In ſeveral of thoſe
' texts, the verb λαμβανω is joined with a *perſon :*
' And in theſe it cannot mean to *improve*, this
' being only reſtrained to *things* ; for I think it is
' improper to ſpeak of improving or making a
' good uſe of *perſons.* To receive a perſon, in the
' New Teſtament, means either to admit him in
' the character he ſuſtains, or to give him a kind
' entertainment; as was obſerved before. In all
' their other texts, this verb is joined with the
' nouns, *teſtimony*, or *words :* To *receive which*
' is to *admit them for true* ; which may be done
' without *improving* them. And this is plainly
' the caſe in one of their texts, Matt. xiii. 20 ;
' as appears from the next verſe. In both theſe
' caſes there ſeems to be nothing like the idea of
' *improving :* Nor are theſe uſes of the verb λαμ-
' βανω ſimilar to the uſe of it, when joined with
' *grace*, or *gift* ; as in the text now in queſtion :
' To *receive* either of which, in all the other places,
' where it is uſed, means ſimply to *have it beſtow-*
' *ed.* This verb is joined with χαρις in John i. 16,
' where,

' where, I think, there can be no doubt but that
' it means simply *receiving*; and again in Rom. i. 5,
' where it plainly has the same meaning, St. Paul
' speaking there of the favor he had received from
' God, in being made an apostle. It is joined with
' δωρεα in Acts ii. 38, and x. 45, compared with 47,
' in both which places it most evidently has the
' same meaning. These four are the only places
' I can find, where λαμβανω is joined with χαρις
' or δωρεα. I find χαρις in one place, namely
' 2 Cor. vi. 1, joined with δεχομαι, a verb of like
' import, though not of so general a signification,
' as λαμβανω; being never used for *taking by force*,
' or *against the consent* of another. But neither is
' there any reason to think, that this verb ever
' carries in it the idea of *improving the thing re-*
' *ceived.* Most certainly it does not, in the place
' just referred to; for the apostle is there exhort-
' ing the Corinthians to improve the grace of God
' which they had received.

' Upon the whole, I have satisfied myself, that
' the proper meaning of λαμβανω is only to *take*,
' or *receive*; and that there is not one place in the
' New Testament, where it signifies *improving*, or
' *making a good use of the thing received.* And, in
' some places, and such too as are similar to this
' in Romans, to understand it of *improving* would
' be highly absurd. Thus, in the parable of the
' talents, Matt. xxv. 16, he that *did not improve*
' *his talent* is said to *have received it*, as well as
' those who did improve theirs. *Receiving* there-

F   ' fore,

' fore, not *improving*, is the true meaning of λαμ-
' βανοντες, in Rom. v. 17, if we may judge by the
' conftant ufe of this word in the New Teftament.
' And the connection of the difcourfe here ftrong-
' ly confirms it. To what you have urged on this
' head, page 58—62, it feems to me may be
' added, that " receiving the abounding of grace,"
" and of the gift of righteoufnefs," in this 17th
' verfe, muft mean the fame thing (only in the
' more glorious fenfe explained in ver. 15, 16)
' as " receiving the reconciliation," ver. 11th;
' where it is impoffible to conftrue ελαβομεν, *by*
' *whom we have now* improved *the reconcilia-*
' *tion.*

' I obferve laftly, that it is not pretended, that
' the apoftle Paul ever ufes λαμβανω in the fenfe of
' *improving*, except in the place now in queftion ;
' not one of the texts alleged, in fupport of this
' meaning, being taken from him : Though he
' ufes this verb forty times; and, if the Epiftle to
' the Hebrews be his, near fixty times.'

Thus my ingenious friend, and, I fhould think,
to the entire fatisfaction of every attentive reader.

(14) *And of the gift that fhall make them righteous.*] The words της δωρεας της δικαιωσυνης, are
capable of being conftrued, (as Dr. Taylor conftrues them) *of the gift of juftification.* They
may likewife be rendered, *of the gift of mercy.*
And I was once inclined to take this to be the
true rendering; as it agrees fo well with the
η δωρεα εν χαριτι, *the gift by grace,* in the 15th
verfe.

verfe. But I now prefer the tranflation in our
Bibles, *the gift of righteoufnefs*; meaning by it,
the gift which will make men righteous, produce in them, fooner or later, a conformity to
the rule of right, the law of righteoufnefs, in this
way forming them to a meetnefs for an eternal
reign in life, as in the paraphrafe. And I the
rather give in to this fenfe of the words, becaufe
the " abounding of the gift " towards mankind,
in the foregoing verfe, with which this is clofely
connected in point of argument, is made to confift
in its terminating in their juftification, that is,
[as we have feen note (11)] in their reigning in
life as righteous perfons, in fpite of all the fins
they may commit in confequence of the lapfe.

(15) *I fay therefore.*] This *therefore* is the
fame which began the 12th verfe. The Protafis,
or firft part of the comparifon, was there entered
upon; but left unfinifhed. 'Tis here refumed;
" I fay, therefore, as by the offence of one man,"
&c. Then follows the Apodofis, or latter part
of the comparifon, " even fo [ουτω και] by the
" righteoufnefs of one," &c. This I take to be
the true conftruction; looking upon the difcourfe,
from the 13th to the end of the 17th verfe, to be
an interpofed parenthefis. See note (2). Though
it may be worth obferving here, it will make no
effential difference in the apoftle's reafoning, if we
fhould fuppofe (as fome do) that the fenfe of ver.
12th is compleat in itfelf, and that the 18th and
19th verfes, introduced with αρα ουν, are a con-

F 2   clufion

clufion from the three foregoing verfes, giving a
fummary reprefentation of the comparifon between
Adam and Chrift. The grand fcope of the
Apoftle, and the force of his arguing, will be
much the fame upon either conftruction. Only,
it fhould be heedfully minded here, though the
apoftle, whichever conftruction of his words be
preferred, is certainly pointing out, in the 18th
and 19th verfes, the *refemblance, likenefs, correfpondence,* there is between Adam and Chrift, or
rather between the confequences of the offence of
the one, and of the obedience of the other; yet
this likenefs, or correfpondence, ought to be
confidered with *all the abounding advantage* which
had been given to Chrift, on his fide of the comparifon, in the foregoing 15th, 16th, and 17th
verfes. For the view of the apoftle, in interpofing
thefe verfes, giving us to underftand, that the
gift through Chrift *exceeded, abounded beyond,* the
damage through the lapfe of Adam, was, that he
might argue from the gift in this *abounding* fenfe,
when he came to profecute the comparifon between
Adam and Chrift. Why elfe fhould he ftop to
point out this *abounding advantage* of the gift on
Chrift's part of the comparifon? And if the " gift
" through Chrift" might reafonably be fuppofed
to *abound* towards men *beyond* the damage of the
lapfe, in the 15th, 16th, and 17th verfes, why not
in the 18th and 19th? 'Tis certain, if we take the
" gift through Chrift," in the 18th and 19th verfes,
in all its *abounding* glory, the reafoning of the

apoftle

apoftle will be more uniform and confiftent ; more honor alfo will be reflected on God, and his fon Jefus Chrift, and greater benefit redound to man ; and, in a word, a very natural and rational account will herefrom arife, why the apoftle fhould make a paufe to infert the intervening important thought, contained in the 15th, 16th, and 17th verfes : Whereas, upon any other fcheme of interpretation, it will be difficult, if not impoffible, either to account for this intervening thought, or to make out a good connection between the feveral parts of this paragraph.

In confideration of thefe things, I cannot but wonder, that Dr. Taylor fhould take fo much pains, in his *Scripture Doctrine of Original Sin,* to prove, that the comparifon on Chrift's part, in the 18th and 19th verfes of this chapter, does not take in the whole advantage of the gift, or the gift in all its *abounding* glory. What he has offered, upon this fame head, in his paraphrafe and notes upon Romans, has increafed my wonder; for he has here added arguments, to thofe he had urged before, to make it ftill further evident, that the comparifon, in thefe verfes, on Chrift's part, is not to be underftood in its *abounding* fenfe : And yet, in thefe very notes, he has virtually given up all his arguments, declaring them to be infufficient to the purpofe for which he had brought them. For he fays exprefsly, page 286, ' Sup-
' pofing the apoftle, in the letter of the 18th and
' 19th verfes, compares the confequence of Adam's
' offence and Chrift's obedience, only fo far as the

' one

' one is commenfurate to the other; yet his rea-
' foning, ver. 15th, 16th, and 17th, plainly fhews
' it is his meaning and intention, that we fhould take
' into his conclufion the *whole of the gift,* fo far as
' it can reach to all mankind.' And again, page
291, ' But after all, I am perfuaded, the *fenfe* of
' ver. 15th, 16th, and 17th, is *intended,* and *under-*
' *ftood,* in ver. 18th and 19th; and that the *drift*
' of the apoftle's conclufion is to fhew, that the
' gift, in its *utmoft extent,* is free to all mankind.'
And this is undoubtedly the real truth of the cafe.
It was the apoftle's intention, and indeed the main
thing he had in view, to take into the comparifon,
in the 18th and 19th verfes, the *gift* in its *utmoft
extent :* Nor is it otherwife conceivable, what end
he could propofe in making a ftop, in his reafoning, to bring in the 15th, 16th, and 17th verfes,
the moft important of any in this whole paragraph.

(16) *By the lapfe of the one man Adam.*] I am
fenfible, the words δι ενος παραπλωμαλος, in this part
of the comparifon; and confequently the words
δι ενος δικαιωμαλος, in the following branch of it,
may properly be rendered, *by one lapfe,* by one
aÆ of conformity to the rule of righteoufnefs :
Nay, this is the moft natural, as well as grammatical, tranflation of the phrafes, confidered fimply
in themfelves. But this notwithftanding, if we
confider thefe phrafes as parts of a difcourfe,
containing a comparifon between *the one man
Adam* and *the one man Jefus Chrift,* in which
comparifon

comparifon δι ενος [oftener without than with the fubftantive ανθρωπου expreffed] is the phrafe that points out *the one man*, either *Adam* or *Chrift*, and is certainly ufed *eight* times in this very paragraph to this purpofe : I fay, if we confider this, it will perhaps appear both moft natural and reafonable to conftrue δι ενος, in this verfe, as alfo in the abovementioned 16th verfe, [three other places where it is ufed in this paffage, and the only dif-putable ones] as in the paraphrafe, *by the lapfe of the one man Adam*, *by the righteoufnefs of the one man Jefus Chrift*. I cannot but think, both Mr. Locke and Taylor have overlooked the true emphafis of thefe phrafes, by their not underftand-ing them in this fenfe ; which they were very obvioufly led to do, as they make the beginning of this 18th verfe a repetition of the Protafis, or firft part of the comparifon, in the 12th verfe ; where ανθρωπου is exprefsly joined with ενος. And this, it feems to me, fhould put the matter out of all doubt with thofe, who connect this 18th verfe with the 12th, in the manner that thefe great men do. I may properly add yet further, it is not the truth of *fact*, that it was *by one act of righteouf-nefs*, on Chrift's part, that the *gift of juftification is come upon all men*. 'Tis true, that one great act, of Chrift's righteoufnefs, his freely fubmitting to die on the crofs, is often mentioned fingly, or by itfelf, as the ground of this gift. 'Tis twice thus mentioned in this chapter, ver. 9, " being " now juftified by his *blood* ;" and, ver. 10,

" reconciled

" reconciled by the *death* of his Son." But whenever the *blood, death,* or *facrifice* of Chrift are
lingly mentioned as the ground of the gofpel donation of benefits, they are to be underftood as
including his other acts of righteoufnefs in the
capacity of mediator ; one eminent act being, by
a common figure, put for the whole. For it
is certain, that his other acts of conformity to
the law of righteoufnefs, together with this, are
the proper ground of the " gift of juftifica-
" tion." See Philip ii. 6 to 10 ; where his willingnefs to become incarnate, with all his humilia-
tions in this ftate, as well as his humiliation to
death, are exprefsly made the reafon or ground
of his *exaltation,* which virtually means the fame
thing with what is here called *the gift of juftification.* His death had eminently an influence
in the beftowment of this gift, being the moft
fignal act of fubmiffion to the governing will of
God he was ever called to exercife ; and therefore it is often fingled out, not to exclude, but
include the reft, by putting one eminent part for
the whole ; which is common in all language, prophane, as well as facred.

(17) *The judicial act came upon all,* &c.] The
Englifh reader has doubtlefs obferved, that the
words, *judgment came,* in the former part of the
apoftle's comparifon, as well as the words, *free
gift came,* in the other part, are printed in a different character from the reft of the verfe. The
reafon is, becaufe they are not in the original, but
                                        fupplied

fupplied by the tranflators.   And as this verfe, in
both parts of the comparifon it contains, is elliptical, it muft be fupplied fomehow or other.   And
perhaps it could not have been fupplied better
than by the word *judgment*, κριμα, in the *protafis*,
and the word *gift*, χαρισμα, in the *apodofis*, as in
the common Englifh verfion.   The connection of
this verfe, with the paragraph of which it is a
part, makes this fupply, or fome other analogous
to it, no matter in what words it is expreffed, neceffary to compleat the apoftle's fenfe.

   (18) *Which delivers them from death to reign in
life.*] The critical reader will perceive, that I
don't take fo much into the meaning of the word
δικαιωσις in this verfe, as I gave to the word
δικαιωμα in the 16th verfe; as alfo, that I take
the word κατακριμα here in a lefs extended fenfe,
than I underftood it there: The reafon is this,
and I defire it may be ftrictly examined, as being a very important point in order to the true
underftanding of this paragraph.   The apoftle, in
the foregoing 16th verfe, is certainly fpeaking of
the whole damage introduced by the lapfe of the
one man Adam; [See note (11)]; but then, inftead of particularly branching this damage into
its two grand parts, as he had done in the 12th
verfe, he generally includes them in the word
κατακριμα, *condemnation*, as, I think, is made evident in the note juft referred to.   In like manner, when he goes on, in the other part of the
comparifon, to defcribe the oppofite abounding
                                              advantage

advantage of the gift through the one man Jeſus Chriſt, he does not particularly branch it into its two oppoſite correſponding parts, but generally includes them in the word διχαιωμα, *juſtification,* as has been explained in the paraphraſe and note on that verſe. Whereas, in the 18th and 19th verſes, he proceeds diſtinctly and particularly to point out the correſpondence there is between the effects of Adam's lapſe, and of the gift through Chriſt. Accordingly, in the 18th verſe, he runs the compariſon between Adam and Chriſt, with reſpect to *death* and *life*; as he does, in the 19th verſe, with reſpect to *ſin* and *righteouſneſs,* ſeparately and particularly taking into the compariſon *both the diſadvantages* through the lapſe, together with the *two oppoſite correſponding advantages* through the gift. It ought to be heedfully minded here, the apoſtle, in the 12th verſe, had begun the compariſon on Adam's part, making the damage, occaſioned through his lapſe, to conſiſt in *two things,* namely, *ſin* as well as *death.* As therefore, in the 18th and 19th verſe, he has reſumed and compleated this compariſon, it may reaſonably be expected, that he ſhould mention *two advantages,* on the ſide of Chriſt, as counterparts to the *two diſadvantages,* on the ſide of Adam. This is accordingly done, in the view we have given of theſe verſes; and it makes out a beautiful and ſtrong conſiſtency between theſe verſes and the 12th: Whereas, upon other ſchemes of interpretation, particularly Mr. Locke's and

7   Taylor's,

Taylor's, there is nothing in thefe verfes to anfwer to that part of the comparifon, on Adam's fide, in the 12th verfe, εφ ω παντες ημαρτον, *whereupon all have finned.* This important point will be further illuftrated in the following notes, which the reader is defired to compare with this.

I would juft add here, though, with Mr. Locke and Taylor, I confider the word κατακριμα, *condemnation,* in this 18th verfe, as fignifying nothing more than the death which Adam's pofterity were fubjected to in confequence of his *one offence*; yet I differ from them as to the *juftification of life,* fignified by the oppofite phrafe δικαιωσιν της ζωης. They confine it to *mere deliverance from death :* Whereas, I extend it to a *reign in life for ever*; and for this very good reafon, becaufe the gift, on Chrift's part of the comparifon, ought [as we have proved note (15)] to be taken here in its *abounding* fenfe : Nor otherwife can the correfpondence between Adam and Chrift, with refpect to their being the fources of *death* and *life,* be connected with the foregoing verfes, particularly the 17th, where, not *mere deliverance from death,* but *reigning in life,* is the *abounding advantage* by Chrift, oppofed to the death by Adam.

(19) *Became finners.*] The apoftle certainly means the fame thing, in this 19th verfe, when he fays, " by the difobedience of one, the many," or all men [κατεσταθησαν αμαρτωλοι] " are made finners," as when he fays, in the 12th verfe, " and thus, *in*
" *this*

" *this way,* death hath paſſed upon all men," [εφ
ω παντες ημαρτον] " *whereupon, upon which,* in con-
" *ſequence of which,* all have ſinned."   If therefore
we may interpret this 19th verſe, by the foregoing 12th verſe, the ſenſe will be as expreſſed in
the paraphraſe.   And the truth is, this firſt clauſe
in the 19th verſe is a repetition of the latter part
of the compariſon begun, but left unfiniſhed, in
the 12th verſe, in like manner as the firſt clauſe
of the foregoing 18th verſe, is a repetition of the
former part of that ſame compariſon : For which
reaſon, the former part of this 19th verſe, and the
latter part of the 12th, muſt mean preciſely the
ſame thing, as I have made it to do.   And 'tis obſervable, in this way of interpretation, I not only
make out a clear and ſtrong connection between
the 12th, and the 18th and 19th verſes, which
anſwer to it, and reſume and compleat the compariſon that was there begun; but give the phraſes,
" all have ſinned," and " the many are made ſin-
" ners," their full natural force ; and cannot be
complained of for making *ſin,* by a harſh me-
tonymy, to ſignify *mortality.*

   (20) *Shall become righteous perſons.*] This part of
the gift, on Chriſt's ſide of the compariſon, muſt
mean our being made ſubjectively righteous, in
conſequence of his obedience, and the conſtitution
of God grounded thereon, in order to its being
a counterpart to the damage in *conſequence* of
Adam's diſobedience, mentioned in the foregoing
branch of the compariſon on his ſide, if I have
                                                given

given a juſt idea of that; as, I truſt, I have, and
have ſaid enough to make it evident that I have.
However, I would go on, and ſay further;—In
the light I have ſet theſe two verſes, they perfectly harmoniſe with each other, and with the
12th verſe; and, what may be worthy of ſpecial
notice, the connecting particle γαρ, *for,* which introduces this 19th verſe, has its proper force and
emphaſis, and makes this verſe, as it ought to do,
a reaſon, and a very good one too, of that which
immediately preceded: Whereas, if the phraſes,
αμαρτωλοι κατεσταθησαν, and δικαιοι κατασταθησονται,
are interpreted, as Mr. Locke and Taylor interpret
them, in the metonymical ſenſe, this 19th verſe
will exhibit no reaſon at all of the foregoing
18th verſe, though inſeparably joined with it by
the particle γαρ, or *for*; but will be a mere tau-
tology. For if, by all men's being *made ſinners*
through the diſobedience of Adam, and their being *made righteous* through the obedience of
Chriſt, nothing more is meant than their being
made mortal, or *ſufferers as far as death*, and being *reſtored back again to life*, this 19th verſe,
containing theſe words, cannot be a reaſon of the
18th. According to this ſenſe of thoſe phraſes,
the ſame thing is only repeated in the 19th verſe,
which had been affirmed in the 18th; and the
19th verſe, inſtead of being a reaſon or argument,
illuſtrating and confirming the 18th, (as it ought
to be, to give the connecting γαρ its juſt force) is
a needleſs repetition of one and the ſame thing;

as

as it is really made to be in the paraphraſes of both the above-named expoſitors: Nor, as I imagine, could it have been otherwiſe according to their conſtruction of the words.

Upon the whole, it ſhould ſeem indiſputably evident, that theſe verſes [the 18th and 19th] are brought in to compleat the compariſon between Adam and Chriſt, which was begun, but left unfiniſhed, in the 12th verſe: Conſequently, as *ſin* and *death*, that is, ſin upon death, in conſequence of death, are the *two grand diſadvantages*, on Adam's ſide of the compariſon, in the 12th verſe; the *ſame diſadvantages* muſt be meant in the repetition of the compariſon in the 18th and 19th verſes. This being ſo, the *advantages*, on Chriſt's ſide of the compariſon, being *counter-parts* to the *diſadvantages* on Adam's ſide, muſt mean *life* and *righteouſneſs*, anſwering to *death* and *ſin*; and this (if we would connect the 18th and 19th verſes, with the 15th, 16th, and 17th, verſes) in a ſenſe that will make theſe *advantages* to *exceed, overflow, abound beyond*, the diſadvantages by Adam, and to *mankind univerſally*, and in oppoſition to *all their own ſins* as well as his. In this view of the paragraph, its ſeveral parts are well connected with each other, with the preceding context, and whole foregoing epiſtle; and exhibit an eaſy, clear, and conſiſtent ſenſe, as well as a moſt glorioully important one: And, I will venture to ſay, no other ſenſe that has yet been put upon it, at leaſt that I have ſeen, will make

it

it either confiftent with itfelf, or the foregoing difcourfe, or give an intelligible meaning to the words in which it is delivered.

(21) *Now.*] The word, in the original, is *δε*; which, I think, fhould be tranflated *now*, (as it often is elfewhere) and not *moreover*. This 20th verfe will then naturally be connected with the foregoing difcourfe, as in the paraphrafe.

(22) *That fin—might abound*, &c.] Mr. Locke and Taylor do both of them underftand, by the *abounding of the offence* by the *entrance of the law*, ‘ an increafe or multiplication of fuch offence ‘ as Adam’s was ; fuppofing that the offence, with ‘ the penalty of death annexed to it, was but óne, ‘ namely, the offence of Adam, before the intro- ‘ duction of the law ; but that, by the introduc- ‘ tion of the law, the offence abounded, that is, ‘ was increafed and multiplied to be as numerous ‘ as all the tranfgreffions of the law which the ‘ Jews were guilty of.’ I have, in the work be- fore referred to, largely endeavoured to fhow this to be a miftake ; and fhall therefore only fay at pre- fent, that if the words, “ the law entered that fin “ might abound,” be compared with Rom. vii. 5, 6, 7, 8, 9, 10, 11, the fenfe will appear to be that which is given in the paraphrafe. The *ινα*, here pointing out the defign of the entering of the law, does not intend, that the law was given, that men might fin ; but, if they did fin, that their guilt might hereby be increafed. And this, by the way, is one of the fenfes in which the *law* was

a *fchool-*

a *school-master to bring the Jews to Christ*, as the apostle's language is, Gal. iii. 24.   By increasing their guilt, it shewed them more strongly the necessity of grace, that grace which is manifested towards men through Jesus Christ.

(23) *Abounds much beyond the utmost*, &c.] The apostle had evidently a view, in these words, to the 15th, 16th, and 17th verses, particularly the 16th, where he had made the abounding of the gift by Christ, to consist in its *surpassing all the sins of men in their own persons*, under all dispensations, as well as the lapse of the one man Adam.   The word, υπερεπερισσευσεν, here used, is emphatically strong.   Grotius, *in loc.* says ' Non satis ha-
' buit dicere επερισσευσεν, sed prepositionem augen-
' tem addidit, ut intelligeretur multò illustriùs ap-
' paruisse Dei benevolentiam quam ante apparuerat
' peccati turpitudo.   Amat tales compositiones
' *Paulus.*'   A number of instances he has accordingly there produced.

(24) *Unto eternal life through Jesus Christ.*] It may be worthy of particular remark, the apostle, while closing, or rather summing up, his whole argument upon the comparison he had been running between Adam and Christ, opposes, in this 21st verse, *an eternal reign in life* to the *reign of sin by death*; and not only so, but this *reign in life* he expressly declares to be *as extensive* as the *reign of sin by death*: And consequently, the latter being *absolutely universal*, the other must *be so too.*

The

The preceding TEXT, PARAPHRASE, *and* NOTES,
  applied to the MAIN ARGUMENT.

The reader is now defired critically to view the
two grand counterparts of the fcheme of providence, in the correfpondence they are reprefented, in the above paffage of fcripture, to have to
each other : upon which he will eafily perceive,
on the one hand, that Adam is confidered as the
fource of damage to mankind univerfally : On the
other hand, that Chrift is a like fource of advantage
to the fame mankind ; but with this obfervable difference, that the advantage, on the fide of Chrift,
exceeds, overflows, abounds beyond, the damage on
the fide of Adam ; and this to *all mankind.* Thus
much fhould feem indifputably clear and certain.
The 15th, 16th, and 17th verfes, in which the
apoftle has defcribed, *ex profeffo,* the *abounding advantage* of the gift through Chrift, *beyond* the damage
through Adam, are abfolutely unintelligible upon
any other interpretation.—To be yet more particular.

The apoftle here makes the damage, on the
fide of Adam, to confift in *two things,* namely, the
fubjection of *all men* to a *frail mortal life* here on
earth, and a *liablenefs thereupon,* or in *confequence
thereof,* to be drawn into the commiffion of that
which is *finful.* [The reader is defired carefully
to attend to the foregoing notes, on which the
proof of what is here offered is principally refted.]
The *oppofite fuper-abounding* advantage through
Chrift, he accordingly places in *two things,* name-

G   ly,

ly, a *reign in life*, and a being formed to a meetneſs for this mercy by being made *righteous per-*
ſons; and this, notwithſtanding the influence of
all the ſins that are conſequent upon Adam's ſin,
whether in point of power, or demerit. And, remark well, this ſuperabounding advantage through
Chriſt, in *both its branches*, is extended to the
ſame mankind who have ſuffered the oppoſite damage through Adam. Thus, in the 16th verſe,
the *gift through Chriſt*, [εις δικαιωμα] terminating in a reign in life as righteous perſons, is applied to the ſame mankind who were ſpoken of, in
the foregoing clauſe of that verſe, as ſubjected to a
ſentence [εις κατακριμα] terminating in the whole
damage through Adam. This matter is yet more
diſtinctly and clearly ſettled in the 18th and 19th
verſes, where the damage through Adam, and the
advantage through Chriſt, are ſeparately and particularly treated of in both their grand parts, and
oppoſed to each other. In the 18th verſe, the damage through Adam, is *judgment to condemna-*
tion; the oppoſite advantage through Chriſt, is
the *juſtification of life*: And the juſtification of
life is directly ſaid to have come upon the *ſame*
all men that were under the judgment to condemnation. In the 19th verſe, the damage through
Adam is *ſin*; the advantage through Chriſt is
righteouſneſs: And the *ſame many*, or *all men*, who,
in conſequence of Adam's diſobedience, are made
ſinners, are, in conſequence of Chriſt's obedience,
made righteous. The damage through Adam,

and

and the advantage through Chriſt, in both their branches, are preciſely of the *ſame extent*; reaching, not to ſome only among men, but to the *whole human race*, mankind univerſally, without exception, or limitation.

And it may be worthy of further ſpecial notice, the *ſuper-abounding advantage*, on the ſide of Chriſt, together with the damage on the ſide of Adam, are equally ſpoken of as *certain* with reſpect to their *event*, or actually coming into *effect*. Is the " judgment to condemnation come upon all " men?" So is " the juſtification of life," ver. 18 ; that is to ſay, all men are as certainly put into ſuch circumſtances through Chriſt, as that they ſhall reign in life, as they are through Adam ſubjected to death. Are *the many*, or all men, made ſinners, in conſequence of Adam's diſobedience ? It is as peremptorily and abſolutely declared, that the *ſame many*, or all men, ſhall be made righteous, in conſequence of the *obedience of Chriſt*, ver. 19. Theſe advantages through Chriſt are as *certain* with reſpect to their *event*, or coming into *fact*, as the oppoſite diſadvantages through Adam. They are indeed, to ſpeak plainly, *the abſolutely free gift of God through Jeſus Chriſt*, and will be carried into *effect*, ſooner or later, with reſpect to the *whole race of men*. This is the plain, natural, moſt obvious, meaning of this ſcripture paſſage ; and it can, as I imagine, have no other intelligible conſiſtent ſenſe put upon it.

Only, let it be heedfully obſerved here, *death*,

being

being a natural difadvantage, may come upon mankind by the appointment, or conftitution, of God, without the intervening confideration of their own mifufed agency. In like manner, fimple deliverance from death, being a natural advantage, may, by a like conftitution of God, be fecured to the fame mankind without any regard had to their own well-ufed agency. And accordingly, this is the real truth of the cafe. The human race come into the world under the difadvantage of being fubjected to death, in virtue of a divine conftitution, occafioned folely by the offence of the *one man Adam* ; and they come into exiftence likewife under the advantage of an abfolute affurance, that they fhall be delivered from death, in virtue of a divine conftitution, occafioned folely by the obedience of the *one man Jefus Chrift.* Deliverance from the power of the grave is *as abfolutely* and *certainly* the advantage even *all men* are under through Chrift, as fubjection to death is the difadvantage that has come upon them through Adam. The advantage is no more connected with their own agency, than was the difadvantage ; but, be their character what it will, they fhall as furely hear the voice of the Son of God, and come forth from their graves, as they went down into them. This is as evident as that there fhall be a *general refurrection* from the dead.

But the cafe is quite different, with refpect to the other difadvantage through Adam, and its

oppofite

oppofite advantage through Chrift, namely, *fin*
and *righteoufnefs*. Adam's lapfe became a difadvantage to all men, with refpect to their being
finners. This is plain from the 12th and 19th
verfes. But how did it become a difadvantage?
Evidently, as they derived from him, in confequence of his lapfe, a frail mortal nature, *whereupon, from whence,* they took occafion to fin themfelves. The obedience of Chrift, on the other
hand, becomes an advantage with refpect to their
being righteous. But how? Evidently, as, in confequence of this obedience of his, and the conftitution of God grounded thereon, they will be
wrought upon, fooner or later, in a moral way, fuch
an one as is adjufted to moral agents, to become
righteous perfons. For it ought always to be
kept in mind, that righteoufnefs is as truly a
moral good quality, as fin is a moral evil one.
They are both connected with perfonal agency,
and abfolutely dependent on it. We can no more
be made righteous by the righteoufnefs of another
transferred to us, and reckoned our's, than we can
be made finners by the fin of another transferred
in like manner. They are both moral impoffibi-
lities, and equally fo.

That part therefore of the advantage through
Chrift, which confifts in our being made righteous, and in this way becoming qualified for an
happy reign in life, after we are delivered from
death, effentially fuppofes the *ufe of means,* and
fuch too as are proper to be ufed with moral
agents, in order to their being formed, agreeably

G 3

to

to their natures, into righteous perfons, or, what means the fame thing, a meetnefs for an eternal reign in happy life. And this, at once, lets us into the true reafon of the erection of the gofpel-kingdom, with all its means, privileges, bleffings, and motives. And this alfo, I would add, is the true reafon of *ftill other difpenfations*, which will (as we fhall fee by and by) hereafter take place, that fo mankind univerfally may, at length, be wrought upon, and in a rational way, to become righteous perfons. For it is *as abfolutely* declar-ed, in this paffage of fcripture, that they *fhall be made righteous*, as that they are *made fin-ners*. And unlefs they are thus *made righteous*, before the time of the end, that they may be fitted to reign in life, the advantage through Chrift, inftead of *exceeding*, *abounding beyond*, the damage through Adam, will really fink below it; which is a flat contradiction to the main fcope of the apoftle's argument in this paragraph, more efpecially the 15th, 16th, and 17th verfes. The plain truth is, *final everlafting falvation is abfolutely the free gift of God to all men through Jefus Chrift*; that is to fay, he has *abfolutely* and *unconditionally* determined, of his rich mercy, through the inter-vening mediation of his Son Jefus Chrift, that *all men*, the *whole race* of lapfed Adam, fhall *finally reign in life*, and be *prepared for that ftate* by being formed into *righteous perfons*. The whole fcope of the apoftle's difcourfe leads to fuch a conception of the matter : Nor can it, upon any other inter-pretation, as I freely own it appears to me, be poffibly poſſibly true, that *the gift, through the one man Jeſus Chriſt, hath* ABOUNDED BEYOND, EXCEEDED, *the damage through the one man Adam :* Nay, the apoſtle's reaſoning, upon any other ſuppoſition, ought, in all reaſon and juſtice, to be inverted, and the advantage, in the parallel he is running, be given to Adam inſtead of Chriſt : For the damage by Adam *certainly* and *univerſally* comes into *event* ; and if this never is to be the truth with reſpect to the advantage through Chriſt, how can it be but that the damage ſhould *exceed, ſtretch beyond,* the gift ?

The ſhort of the caſe is, the *abounding glory* of the gift through Chriſt lies in this, that it *abſolutely* places all mankind under circumſtances, with reſpect to an eternal reign in happy life, that *ſurmount, go beyond, ſurpaſs,* all their diſadvantages, whether occaſioned by the lapſe through Adam, or their own ſins conſequent thereupon. No other idea of the grace and gift through Chriſt will give a conſiſtency, much leſs an emphatical cogency, to the apoſtle's reaſoning here. Infallibly, if the greater part of the human kind, notwithſtanding this gift, and the *abounding* of it, are left to periſh eternally, in conſequence of the lapſe through Adam, a broader foundation is really laid for their groaning under the damage by him, than for their rejoicing in the oppoſite advantage derived to the world through Jeſus Chriſt : Nay, it will demonſtrably follow, that Adam has done *more hurt* than Chriſt has done *good* ; and conſe-

quently,

quently, that the race of men have more reaſon for complaint on account of his diſobedience, than they have for thankfulneſs on account of Chriſt's obedience: Which is a thought as far from re-dounding to the honor of God, or his ſon Jeſus Chriſt, as it is with ſuiting the main drift of the apoſtle's arguing in this portion of ſcripture we have been thus long conſidering.

The only difficulty the above interpretation is liable to, that I know of, is this ;—that it ſeems inconſiſtent with the general run of ſcripture, which threatens a miſimprovement of the goſpel, and its means, advantages, and bleſſings, with certain death after the reſurrection at the great day, when all men ſhall be reſtored to life.   And how, it will be aſked, can men univerſally reign in life for ever, when ſo many are finally diſobedient to the goſpel, and muſt, for that reaſon, ſuffer the pains of the ſecond death ?   This, I own, is a difficulty ; and it is the very one that has put interpreters upon conſtruing the apoſtle's words, in this paragraph, quite differently from what they would otherwiſe have done.   And the truth is, they have greatly perplexed his reaſoning, and ſadly tortured his words, in order to reconcile what he has here ſaid with the ſcripture account of that death, or miſery, which wicked men ſhall ſuffer after the general reſurrection.   But this difficulty, it is hoped, we ſhall, in the progreſs of this work, intirely remove away, by ſhowing, in fact, how wicked men may univerſally reign in life, through Jeſus Chriſt,
though

though many of them will firft fuffer the fecond death for their fin and folly in this prefent ftate.

I cannot proceed to the other texts under this propofition, till I have fuggefted this further thought in confirmation of the fenfe we have put upon the above paffage, namely, its giving a fin-gular pertinency to the immediately following words, which begin the next chapter; " What fhall " we fay then ? fhall we continue in fin, that grace " may abound ? God forbid !" For they will now be brought in to guard againft the ill ufe, that might be apt to be made of the foregoing doctrine of univerfal grace. And thus introduced, there will be a fingular juftnefs in them, which there is not in the other ways of interpretation. . If the *abounding of the grace,* and of *the gift through Chrift,* of which the apoftle had been fpeaking, was only a conditional offer of life, (as Dr. Tay-lor fuppofes) that is, the offer of it in cafe men would improve their gofpel-advantages, which if they did not, they muft certainly perifh notwith-ftanding this offer; I fee not with what propriety any could be introduced, from this doctrine of his, as pleading, that *they might continue in fin that grace might abound:* Whereas, upon our interpre-tation, which makes the *abounding of the grace through Chrift* to iffue finally in men's *univerfally reigning in life,* notwithftanding all their *own fins,* as well as the *one lapfe of Adam,* this is an obvious and natural pretence; and it might indeed be
reafonably

reasonably expected, that the apostle should take care to guard against the undue influence of it: Which he accordingly does, in this sixth chapter, by a variety of considerations; among which, that, in the 21st and 22d verses, is one, and not the least weighty, " What fruit had ye in those things " whereof ye are now ashamed? For the end of " those things is death. But now being made free " from sin, and become servants to God, ye have " your fruit unto holiness, and the end everlasting " life." His design, in these words, plainly is to discourage men from abusing the *grace of God through Christ*, by pointing out, on the one hand, the evil effects that would follow upon their indulging to sin, notwithstanding what he had said of the *abounding of the grace of God*, viz. *shame* in *this* world, and the *second death* in the *next*; and, on the other hand, the *happy effects* that would follow upon their approving themselves the faithful servants of God, viz. their being *immediately* instated in *eternal life* upon their *resurrection* at the great day. This same thought he further enforces, in the 23d verse, in these words, " For the wages " of sin is death; but the gift of God is eternal " life, through Jesus Christ our Lord;" that is, If men continue the servants of sin, the wages they shall receive, before the gift through Christ is conferred on them, will be the *second death*; whereas, if they become the servants of God, this gift through Christ will issue in their eternal life without their passing through the second death.

This,

This, I am fenfible, will be called a novel interpretation; but it may notwithftanding be the true
one: And, I believe, it will be found, upon examination, to be the only one that is fo. For it is
to be remembered, an eternal reign in life is the
grant of God's free favour to all men, as grounded
on the obedience of Jefus Chrift, according to the
whole tenor of the apoftle's arguing in the foregoing chapter; and therefore, when, in order to
guard againft the ill ufe that might be made of this
abounding favor of God, he fays, that, if men
encourage themfelves herefrom to continue the
fervants of fin, their folly will end in *death*; whereas, if they are wrought upon, by this grace, to become the *fervants of God*, the end will be *eternal
life*: I fay, when the apoftle fpeaks thus, he can
mean, in confiftency with himfelf, and to the purpofe of his argument, nothing more, with refpect
to the *fervants of fin*, than *death previoufly to a reign
in life*; and with refpect to the *fervants of God*, an
inftatement *in life without paffing through the fecond
death.*—But the reader may not be, at prefent,
prepared to difcern the propriety of this interpretation, or the force of the argument grounded on
it. He may therefore, if he pleafes, fufpend his
judgment till he has gone further into the fcriptures that fupport the fcheme we are upon.

Another text, to the purpofe of our prefent argument, we meet with in Rom. viii. from the 19th
to the 24th verfe; which, according to the foregoing

going method, I ſhall firſt lay before the reader's view with a paraphraſe ; then juſtify the paraphraſe by correſponding notes ; and finally ſhew the pertinency of the text, as explained in the paraphraſe and notes, to the main point in proſecution.

TEXT.	PARAPHRASE.
19. *For the earneſt expeſtation of the creature waiteth for the manifeſtation of the ſons of God.*	For (26) the creature, the rational creature, mankind in general (27), waits in earneſt expeſtation for the time when it ſhall be revealed that they are the *ſons of God* by being made *glorious̄ly immortal* (28). And they may with good reaſon, upon a juſt and ſolid foundation,
20. *For the creature was made ſubjeſt to vanity, not willingly, but by reaſon of him who ſubjeſted the ſame in hope,*	thus wait ; FOR (29) the rational creature, or mankind, was ſubjeſted to the infeliciłies of this preſent vain mortal life (30), not through any fault of its own (31); but by the judicial ſentence of him who ſubjeſted it (32), not *finally* and *for ever*, but *in conſequence* of a *previous hope*, having firſt given reaſon to
21. *Becauſe the creature itſelf alſo ſhall be delivered from*	expeſt (33) *that* (34) even *this very* creature, the *ſelf ſame* mankind (35), ſhould be delivered

TEXT.

from the bondage of corruption, into the glorious liberty of the children of God.

22. *For we know, that the whole creation groaneth, and travaileth in pain together until now.*

PARAPHRASE.

delivered from its *flavery* through the influence of a *frail mortal corruptible body* (36), into the freedom of thofe, who, as the fons of God, fhall, in proper time, be clothed with *immortal incorruptible bodies* (37). I had faid, in the 19th verfe, that mankind wait, with earneft expectation, for the revelation of the fons of God; and I have proved, in the 20th and 21ft verfes, that they might reafonably thus wait with expectation: I now come to fpeak to the truth of the fact itfelf, to fhow that they *are really waiting* for this revelation of fons; upon which much need not be faid, FOR (38) it is a certain truth, we all know, that the whole rational creation, even all mankind, feel the vanity of this prefent ftate, and have all along done fo from the entrance of fin and death into the world; infomuch that they have groaned un-

der

TEXT.	PARAPHRASE.
	der it, and been in pain, like a woman in labour, longing to be delivered (39). Now (40) fuch is the conftitution of things, in the all-wife go-
23. *And not only they, but ourfelves alfo, which have the firft fruits of the Spi- rit, even we our- felves groan within ourfelves, waiting for the adoption, to wit, the redemption of our body.*	vernment of God, that not only mankind in general, but we Chriftians alfo, who have had the " firft fruits of the " fpirit (41)" beftowed on us, even we ourfelves do groan under the preffures of this vain life, which groaning of ours is a virtual and con- ftructive waiting for the adoption, I mean, the deli- verance of our *bodies* from their *mortal corruptible* con- dition, when they fhall be cloathed with *immortality* and *glory.*

NOTES *juftifying the foregoing* PARAPHRASE.

(26) *For,* γαρ.] This illative particle denotes an argumentative connection between the para- graph beginning with the 19th verfe, and the preceding difcourfe; which appears to me to ftand thus. In the 17th verfe, the apoftle had argued, with refpect to himfelf and all good Chriftians, whom

whom he had been speaking of as *children* ; I say, he had argued, " if children, then heirs," that is, to some valuable inheritance ; " heirs of God," that is, to an inheritance worthy of so great and munificent a father ; and " joint heirs " to it " with Christ ; inasmuch as," or since *(a)* " we " suffer with him, that we may be also glorified " together." In the 18th verse, he had argued *(b)* still further, " that the sufferings of this " present

(a) So I think the conjunction ειπερ should have been translated, and not, *if so be.* 'Tis certain it may properly be thus translated ; and if it *may,* it ought to be so here. For it may be worth observing, the *force* of the apostle's reasoning (which perhaps has not been attended to, if perceived, by expositors) from *sonship* to *heirship* lies in this, that the *children* are, at present, in *suffering* circumstances. Were we wholly exempt from *sufferings here,* we could never argue, from our being the *children* of God, that we were *heirs* to any *better* or *higher* state *hereafter.* There would then have been no foundation, in reason, to think, but that this was to be our *final* state. But taking in the consideration of our *sufferings,* the conclusion is just, and the argument stands thus ; *Since we are the children of God,* and yet in a *state of suffering,* we may argue, that we are *heirs to a better state,* inasmuch as God placed us in this state of *suffering* with this view, and for this end, that we might be fitted for, and at length introduced into, a state of *glory.* Thus we may argue *now* ; but when we have attained to this *glorious state,* we can no longer argue, *if children, then heirs.*

(b) So this 18th verse is introduced. *I argue,* λογιζομαι. This verb, when used *passively,* signifies to *be reckoned,* or *put to account* ; and thus it is frequently used in this epistle, and elsewhere. But when it is used *actively,* it also signifies to *think,* to *reason,* to *argue,* to *prove,* to *conclude by argument.* This

" prefent time are not worthy to be compared
" with the glory that fhall be revealed [εις ημας,
" not *in,* but] *to us.*" Particularly remark here,
the *glory,* the apoftle is treating of, is glory in
futurity; glory that is the object, not of fight,
but of hope ; glory that is not at prefent enjoyed,
but muft be waited for till the proper time of its
revelation. The apoftle emphatically enlarges
upon this thought, in the 24th and 25th verfes,
which ought to be read, and compared, with this,
as they are a clear and full comment upon it. In
this manner, the 19th verfe, and the following
one, of which it is a part, are introduced ; and,
as I imagine, with a double view ; 1. To fhew
the reafonablenefs of what the apoftle had been
juft arguing, namely, that thofe who are the children of God are heirs to glory, glory incomparably
more than a balance for their fufferings ; 2. To
reconcile them to the thought of its being glory,
not in poffeffion, but expectation only ; what they
do not actually enjoy, but muft patiently wait for.
And, in both thefe views, there is a fingular pertinency and force in what the apoftle advances in
this paragraph. For if *the creature,* the rational
creature, mankind in common [fee note (27)] are
the fons of God, his fons fo as that glory fhall be

This fenfe it has in Mark xi. 31. Rom. iii. 28. Heb. xi. 19.
and in other places. And in this fenfe it ought to be taken
here. As if the apoftle had faid, ' I argue, reafon, or con-
' clude, from our being the children of God, *that the fufferings*
' *of this prefent time, &c.*'

revealed

revealed to them [fee note (28)]; *much more* shall this be the cafe of thofe who are the children of God, as having the " fpirit of adoption," as being formed to a refemblance of their heavenly Father in his moral image. And if it is the wife conftitution of God, with refpect to the whole rational creation in this lower world, that glory is the object of their hope only; what they do not at prefent enjoy, but muft come to through fufferings, after long and patient waiting: I fay, if God has thus conftituted things, thofe who are his children, as being partakers of his nature, fhould not complain, they have no reafon to complain, that the like conftitution takes place with regard to them. This I take to be the ground of connection between the paragraph we are now entering upon, and the preceding verfes in this chapter, which I defire may be carefully attended to.

(27) *The creature, mankind in common.*] Some, I am fenfible, by η κλισις in this 19th verfe, and πασα η κλισις in the 22d verfe, underftand the inanimate creation; which, fay they, was fubjected to vanity, through the lapfe of the one man Adam, and fhall finally be delivered from it. They accordingly fuppofe, that the apoftle here brings in this whole creation, by a ftrong rhetorical figure, as groaning under its prefent vanity, and longing, and waiting for the time when it fhall be reftored to its original ftate. And fhould this be the thing intended by the apoftle, it would rather ftrengthen, than weaken, the grand point I am aiming to prove. For

H   furely,

surely, if πασα κλισις is extended in its meaning so as to take in the inanimate part of the creation, the rational or moral part ought *much more* to be comprehended. For though, on the one hand, the rational part of the creation may properly enough be ſtiled πασα η κλισις, without including the inanimate part ; yet it would be highly incongruous, on the other hand, to give this ſtile to the inferior, or leſs valuable part, wholly leaving out the moſt excellent : eſpecially would it be ſo here, if it be remembered, that the judicial act of God, ſubjecting the creation to vanity, was *ultimately* pronounced againſt the rational creation, or mankind : and reſpected the creation, as to its inanimate part, no otherwiſe than as a *means* to carry this ſentence againſt mankind more effectually into execution. The rational creation therefore, or mankind, ought to be conſidered as the *ultimate object* of the deliverance from vanity here treated of ; and the creation, in the more extended ſenſe, no otherwiſe, than as its deliverance might be a *means* ſubſervient to the great end of delivering mankind. Thus the above interpretation is no ways inconſiſtent with the argument I am upon. But yet, I am fully perſuaded, it is not the true one.

It does not agree with the other parts of this ſame paragraph. The phraſes, *earneſt expectation, waiting, groaning, travailing together in pain*, are more naturally and obviouſly applicable to the *rational* than *inanimate* creation ; and do not call

for

for fo bold a figure in fupport of their propriety. Befides, which is of far greater importance, it is exprefsly faid of this creature, or whole creation, that it was fubjected to vanity, ουχ εκουσα, *not wil-fully* [fee note (31).] But the rational creature, or creation, is the only creature, or creation, that could poffibly be thus fubjected to vanity. Further, it is affirmed of the creature, and whole creation, that it fhall be " delivered from the bon- " dage of corruption," that is, its flavery, through the influence of a frail corruptible body, " into the " glorious liberty of the children of God," that is, the freedom of thofe who, as God's fons, fhall be cloathed with immortal incorruptible bodies [fee notes (36) (37)]; but no creature in this lower world, befides man, no creation but that which is intelligent and moral, can, with any propriety of fpeech, have fuch things affirmed of them. Moreover, the comparifon in the 23d verfe, between " we ourfelves, who have the firft fruits of the " Spirit," and the *creature*, or *whole creation*, will be eafy and natural, if we underftand by the phrafes, the *rational* creature, and creation; but uncouth and harfh, if we extend their meaning any further.

But what is moft of all worthy of notice is, that the phrafe πασα κλισις is never ufed [one difputed text only excepted, Col. i. 15, fee note (41)] in all the New Teftament, to fignify more than the *whole moral creation*, or *all mankind*. And 'tis remarkable, when the apoftles were commiffioned

H 2

to preach the gofpel to *all mankind,* the words are,
Mark xvi. 15, πασꞥ τꞥ ϰλισϵι.   So, when the gofpel
is faid to have been preached, in confequence of
this commiffion, to *all mankind,* the fame words
are ufed, πασꞥ τꞥ ϰλισϵι, Col. i. 25.   And .that the
rational creature, or mankind, is the *only* meaning
of thefe words, may certainly be collected from
Matt. xxviii. 18, and Luke xxiv. 47, where the
gofpel is fpoken of as entrufted with the apoftles,
to be preached, ϵις πανϊα τα ϵθνꞥ, that is, *to all
nations of men.*   So that it is the *rational* creature,
the *rational* creation, or *all mankind,* that the apoftle
is here fpeaking of.

(28) *Revealed to be the fons of God, &c.*] That
by the phrafe, τꞥν αποϰαλυψιν των υιων του Θϵου, is
meant fuch a *revelation of the fons of God* as imports
their *glorious immortality,* is evident from the
whole fcope of the apoftle's reafoning in this paffage, as well as from its connection with the preceding verfes.   Nor will this be difputed.   'Tis
the fenfe in which the words are commonly underftood.   The only controverfy here is, whether
thefe words are to be connected with the *creature,*
the *rational creature, mankind in common* ; as fignifying, that the time will come, when THEY
fhall be *revealed to be the fons of God* by being
made *glorioufly immortal.*   And it evidently appears
to me, that this is the apoftle's meaning : Nor
will any other meaning, as I imagine, make out
an *argumentative* confiftency between this *verfe*
and the *other verfes* it is connected with, whether
thofe

thofe that go before, or follow after it. The apoftle had been arguing, in the *foregoing* verfes, that the *fufferings* of *good Chriftians* fhould be *over-balanced* with a *future weight* of *glory*; and very juftly, if the time is coming when the *creature*, that is, mankind in common, fhall be *revealed to be the fons of God*, notwithftanding all the *fufferings* they may groan under, by being admitted to *immortality* and *glory*: For this is arguing, and very ftrongly too, *à fortiori*. But, if this *revelation of fons* is a revelation that the *creature*, or mankind, will not be *finally* benefited by, why are their groanings, under the preffures of this vain life, reprefented as a *longing*, and *waiting* for it? Why fhould they *long* and *wait* for a *revelation of glory* that will be, as to them, of no manner of fervice? And how can their waiting for that which they will never obtain, be an *argument* [as it ought to be, to give the connecting γαρ its proper force, fee note (26)] that the *fufferings* of *good Chriftians* are not *worthy to be compared with the glory that fhall be revealed to them?* Befides, which ought to be well regarded, *the revelation of the fons of God*, in this 19th verfe, means the fame thing with *deliverance from the bondage of corruption into the glorious liberty of the children of God*, in the 21ft verfe; to be fure, thefe *latter* words include in them as much as the *former*, and neither of them comprehend lefs than a *glorious immortality*. Now, the *creature*, *the whole creation*, even *mankind univerfally*, is exprefsly made, in this 21ft verfe,

the

the SUBJECT of this *glorious immortality* ; yea, it is
affirmed here of the *ſame creature*, the *ſelf-ſame
mankind*, which had been *ſubjeĉted to vanity*, ver. 20,
that it ſhall be *delivered from it* ſo, as to be *glorȳouſly
immortal* This *immortality* therefore is *the revelation of ſons* ſpoken of in the 19th verſe, which *the
creature*, or *mankind*, are *longing* and *waiting* for.
The words, conſidered in this view, make out a
ſtrong connection between the ſeveral parts of the
apoſtle's diſcourſe here, which cannot otherwiſe
conſiſt together.

(29) *For.*] The particle *for*, γαρ, evidently
ſtands here to denote that this, and the following
verſe, are brought in as the *reaſon*, or *argument*,
why *mankind* earneſtly expect *the revelation of God's
ſons*, its being made to appear that they are *his
ſons* by their being crowned finally with *immortality* and *honor* ; namely, becauſe they were *ſubjeĉted
to vanity*, not *through their own fault*, but in virtue
of a *divine conſtitution*, which conſtitution did not
take place till *juſt ground* had been *firſt given for
this expeĉtation* [ſee note (33)]. 'Tis obſervable,
the arguing here, as to its true import, is preciſely
the ſame with that in Rom. v. 15, *If through the
offence of one the many*, or all men, *are dead* ; MUCH
MORE *hath grace* ABOUNDED *to the* ſame *many*, or
all men ; that is, 'tis much more credible to
ſuppoſe it, 'tis much more reaſonable to believe it.
And the arguing is ſtrictly concluſive. For if
mankind were ſubjeĉted to a ſtate of *ſuffering*, not
through any *wilful diſobedience* which they themselves

felves had been *perfonally* guilty of, it is congruous
to reafon to think, that they fhould be fubjected
to it, not *finally* and *for ever*, but with room for
hope that they fhould be delivered from it. And
was it not for this *hope*, it cannot be fuppofed, it
ought not to be fuppofed, it would be a reflection
on the fupremely perfect benevolence of the Deity
to fuppofe, that they would have been fubjected to
it. Sherlock, Bifhop of *London*, very juftly
argues upon this head, [*Ufe of Prophecy*, page 284]
' Whoever views mankind in their prefent ftate,
' into which they came by no voluntary act of
' their own, but were placed in it by him who is
' their maker, and will be their judge ; fubject to
' ignorance, and fuperftition, by a kind of neceffity
' of birth and education ; furrounded with many
' natural infirmities and paffions, arifing from no
' *crime* of which they are *confcious* ; and, at the
' fame time, confiders the benignity of the divine
' nature, and the love of God towards his crea-
' tures, of which the affection of natural parents is
' but a faint refemblance, will eafily fee that the
' condition of man pleads ftrongly for mercy ; that
' nature, with unutterable groans, calls for help
' and deliverance for her children ; and that there
' is great reafon to expect, from the goodnefs of
' God, that he will not be deaf to their cries.'
And indeed [as he goes on, page 291] ' Were it
' not for a juft expectation, from the promifes of
' God, that all the miferies and confufions in the
' world fhall *finally* end to the glory of God, and

' the

' the good of thofe who continue with patience
' in well-doing, [he might with the fame force of
' argument have fpoken as *extenfively* as I do; nor
' indeed is his argument otherwife conclufive] it
' had been far greater mercy to have put an end to
' two wretched lives, than to continue them, for the
' propagation of wickednefs and mifery, to a thou-
' fand generations.' Nor can it be thought, [as
this fame author fays, page 286] ' that God would
' have fuffered the world to have been filled with
' weak miferable creatures, had he not intended
' them for *objects of his mercy.*'

   (30) *Was fubjected to vanity.*] This vanity includes
in it not only *mortality*, but all the *unavoidable
unhappinefs* and *imperfection* of this prefent *weak,
frail, mortal* ftate. We cannot conceive more
juftly of the thing aimed at by the apoftle than
by confulting *Solomon's* book of *Ecclefiaftes*, which
muft fatisfy us, that man's life on earth is fufficiently *vain*; efpecially, if we compare what is
there faid with what we feel within ourfelves.

   (31) *Not through any fault of its own.*] This I take
to be the true import of the words ουχ εκουσα ;
which cannot be better illuftrated than in Dr. *Taylor's* words. He fays (in loc.) ' εκουσα feems to
' have the fame fignification as εκουσιως, *wilfully*,
' Heb. x. 26; or as θελοντας, 2 Pet. iii. 5. *this
' they are* WILFULLY *ignorant of.* What we render *lie
' not in wait* (Exod. xxi. 13) the Seventy render ουχ
' εκων, *not wilfully*, in oppofition to *prefumptuoufly*,
' in the next verfe. Thus εκουσα denotes a *cri-
                                              ' minal*

'*minal choice,* and in an high fenfe too, [carefully
'obferve how εκουσιως ftands, Heb. x. 26] name-
'ly, a tranfgreffion fubjecting to wrath. *The crea-*
'*ture was made fubject to vanity,* not by its *own*
'*criminal choice,* not by *finning after the fimilitude*
'*of Adam's tranfgreffion.* Rom. v. 14.'

(32) *But by the judicial fentence,* &c.] The apoftle
having faid, *negatively,* in the foregoing words,
how mankind were not fubjected to vanity, declares here, *pofitively,* how they were, namely, δια
του υποταξαντα, *by* or *through him who fubjected them.*
Mr. *Locke* fuppofes, with fome others, that the
devil was the *him through whom* mankind were
fubjected to vanity. And it is true, it was through
the *devil's* fubtlety, in managing the *temptation*
with which he affaulted our firft parents, that
fin was introduced into the world, *that fin* which
gave rife to this *fubjection to vanity.* But though
the *devil's* temptation was the occafion of fin, and
fin the occafion of mankind's fubjection to vanity; and fo the *devil* may (as well as our *firft*
parents) in a fenfe, be faid to have been the *au-*
thor of this *fubjection:* Yet the WILL OF GOD,
publifhed in the JUDICIAL SENTENCE taking rife
from *Adam's lapfe,* was THAT, and THAT ONLY,
which really *fubjected mankind to vanity.* This
WILL or CONSTITUTION of God therefore, thus
taking rife from *Adam's lapfe,* muft be the thing
intended by the apoftle: Nor will there be any
room for doubt upon the matter, if we compare
what is here faid with this apoftle's more enlarged

declaration

declaration upon this ſame point, in the 5th *chapter* of this *epiſtle*, where he ſays, ver. 16, " The JUDG- " MENT came by one to CONDEMNATION ;" and yet more fully, ver. 18, " By the offence of one JUDG- " MENT came upon all men to CONDEMNATION." The plain meaning of which texts is—that mankind univerſally were *ſubjected to vanity*, or *mortality*, with all the appendages of them, by the JUDICIAL SENTENCE OF GOD, taking riſe, not from their *own* diſobedience, but the *ſin of the one man Adam*, their common father.

(33) *In conſequence of a previous hope.*] This, I am fully perſuaded, is the true meaning of the phraſe, επ ελπιδι. The prepoſition επι has this force, when uſed with a dative caſe, moſt com- monly throughout the New Teſtament. [See note (3) on *chapter* 5th, ver. 12th.] And perhaps επι, rather than any other prepoſition, was here joined with ελπιδι, to ſignify, that the *judicial ſen- tence*, ſubjecting mankind to vanity, was not *merely poſterior*, in point of time, to the *hope* of *deliver- ance*, but *conſequent upon it* in the purpoſe of God ; *ſo conſequent* as that he never would have paſſed the ſentence, had he not intended to have given *reaſon* for this *hope*. It may be worthy of ſpecial notice here, the *judicial ſentence* of God, which ſub- jected mankind to vanity, that is, the infelicities of this vain mortal life, was not pronounced till a SAVIOUR HAD BEEN PROMISED, and proviſion ac- tually made for their *deliverance*, not only from the *final conſequences* of this ſentence, but for their reinſtatement

reinftatement univerfally in *immortal happinefs*.
For, if we turn to the *third chapter* of Genefis,
we fhall find, that *the feed of the woman to bruife
the ferpent's head* was promifed BEFORE the *fentence*, dooming the race of Adam to vanity, was
given out. And this *promife* contains *fummarily*
that *difpenfation of grace* which mankind, from the
lapfe of Adam, have all along been under, though
perhaps few of them have known it; and in *confequence* of it they have all along been interefted in
the gift and grace through Chrift, which the apoftle
treats of in the 5th chapter of this *epiftle*; and in
the *deliverance from the bondage of corruption into
the glorious liberty of children*, of which he is
fpeaking in the paffage under debate. We fhall
have occafion to fhew more particularly afterwards, that this is the true import of the promife, " the feed of the woman fhall bruife the fer-
" pent's head."

I fhall only add here, Mr. Locke, Albertus,
and fome others, had no need to make the 20th
verfe a *parenthefis*, that fo they might join the
words εϖ ελπιδι, with the verb αϖεκδεχεται. This
conftruction is lefs agreeable to the fyntax of
the paffage than the common tranflation, which
connects *in hope* with the foregoing words, *fubjected the fame*. And the *fenfe* abfolutely requires
this conftruction, if there be any truth or pertinency in what has been above advanced, which
is left with the reader to judge.

(34) *That.*] It would be an affront to thofe, in
any

any meafure verfed in *Greek*, to point out places, where the particle οτι is ufed precifely in the fenfe which I have here given it. Scarce a paragraph of any length can be met with, throughout the New Teftament, without an inftance to this purpofe. It is a wonder to me this word was *here* tranflated *becaufe*. Not that this is not fometimes its proper meaning; but not in this place: And it fo perplexes the fenfe, that it is, I believe, impoffible a merely *Englifh* reader fhould ever underftand the apoftle.

(35) *Even this very creature.*] The repetition of this word *creature* [κτισις] feemed quite harfh to Erafmus. Beza thought it was brought in *more Hebraico.* Zech. Pierce fuppofes it was originally a *marginal glofs*, and from thence too haftily taken into the text; but he does not feem to have good reafon for this thought, as κτισις is inferted in all the *copies* and *verfions*. Vide Wolfii. Cur. Philolog. *in loc.* And it appears to me, that, upon the fcheme of interpretation I am explaining, it is emphatical; efpecially as it is not a fimple repetition, but a repetition joined with και αυτη. The apoftle, as I imagine, would fuggeft, by the words και αυτη η κτισις, that *even that very creature, the felf-fame mankind,* who was *fubjected to vanity,* fhould be alfo *delivered from it*; which is expreffed far more ftrongly by the repetition of κτισις with the pronoun αυτη, than it would have been without it.

(36) *Shall be delivered from the flavery, &c.*] It would not affect the main argument I am purfuing,

ing, if I fhould allow the common interpretation of the words ελευθερωθησεται απο της δουλειας της φθορας to be the true one. But I am clearly fatiffied it is not ; and that the fenfe given in the paraphrafe ought to be preferred. For it is evident, from the whole run of the apoftle Paul's writings, not only that the *creature*, or man, is under *bonds to death*, that is, fubjected to a frail, mortal, corruptible condition ; but that, *in confequence* of this *bondage*, he is, upon the foot of *mere law*, and without the fuppofition of *grace* or *gofpel*, in *bondage* alfo to *bodily* or *animal appetites* and *inclinations*. [This I have proved at large in the *book* feveral times before referred to.] Both thefe fenfes of *bondage* are certainly included in that *vanity the creature is fubjected to.* They ought therefore to be Both comprehended in the *oppofite deliverance* here fpoken of. The plaifter, in this cafe (to ufe a vulgar comparifon) will be as broad as the fore ; but not otherwife. So it is exprefsly reprefented to be (which ought to be remembered here) by this fame apoftle, in the 5th chapter of this fame *epiftle*, as we have before feen ; and I am perfuaded he had the fame thing in view here.

(37) *Into the freedom of thofe*, &c.] The paraphrafe here is certainly juft, if I have given the true fenfe of the creature's deliverance from the *bondage of corruption*. The interpretation of both parts of the fentence is grounded on the fame reafon. And it may be worth obferving, the fenfe we have given of thofe verfes makes out a per-

fect

fe&t analogy between the apostle's discourse *here,*
and in the 5th chapter of this *same epistle.* The
creature's subjection to vanity, in the 20th verse of
this chapter, is the same thing with *death's having passed upon all men, whereupon they have all sinned,* in the 12th verse of the 5th chapter. And
the *deliverance* of THIS VERY CREATURE, that was
subjected to vanity, from the *bondage of corruption
into the glorious liberty of the children of God,* ver.
21st of this 8th chapter, is precisely the same
thing, in import, with the *free gift that is come
upon all men unto justification of life,* and that will
qualify them for it by *making them righteous
persons,* in the 18th and 19th verses of the other
chapter. The apostle, without all doubt, had the
same general thought in his mind, while he was
writing both these paragraphs ; as may more fully
appear presently.

(38) *For.*] Expositors, as it seems to me, have not
duly attended to the true connection of this particle *for,* γαρ ; which ought not to be joined either
with the preceding 21st or 20th verses, but with
the 19th, as in the paraphrase. The apostle had
said, in the 19th verse, in order to illustrate the 17th
and 18th verses, that *the creature earnestly expected,
and waited for, the manifestation of the sons of God.*
Before he proceeded to prove that the creature
thus *actually waited,* he interposes the 20th and
21st verses, which may very well be considered as
a *parenthesis,* to shew that it might *reasonably,* or
upon *just grounds,* thus wait in expectation. And,
having

having difpatched this, he now goes on, in the
22d verfe, to the proof of the *fact* he had afferted
in the 19th verfe. In this view of the words, the
for in the 20th verfe, as well as in the 22d, is
joined in conftruction with the 19th verfe; but
not to prove the fame thing. The *former* is intended to denote the *reafonablenefs* of what he had
afferted; the *latter*, its truth in point of *fact*:
And, in this method of connection, there is a propriety, confiftency, and force, in both thefe *fors*,
and the whole paffage of which they are parts.

(39) *Have groaned—longing for deliverance.*] This
deliverance, the *whole creation*, or *all mankind*, are
reprefented as *longing for*, refpects the *manifeftation of the fons of God*, their *freedom from corruption*, and being made *glorioufly immortal*, as has
been explained in fome of the above notes.
The connection of the difcourfe makes this neceffary.

But how, you will afk, can this be? How can
even *all mankind long and wait for this deliverance*,
when but a very fmall part of the world of men
know any thing of the *obtainablenefs* of *fuch a deliverance?* To which Dr. Taylor, in his *note* upon
this place, has, in my opinion, given a very clear
and fatisfactory anfwer. He fays, ' We know,
' as the apoftle fays, ver. 22, that all mankind
' do groan under the afflictions and preffures of
' this prefent world, fenfible of its imperfections
' and vanity, and confequently muft defire fome-
' thing better. And although they may not know

3   ' what

‘ what that *better thing* is, yet the apoftle knew
‘ it ; and he fpeaks according to his own know-
‘ ledge, and not theirs. He affirms, of his
‘ own knowledge, what their expectations would
‘ iffue in. Their *earneft waiting* was in fact,
‘ however they might be ignorant of it, a
‘ *waiting for the manifeftation of the fons of God.*
‘ And he proves this [I would rather fay, the
‘ *reafonablenefs* of it. See note (38)] ver. 20,
‘ 21 ; as fuppofing the Chriftians, to whom he
‘ wrote, might be ignorant of it : Which fhews,
‘ that when he affirms, the *earneft defire* of man-
‘ kind after a releafe from the *fufferings* of this
‘ *vain* life, he fpeaks not of what *Heathens,* or
‘ even *Chriftians,* underftood, or believed, to be
‘ true. Further, Dr. Whitby, upon the place,
‘ juftly obferves, that, in the facred dialect, *defire*
‘ and *expectation* is afcribed to creatures in refer-
‘ ence to things they want, and which tend to
‘ their advantage, though they *explicitly* know
‘ nothing of them. Thus the *Meffiah,* before
‘ he came, is called *the defire of all nations,*
‘ Hag. ii. 7.’

(40) *Now.*] The word, in the original, is
δε; which, I think, ought to be rendered *now,*
and not *and,* as in our Bibles, and by moft commentators. The apoftle, as it appears to me,
comes, in this verfe, to apply the *argument* he had
been purfuing to the cafe of *Chriftians,* for which
he had brought it. As if he had faid, “ You fee
that even the *whole world* of mankind do *virtually*
declare,

declare, by their groanings under the *sufferings* of this vain life to which they are subjected, that they desire, long after, and wait for, some *better state:* Now, this is the truth with respect to *us Christians* also. The all-wise God has so constituted things, that *even we likewise* groan under the various pressures of life, which is a *fact implicitly* signifying, or declaring, that we *wait for redemption*, not being as yet actually possessed of it."

(41) *Who have had the first-fruits of the Spirit.*] Perhaps, the apostle may intend, by the words, την απαρχην του πνευματος, more than expositors commonly take into it. He certainly here alludes to the *Jewish* custom of offering the *first-fruits* of their increase; which oblation sanctified not only *these fruits*, but *all the rest*. And might he not, by this allusion, have it in view to lead us to think, that *these Christians* were not merely the *first* that had received the *gifts* and *graces of the spirit*; but that these gifts and graces, bestowed on them, were a *specimen, pledge*, or *earnest*, of what should be bestowed, in God's time, and way, upon the *rest of mankind?* If *these Christians* are thus looked upon as the *first fruits*, and the *whole race* of men as the *following harvest*, it will admirably suit the apostle's argument, and give a noble sense to his words. And there are other texts which seem to countenance this interpretation. The apostle James, in the 18th verse of the first chapter of his Epistle, says of *himself*, and the *Christians* he was writing to, " Of his own will begat he us with the

I " word

" word of truth" [εις το ειναι ημας απαρχην τινα των αυτου κτισματων] THAT *we might be a certain first-fruits of his creatures.* To what had God begotten these Christians ? If we may answer in the words of the apostle Peter, second Epistle i. 3, 4, 5, it was, *to a lively hope.* Of what ? " An inheritance in-
" corruptible, undefiled, and that fadeth not away,
" reserved in heaven for us, to be revealed in the
" last time." And as they were thus begotten, THAT they might be the *first-fruits* [των αυτου κτισματων] *of God's creatures,* his *rational* creatures, *mankind,* I see not but *these creatures,* in relation to whom *these Christians* are called the *first-fruits,* must partake in the same common hope, so as finally to enjoy the thing hoped for. The allusion to the *Jewish first-fruits* naturally and obviously leads to this thought : Nor can it be so easily explained any other way. It may tend still further to strengthen this sense of the apostle's allusion, if we attend to the thing meant, when *Christ* is called, 1 Cor. xv. 20, απαρχη των κεκοιμημενων, *the first-fruits of them slept.* Surely, the thing intended, by this mode of expression, is not that Christ was the *first* that was raised from the dead ; but that he was the *first* that was raised as a *pledge, earnest,* or *assurance,* that mankind *universally* should be raised also. His *resurrection,* in analogy to the *first fruits* under the law, *consecrated the whole world of men,* and was designed, by God, as an intimation, that the *resurrection of all men* should as surely follow the *resurrection of Christ,* as the *whole harvest* followed

lowed the *firſt-fruits*. And this alſo is the true
meaning of that ſtyle which is given to Chriſt,
Col. i. 18—Rev. i. 5, πρωτοτοκος εκ των νεκρων, *the*
firſt-born from the dead. So the common tranſlation has it; and very juſtly, if by the *firſt-born* be
meant, not *merely* the *firſt* that was raiſed from the
dead; but the *chief*, the *head*, the *firſt in pre-*
eminence, of *that family*, of *thoſe children*, who
ſhall live again after death; the *reſurrection* of
Chriſt being here conſidered as the *pledge* of their's.
And this, by the way, may ſerve to lead us into
the true ſenſe of that controverted text, Col. i. 15,
where the apoſtle, ſpeaking of Chriſt, calls him
πρωτοτοκος πασης κτισεως, *the firſt-born of every crea-*
ture, as it is rendered in our Bibles; and with
propriety, if, by *every creature*, we underſtand
every *rational* creature in this lower world; [This,
as we have ſeen *note* (27) is the meaning of the
phraſe πασα κτισις in the New-Teſtament writings]
and if, by *firſt-born*, we underſtand, not the *firſt*
creature that was born; but the *firſt in pre-eminence*,
the *chief* among mankind; the *eldeſt ſon*, with
whom is the right of *primogeniture*; that glorious
perſon whom God made the *firſt heir of all things*,
and the *other children*, the *reſt* of *the family*, heirs
through him, or on *his account*, ſo heirs as that they
ſhall *finally* come to poſſeſs the *inheritance* with
him. The phraſe, πρωτοτοκος εν πολλοις αδελφοις,
in Rom. viii. 29, may properly be explained by
this in Col. i. 15. The *many brethren* there, may
mean the ſame thing with *every creature* here, that

is,

is, every *rational* creature, all mankind. For it is to be remembered, the *special reason* given, why Chriſt *became a partaker of fleſh and blood*, is, as the author of the Epiſtle to the Hebrews expreſſes it, chapter ii. 14, " becauſe the children were par-" takers thereof." The *children*, that is, *every ſon* and *daughter* of *Adam*, the *whole human race* ; for it was with a view to EVERY MAN, in order to his being qualified to give his life a *ranſom* FOR EVERY MAN, that Chriſt was *made for a while inferior to the angels*, or, what means the ſame thing, became man, *partook of fleſh and blood*, as in the 9th verſe of this chapter. Upon the whole, it ſhould appear highly probable, to ſay the leaſt, that the apoſtle, by uſing the phraſe, *the firſt-fruits of the Spirit*, with reference to the *gifts* and *graces* be-ſtowed on the *firſt Chriſtians*, intended an inſinuation as though *theſe gifts and graces* would be be-ſtowed on *mankind univerſally* ; or that *theſe Chriſtians* were, with relation to *all men*, what the *firſt-fruits* were, among the *Jews*, with reference to the following *whole harveſt*.

OBSERVATIONS *deduced from the foregoing* TEXT, PARAPHRASE, *and* NOTES.

Upon a careful peruſal of the above paſſage of ſcripture, with what has been offered in illuſtra-tion of it, it is eaſy to obſerve,

That the *race of men*, mankind *univerſally*, are *the creature*, and *the whole creation*, the apoſtle is

treating

treating of in this place. It may poſſibly ſeem harſh to an *Engliſh* reader to underſtand, by *the whole creation*, nothing more than *mankind*; and, being always uſed to interpret the phraſe in a more *extended* ſenſe, he may have a ſecret prejudice in his mind againſt this *reſtrained* one. But it is certain, the *Greek* phraſe, πασα η κτισις, has not the ſame force, in the New-Teſtament writings, with the *Engliſh* one, *the whole creation*. The idea obviouſly conveyed, and intended to be conveyed, is this, and only this, the whole *rational* creation, the *whole world of mankind*.

It is further obſervable, TWO GRAND THINGS are here ſpoken of, as referring to this *whole creation*, or *all mankind*, namely, their SUBJECTION TO VANITY, and their DELIVERANCE FROM IT.

On the one hand, it is affirmed of *the creature*, that is, of *mankind in general*, that they are *ſubjected to vanity*, that is, the imperfections and infelicities of a vain mortal life here on earth. And, it is worthy of ſpecial notice, their ſubjection to this vanity is ſaid to have been faſtened on them, not through any *default of their's*, not by *any wilful act of diſobedience* they had been *perſonally* guilty of; but in virtue of a *divine conſtitution*, by *God* who was pleaſed thus to ſubject them. And why did he thus ſubject them? Not arbitrarily; not in a mere ſovereign abſolute way: But upon occaſion of the *lapſe* of *the one man Adam*, their common progenitor; as this ſame apoſtle had before, in the fifth chapter, particularly related. And here

I 3　　　　　　　I cannot

I cannot but obferve, and point out, the perfect analogy there is between his difcourfe in *this paragraph*, and *that* remarkable chapter. He fpeaks indeed the fame thing, expreffes the fame fentiments, though in different words. What he *here* calls the *creature's fubjection to vanity*, he *there* calls *all men's coming under condemnation*; *death's reigning over them*; *death's having paffed upon them, whereupon they have all finned*. And whereas he *here* fays, the creature was fubjected to vanity, *not* WILFULLY, not by *any fin of their's*; but through the *will of him who fubjected them*: He *there* declares the fame thing, only in a more full and explicit manner; afcribing this fubjection of all men to *mortality*, or vanity, with the confequences thereof, not to their having *finned after the fimilitude of Adam's tranfgreffion*; but to the *conftitution of God*, occafioned by, and taking rife from, *the one man that finned, the one offence of the one man Adam.* The general idea intended to be communicated both *there* and *here,* is evidently the fame, fo evidently that one can fcarce help difcerning the *identity* of fentiment.

On the other hand, it is as pofitively affirmed of *the creature,* or mankind in general, that they were not fubjected to this vanity FINALLY, and FOR EVER, but IN CONSEQUENCE OF HOPE, not only that they fhould be *delivered from this unhappy fubjection,* but be inftated in *immortal glory as God's fons.* For fo the words are, in the 20th and 21ft verfes; " who fubjected the fame in hope, THAT
" the

" the creature itself also," *even this very creature,
the self-same mankind,* " shall be delivered from the
" bondage of corruption into the glorious liberty of
" the children of God ;" directly and plainly affirming, that mankind was not subjected to the infelicities of this present vain life as a *final condemnation,*
but upon the foot of a *previous hope* that they should,
in due time, be *delivered,* and with *advantage too.*
For observe, what is the *object* of this hope ? Not
merely deliverance from the *bondage of corruption,*
but an enlargement into the *glories of an immortal
life.* And who are the *subjects* of it ? Why, *the creature,* the *whole creation,* that is, mankind, the whole
race of men. For, remark, *the very same creature,* the *self-same mankind,* who was subjected to
vanity, was subjected to it IN HOPE. In hope of
what ? Not only of a *deliverance from this vanity,*
but a deliverance from it that should be accompanied with an *immortality in glory and honour.*

The attentive reader will, upon this explanation, very easily perceive, that the OBJECT OF
HOPE, in this passage, is precisely the same thing
with the ABOUNDING GIFT AND GRACE THROUGH
CHRIST, in the foregoing fifth chapter ; and that
η κτισις, and πασα η κτισις, *the creature,* and *the whole
creation,* spoken of *here,* mean the same thing with
οι πολλοι, and παντες ανθρωποι, *the many,* and *all men,*
upon whom the ABOUNDING GIFT through Christ
is *there* bestowed. And further, if, by deliverance
from the *bondage of corruption* into the *glorious
liberty of the children of God,* we understand *here*

I 4   deliverance

deliverance from *fuch bondage* into *fuch freedom* as is mentioned in the paraphrafe, the analogy will be ftill more obfervable, and may, in this refpect, be feen pointed out in *note* (37). The truth is, one can fcarce critically compare what the apoftle fays *here*, with what he has advanced in the foregoing fifth chapter, and be afterwards at a lofs to determine, that he was purfuing the *fame thought* in both thefe places. It is certain, if we interpret thefe places by *one another*, making them to fignify *one* and the *fame thing*, we fhall give a very juft and confiftent fenfe to the apoftle's words, and, I believe, the moft natural and obvious one that can be pitched upon: Yea, this paffage, in this point of view, will appear quite eafy and intelligible; and we fhall have no reafon to rank it, as fome have done, among the *chief* of the *Pauline* δυσνοντα, or *things hard to be underftood.*

The fum of the matter is, the apoftle, comparing his difcourfe *here*, with his difcourfe in the fifth chapter, from the 12th verfe, is evidently fpeaking of the *whole human race.* And what he fays of them is, that they are fubjected to a *fuffering ftate*; that they were fubjected to it, not on the account of *any fin*, or *fins*, they had been guilty of *previous* to this fubjection, but by the *will of God*, taking rife from, and grounded on, the *fin of the one man Adam*; and that he fubjected them to this *fuffering* condition, not as a *final condemnation*, but upon having *firft* given them reafon to *hope*, not only that they fhould be delivered from their

fufferings,

sufferings, but with ABOUNDING ADVANTAGE, by being *finally* made meet for, and then crowned with, *immortality* and *glory* as the sons of God. This is the plain natural sense of *this* passage of scripture, compared with the *other*; and it is the most consistent sense also, that which gives not only the strongest energy to the argument the apostle is upon, but the best connection between the several parts of his discourse.

I shall only add, that the apostle's way of arguing *here*, as also in the foregoing fifth chapter, is very unlike to *that* which is commonly to be met with in commentators, and other Christian writers. *They* GROUND the *suffering* state mankind are subjected to, on the *sin* which *they themselves* have been guilty of; representing the *whole human race* to have *sinned in*, and *fell with*, the one man Adam in his *first transgression:* And having *thus sinned* by his sinning, they suppose *they* have merited all this *unhappiness*, and that it is fit and proper they should *suffer* it, as being a just testimony of the displeasure of God against the *sin*, they *themselves* are chargeable with : Whereas the *apostle* speaks very differently upon the matter. He frees *mankind* from all *blame* on account of the *offence* of their *first father*; acknowledging indeed that this offence of his was the *occasion*, *ground*, or *reason*, of that subjection they are under to *vanity* and *mortality*, and the *unavoidable* appendages of them; but affirming, at the same time, that they were thus subjected to suffering, not *remedilessly*, but

but with an *intention of mercy*; and that their *ſufferings* ſhall finally terminate in their *ſuper-abounding advantage*; yea, and that it was highly congruous to *reaſon* to conceive thus of the matter. And it is this thought only, ſo far as I am able to judge, that can reconcile the *unavoidable ſufferings* of the race of men, as occaſioned by, and taking riſe from, the *lapſe* of their common father *Adam*, with the perfections of God, particularly his infinitely perfect and unbounded benevolence. And this, as I imagine, will effectually do it. The grant of exiſtence, in this point of light, appears, at the firſt glance, to be an unſpeakable benefit, and what calls for the moſt grateful acknowledgments from all the ſons of *Adam*, notwithſtanding all the *ſorrows*, and *trials*, they are ſubjected to, and muſt paſs through; as they will *end* in their *reigning in happy life for ever*. But, upon any other view of the caſe, I ſee not, I freely confeſs, for my own part, that the *gift of exiſtence*, all things conſidered, is a *valuable* one, or what we can *rationally* be *thankful for*. According to the common way of explaining the *fall of Adam*, there is moſt certainly juſt ground for *complaint* on account of the *diſadvantageous* circumſtances his *poſterity*, by this means, have been ſubjected to: Nor is this ground for complaint in the leaſt removed away by *the gift and grace through Chriſt*; for, with reſpect to the *greater part* of the human race by far, their caſe is as *remedileſs* as it would have been, had *no grace* been ever maniſeſted

fefted towards men in Jefus Chrift : Nay, what
is worfe, their cafe, by means of Chrift, is made,
in the end, more *aggravatedly miferable*, though
not lefs *remedilefs :* The reverfe of all which is
evidently the *great fcope* of the apoftle's reafoning
in this eighth chapter of his Epiftle, as well as in
the foregoing *fifth* ; which ought always to be
read together, as they exprefs the fame fentiments,
and mutually and clearly illuftrate each other.

Another *text*, falling in with the general head
we are upon, occurs in Col. i. 19, 20. "For it
"pleafed the Father that in him fhould all fullnefs
"dwell. And (having made peace through the
"blood of his crofs) by him to reconcile all things
"to himfelf, by him, I fay, whether they be
"things in earth or things in heaven."

Caftellio, and, from him, Mr. Pierce, and the
author of the new edition of the New Teftament
in Greek with an Englifh verfion, tranflate thofe
words, in the 19th verfe, εν αυτω ευδοκησε παν το
πληρωμα κατοικησαι, thus, *it pleafed the Father by him
to inhabit all fullnefs.* It is of no importance, in the
prefent argument, whether *this*, or the rendering
in our *Bibles*, be adhered to : For which reafon,
waving all difpute upon fo critical a point, I fhall
retain the verfion that is commonly received. The
only thing then needful to be fettled in ver. 19th,
is, what the apoftle means by the phrafe, παν το
πληρωμα, *all fullnefs.* And he plainly means by it,
as I conceive, *fuch a fullnefs* of *gifts* and *grace*, as
fhall be *fufficient*, and *effectual*, to repair the *damage*
of

of the *lapse,* and *all* that has been *consequent* upon it, with *abounding advantage,* even to *all* mankind. I shall set this matter in as clear and strong a light as I am able. In order whereto let it be carefully observed,

The apostle *Paul,* speaking of *Christ,* says, in the *second chapter* of this *epistle,* the 9th verse, " in him dwelleth all the fullness of the Godhead " bodily." By this *fullness of the Godhead* we are to understand, not that *absolute fullness of all perfection* which belongs to the *Deity,* but that *fullness of gifts and grace,* which the *Godhead* intends *by him* to impart to *others.* See this verse illustrated by Mr. Pierce, as I think, beyond all reasonable dispute. Agreeably, when it is said, that *the fullness of the Godhead dwelleth in Christ bodily,* the meaning is, that he is *really* and *truly* possessed [See this same expositor on the word σωματικως] of *all the transient fullness of God,* or, as the same thought may be expressed in other words, that he is the glorious *person in whom* God has *really lodged,* and *through whom* he will actually communicate *all that fullness* wherewith he intends this *lapsed world* shall be *filled,* in order to its *restoration.* In conformity to this sense of the word *fullness,* it is said, in the immediately following verse, και εστε εν αυτω πεπλη-ρωμενοι, not, *and ye are compleat in him,* but, *and ye are filled by him.* In like manner, it is observed of Christ, not only that he was " full [πληρης] of " grace and truth;" but that [εκ του πληρωματος αυτου] " of his fullness we have all received, and " grace

" grace for grace," John i. 14, 16. And it is with
reference to this ſame *fullneſs* that has been lodged
in Chriſt, to be imparted by him to the *race of lapſed
man*, that we read of " the fullneſs of him who fil-
" leth all in all," Eph. i. 23. Mr. Pierce, in contradiction to Mr. Locke, and moſt interpreters, underſtands theſe words, *who filleth all in all*, not of
Chriſt, but of *God the Father*. He ſays, in his *note*
upon Col. i. 19, 'Conſidering the lofty terms wherein
' he [the apoſtle] had juſt before ſpoken of God
' the *Father*, deriving all things from him that were
' even in Chriſt himſelf, and comparing this ex-
' preſſion with what he ſays of the *Father*, Eph. iv. 6,
" One God and father of all, who is above all, and
" in you all," and with 1 Cor. xii. 6, " It is the
" ſame God who worketh all in all :" I ſay, con-
' ſidering theſe things, I am much rather inclined
' to underſtand the *Father* to be meant by *him that
' filleth all in all.*' But ſurely this accurate ex-
poſitor did not duly conſider, though the *Father*
is *above all, in all*, the *Father of all*, and *worketh
all in all*; yet that he does nothing by himſelf
immediately, but all *through* and *by* the *intervening
agency* of his Son *Jeſus Chriſt*. For *all the tranſient
fullneſs of the Godhead dwelleth in him*, and was
made to dwell in him for this very purpoſe, that
it might *by him* be communicated to the *lapſed
creation*. And, in truth, Chriſt, having this *fullneſs* lodged in him, *aſcended up far above all heavens* [ινα πλη ρωση τα παντα] THAT HE MIGHT
FILL ALL THINGS, as the apoſtle expreſsly affirms,
Eph.

Eph. iv. 10. And as the *filling all things*, that is, in the *lapfed world*, that they might be *reftored*, was the FINAL CAUSE of the *afcenfion* of Chrift up to heaven, *all things* muft accordingly be *filled in fact*, by him, fooner or later. The apoftle therefore obferves, in the following verfes, not only that he had imparted *gifts*, in profecution of this *end* of his exaltation ; but that, in order to the full accomplifhment of it, he would go on to impart them, " TILL WE ALL COME to the unity of the " faith, unto a perfect man, unto the meafure of " the ftature of the fullnefs of Chrift." [Read what is further faid upon this matter, under Eph. i. 9, 10.] And it was, as I fuppofe, with a direct view to Chrift's thus *filling all things*, that the apoftle fpeaks of him, in the words we are now confidering, as that *glorious perfon in whom it has pleafed the Father that all* communicable *fullnefs fhould dwell*. I need not fay, that this interpretation gives the phrafe, *all fullnefs*, a very emphatical, and moft glorioufly fignificant meaning. And I am the rather fatisfied, that this is its true meaning, as it fo admirably agrees with the following verfe ; in which the apoftle goes on to fpeak of the *Father's reconciling all things to himfelf by Jefus Chrift, whether they be things in earth, or things in heaven.*

This verfe has been vaftly puzzling to expofitors. Scarce a text in all the Bible has more exercifed their talents, or given occafion for greater variety in their fentiments. Grotius interprets it one way, Dr. Hammond another,

Dr.

Dr. Whitby another, Mr. Locke another, Mr. Pierce another. Dr. Taylor, fpeaking of this text, plainly fays, [in his book on Romans, page 282], 'that he does not underftand it.' And, fo far as I can judge, it is really inexplicable upon the common fchemes of divinity; but yet obvioufly capable of an eafy, and yet noble and fublime fenfe, if underftood conformably to the fenfe we have given of the preceding words.

The idea I have of it, without troubling my-felf, or the reader, with what others have faid upon it, is plainly this. By *the things in earth,* and *the things in heaven,* I underftand this *whole lower creation,* both *animate* and *inanimate,* both *men* and *things,* whether in the *earth* or the *aerial heaven* that furrounds it. By *God's reconciling thefe things to himfelf,* I underftand *his changing them back again to their former* or *original ftate.* And whereas he is faid *to reconcile* or *change the ftate* of thefe things *by Jefus Chrift, having made peace by the blood of his crofs;* I fuppofe the thought in-tended to be conveyed is, that Chrift, having, by *his death on the crofs,* laid a juft foundation for *peace with God,* is the glorious perfon, by whom, as the prime minifter of God, *this change* was brought into effect. As if the apoftle had faid, to fum up the meaning of thefe verfes in the fol-lowing paraphrafe, " It pleafed the Father, that all *communicable fullnefs* fhould be lodged in his Son *Jefus Chrift,* and *by him,* as his *great agent,* (hav-ing prepared the way for it by his blood fhed

on

on the crofs) to *change back again all things to himfelf*; I fay, *by him* it pleafed the Father to *change the ftate* of this *lower world*, of *the men* and *the things of it*, whether they be on *the earth*, or in *the heaven* that encompaffes it."

In fupport of this interpretation it is fcarce needful to fay, that ουρανος may fignify the *aerial heaven*, the heaven that furrounds this earth, fince we fo frequently read of the *rain of heaven*; of the *clouds of heaven*; of the *fowls of heaven*; of *the heaven* as covered *with blacknefs*, as cloathed *with darknefs*, and the like. It will be of more importance to go on, and fhow, that the word καταλλασσω, a derivative from αλλος, and a compound of κατα and αλλασσω, properly fignifies to *re-change*, or *bring back again to fome former ftate*. Thus it is ufed in 1 Cor. vii. 10, 11. "Unto the " married I command, yet not I, but the Lord, that " the wife be not feparated [χωρισθηναι] from her " hufband: But if fhe be already feparated [εαν δε " και χωρισθη], let her remain unmarried, or let her " be reconciled [καταλλαγητω] to her hufband;" that is, let her *be rechanged, return back to her former ftate of living with him*. In all other places in the New Teftament, this word is ufed with reference to the great affair of *falvation by Jefus Chrift*; but ftill, it has the fame general fenfe, at leaft one that obvioufly coincides with it. This is its meaning here. And we fhall the more readily perceive it to be fo, if we call to mind,

That a *change*, by means of the *offence* of the
one

one man Adam, and the *condemnatory sentence* of
God taking rife therefrom, was introduced, not
only in the *ftate of all his pofterity*, but of *all
things elfe* in this lower creation, that is, in *the
things of the earth, and the things in the heaven* that
furround it, as it is here expreffed. It was indeed
by *this change* of the *earth* and *heaven* from their
original ftate, that they became fitted to be the *occafion* of that *vanity, forrow,* and *death,* to which
it pleafed God to fubject the *whole human kind.*
It is true, the *earth* only is mentioned, in the third
chapter of Genefis, as that which was *curfed for
man's fake,* that is, *changed* from its *original ftate,*
that it might be adapted to be an *occafion* of forrow and death to the *race of lapfed man :* But the
earth here is to be underftood as meaning the
whole lower world, not only the *earth itfelf,* but
the *heaven* that environs it. Accordingly, when it
is faid, " It has pleafed God to reconcile all things
" to himfelf, the things in earth, and the things in
" heaven ;" the obvious meaning is, that he has *rechanged their ftate, brought them back to that they
were originally in.* And having done this, he will
take effectual care to accomplifh the defign of
his mercy herein. And this interpretation of the
words wonderfully coincides with what the fcripture elfewhere fays with reference to *all things,*
underftanding hereby the *inanimate world,* and
mankind the principal inhabitants of it. We fhall
be a little particular in the illuftration of this important point.

This is the *fenfe* of fcripture with refpect to *all*
K *things*

things in the inanimate world. Hence thofe words of
our Saviour, Matt. xix. 28, " Ye which have fol-
" lowed me, *even ye,* IN THE REGENERATION, ſhall
" ſit upon twelve thrones——." The word παλιγγενεσια, here tranſlated *regeneration,* is the very word
that is uſed (as Dr. Burnet obſerves) both by the
Greek philoſophers, and the Greek chriſtian fathers, for the RENOVATION OF THE WORLD. And
doubtleſs the *new form of exiſtence* that is to be given
to *all things,* their being, as it were, *born again to
another and better ſtate,* is what our Saviour has here
in view. Hence alſo thoſe words of the apoſtle
Peter, Acts iii. 21, αχρι χρονων αποκαταστασεως
παντων, *until the* times of THE RESTITUTION OF ALL
THINGS. And this ſame apoſtle ſays, 2 Pet. iii. 13.
" According to his promiſe we look for NEW HEA-
" VENS, and a NEW EARTH;" probably alluding to
thoſe words of the prophet, Iſa. lxv. 17, " Behold,
" I create NEW HEAVENS, and a NEW EARTH; and
" the former ſhall not be remembered, nor come to
" mind." And the apoſtle John points our view to
the time when " there ſhall be NO MORE CURSE,"
Rev. xxii. 3; when the " OLD HEAVENS and EARTH
" ſhall FLEE AWAY," chap. xx. 2; when there ſhall
be " a NEW HEAVEN, and a NEW EARTH, for that
" the FIRST HEAVEN, and the FIRST EARTH are
" PASSED AWAY," chap. xxi. 1: Upon which,
he that ſitteth on the throne is introduced, ſaying, as
in the 5th verſe, Ιδου, καινα παντα ποιω, BEHOLD, I
MAKE ALL THINGS NEW. Thus *the things in
earth,* and *the things in heaven,* meaning hereby the
inanimate parts of this lower world, are *reconciled*

to

to God : And they may, with as much propriety, be faid to be fo, as they are faid to have been *curfed by him.* Their ftate was *changed* by means of the *curfe,* occafioned through the *lapfe* of the one man *Adam* ; and they are *changed back again to their former* or *original ftate.* This lower world now is, and has been, all along, from the days of Adam, in the *unhappy ftate* [unhappy, I mean, with refpect to us men] it *was changed to* by rea-fon of the *fall :* But the time is coming when it fhall be *changed into another ftate,* that is, be erect-ed into a NEW WORLD, a NEW HEAVEN and a NEW EARTH. And becaufe this certainly WILL BE, yea, NOW is in the PURPOSE of God, it is fpoken of in this place, as though it *actually was.* So it is faid of Chrift, Heb. ii. 8, " Thou haft put all " things in fubjection under his feet :" Not that this is, at prefent, the real truth of *fact* ; for, as it is added, in the latter claufe of this fame verfe, " we fee not " YET all things put under him :" But they certainly SHALL BE ; and that which certainly SHALL BE is fpoken of, for that reafon, as though it ACTUALLY WAS.

This alfo is the fenfe of fcripture with reference to *mankind,* the principal inhabitants of this lower world. It fpeaks of God, in other places befides this we are confidering, as having *reconciled them to himfelf,* that is, *rechanged, brought them back to their former* or *original ftate.* By the *lapfe* of their firft father *Adam,* their *ftate was changed,* that is to fay, they came into being under quite different

circumftances

circumstances from what they would otherwise have done, under the *condemnatory sentence* of God, and in such a state, in one word, as that it was impossible they should be saved. But *by Christ their state was changed,* they were absolutely *brought back to the condition they would have been in* had it not been for the *lapse*; what I mean is, that they were ABSOLUTELY and UNCONDITION- ALLY put into *salvable circumstances,* notwithstand- ing the *condemnation through the lapse,* and all that could be *consequent* upon it. And it is upon this foundation, and this only, that they are become *capable of a future immortality*; and that a *scheme* has been erected, under the ministration of *Jesus Christ,* in the final issue of which they shall *all,* notwithstanding the *lapse,* and what has followed upon it, *reign in life as righteous persons.* All the passages, in the New Testament, where the words *reconciliation, reconcile, reconciled,* are used, with re- ference to the affair of *salvation,* admirably coin- cide with this sentiment. We shall briefly con- sider them all, so far as is necessary to illustrate the present point.

The first we have in Rom. v. 10. " For if, " when we were enemies, we were reconciled to " God by the death of his Son ; MUCH MORE being " reconciled we shall be saved by his life." The words, *while we were enemies,* point out the *state* mankind were *changed to,* in consequence of the *lapse* through the one man *Adam.* While mankind were thus *enemies,* in the view of God, they *were re-*

conciled

conciled to him, that is, *changed in their ſtate,* ſo changed as to be *abſolutely put into a ſalvable con-dition,* the condition they *would have been in* had it not been for the *lapſe.* And as this *change of ſtate* was effected by the *Son of God's death for them,* and this while they were *enemies,* and as ſuch in a *ſtate of condemnation,* the apoſtle therefore argues in that moſt ſtrong and concluſive manner, " MUCH MORE being reconciled we ſhall be ſaved " by his life." As if he had ſaid, " Foraſmuch as God, while mankind were in the unhappy ſtate of *enemies,* and *under condemnation,* was pleaſed FREELY and ABSOLUTELY to *rechange their ſtate,* putting them into a *ſalvable condition,* and in no leſs aſtoniſhing a way than *by the death of his own Son;* MUCH MORE will he, now that he has *raiſed* his Son from death to *live* at his own right hand, cloathed with all power in heaven and earth, *finally* accompliſh their *actual* and *eternal ſalva-tion."*

The word *reconciliation* is again [in the *ori-ginal*] uſed in the next verſe; where the apoſtle, in the name of believers, ſays, " By whom [that is, " Jeſus Chriſt] we have now received the reconcilia-" tion," that is, [See note (1) where this text is par-ticularly conſidered] the *change of ſtate* ſpoken of, and argued from, in the preceding verſe.

It may be worthy of ſpecial notice here, the apoſtle having, in *this* and the *preceding verſe,* ſpoken of the affair of *mankind's reconciliation,* or *rechange of ſtate by Jeſus Chriſt,* goes on, in the

following ones, to lead us into a juft and full idea
of this whole matter. He tells us, in the 12th
verſe, not only that mankind were *changed from
their original ſtate*, but acquaints us with the *way*
and *means* by which this was brought about, namely,
the *lapſe of the one man Adam*. And left any
ſhould miſtake his meaning, and argue, from his
having uſed the words καταλλασσω, and καταλλαγη,
in the 10th and 11th verſes, that Chriſt had *rechanged their ſtate* ONLY SO FAR as to put them into
the *like ſalvable condition they would have been in*, had
it not been for the *lapſe*, and the *condemnation through
it*; he immediately, before he has finiſhed one
ſentence, goes off into a *parentheſis* to guard againſt
any ſuch thought, ſhewing that the *gift through
Chriſt* EXTENDED FAR BEYOND THIS, changing
them into a *better* than their *original* ſtate; a ſtate
that would certainly, in the final operation of the
ſcheme of God, as in proſecution by his Son Jeſus
Chriſt, iſſue in their actually *reigning in life for
ever*, being previouſly changed into a *meetneſs* for
it. This the reader ſhould particularly keep in
view; and he will then ſee, that the *reconciliation*,
here treated of, is *ſuch a change of ſtate*, with reſpect to even *all mankind*, as virtually includes in
it their *final ſalvation*. It is, in one word, a reſtoration to *their firſt ſtate*, with all the ABOUNDING
ADVANTAGE deſcribed in the 15th, 16th, and
17th verſes.

The next place that mentions *reconciliation* is
Rom. xi. 15; where the apoſtle, ſpeaking of the
rejection

rejection of the Jews, says, " If the cafting away of
" them be [καταλλαγη του κοσμου] the reconciliation
" of the world—"; that is, a *mean* to promote *fuch*
a change in their tempers and manners as fhould
make them *meet for,* and *intereft them in,* an *actual*
right to *eternal life.* Let it be remarked here,
though the *world, mankind univerfally,* were fo
changed in their ftate by the *death of Chrift,* as that
they were in a *falvable condition,* notwithftanding
the *lapfe,* yet it was neceffary they fhould be *morally fit* for falvation before it could *actually* be
beftowed on them; and the *gofpel-difpenfation* was
the *grand mean* the wifdom of God had contrived
to this end. Now the *rejection of the Jews* was an
occurrence fitted to *extend* the *gofpel-difpenfation,* and
in this way to promote the *reconciliation of the*
world, that is, *their change of ftate,* in point of *meetnefs for,* and an *actual intereft in,* the *falvation of*
heaven. The word *reconciliation,* in this text, has,
as I imagine, a meaning fomewhat different from
the *fame word,* or the word *reconciled,* in the
texts before mentioned. There is indeed, in the
fenfe of the apoftle Paul, a *double reconciliation,* as
well as *juftification.* The *one* means *that change of*
ftate all men ABSOLUTELY are brought into by the
death of *Chrift;* and is oppofed to the *condemna-*
tion through the *lapfe* of the one man *Adam.* The
other is that *change of ftate* which is connected with
an *actual meetnefs for,* and *prefent intereft in,* eternal
life. The *latter,* I fuppofe, is fpoken of in this
text:

text: Though it ought to be remembered, the *former* is connected, in the ſcheme of God, with the *latter*; and will *finally* iſſue in it, as the apoſtle has abundantly explained this matter, Rom. v. 12, and onwards; which has been taken notice of already.

The words *reconciliation, reconciled, reconciling,* are all uſed, and repeated, and ſo as to confirm what I juſt now obſerved of a *double reconciliation,* in 2 Cor. v. 18, 19, 20. "And all things are of "God, who hath reconciled us to himſelf, by "Jeſus Chriſt, and hath given to us the mi-"niſtry of reconciliation. *As* (becauſe (42) God "was

___

(42) *As, becauſe.*] So, I think, ως οτι ought to be rendered, and not, *to wit, that,* as in our Bibles. If the particle ως ever means *to wit,* it is in ſome rare inſtances, where the ſenſe cannot otherwiſe be made out; which is far from being the caſe here. The ſenſe is rather hurt, than helped, by this tranſlation of the word. It is true, thoſe words, in the beginning of this 19th verſe, *that God was reconciling the world to himſelf,* may be connected with the *miniſtry of reconciliation,* ſpoken of in the foregoing 18th verſe, and conſidered as *explanatory* to it: And in this way there may be a propriety in rendering ως *to wit.* But then the difficulty will be to point out the coherence of the words that immediately follow, *and hath committed unto us the word of reconciliation.* Whereas, if we connect this ως with υπερ Χριστου ουν πρεσβευομεν, in the 20th verſe, making the words from οτι, in the 19th, a *parentheſis,* and tranſlating ως *as,* and οτι *becauſe,* there will not only be good ſenſe, but a noble elegance, in the apoſtle's diſcourſe. According to this conſtruction, the 19th verſe will be

" was in Chrift, reconciling the world unto himfelf,
" not imputing their trefpaffes to them, and hath
" committed unto us the miniftry of reconcili-
" ation) in the ftead of Chrift we do therefore
" come to you with an embaffy ; AS though God
" did befeech you by us, we pray you, in Chrift's
" ftead, be ye reconciled to God." Here it is declared, that God *hath reconciled us to himfelf by
Jefus Chrift* ; the meaning of which is, that he has
by the *death* of his Son *changed the ftate of mankind*, putting them *abfolutely* into a *falvable* condition. In confequence of this, having thus *changed
their ftate*, he has *given unto us* [apoftles] *the miniftry of reconciliation* ; that is, the office or fervice
of acquainting the world that they are abfolutely
changed from the ftate of *condemnation* they were
in, through the lapfe, into a *falvable one* through
Jefus Chrift ; and to prevail upon them to make
a wife and good ufe of this *change of ftate*, that
it may iffue in that *moral internal change*, which
would make them *meet for*, and actually *intereft them in*, the *immortality* and *glory* that is
opened to view in the gofpel. And becaufe
*God was in Chrift reconciling the world unto him-
felf*, that is, had erected the *gofpel difpenfation*,
as a wife and powerful *mean*, under *him*, for ef-

be a reafon, and a very good one, of the ftrong and pathetic
language in the 20th verfe ; and the ως, in the 19th verfe,
will anfwer to the other ως in the 20th, fo as to make out a
very beautiful climax, as in the above tranflation.

fe&ting

fecting such a *moral change* in them, as would
prepare them for, and *actually* interest them in,
that immortal life they had been *absolutely changed*
into a capacity of attaining to ; and because *he
had deposited* in his apostles this *word of reconciliation*, this *gospel-mean* of thus *changing* men into a
meetness for a glorious immortality, *they* are here
brought in as *beseeching* men, in the strongest and
most pathetic language, *to be reconciled to God*,
that is, to suffer themselves, in a *willing way*, as
moral agents, to have this important *change* wrought
in them.　It appears to me absolutely necessary
to understand the words *reconciliation*, *reconciled*,
reconciling, in this passage, in this latitude of sense,
in order to make out an intelligible and consistent
meaning.　And taken thus, they obviously afford
such an one.　If mankind have been really *so
changed* in their state, by the *death* of *Christ*, as
that they are *now* in a *salvable* condition, a just
foundation is laid for the erection of a *dispensation*,
with proper *ministers*, in order to *change* them in
a *moral* way, which is the only suitable one, into
an *actual meetness* for *salvation* : Nor could it have
been erected upon any other foundation.　In vain
would it be for God to erect such a *dispensation* as
the *gospel* one is, furnished with all desirable *means*
and *motives* to *change* men into a *meetness* for *salvation*, if they were not *first changed* from that state
of *condemnation* they were in through the *lapse*.
And, unless this be supposed, vain would it be also
in apostles, or prophets, or pastors, or teachers,

to

to " befeech men, as in Chrift's ftead, to be recon-
" ciled to God," to be *willingly changed* into the difpofitions of virtue. The *gofpel-miniftry*, and indeed
all its *means*, *advantages*, and *motives*, are to be confidered as a *fuperftructure* upon that *abfolute change
of ftate* which mankind have been brought into
by the death of Chrift. And this *abfolute change*,
as it has been argued from, and explained at
large by the apoftle *Paul* in his fifth chapter to
the Romans, it is to be remembered, will *finally*
iffue in that *moral one* which will prepare them to
reign in life as righteous perfons. This, it is true,
may fail of being the effect, by any of the *means*
that will be ufed under the *prefent* difpenfation
of the kingdom of God; but OTHER MEANS, in
STILL FUTURE DISPENSATIONS, will be ufed, and
fuch too as fhall FINALLY PROVE EFFECTUAL ; as
we may fee afterwards.

Another text that fpeaks of the affair of reconciliation, is Eph. ii. 16. " And that he might re-
" concile both unto God in one body, by the
" crofs, having flain the enmity thereby :" The
meaning of which words, and of the whole context they are related to, is, that God, having by the
death of Chrift *rechanged the ftate of all mankind*,
had, in confequence of this, and as a wife *mean*
to accomplifh his merciful intention herein, taken
away the *diftinction* he had formerly made between
Jews and *Gentiles* ; erecting a *difpenfation*, with his
own Son at its head, under which they fhould be
no more *twain*, but *one body*, or political commu-
2   nity,

nity: The *breaking down the partition-wall* between *Jew* and *Gentile* is not the thing *ultimately* meant by the *reconciliation* treated of in this *chapter*. This is rather to be confidered as a *mean,* in the fcheme and government of God, in order to carry into effect his *grand defign* of mercy in having *rechanged the ftate of all mankind by his Son's death.* It would convey, comparatively, but a poor lean idea of the fcheme of God, to underftand the apoftle in any lower fenfe.

These now are all the texts in which we meet with the words *reconciliation, reconcile, reconciled,* exept one, which I fhall have occafion to mention prefently. And though they do not, in every place, mean precifely the fame thing ; yet they are always *connected with,* and *grounded on,* that RECHANGE OF STATE common to ALL MANKIND, with reference to which the apoftle Paul has taught us to argue, MUCH MORE IF WE ARE THUS CHANGED SHALL WE FINALLY BE SAVED BY CHRIST : Declaring, at the fame time, that the PECULIAR ADVANTAGE of this *rechange of ftate* lies in this, that it has placed us in *better circumftances* than we fhould have been in had it not been for the *lapfe* ; for that it will certainly terminate, in the final operation of the fcheme of God, in our *reigning in life for ever as righteous perfons.*

I fhall only add, the context that follows the paffage we have been thus long illuftrating very much favours the fenfe we have given it. For
the

the apostle having said, " It pleased the Father, by
" Jesus Christ, to reconcile all things to himself,"
immediately subjoins, applying himself to the *Gentile*
converts, " and you that were some time alienat-
" ed, and enemies in your mind by wicked works,
" yet now hath he reconciled, in the body of his
" flesh through death, to present you holy, and un-
" blamable, and unreprovable in his fight ; if ye
" continue in the faith, grounded and settled, and
" be not moved away from the hope of the gospel,
" which ye have heard."—As if he had said, "You
Christian Gentiles, to whom I am writing, are an
evidence of the truth of what I just now observed, namely, that it hath *pleased the Father by Jesus
Christ to reconcile all things to himself;* for though
you were ONCE [ποτε] seemingly left of God, being estranged from his church, [*aliens from the
commonwealth of Israel,* as it is expressed, Eph. ii.
12.] and enemies to him in your mind by wicked works ; yet NOW, in these *gospel-days,* hath he
placed *you* equally with the *Jews* under the powerful *method of reconciliation* his wisdom hath contrived, and goodess erected, through the death of
the fleshly body of Christ, in order to your having that *moral change* effected in you which shall
make you *holy, unblamable,* and *unreprovable* in his
fight : And this will be the effect of your being
placed under the *gospel means of reconciliation,*
if ye continue in faith, grounded and settled, and
be not moved away from the hope of the gospel
which ye have heard." The apostle goes on to
say,

say, that the *gospel*, which these *Coloſſians* had heard, had, in consequence of God's pleasure to *reconcile all things*, been preached to *every creature under heaven*. He then speaks of himself as a *miniſter of this goſpel*, and as *made a miniſter* of it to *fulfil the word of God, even the myſtery that had been hid from ages and generations*. What *myſtery* was this? Expositors commonly understand by it the purpose of God to admit the *Gentiles into his viſible kingdom*. But surely, it ought to be interpreted in an higher and more significant sense. In one word, this *secret* to former ages, was the purpose of God to *rechange the ſtate of the whole world* by the *death* of his Son *Jeſus Chriſt*, in the sense that has been explained. Accordingly, this is the *secret* which has now, in the gospel-days, been made manifeſt. For in execution of the *pleaſure of God to reconcile all things*, the diſtinction between *Jew* and *Gentile* has been taken away, and *Chriſt the hope of glory* preached equally to ALL MEN: So speaks the apoſtle, ver. 28, "Whom "we preach, warning EVERY MAN, and teaching "EVERY MAN, that we may preſent EVERY MAN, "perfect in Chriſt Jeſus." We ſhall have occaſion more fully to *explain* and *confirm* theſe things under the next scripture paſſage pertinent to the *general propoſition* we are upon; to which I accordingly now proceed.

It is in Eph. i. 9, 10, "Having made known "unto us the myſtery of his will, according to his "good pleaſure, which he hath purpoſed in him-
"ſelf,

" felf, that, in the difpenfation of the fullnefs of
" times, he might gather together in one all things
✝ in Chrift, both which are in heaven, and which
" are on earth, even in him." The fame thing is
meant *here*, by the *things in heaven and on the
earth*, that is intended by them in the *foregoing
text*. So that we need not be at any lofs to know
their meaning in *this place*, if we have interpreted
them right in *that*. And what is *there* called
God's *reconciling thefe things to himfelf*, is here
fpoken of as *his gathering them together in one* :
So the words, αναχεφαλαιωσασθαι τα παντα, are
tranflated in our bibles. In order to a clear underftanding of the thing meant by the apoftle, it may
be proper to fay,

Κεφαλαιον, from whence αναχεφαλαιωσασθαι is derived, is that fum of any thing which is the refult of feveral particulars united. In figures,
χεφαλαιον is the *fum* arifing from feveral numbers
collected into one. In money-matters, it is that
fum which is made up of feveral parcels. Hence
thofe words, in Acts xxii. 28, " with a great fum
" [πολλου χεφαλαιου] obtained I this freedom." In a
difcourfe, it is a *fummary* reprefentation of things.
Hence Heb. viii. 1. " Now, of the things which we
" have fpoken, this is [χεφαλαιον] *the fum*." Accordingly, the compound verb, αναχεφαλαιοω [fumma-
tim repeto, in fummam redigo] fignifies to *fpeak
fummarily*, to *reduce that which was before in particulars into one whole*. So, when the apoftle Paul
had enumerated the feveral duties we owe to our
neighbour,

neighbour, he fays, Rom. xiii. 9. " if there be any
" other, [ανακεφαλαιουται εν τω] it is fummarily
" comprehended in this, Thou fhalt love thy neigh-
" bour as thy felf." In like manner, when fheep,
in a fcattered ftate, are collected into one flock,
it may properly be faid, ανακεφαλαιουνται. So
when foldiers, that were difperfed from each
other, are reduced into one troop, it may aptly
be expreffed by faying, ανακεφαλαιουνται. And, in
the fame general fenfe, this word may, with as
much propriety, be ufed with refpect to *all things
in heaven and on earth.* By means of the *lapfe,*
and what has been *confequent* thereupon, *thefe
things* were got into a broken, disjointed, diforderly ftate; and the good pleafure of God *to
reduce them* from their prefent feparated diforderly
ftate, *into one duly-fubjected and well fubordinated
whole,* may very fitly be fignified by the phrafe,
ανακεφαλαιωσασθαι τα παντα. And this I take to
be the thing intended here. The thought the
apoftle would convey is the *fame* with *that* in
Col. i. 20. He ufes indeed another word, but of
like general meaning. For they both equally
import, that *the things in heaven and earth* fhall
be *reduced to another ftate than that they were in
through the lapfe;* which is the main thing in view
in both texts.

Some, I am fenfible, chufe to fetch the meaning
of the words, ανακεφαλαιωσασθαι τα παντα εν Χριστω,
from thofe in the 22d verfe; και αυτον εδωκε κεφαλην
υπερ παντα τη εκκλησια, *and gave him to be head
over*

over all things to the church ; explaining them
both (43) by that paſſage of our Saviour,
Matt. xxviii. 18, where, ſpeaking of himſelf, he
ſays, εδοθη μοι πασα εξουσια εν ουρανω και επι γης, *all
power in heaven and earth is given to me.* But
ſhould it be allowed, that the apoſtle has reference
here to the *headſhip of Chriſt over all things*, it is
evident, he is to be underſtood, not merely of the
power *as committed to him*, but *as exerted by him in
reducing all things to their former ſtate of ſubjection.*
By the lapſe, and in conſequence of it, all things
were, as it were, unheaded, not knowing their
place and ſubordination, not moving in that order

(43) *Raphelius,* in his note upon the words, αναπεφαλαιω-
σασθαι τα παντα εν Χριστω, ſays, ‘ Idem hoc eſt cum eo, quod
‘ paulò poſt ſequitur, v. 22, αυτον εδωκεν κεφαλην υπερ παντα τη
‘ εκκλησια. Cujus utriuſque loci interpretationem petendam
‘ arbitror ex Chriſti verbis, Matt. xxviii. 18, Εδοθη μοι πασα
‘ εξουσια εν ουρανω και επι γης. Equidem hoc ipſum verbum in
‘ Xenophonte me legere non memini, cognatum tamen inveni,
‘ et quod ejuſdem planè eſt ſignificationis, συγκεφαλαιουσθαι.”
He goes on to illuſtrate this ſenſe from ſeveral paſſages in
Xenophon and Polybius. *Vid.* Raphel. Annot. Philolog.
vol. ii. pag. 463, 464. Wolfius, having mentioned this ſenſe
of Raphelius, and his illuſtration of it from the uſe of the
word συγκεφαλαιουσθαι, goes on, and ſays, ‘ Neque mirum
‘ cuiquam videri debet, quod apoſtolus non verbo συγκεφαλαι-
‘ ωσασθαι, ſed ανακεφαλαιωσασθαι, utatur ; cum poſterius illud
‘ aptius ſit ad indicandum, per Chriſtum affectum eſſe, ut,
‘ quæ ab hominibus facta erat diſceſſio, tolleretur, et idem
‘ ad unum caput revocarentur.’ *Vid.* Wolf. Cur. Philolog.
in loc.

L   they

they might otherwife have done (44). In this ftate of *all things,* it was the good pleafure of God to *re-head them in Chrift* ; giving him power to *reduce them* under due fubjection to himfelf, and fubordination to each other. In either way of interpreting the words αναχεφαλαιωσασθαι τα παντα, the fenfe will amount to much the fame, and exprefs the very thought that was propofed to be communicated by the phrafe, in Col. i. 20, αποκαταλλαξαι τα παντα.

This text and *that* do yet further harmonife with each other. For as it is faid *there,* fo it is declared *here,* that all thefe things in heaven and earth fhall be reduced, from the ftate they were in by means of the *lapfe,* into a well-fubjected and fubordinated whole, BY CHRIST : So εν τω Χριστω ought, as I think, to be rendered, and not *in Chrift,* as in our Bibles. And the fame may be faid of the εν αυτω ; it ought to be rendered, not *in him,* but *by him,* that is, Chrift. The idea the apoftle would fuggeft is evidently this, that *Jefus Chrift* is the perfon, that glorious agent, whom God would employ in effecting this *reduction,* or *reconciliation.* This is put beyond all doubt in Col. i. 20, for *there* the words are δι αυτου, *by him,* that is, Chrift : Nay, the apoftle, that he might exprefs himfelf in

---

(44) It is accordingly obfervable, they are reprefented, in chap. ii. ver. 2. of this Epiftle, as in a ftate of *difobedience* to God's authority, and of *fubjection to a foreign head,* an ufurping power ; *the prince of the power of the air.*

an

àn emphatically ftrong manner, upon this point, repeats the words; I fay, δι αυτου. And as εν αυτω, in this text, is brought in, by way of repetition, after it had been faid εν τω Χριστω, it fhould feem paft all difpute, that it ought to be conftrued *by him,* that is, Chrift; as the δι αυτου muft be in the parallel one.

It may be ftill worthy of notice, this reduction of all things is fpoken of, as what it is the good pleafure of God to accomplifh, εις οικονομιαν του πληρωματος των καιρων, *in the difpenfation of the fullnefs of times*; that is, in the *times* that are under the *adminiftration* of *Jefus Chrift:* For, as this fame apóftle obferves, Gal. iv. 4, " God fent forth " his Son, οτε ηλθε το πληρωμα του χρονου, when the " fullnefs of the time was come." The fame *general period* is meant in both thefe texts, viz. *the time when God's kingdom is in the hands,* or *under the adminiftration of Jefus Chrift.* And it is called *the fullnefs of the time,* or *times,* becaufe it did not come on till the *times* introductory to it, in the appointment of God, were *fully run out, compleated,* or *filled up* (45). Only let it be particularly regarded here, *this*

(45) It is a juft obfervation of Raphelius, ' Tunc plenitudo ' temporis veniffe dicitur, quandò extremum, quod præfinitum ' erat, fpatium ejus exactum eft. Ita plenitudo vitæ vocatur, ' cum quis octogeffimum ætatis annum attigit, quod nunc eft ' longiffimum tempus homini ad vivendum præftitutum, ' apud Herodotum, lib. iii. pag. 192.' Æthiopum rex legatos Perfarum interrogabat, Χρονον οκοσον μακροτατον ανηρ Περσης ζωει ? Quod longiffimum tempus a viro Perfo viveretur?

Illi

this time of Chrift's adminiftration ought not to be confined, as moft divines do confine it, to this *pre-fent ftate*; but is to be carried into the *refurrection-world*, and *continued there* till the coming on of *that period*, when the *Son fhall deliver up* the medi-atory *kingdom to the Father*; for, in all this time, he will go on profecuting the grand purpofe of God to *reduce all things to one well-fubjected whole*: Nor will he deliver up his *truft*, as *head* of the media-tory kingdom of God, till he has fully carried this purpofe of God into *effect*; as we fhall have occa-fion particularly and largely to fhow afterwards.

Upon the whole, the juft import of *this fcripture* may, I think, be properly expreffed in the follow-ing paraphrafe, " The thing which God purpofed in himfelf, according to his own good pleafure, and which would have remained a SECRET in his own breaft, but that he hath made it known to us, is, that he will *reduce all things*, both *in the aerial heavens*, and *on the earth*, from their prefent dif-jointed irregular ftate, into one uniform, well-fub-jected, and duly-fubordinated whole; and that he will do this, not by himfelf *immediately*, but by the

Illi refpondebant, Ογδωκοντα ετεα ζωης πληρωμα ανδρι μακροτατον προκεεσθαι, Perfectiffimum diu vivendi fpatium homini proponi octoginta annos. Quare nec hic Hebraifmus ullus eft, ad quem hoc loquendi genus Beza refert. Ufurpatur et nomen πληρωσις, de *pleno tempore*, lib. iii. pag. 214. Ο Μαγος εβασιλευε μηνας επτα τους επιλοιπους Καμβυση ες τα οντα ετεα της πληρωσιος, Magus regnavit menfes feptem, qui reliqui erant ad implen-dum octavum annum regni Cambyfis. *Vid.* Raphel. Annot. Philolog. vol. ii. pag. 445, 446.

agency

agency of his Son *Jesus Christ*, and in *the period of his mediatory administration*, which *commenced* when *the times* preparatory to it were *fully compleated*, or *filled up*, and will *last* till his *delivery of the kingdom to the Father*, when *God* shall be *all in all*."

It will be an additional confirmation of the above sense of this scripture, if we go on, and show its analogy with the *following context*, and indeed this *whole Epistle*. Be pleased then to observe,

The apostle, in these verses, having spoken of the purpose of God to reduce all things by Christ into one well-subjected whole, immediately subjoins, in proof that he was really prosecuting such a *grand scheme*, the following words, " In whom " also we have obtained an inheritance, being pre- " destinated according to the purpose of him who " worketh all things according to the counsel of " his own will; that we should be to the praise " of his glory, who first trusted in Christ: In " whom ye also trusted after that ye heard the word " of truth, the gospel of your salvation ; in whom " also, after that ye believed, ye were sealed with " that holy Spirit of promise, which is the earnest " of our inheritance, until the redemption of the " purchased possession, unto the praise of his glory." As if he had said, " In him we *Gentiles*, in execution of this gloriously extensive plan of God's grace, are, in common with the *Jews*, put into the *gospel-method* of obtaining an inheritance (46),

not

---

(46) *Gospel-method of obtaining an inheritance.*] The word here is εκληρωθημεν; which Mr. Locke, after Dr. Hammond, understands

not like that of the earthly Canaan, but one that is heavenly, incorruptible, and eternal, being before

understands passively, *in whom we became his inheritance*, instead of *in whom we have obtained an inheritance* : ' This being,'
says he, ' the way wherein God spake of his people, the
' *Israelites*, of whom he says, Deut. xxxii. 9, " The Lord's
" portion is his people, Jacob is the lot of his inheritance."
' See also, Deut. iv. 20.—1 Kings viii. 51, and other places.'
But the apostle evidently brings in this, and the following
verses, to illustrate, or prove, what he had just before advanced, namely, that it was God's purpose *to gather all things
into one by Christ*. So, in the above-explained *twin-text*,
Col. i. 19, 20, having observed, that it was the " good plea-
" sure of the Father to reconcile all things to himself," he
goes on to illustrate what he had observed by saying, " And
" you Gentiles, who were once alienated from God, hath he
" now reconciled ———." He plainly intends the same thing
in both places. And what he means is, not that *these Gentiles*
were already possessed of *that change* which made them *meet
for*, and *actually interested them in*, the *heavenly inheritance* ; but
that they were put into the *gospel-method* of having this *moral
change* effected in them, that so, being made *meet for*, they might
become *actually interested in*, this *inheritance*. It is therefore observable, the apostle says, in the former of these places, " IF ye
" continue in faith, and be not moved away from the hope of the
" gospel." And this same *condition* is tacitly understood here. We
" have obtained an inheritance," that is, are put into the *gospel
way* of obtaining it ; and may be said *actually* to have obtained it, *if we continue in the faith*, and *do not renounce the gospel*.
It is not the design of the apostle to give us to understand,
as though the admission of the *Gentiles* into the *gospel kingdom*
was the accomplishment of God's *purpose*, and *good pleasure*, to
gather all things into one, to *reconcile all things* ; for this was a *mean*
only in order to the accomplishment of this *end* : Which *mean*
might, and would, be ineffectual with respect to *many* ; because they would not *continue in the faith*, and remain *unmoved*
from

fore appointed hereto conformably to the design
of him who worketh all things after the counsel of
his own will: And we, the first Gentiles who hoped
for glory in Christ (47), were put into the gospel

from the gospel. But this is no argument that the *grand purpose*
of God to *reduce, reconcile, all things,* shall not be fully carried
into execution. For this is only *one mean* in pursuance of this
great design ; and when it has had its course, some *other dispensation* will open in prosecution of this *same end,* as we shall
see afterwards. Dr. Hammond says, ' The king's MS. has
' not the word εκληρωθημεν, but εκληθημεν, *we were called.*' The
author of the New English version of the New Testament says,
' it is εκληθημεν in Alexand. Germ. Gr. Lat.—Clar. Gr. Lat.—
' Bonner Gr. Lat.' Wolfius's note, *in loc.* agrees herewith,
' Pauci quidem codices legunt εκληθημεν ;' but he justly adds,
' vitio, puto, librariorum, qui verbi alterius notionem non
' satis adsequerentur.' And indeed it is no way likely, that
so uncommon a word as εκληρωθημεν, a word that is used no
where else in the whole New Testament, should creep into any
copy, if it had not been in the original text: Whereas it is
easy to suppose, on the contrary, that εκληθημεν, a very common word, might be substituted by some transcriber, who did
not well know what εκληρωθημεν meant.

(47) *We the first Gentiles who hoped for glory in Christ.*] In
the original it is ημας προηλπικοτας εν τω Χριστω ; the meaning
of which words may be learned from Col. i. 27, where the
apostle, speaking of the gospel which had been preached to
the Gentiles, calls it, Χριστος εν υμιν η ελπις της δοξης, *Christ
among you the hope of glory.* And the Gentiles, who first embraced Christianity, might very fitly be spoken of as those
who *first hoped for glory in Christ,* because, in the second chapter of this same epistle, and 12th verse, *that* is one of the characters the apostle applies to them in their *Pagan* state, ελπιδα
μη εχοντες, *not having hope,* that is, *gospel-hope,* such hope as
the gospel justly lays the foundation for.

way

way of obtaining this inheritance, that we might
be to the praife of God's glory. In Chrift alfo
ye *Ephefian* Gentiles were put into the fame way
of obtaining this inheritance (48), having heard the
word of truth, the glad-tidings of falvation : In
him alfo, having believed, ye were fealed by the
holy promifed Spirit both with *miraculous gifts* and
Chriftian graces (49); which fealing by the promifed

(48) *In Chrift alfo ye Ephefian Gentiles*, &c.] Mr. Locke, as
it appears to me, is right in fuppofing, not only that the
words, εν ω και υμεις, are elliptical, but that they fhould be
fupplied with the verb εκληρωθητε. I have accordingly fo
fupplied them, though in the fenfe in which, I think, this
word ought to be underftood. Not that this *fupply*, or that of
trufted in our Bibles, are either of them abfolutely neceffary;
for the verfe may be thus conftrued without them, "In whom
ye *Ephefian* Gentiles alfo, after that ye had heard the word
of truth, the gofpel of your falvation; I fay, in whom, after that ye had believed, ye were fealed, &c." But the
fenfe will be more eafy, and the difcourfe more emphatical,
if we fuppofe that the apoftle, in the 11th verfe, is fpeaking
of the *firft* Gentiles that believed; and in *this*, of the *Ephefians*
who were believers *after them*; making them both to be
equally put into the gofpel-method of obtaining the inheritance.

(49) *With miraculous gifts and graces.*] It is certain that the
Holy Spirit was promifed, and beftowed, both in *miraculous
gifts* and *Chriftian graces*. And it fhould feem reafonable
therefore to think, that both thefe, the *former* as well as the
latter, are that *fealing by the Spirit*, which is here fpoken of as
an *earneft*, *pledge*, or *proof* of the *future inheritance*. Only, it
ought to be remembered, *miraculous gifts* are a *pledge*, or
affurance, of nothing more than the *truth of the gofpel*, which
declares the *heavenly inheritance* to be an *obtainable good*:
Whereas,

mifed Spirit *is the earneſt*, pledge, or aſſurance, *of our inheritance*, of the inheritance both *we* and *you* were put into the goſpel-way of obtaining ; ver. 11, 13, " unto the purchaſed redemption" (50), or *till the day of redemption* [chap. iv. 30], " the adoption we " are waiting for [Rom. viii. 21. 23], the redemp-

Whereas, the real being of *Chriſtian graces* in the hearts of be-lievers is an *earneſt*, or *pledge*, that they are *now actually* in-tereſted in a *right* to this inheritance.

(50) *Unto the purchaſed redemption.*] In the original it is, εἰς απολυτρωσιν της περιποιησεως. The phraſe has been puzzling to interpreters, if we may judge by what they have ſaid upon it. The true ſenſe appears to me to be given in the para-phraſe. Απολυτρωσις obviouſly means *deliverance, redemption*, the ſame thing with what the apoſtle Paul calls *the redemption of the body, deliverance from corruption into a glorious immortality*. Περιποινσις properly ſignifies *acquiſition, purchaſe, poſſeſſion*. The prepoſition εἰς has often the force of a particle of *time*, anſwering to the *Engliſh* word *unto, until*, as in our tranſlation. Inſtances to this purpoſe are too common to be particularly mentioned. If now we look upon the word περιποινσεως, a ſubſtantive of the genitive caſe, as having the force of an *adjective* [like examples of which are frequently to be met with in ſcripture. We have two in the preceding verſe, *the word of truth* for *true word* ; and *Spirit of promiſe* for *promiſed Spirit*] the phraſe, εἰς απολυτρωσιν της περιποινσεως, may fitly be rendered *unto, until the purchaſed redemption*, that is, the day, the time, when the redemption which Chriſt has purchaſed ſhall be actually poſſeſſed as an inheritance. This ſeems to me to be the moſt eaſy natural conſtruction of the phraſe ; and it perfectly ſuits with the apoſtle's general ſcope in this paſſage of ſacred writ. The tranſlation in our Bibles, to ſay the beſt, is darkly expreſſed, and ſo as to be ſcarcely intel-ligible to many readers. The reader will judge whether I have ſet it in a better light.

tion

" tion of our body," purchafed for us by Chrift, when we fhall be " delivered from the bondage of " corruption into the glorious liberty of the children " of God;" that fo *you* alfo, as well as *we*, may be " to the praife of the glory of God's grace."—The apoftle, after *giving thanks*, and *making prayers*, for thefe believing Gentiles, goes on to fpeak of *Chrift* as that glorious perfon, " whom God has fet at his own " right hand in the heavenly places, far above all " principality, and power, and might, and domi- " nion, and every name that is named, not only " in THIS WORLD, but in THAT WHICH IS TO " COME; and under whofe feet he hath put ALL " THINGS, giving him to be head over ALL " THINGS to the church, which is his body, the " fullnefs of him that FILLETH ALL IN ALL." And furely, God's thus fetting Chrift *far above all things*, and putting *all things under his feet*, and giving him to be *head over all things*, and fo as to deferve the charaćter of *filling all in all*, is fuch a comment on his purpofe to *gather all things into one by him*, as will fully juftify what we have faid upon it.

The apoftle, indeed, has his eye, not only in this chapter, but throughout this *whole epiſtle*, upon the *reduŝtion of all things into one by Jeſus Chriſt*. Hence he fpeaks of the UNITY of every thing that relates to this *grand purpoſe* of God's grace. " There " is," fays he, chap. iv. 4—6. " one body, one " Spirit, one hope, one Lord, one faith, one bap- " tifm, one God and Father of all, who is above all,
                                                    " and

" and through all, and in you all." And as Chrift is " afcended far above all heavens, ver. 10. that he " might FILL ALL THINGS," he will go on imparting *gifts* to this END, ver. 13, μεχρι καταντησωμεν οι παντες εις την ενοτητα——, " until we are ALL arrived at the " UNITY of the faith,—unto a perfect man, unto the " meafure of the ftature of the fullnefs of Chrift." If we confider this impartation of *gifts* in connection with God's *purpofe to gather all things into one by Jefus Chrift*; with Chrift's being that glorious perfon who *filleth all in all*; with his being fet at God's right hand as *head over all things*, and to this end, *that he might fill all things*: I fay, if we confider this beftowment of *gifts* in this view, it will be both reafonable and natural to fuppofe the *continuance* of it, not only through the *prefent* adminiftration of the kingdom of God, but TILL *every individual* of the human kind is arrived at fuch UNITY in faith and knowledge, as to be, in the fpiritual fenfe, a *full grown man*, in fome proportion conformed to the *fullnefs* of the *fpiritual ftature* of Jefus Chrift. No other interpretation will fo well connect the apoftle's difcourfe in this *epiftle*, or give it fo full and noble a meaning.

And it is with reference ftill to this fame *reduction of all things into one whole*, that the apoftle fpeaks of *Jews* and *Gentiles*, chap. ii. 14, as being *made both one*; and, ver. 16, as being *both reconciled to God in one body, by the crofs of Chrift*. It is a great miftake to think, as many commentators

mentators do, that this incorporating both *Jews* and *Gentiles* into *one church*, partaking in common of the visible advantages and privileges of the *gospel kingdom*, is the *only* thing the apostle has in view. This, it is true, is part of his design, but not the whole. One leading step, in consequence of Christ's death on the cross, in order to the accomplishment of the extensively glorious plan of God to *reduce all things into one*, was the breaking down the *partition-wall* he had formerly made, which separated between the *Jews* and *Gentiles*, and putting things in such a situation as that they might both make *one ecclesiastical community*, enjoying in common the privileges, motives, advantages, and hopes of the *gospel-dispensation*. But the accomplishment of this was not the accomplishment of the *purpose* of God to *gather together all things in one*. It was a *mean* only in order to this *end*; which *end*, if it be not accomplished by this *mean* [as it will not] must and will be followed with some *other*, and more *effectual mean*, in some *other dispensation* of the kingdom of God ; as shall be shown in its proper place elsewhere. The MYSTERY therefore spoken of, in this Epistle, with so much affectionate admiration, is not the *admission of the Gentiles into the visible kingdom of God*, in itself simply considered ; but their admission into it as a MEAN that was wisely and powerfully adapted to promote the bringing into *effect* the GRAND PURPOSE of God of which we are treating. It is therefore observable, the apostle

not

not only declares, in the paſſage we have been thus long conſidering, that "God hath made known unto "us the MYSTERY of his will,—which he PURPOSED "in himſelf;" but explains what he means by this MYSTERY, making it to conſiſt in this, namely, "that, in the diſpenſation of the fullneſs of times, "he would gather together in one all things by "Chriſt, both which are in heaven, and which are in "earth." This then is the thing meant by the "MYSTERY, which, in other ages, was not made "known to the ſons of men," that is, *ſo made known to them,* in ſo clear, full, and explicit a manner, "as "it is NOW," under the goſpel, "revealed to the "apoſtles, and prophets, by the Spirit," as the apoſtle ſpeaks, chap. iii. ver. 5. And this is the thing meant by the MYSTERY, which this ſame apoſtle ſays, in the 3d verſe of this chapter, "was made known to him "by revelation, as he wrote afore [that is, chap. i. "ver. 9, 10] in few words;" which MYSTERY, as he opens it, ver. 6, lay in this, that "the Gentiles "ſhould be fellow-heirs, and of the ſame body, and "partakers of his promiſe in Chriſt, by the goſpel." Remark here, the MYSTERY of which the apoſtle is treating, in this *third chapter,* is the *ſame myſtery* of which he had ſpoken in the *firſt chapter* ; for he expreſsly ſays, *that he had wrote before about it in few words.* When therefore he makes *this myſtery,* in this *third chapter,* to conſiſt in this, "that the "Gentiles ſhould be fellow-heirs, and of the ſame "body, and partakers of God's promiſe in Chriſt," the meaning ought not to be *confined* to the ad-

miſſie

miſſion of the *Gentiles* into the *goſpel-viſible-king-dom,* ſo as to be *joint-partakers* with the *Jews* in the privileges of it. This may be *one thing* intended [in the ſenſe that has been explained], but not the *main.* What the apoſtle has *principally* and *ultimately* in view is, that glorious plan of God which he had PURPOSED IN HIMSELF, conformably to which both *Jews* and *Gentiles,* that is, mankind univerſally, were *fellow-heirs,* ſo united together as to make *one and the ſame body,* and *co-partners in eternal life,* which, in Jeſus Chriſt, is the great promiſe of the goſpel. The apoſtle therefore, verſes 8, 9, glories in it as an high honour done him, that God ſhould make him a *miniſter* of this *grand myſtery* of his will. "Unto me," ſays he, "who am leſs than "the leaſt of all ſaints, is this grace given, that I "ſhould preach among the Gentiles the unſearch-"able riches of Chriſt, and make ALL MEN ſee "what is the fellowſhip of [the joint-partnerſhip "in] the MYSTERY, which, from the beginning "of the world, hath been hid in God; who CRE-"ATED ALL THINGS BY JESUS CHRIST." The apoſtle, you obſerve, as God's *miniſter,* was to make ALL MEN ſee their *fellowſhip,* or *joint-partnerſhip, in the* MYSTERY *that had been hid in God,* απο των αιωνων, *from former ages.* What *myſtery* was this? Plainly, the PURPOSE in God's breaſt (as it is expreſſed, chap. i. ver. 9, 10) to "gather together "in one by Jeſus Chriſt all things;" or that purpoſe of his, in which [as it is ſignified in the 6th verſe of this *third chapter*] both *Gentiles* and *Jews,*

2

that

that is, the whole world of men, were made *fellow-heirs, one myftical body,* and *partakers in common of eternal life,* the great thing *promifed,* and aimed at, in the gofpel. And that ALL MEN fhould *fee this myftery,* this purpofe of God, and fo fee it as to *know* their *fellowfhip, joint-partnerfhip,* in it, though it had formerly been a *fecret,* a thing *hidden in God,* is very ftrongly fuggefted in thofe remarkable words, in the 9th verfe, "WHO CREATED ALL "THINGS BY JESUS CHRIST."

Interpreters are much at a lofs to point out the connection of thefe words with the difcourfe of which they are a part. The great Mr. Locke, not perceiving how *God's creating all things by Jefus Chrift,* in the literal common fenfe, could be connected with the argument the apoftle is here purfuing, judged it neceffary to underftand the words *figuratively,* that is, of the *new creation.* ' By interpreting them otherwife, (fays he) we ' fhall make St. Paul a very loofe writer, and ' weak arguer;—bringing in things not at all to ' his purpofe, and of no ufe to the bufinefs in ' hand.' See his note *in loc.* But the view we have given of his difcourfe throws a fingular pertinency upon his here introducing Chrift as the perfon *by whom God created all things,* not *figuratively,* but in the literal fenfe of the words. For, if God *created all things,* in this lower world, *by Jefus Chrift,* he could not employ a more fuitable agent to carry into *effect* the *myftery which he had purpofed in himfelf,* namely, the *reducing them from*

their

their prefent disjointed irregular ftate, into one orderly well-fubordinated whole. And as he is *equally* the creator of *all things* by Jefus Chrift, it is highly reafonable to think, fince he has made him his *great agent,* his *prime minifter,* in the affair of *reftoring the world,* that he will do it UNIVERSALLY; reducing ALL THINGS, as ONE, in *fubjection to God.* If there was any thing, in this lower world, that was not *created* by Jefus Chrift, it might be confidered as an exception in the fcheme of *recovery*; but as ALL THINGS, without limitation, were *created* by him, it is a credible truth, a thing fit, reafonable to be believed, that they fhall ALL by him be *gathered together into one well-connected and duly-fubordinated whole.* In fhort, if God *created all men,* as well as *other things,* in this world, by his fon *Jefus Chrift,* we may eafily collect from hence, how he comes to be their COMMON FATHER, [Mal. ii. 10]; and if their father, how they are his CHILDREN; and if they are children, how fit, proper, and reafonable it is, that they fhould be FELLOW-HEIRS TO, and JOINT-PARTAKERS IN, that *happy ftate* which he has PURPOSED fhall take place, when he has *gathered all things into one,* under the *agency* of that fame *Jefus Chrift by whom he,* at firft, *created them all.* In this view of the apoftle's words, harmony and beauty, wifdom and goodnefs, yea, the riches of them, run through the *plan* of God, and the *execution* of it, with reference to this world of our's: Forafmuch as he not only *made all things* in it by *Jefus Chrift,* but will

will *reduce them all*, from their preſent disjointed diſordered ſtate, by means of the *lapſe*, into *one glorious perfeƈtly ſubordinated whole*; and will do it by the *ſame Jeſus Chriſt*, through whoſe agency he *created them* in the beginning.

And this, it may be noted, is the true meaning of *the myſtery hid from ages and generations*, which is ſo often, and ſo juſtly [upon the preſent ſcheme] mentioned with admiration by the apoſtle Paul in *all his epiſtles*. Well might he ſpeak of it in that ſtyle, Col. ii. 2, 3, " the myſtery of God, even the " Father, and of Chriſt, in which" [ſo *εν ω* ought to be tranſlated, or *wherein*, as in the margin ; and not *in whom*, as in the text itſelf] " are hid all the trea- " ſures of wiſdom and knowledge." Well might he ſay, as in 1 Cor. ii. 7, 8, " We ſpeak the wiſdom of " God in a myſtery, even the hidden wiſdom, " which God ordained before the world to our " glory : which none of the princes of this world " knew ; for had they known it, they would not " have crucified the Lord of glory (51)." In a
word,

(51) It may be worth obſerving, the words, *which none of the princes of this world*, &c. let us into the *true reaſon* why the *purpoſe of God* to *reconcile all things*, to *gather all things into one*, was kept a *myſtery*, a *ſecret*, to *former ages and generations*. The *death* of Chriſt was a *foundation-ſtroke* in the ſcheme of *recon-ciliation*, the *grand mean* in order to its accompliſhment. If this ſcheme of God had been *revealed by the Spirit* to *former ages*, as it *has been ſince*, it could not, humanly ſpeaking, have been carried into *execution :* For *none of the princes of this world*, in that caſe, *would have crucified Chriſt* It was,

therefore,

word, well might he cry out, as in Rom. xi. 33, " Oh the depth of the riches of the wisdom, and " knowledge of God! How unsearchable are his " judgments, and his ways past finding out!" This exclamation took rise from the wonderful way in which *this mystery*, the *salvation* of *Jews* and *Gentiles*, that is, mankind universally, was to be brought about, namely, by their being in their turns generally left to *unbelief*; for, says the apostle, ver. 32, " God hath shut them up all " together [συνεκλεισε τους παντας] in unbelief, that " he might have mercy upon them all." He, I am sensible, is speaking, in this *chapter*, of *Jews* and *Gentiles*, in the *collective* sense; and of their being, in this sense, admitted into, or cast out of, the visible kingdom of God: But it is easy to see that he aims at something far higher; speaking of this conduct of God towards the *collective* bodies both of *Jews* and *Gentiles*, not as his *ultimate intention*, with respect to either of them; but as a wise and well-adapted *mean*, in prosecution of his *grand purpose* to *have mercy upon all*, or, as it is more fully expressed in Col. i. 20, and Eph. i. 10, " to re- " concile all things to himself," to " gather to- " gether all things in one:" Nor will any other interpretation give so *grand a sense*, and so *noble a*

therefore, at least in part, with a view to this leading step in the accomplishment of the affair of *reconciliation*, that it was *hid in God*; and with great propriety, as a clear and explicit revelation of it would have directly tended to counteract, and defeat, this purpose and counsel of God.

pertinency,

pertinency, to the doxology which concludes this chapter, "For of him, and through him, and to "him, are all things; to whom be glory for ever. "Amen."

I shall now finish what I have to offer, in proof of the present proposition, with a few touches upon those observable words, in 1 Tim. ii. 4, ος παντας θελει ανθρωπους σωθηναι, "who is willing, "desirous, that all men should be saved." Now, if such a Being as we justly conceive God to be, is *really willing, sincerely desirous*, that *all men should be saved*, they *certainly shall be saved*.

Two things are objected against this reasoning, the answer whereto will set the text upon which it is grounded in a clear and full point of light.

It is said, in the *first* place, the apostle is here speaking *de hominum generibus, non singulis personis*; that is, of *all ranks* or *sorts* of men, not of *all individuals*. In order to our forming a right judgment of this plea, we must consult the whole paragraph, of which the words in debate are a part. It runs thus : "I exhort, therefore, that, first of all, "supplications, prayers, intercessions, and giving "of thanks, be made for ALL MEN; for kings, "and for all that are in authority, that we may "lead a quiet and peaceable life in all godliness "and honesty. For this is good and acceptable "in the sight of God our Saviour; who will "have ALL MEN to be saved, and to come to the "knowledge of the truth. For there is ONE "GOD, and ONE MEDIATOR between God and

M 2   "man,

" man, the man Chrift Jefus; who gave himfelf
" a ranfom FOR ALL, to be teftified in due time."
The queftion now is, Who are meant by the ALL
MEN God is willing fhould be faved, whether all
men *individually*, or *generically?* It fhould feem
paft all difpute, that the apoftle intends the *former*;
and for thefe two reafons.

1. God's willingnefs that *all men* fhould be
faved is brought in as an argument to enforce the
foregoing duty of *praying for all men.* Confequently, we muft underftand, by *all men*, the fame
perfons in the *motive,* that are intended in the
duty: Otherwife, we fhall make the apoftle argue
inconclufively. Now, all men *univerfally* are the
objeƈt of the *duty* here enjoined. It is for all men,
without exception, that we are exhorted to pray.
All men therefore, *without exception*, are the perfons
meant by the *all men* God is willing, or defires,
fhould be faved.

2. The *reafon* given, why God defires the falvation of all men is, becaufe there is *one God*, and
*one mediator between God and men, the man Chrift
Jefus.* Now, this is a reafon that extends *equally*
to all men without limitation.

There is one God, (i. e.) all men have one God
and Father. God is as truly the God of one man
as of another; and there is therefore the fame reafon
to think, that he fhould be defirous of the falvation
of *every man*, as of any man. We may colleƈt the
juft fenfe, and full force, of thefe words, from thofe
fimilar ones, Rom. iii. 29, 30, " Is he the God
" of

" of the Jews only ? Is he not the God of the
" Gentiles alfo ? Yes, of the Gentiles alfo : Seeing
" it is ONE GOD that juftifieth the circumcifion by
" faith, and the uncircumcifion through faith (52)."
In like manner, we may argue here, Is he the
God of a *fmall portion* of mankind only ? Is he not
the God and Father of *all men ?* Surely he is ; and
equally willing to juftify them *all* through the faith
of the gofpel.

The other branch of the reafon, " There is one
" mediator between God and men, the man Chrift
" Jefus," equally extends alfo to *all men.* The
parties between whom the man Jefus mediates are
God and *men* ; that is, men *univerfally,* the *whole
race* of men ; not fome men, in diftinction from
others. No reafon, to be fure, no good reafon,
can be affigned, why the *man Chrift Jefus* fhould
mediate between *God* and *fome men only,* to the ex-
clufion of others. And indeed he is probably
fpoken of under the ftyle of the *man* Jefus, to
intimate, that *man,* the *whole human kind,* is one of

(52) Dr. Benfon, in his note *(b)* on 1 Tim. ii. 5, tranflates
this 30th verfe thus : *For it is one and the fame God who will
juftify* [περιτομην εκ πιστεως] *the believing Jew,* [και ακροβυστιαν,
fcil. εκ πιστεως] *and the believing Gentile* [δια της πιστεως] *by
the faith of the gofpel.* I was at once ftruck with the propriety
of this verfion, though the Dr. barely mentions it, without
offering any thing to fupport it. And it is the only one I
ever faw that I could reft fatisfied in. Were this a fit place
for it, I could eafily point out the preferablenefs of *this* to
the *common* tranflation, and juftify it againft all the objections
I am aware could be made to it.

M 3 the

the parties, on whofe behalf he has undertaken the office of a *mediator.* So that there is no reafonable room to queftion, whether, by *all men* we are here to underftand *mankind univerfally.* This fhould feem to be undeniably evident.

It is pleaded, in the *fecond* place, there is no *certain connection* between God's being *willing* that all men fhould be *faved,* and their being *eventually faved* ; becaufe this *defire* of God, however ftrong and hearty, may be counteracted by men themfelves. He may, in confequence of this defire, ufe proper *moral means* that all men might be faved ; but, as men are *free agents,* they may *mif-improve* thefe means, and bring *final ruin* upon themfelves, notwithftanding God's *willingnefs* they fhould be faved.

I readily own, in anfwer hereto, that men, as they are *free agents,* have the power of *refifting,* or *oppofing,* thofe *means,* which God, from his *defire* of their falvation, may fee fit to ufe with them ; which power ought not to be *over-ruled,* nor indeed can it be in confiftency with *moral agency.* But then it muft be affirmed, at the fame time, that they have power to make a *good* as well as bad ufe of thefe means ; and of exerting it with the full confent of their wills. And if God *really defires* their falvation, why need it be fuppofed, that his defire fhould be *finally* and *everlaftingly fruftrated* through men's non-compliance with the means ufed in order to its accomplifhment? Is infinite wifdom, excited by infinite benevolence, and

and accompanied with infinite power, incapable of devising, and then executing, a scheme, with reference to *all men*, which shall, in *event*, without breaking in upon their *liberty*, or using any *means* but such as are *moral* and *rational*, and therefore adjusted to their character as *moral agents*, infallibly issue in their salvation? It appears to me a gross reflection on that Being, who is infinitely perfect, to suppose him *unable finally to counteract*, and in a *moral* way too, the weakness, and folly, and obstinacy, of such poor inferior creatures as men are. And if he is able, in consistency with men's make, as *moral* and *intelligent agents*, to effect their *salvation*, I see not, I own, when it is said, *he desires they should be saved*, but that such a declaration virtually and constructively amounts to the same thing as if it had been said, *he would save them in event and fact.* For if God is really *able* to save them, his *desiring they should be saved*, and his *eventually saving them*, are convertible terms : Unless we absurdly suppose, that God can be *heartily desirous* they should be saved, and yet not use *those means* in order thereto, which it is in his *power* to use, and which, if he should use, would bring their salvation into *event* or *fact*. I am free to declare, for myself, that a *revelation*, from such a Being as God is, directly affirming, that he *desires all men should be saved*, is, with me, a sufficient inducement to believe, that they *eventually* shall. For if he is *sincere* in this desire, what should hinder its coming into *fact*? Shall we set up *man* in opposition to

God,

God, and say that his *foolishness* and *obstinacy* are an overmatch for the infinite wisdom, knowledge, and power of God? The bare mentioning such an absurdity is a sufficient confutation of it.—But it will more fully appear, that God's *desiring* the salvation of *all men* is certainly connected with their *final salvation*, when we come to shew, as we shall by and by, that, in consequence of this *desire*, or *willingness*, in God, such *means* will be used, in fact, as shall *prevail* upon *all men*, and prepare them, in a *moral way*, as *moral agents*, for an *eternal reign in happy life*.

In the mean time, I would subjoin here to what has been already said, that those words in ver. 6, " who gave himself a ransom for all," exceedingly favour the interpretation we have given of the preceding words, ver. 4, " who desires that all " men should be saved." For they are, in their connection, assigned as an argument in justification of their truth. As if the apostle had said, " I had affirmed, in the 4th verse, *that God desires all men should be saved*, and you may give full credit to my affirmation; for Jesus Christ, in consequence of this *desire*, and that it might be complied with, *gave himself a ransom for all*." Now, if God *desires the salvation of all*, and Christ died that this *desire* of God might be complied with, is it credible that a *small portion* of men only should be saved in *event*? Can it reasonably be supposed, when the all-merciful God has expressed his *desire* that *all men*, the *whole race* of *Adam*, should be saved, and has

has actually sent his son Jefus Christ to *give his life a ranfom for them all*, that both the *defire of God*, and the *confequent death of his own Son*, fhould, in *event* and *fact*, be of *no fignificancy* with refpect to the *greateft part* of the fons of men, as they certainly will be, if they *finally* and *eternally perifh*? No, fays the apoftle, the contrary to this fhall be fully *evidenced in proper time*. This, as I imagine, is the true import of thofe obfervable words, which are added to the 6th verfe, το μαρτυριον καιροις ιδιοις, *a teftimony in due time* (53). The fentence is fomewhat

what

(53) Dr. Benfon tranflates the words, το μαρτυριον καιροις ιδιοις, *a teftimony to his times*; fuppofing the apoftle would hereby fuggeft, that Chrift not only *gave his life a ranfom for all*, but that by his death he was " an eminent and ftedfaft witnefs of the truth *to the age* in which he lived." And it is readily acknowledged this is the truth of *fact*; but I cannot, at prefent, be perfuaded to think, it is the truth intended to be communicated in this place. The word *teftimony*, το μαρτυριον, as it appears to me, ftands connected, in this paffage, not *fimply* with the *death of Chrift*, but with the *thing* affirmed of his death, its being *a ranfom for all*. His *giving his life a ranfom for all* is therefore το μαρτυριον, *the teftimony*, here fpoken of. And the truth it is *a teftimony to* is, that *God defires the falvation of all men*: Which teftimony, it is faid, fhall be fully exhibited καιροις ιδιοις, *temporibus propriis, congruentibus, convenientibus*, in *proper feafon, in meet, fit, due time*, as in the tranflation of our Bibles. Some chufe to render the phrafe *fuis temporibus, in his times*, that is, the *times of Chrift*, within the general period of the adminiftration of God's kingdom in his hands. Either tranflation, as it feems to me, is juft: Nor is it of any importance which of them be preferred. The fame thing, without all doubt, is intended by καιροις ιδιοις

what abrupt and fufpended; but its meaning, fupplied, and placed in due order, agreeably to its connection with the other part of this paffage, is obvioufly this, namely, that Chrift's being a *ranfom for all* fhould, *in its feafon, in proper, due time,* be an *evidence*, or *teftimony*, glorioufly convincing to all, that *God was really willing, heartily defirous,* that *all men fhould be faved*. In agreement with this fenfe, the apoftle obferves, in the words that immediately follow, "whereunto" [εις ο, *to which tef-timony*, that is, to make it appear a juft and full one] "I am ordained a preacher and an apoftle." And, in the execution of his truft as fuch, he has made it *manifeft*, that Chrift's giving his life *a ranfom for all* is a *clear evidence*, a *juft teftimony*, that God is *willing that all men fhould be faved*: Though, I would add here, this will not be fet in its *fulleft* and *ftrongeft* point of light, till the commencement of THAT PERIOD, or DISPENSATION, when *God*, even the *Father*, fhall BE ALL IN ALL; which we fhall have occafion largely to explain under the next propofition; to which I accordingly now proceed.

PROPOSITION V.

"As a mean in order to men's being made "meet for falvation, God, by Jefus Chrift, will, "fooner or later, in THIS STATE or ANOTHER,

ιδιοις here, which is intended by πληρωμα του χρονου, Gal. iv. 4; and εις οικονομιαν πληρωμαλος των καιρων, Eph. i. 10, as thefe phrafes have been before explained.

"reduce

" reduce them all under a WILLING and OBEDIENT
" SUBJECTION to his moral government."

The grand difficulty that lies in the way of
men's being *univerfally* faved is, that *moral depravity*
fo many of them have funk into by vicious living.
And it is readily confeffed, that, if any of the race
of men have fo *corrupted* their minds, and *vitiated*
their tempers, as that they are REALLY INCURABLE
by any *moral* means that can be ufed with them,
in order to their recovery, their ftate muft be
HOPELESS : It is impoffible, in this cafe, confiftently
with reafon, that they fhould be FINALLY HAPPY.
My defign therefore, under this general head, is to
make it evident, from the fcriptures, that mankind
are fo far from being INCURABLE in degeneracy, that
they fhall ALL, fooner or later, be RECOVERED IN
FACT to a virtuous temper of mind, and fo made
meet for *happinefs* in a ftate that will laft for ever.

And thus much, I think, is the obvious natural
import of thofe texts, which fpeak of the *deftruction of fin*, the *faving men from their fins*, the *taking
away their fins*, as the *great defign* of the mediatorial
miffion of Jefus Chrift into our world. The texts
that carry in them this fenfe are numerous. The
apoftle fays, 1 John iii. 8, " For this purpofe was
" the Son of God manifefted, that he might deftroy
" the works of the Devil," that is, vice and
wickednefs. Parallel whereto are thofe words, in
the 4th verfe of this fame chapter, " He was ma-
" nifefted to take away our fins." Hence *John
the*

the Baptist speaks of him in that language, John i. 29, " Behold the Lamb of God, which " taketh away the sins of the world." And the name *Jesus* is said to have been given to him for this reason, Matt. i. 21, " because he shall save " his people from their sins."

These texts, if interpreted according to the natural and genuine force of the words in which they are expressed, do certainly give us to understand, that it was one great part of the *design* of Christ's manifestation in our flesh, to put an end to the reign of *sin*, by *universally destroying* its *influence* over the hearts of men. But, as it is seen in *fact* that this *design* is not accomplished *at present*, with respect to a great many among mankind, the meaning commonly put upon these and such like texts is—that Christ was manifested, not to *destroy sin* in *certain fact*, but only to make use of proper and well-adapted *means* in order to the attainment of this *end*, which end may *finally* fail of being attained, and will not, in *event*, be attained with respect to multitudes. But why should these texts be thus restrained in their sense? What need is there of thus limiting their meaning? May we not, yea, ought we not, to argue rather after this manner? " As it was the *design* of Christ, in coming into the world, *to destroy sin*, it must certainly be destroyed ; and since it is not destroyed in this *present* state, we may reasonably look for *another*, when this *design* of his *mediatory manifestation* shall be fully accomplished." This, I should think, is

the

the moſt natural and confiſtent way of reconciling *preſent faƈt* with the moſt *obvious ſenſe* of theſe texts. And that this is not only their *true ſenſe,* but the *true way* of reconciling their *ſenſe* with *preſent faƈt,* we ſhall be at the pains particularly and largely to prove, by an enumeration of ſeveral paſſages of ſcripture, which peremptorily declare, either in ſo many words, or by juſt and unavoidable conſequence, that *mankind univerſally,* before the ſhutting up of the ſcheme of God, as conduƈted and managed by his Son Jeſus Chriſt, in order to their ſalvation, ſhall CERTAINLY, or in EVENT and FACT, be RECOVERED FROM THE REIGN OF SIN, and reduced under a WILLING and OBEDIENT SUB-JECTION to the divine government.——The texts to this purpoſe are theſe that follow.

The firſt is Pſal. viii. 5, 6, as explained, and argued from, Heb. ii. 6—9. Inſpired David is ſpeaking in this place concerning *Chriſt*; and ſays, in the language of prophecy, "Thou haſt made "him a little lower than the angels, and haſt "crowned him with glory and honour. Thou "madeſt him to have dominion over the works of "thy hands: THOU HAST PUT ALL THINGS UNDER "HIS FEET." That theſe words were ſpoken, not of *Adam,* nor of any ſon of Adam by *ordinary generation,* but prophetically of *Chriſt,* we are aſ-ſured by the writer of the Epiſtle to the Hebrews, in his ſecond chapter. It would be too great a digreſſion, and, it may be, a needleſs one, to ſtop here to juſtify this application of the paſſage; as I
have

have now to do only with thofe who believe the divine infpiration of the *author* of the Epiftle to the Hebrews: Though, if any fhould defire to fee this done, they may confult, as I think, to their full fatisfaction, Dr. Owen, or Mr. Pierce, who have fet this matter in a very clear and ftrong point of light. At prefent, I take it for granted, upon the authority of this writer, that the paffage was *prophetically* fpoken of *Chrift.* And he applies it to him in fupport of his argument, tending to prove the *fuperiority of Chrift to the angels.* For having faid, ver. 5, " unto the angels hath he not put in " fubjection the world to come," he then introduces this paffage in the Pfalms concerning Chrift : And, having mentioned thofe words in it, THOU HAST PUT ALL THINGS IN SUBJECTION UNDER HIS FEET, he goes on, and argues, as in the 8th and 9th verfes, " For in that he put all in fubjection " under him, he left nothing that is not put under " him. But now we fee not yet all things put " under him. But we fee Jefus, who was made a " little lower than the angels, for the fuffering of " death, crowned with glory and honour, that he " by the grace of God fhould tafte death for " every man." The true import of which words, I fhall take leave to exprefs in the following paraphrafe :—" In proving the *fuperiority* of *Chrift* to the *angels,* I had faid, ' unto them God had not put ' in fubjection the world to come,' and with very good reafon ; for in that paffage, in the eighth Pfalm, which fays, in thofe extenfive words, ' thou
‘ haft

' haſt put all things in ſubjection under him,' even
the *angels* themſelves are included. For when it
is ſaid, without limitation, ALL THINGS ARE PUT
UNDER HIM, it is manifeſt there is no room for any
exception; but God muſt be ſuppoſed to have left
NOTHING UNSUBJECTED TO HIM. It is true, we
do not YET ſee all things reduced under ſubjection
to him: But this ought not to be conſtrued an
argument againſt the *above extenſive application* of
the Pſalmiſt's words to him; becauſe, though we
do not at preſent ſee all things brought into ſubjection to him, yet we ſee Jeſus, who, for a little
while (54), was made inferior to the angels, that
he might be qualified for the ſuffering of death (55),

crowned

(54) *For a little while.*] So βϱαχυ τι may properly be tranſlated, as it is in the margin of our Bibles. Eraſmus and Beza
render it *pauliſper*; Grotius, *ad breve tempus.* And it muſt be
taken in this ſenſe Acts v. 34, " And he commanded to put
" the apoſtles forth, [βϱαχυ τι] for a little ſpace." And it
ought to be thus tranſlated here; for it can ſcarce be ſaid of
Chriſt with truth, to be ſure, not with accurate propriety,
that he was made a *little lower* (for it was a great deal) *than
the angels:* Whereas it is ſtrictly juſt to ſay of him, that he
was, for a *little ſeaſon*, a *ſhort time, made inferior to them.* And
it is obſervable, the Hebrew word מעט, in the 8th Pſalm,
which anſwers to the Greek phraſe βϱαχυ τι in this place, is
uſed in the ſame manner, as will be evident to any who will
be at the pains to compare Job xxiv. 24, Iſa. x. 25.—xxix. 17.
Jer. li. 33, Hoſ. i. 4, Hag. ii. 6. Junius and Tremellius
accordingly tranſlate the Hebrew word by *pauliſper*, *a little
while.*

(55) *That he might be qualified for the ſuffering of death.*]
This is the ſenſe I would chuſe to give the words, διᾰ το
παθημα

crowned with glory and honour, that he might profecute the grand intention of his death (56), which by the grace of God he tafted for every man.

The following things, to our purpofe, are obvioufly difcernible in this paffage of fcripture. 1. That thofe words, in the eighth Pfalm, " Thou " haft put all things in fubjection under his feet,"

παθημα τȣ θανατȣ. I am fenfible they may be joined with the preceding words thus, *who for a while was made inferior to the angels by fuffering of death:* So Mr. Pierce joins them. Or, they may be connected with the fubfequent words in this manner, *who upon the account of his fuffering was crowned with glory and honour*; which well agrees with the fcripture account of the *reward* of Chrift's humiliation to death. But they may alfo be conftrued in the fenfe I have put upon them; and perhaps in ftricteft conformity to the proper force of the prepofition δια, when joined with an accufative cafe. And thus interpreted, their meaning will be the fame with the 14th verfe, which I take to be a juft comment upon them, " For-" afmuch as the children were partakers of flefh and blood, " he alfo took part of the fame, that [being now qualified " for it] he might through death deftroy him that had the " power of death."

(56) *That he might profecute the intention of his death.*] This thought I have borrowed from Mr. Pierce; who, in juftification of it, fays, " that fuch an *ellipfis,* or *fyllepfis,* is to be met with both in prophane and facred writers;" and refers us to Gatak. adverf. Mifcel. Poet. c. 31; where there is produced a great many inftances of this kind, two of which he mentions from him. See his *note* upon this text. So that the fenfe of the words is this, " That God crowned Jefus with glory and honour, that fo he might be qualified to purfue the *great end* of his death for *all men,* in bringing them *into fubjection to him.*"

are

are juſtly applicable to Chriſt, and in their ſtrict and full ſenſe. 2. That, when *all things* are ſaid to be *put under him*, the words, ALL THINGS, muſt be underſtood in the GREATEST LATITUDE, ſo as to include [God only excepted] ALL THINGS WHAT-SOEVER. So they are moſt accurately explained in what follows: " For in that he put all in ſubjec-" tion under him, he LEFT NOTHING THAT IS NOT " PUT UNDER HIM." 3. That all things, in this latitude of ſenſe, are not AS YET actually reduced under ſubjection to Chriſt. So it is moſt peremp-torily and directly declared in the words that im-mediately follow, νυν δε ουπω ορωμεν, " But now we " ſee NOT YET all things put under him." 4. That our not ſeeing all things, *at preſent, as yet,* actu-ally ſubjected to Chriſt, is not an argument of any force againſt the application of the Pſalmiſt's words to him in their *full* and *moſt extenſive* meaning ; be-cauſe, 5. We ſee that " ſame Jeſus, who, for a " little while, was made inferior to the angels, " CROWNED WITH GLORY AND HONOUR."

But how, you will aſk, is this a *proof*, that ALL THINGS ARE PUT UNDER SUBJECTION TO CHRIST, according. to the EXTENSIVE MEANING of the Pſalmiſt, as above explained ? I anſwer, The Pſal-miſt ſpake of that which *certainly would be*, as though it *was already in fact*. And though Chriſt's being " crowned with glory and honour " is not a *proof*, that all things are *already* ſubjected to him, yet it is a ſure argument, that this is *now in proſecution*, and that it *will*, in proper time, be actually carried

N

into *effect.* " We fee Jefus crowned with glory and
" honour." The proper force of the apoftle's argument herefrom is this ;—We fee, by the light of
fcripture, that Chrift has been exalted to the right
hand of dignity and power in the heavenly world,
and we may fee as clearly, by the fame light, that
it is his *proper work,* in this exalted ftate, to *reduce
all enemies,* bringing them under *fubjection to him,*
and that he will *fo* ufe his regal dignity and power
as *certainly* and *eventually* to *accomplifh* this *end.*—
This is the apoftle's argument. And its pertinency
and ftrength, to the purpofe for which he brought
it, lies in the CONNECTION God has eftablifhed
between *Chrift's exaltation to kingly glory and power,*
and the *certain actual reduction of all things under
fubjection to him* in due time ; infomuch that we
may infallibly conclude, fince *we fee Chrift crowned
with glory and honour,* that the FINAL EFFECT of
it will be, the fulfilment of the Pfalmift's prophecy, when it fhall be literally and ftrictly true,
that ALL THINGS, in the full and extenfive latitude of the words, are ACTUALLY, or in EVENT,
fubjected to him. Compare this argument of the
apoftle with what is afterwards faid upon 1 Cor. xv.
22—28, and we fhall not be at a lofs to determine, that this is its true fenfe.

To apply now the above proof of the *final fubjection of all things to Chrift* to the purpofe of our
prefent argument.——And the reafoning here is
quite eafy, and yet ftrictly juft, and ftrongly conclufive. If ALL THINGS *fhall be fubjected to Chrift,*

2

and

and in a ſenſe ſo *univerſally extenſive* as that
NOTHING SHALL BE LEFT UNSUBJECTED, the time
will then come, and muſt come, when SIN, among
other things, ſhall be *ſubjeſted to him.* This is certainly one of the *things,* which greatly needs to be
reduced under ſuch ſubjeſtion : For it is *an enemy;*
yea, a *principal enemy* ; emphatically *that enemy,*
which Chriſt came into the world to *deſtroy,* according to thoſe fore-cited expreſs words of the
apoſtle, 1 John, iii. 8, " FOR THIS PURPOSE, the
" Son of God was manifeſted, THAT he might
" deſtroy the works of the Devil," that is, ſin and
wickedneſs. Now, how can *ſin be deſtroyed,* or,
what means the ſame thing, *be ſubjeſted to Chriſt,*
but by effeſting ſuch a *change* in ſinners as ſhall
make them, inſtead of *rebels againſt God,* his
willing and *obedient people ?* There is no other
poſſible way in which an *end* can be put to the *dominion of ſin,* and *moral ſubjeſtion* to the government
of God ſubſtituted in the room of it. The truth
of the matter is plainly this :—Men, by ſinning,
oppoſe the *government* of God : Not his government
of *power,* for this ever was, and ever will, and ever
muſt be, ſubmitted to ; but that *moral* government which he exerciſes over *intelligent* and *free
agents.* Here is room for *oppoſition.* Men may
reſiſt, they have it in their *power* to reſiſt, *that will*
of God which requires their *obedience* as *moral
agents.* And herein, properly and accurately
ſpeaking, and herein only, lies the *eſſence* of *ſin,* or
vice : Nor can it be *deſtroyed,* or *reduced under*

N 2 *moral*

moral subjection, but by application to the *wills* of sinners so as to gain their *free* and *full consent* to become the *obedient servants of God*. Now *Christ*, that he might thus *destroy sin* by making mankind the *obedient subjects* of God, in order to his being *qualified* for this *great* and *noble work*, and placed under suitable circumstances for the *effectual accomplishment* of it, was, after he had *tasted death for* EVERY MAN, *crowned with glory and honour* *. And, in

---

* This same thought is very clearly and fully expressed by Dr. Samuel Clarke, though with no view to establish the *present doctrine*, of which I cannot collect from his writings, that he had any notion. His words, which may be the more regarded, because he was so great a man, are [vol. i. of his *works*, pag. 197, 198] these : ' The kingdom of God *princi-* ' *pally* consists, in his government of *reasonable* and *intelligent* ' creatures ; in his being *served* and *obeyed* by those, who, at ' the same time, are capable of *disobeying* ;—who, in their ' several stations and degrees, according to the light that is ' afforded them, *discern* what is *right*, and *approve* what is ' *good*, and *act* by their *free power*, and are *conscious* of the excel- ' lency of *virtue*, and *love* him whom they obey, and are ' made *happy* by the participation of his perfections. This is ' *that*, wherein *principally* consists the kingdom of God.—By ' *sin*, this kingdom of God, this his government over the ' *hearts* and *wills* of the rational part of the creation, is *opposed* ' and *withstood*. For his *natural kingdom*, the kingdom of his ' *power*, *cannot* be resisted. In this respect, the whole world is ' in his hand as a dust of the balance ; he can withdraw from ' all things their very *being* itself, and, with a blast of his ' mouth, whenever he pleases, reduce them all into nothing in ' a moment. So that it is a very *absurd* notion, which some ' have entertained, from certain figurative expressions of scrip- ' ture very much misunderstood ; as if the Devil had at- ' tempted

in truth, this is the only *fubjection*, it can reafonably
be fuppofed he fhould be advanced to *regal dignity*
and

' tempted to oppofe the Almighty with *force*, and had contended
' with him for the *dominion of the univerfe.* No : Such repre-
' fentations as thefe are only the fictions of the poets. The
' Devil indeed *rebelled* againft God; but in the fame fenfe
' wherein wicked men *rebel* againft him : Not by thinking to
' refift his *power*, but by prefumptuoufly venturing to *difobey*
' *his will*, in thofe things wherein the *nature* of *virtue* and
' *vice*, and the very *effence* of *moral government*, neceffarily
' require that they fhould not be over-ruled and compelled by
' *force*. For here, the thing which God requires is the *free*
' *confent of the will* ; which, in the nature of things, is not
' fubject to *compulfion : Obedience itfelf* being *no obedience*, where
' there is no poffibility of having *difobeyed*. By *fin* therefore
' this *moral kingdom* of God began to be *oppofed*; by the fins of
' *evil angels*, and by the *fins* of *wicked men :* Among whom, as
' they corrupted themfelves by degrees, in departing from
' the living God, the Devil fet up a kingdom of *idolatry* and
' *great wickednefs*, in oppofition to the kingdom of God. In
' order to *deftroy* which *works of the Devil*, [to deftroy them,
' not by the exercife of OMNIPOTENCE, but by the ESTAB-
' LISHMENT OF VIRTUE AND TRUE RELIGION, which is
' the PROPER, and ONLY PROPER DESTRUCTION OF IMMO-
' RALITY AND VICE] God was pleafed to give affiftance and
' ftrength to the light of *nature* and *reafon*, by making
' *revelations* of himfelf, from time to time, to the degenerate
' world ;—firft by the *Patriarchs* ;—then by Mofes and the
' prophets ;—and at laft by his *own Son*, who came into the
' world, and *was manifefted* (as St. John affures us)· '' for this
'' caufe, that he might deftroy the works of the Devil ;'' that
' is, that he might root out idolatry and fuperftitious worfhip,
' and reform men from debauchery and all unrighteous prac-
' tices ; that by the knowledge, worfhip, and love of the one
' true God, and maker of all things, in purity and holinefs of

' life,

and *power*, at God's right hand in heaven, that he might accomplish. Sinful men were *before* abfolutely in fubjection to the *kingdom of God's power*, as being unable to make the leaft *refiftance* to any of its difplays, however fatal they might be in their tendency. There was no need therefore of *Chrift's exaltation*, in order to *force* finful men to *fuch* a fubjection as this. The great thing neceffary was, as they were *free agents*, to make them a *willing people*, in confiftency with their *liberty*. And to *this end* it was, that Chrift was *crowned with glory and honour :* And this *end* he muft accomplifh, before it can be faid, either with propriety or truth, *that* ALL THINGS *are fubjected to him*, in that latitude of fenfe, in which the *writer* of this *epiftle* has explained thefe words, and, *ex profeffo*, directed us to underftand them.

The plain truth is, if ALL THINGS fhall finally be *fubjected to Chrift*, as they muft be, or this

‘ life, in juftice, meeknefs, and univerfal charity and good-
‘ will towards each other, he might bring them back from a
‘ ftate of general corruption, to become worthy and obedient
‘ fubjects of his father's kingdom of righteoufnefs.’ The
Doctor has here exhibited a true and juft idea of God's *moral
kingdom*, his principal glory ; and of *fin*, by which *only* it is
oppofed and *withftood*; and of the *deftruction of fin*, which is
precifely the *fame thing* with the *eftablifhment of real virtue*.
And his whole difcourfe here is a clear and ftrong illuftration
of the *truth* we are upon : Though he did not perceive it ;
which to me is exceeding ftrange, as it is fo obvioufly and naturally connected with the *notion* he has given us of the *deftruction of fin*, on which alone God's *moral kingdom*, which is his
principal one, can be erected, in this *finful* and *degenerate* world.

writer

writer has not argued juftly and fairly; I fay, if
ALL THINGS, without any limitation, or exception,
fhall be brought under *fubjection to Chrift*, then the
time muft come, fooner or later, in this ftate or
fome other, when there fhall be no *rebels* among
the fons of *Adam*, no *enemies* againft the *moral* government of God. For there is no way of *reducing
rebels*, fo as to deftroy their character *as fuch*, but
by making them *willing* and *obedient fubjects*. And
with what truth can it be affirmed, that ALL THINGS,
leaving *nothing in referve to be excepted*, [for the
apoftle, it is to be remarked here, is exprefsly fpeaking of all things in this *unlimited fenfe*] *are fubjected
to Chrift*, when millions of finners (according to
the common opinion) are finally left to blafpheme
both *his* and his *father's* name, as being prompted
thereto by the UNSUBDUED UNCONQUERED ENMITY
of their hearts?

It will, doubtlefs, be faid here, thefe *rebels* will
all be confined, at the great and laft day, in the
prifon of hell, and in this fenfe be brought under
fubjection to Jefus Chrift. But, *this fubjection* notwithftanding, they will ftill continue the *enemies of*
God, and as much unfubjected to the government
of Chrift, as his *willing* and *obedient* fervants, as
ever. How then can it be affirmed, that ALL
THINGS *are brought under fubjection to Chrift?* If
thefe finners ftill continue in their *rebellion*, and are
really (though in hell) the *willing fervants*, not of
God, nor of his Son *Jefus Chrift*, but of *fin* and the
Devil, they are infallibly *as yet* in a ftate of *non-*

N 4 *fubjection*

subjection to the government of Heaven, in a true and proper fenfe ; yea, I may juftly fay, in that very fenfe in which they were fo when Chrift came into the world *for their reduction*. It may therefore, with as much truth be faid THEN, as *now* ; nay, with much more, *we fee* NOT YET *all things put under fubjection to Chrift :* Neither (according to the generally prevailing doctrine) fhall we *ever fee this,* though we have feen *Jefus crowned with glory and honour :* To be fure, we fhall never fee this, in that *latitude* of fenfe, in which it is here faid, *all things are fubjected to Chrift* ; which things are fpoken of, in the prefent tenfe, as *actually in a ftate* of fubjection to him, becaufe, in the final iffue of his adminiftration, they *certainly will be.*

I may add here, with great propriety, as well as ftrength of argument, if ALL THINGS, without exception, fhall be *fubjected to Chrift,* then *death,* the SECOND as well as the *firft death,* will be finally fwallowed up in *victory.* None doubt but that the *firft death* will be fo far deftroyed, even with refpect to the *wicked,* as that they fhall be again reftored to life. And it fhould feem as juft and neceffary a confequence from this fcripture, that the SECOND DEATH alfo fhall be deftroyed. For *this* is as truly an *enemy,* in every fenfe that can be affigned, as the *firft death.* And as the *firft death* is one of the THINGS that fhall be *fubjected to Chrift,* that is, *be deftroyed* ; the argument holds as ftrong for his *conqueft of the* SECOND DEATH, becaufe ALL THINGS muft be *fubjected to him,* fo *univerfally,* in a
fenfe

fenfe *fo unlimited*, as that *nothing fhall be left un-fubjected*. If any fhould be difpofed to fufpect, that this reafoning lays too great an *emphafis* upon the words, ALL THINGS, and is *too rigorous* in *extending* the fenfe of them, I truft he will acquit me of all blame upon this head ; for, if there is juft reafon for blame, he muft throw it upon the *author* of this *epiftle*, and not upon me : For I only ufe his argument, which, I am fure, concludes thus much, if it concludes any thing at all.

I fhall only fubjoin to what has been hitherto faid, that if I have given the true meaning of the 9th verfe, which is thus rendered in the para-phrafe, *We fee Jefus, who, for a little while, was made inferior to the angels, that he might be qua-lified for the fuffering of death, crowned with glory and honour, that he might profecute the grand inten-tion of his death, which, by the grace of God, he tafted for every man :* I fay, if we have given the true fenfe of this verfe, more efpecially the laft claufe of it, it will very much favour that *univerfal fub-jection to Chrift* we have been pleading for. For, according to this conftruction, *the grace of God*, his love, good-will, or kindnefs, is the original *fpring*, or *fource*, of the *death of Chrift* : Now, this love of God being *univerfal*, the *death of Chrift* was *uni-verfal* too ; and having died *for all*, he is *crowned with glory and honour*, that he might profecute the benevolent intention of his death, which was, *the final falvation of all*, by reducing *all under fubjection to God* as his *willing* and *obedient fervants.*

The

The *sense* we have put upon the paffage of fcripture we have been confidering, will be very much illuftrated and confirmed by proceeding to the *next* that deferves particular notice upon this occafion ; which is that parallel one, in the fecond chapter of the epiftle to the Philippians, where the apoftle, having fpoken of the *humiliation* of Chrift, even to the death, goes on, and fays, ver. 9, 10, 11, " Wherefore God hath highly exalted him, " and given him a name which is above every " name, that, at the name of Jefus, every knee " fhould bow, of things in heaven, and things in " earth, and things under the earth ; and that " every tongue fhould confefs that Jefus Chrift is " Lord, to the glory of God the Father." The following things are eafily obfervable in this text :

1. That the *exaltation* of Chrift was not *merely confequent* upon his humiliation to death, but the *reward* of it. This will readily be acknowledged a point beyond all difpute.

2. That this exaltation of Chrift confifted in God's *giving him a name above every name* ; that is, dominion fuperior to all other. For 'tis plain, by *name* we are here to underftand *authority, power, dominion.* Hence, in Heb. i. 4, Chrift's fuperiority to the angels, in point of dignity and power, is expreffed by his having *obtained a more excellent name than they.* Hence alfo our Saviour, fpeaking of this *name* which had been given to him, fays, Matt. xxviii. 18, " All power in heaven and earth " is

" is given to me." And what is here called God's *giving him a name above every name,* is expreſſed, Eph. i. 20, 21, by his " ſetting him at his own " right hand, in the heavenly places, far above all " principality, and power, and might, and do- " minion, and every name that is named, not only " in this world, but in that which is to come." The *name* then given to Chriſt, in reward of his ſufferings and death, was *univerſal dominion.* To be ſure, none will exclude *this,* whatever elſe they may include in its meaning. And this is all I con- tend for.

3. That the FINAL CAUSE of God's giving to Chriſt this *univerſal dominion* was, that he might *univerſally* reduce things under *ſubjection* to the *moral kingdom* of God, which was now under his *adminiſtration.* This is fully and ſtrongly ex- preſſed in thoſe words, " God hath given him a " name—THAT, at the name of Jeſus, every knee " ſhould bow, of things in heaven, and things in " earth, and things under the earth ; and THAT " every tongue ſhould confeſs that Jeſus Chriſt is " Lord, to the glory of God the Father." Inter- preters differ (57) as to the preciſe meaning of the

(57) *Interpreters differ*] Dr. Whitby, by *things in heaven,* underſtands the holy angels; by *things in earth,* men ; by *things under the earth,* the dead, who, being raiſed by Chriſt, ſhall acknowledge his power. Mr. Peirce paraphraſes *the things in heaven and earth,* ' heavenly and earthly beings ;' that is, as I ſuppoſe, angels in heaven, and men on earth. By *the things under the earth,* ſays he, ' are included the dead, as
' Chriſt

the enumeration here, " things in heaven, and
" things in earth, and things under the earth :"
                                            But

' Chrift is " *made Lord of both the dead and living,*" Rom.
' xiv. 9 :' Though, as he adds, ' I fee no neceffity of con-
' fining this expreffion to them ; for the fallen angels may be
' alfo comprehended in it.' Wolfius is of the fame mind,
thinking *the things in heaven, and earth, and under the earth,*
may well be explained by the fimilar phrafes that are ufed,
Rev. v. 13. He fays, ' Hæc omnium optimè ex fimili phrafi
' Joannis, Apoc. v. 13, exponi poffe videntur : Και παν
' κλισμα, ὁ εσλιν εν τω ουρανω (en επουρανια), και εν τη γη (en επιγεια),
' και υποκαλω της γης (en καλαχθονια)—ηκουσα λεγονλας—' And
this was the opinion of moft of the ancients, as this author
fummarily reprefents their fenfe in the following words
of Chryfoftom : ' Τουλεσλιν ο κοσμος πας, και ανγελοι, και ανθρωποι,
' και δαιμονες, ἡ ὁλι και οι δικαιοι, και οι αμαρλωλοι.' But the moft
eafy, natural interpretation of thefe phrafes, is given by Mr.
Hallet, in his *Notes on particular texts,* vol. i. page 27. ' It is,
' (fays he) an old and common method to divide the world into
' three parts, *heaven, earth,* and a *place under the earth.* By
' the *laft,* I apprehend, is meant the *fea.* This feems to
' appear from the following paffages : Exod. xx. 4, " The
" likenefs of any thing that is in *heaven* above, in the *earth*
" beneath, or in the *water under the earth.*" Nehem. ix. 6,
" Thou haft made *heaven,*—the *earth,*—the *feas.*" Exod.
' xx. 2, " For in fix days the Lord made *heaven,* and *earth,*
" the *fea,* and all that in them is." Pfal. lxix. 34, " Let
" the *heaven* and *earth* praife him, the *feas,* and every thing
" that moveth therein." Rev. v. 3, " And no man in
" *heaven,* nor in *earth,* neither *under the earth,* and fuch as
" are in the *fea.*" From thefe texts it feems plain to me, that
' *the things under the earth* muft be the things in the *waters*
' which are under the earth, as the expreffion is in the fecond
' commandment. From comparing the former texts, we fee
' what fome call *under the earth,* the others call the *feas,* or *the*
                                            " *waters,*

But yet, they all as one agree that *mankind univer-sally*, whether *living*, or *dead*, are comprehended in it, which is as much as the prefent argument requires. The great and only queftion therefore to be debated is,

What are we to underftand by that *fubjection*, Chrift was exalted that he might reduce *mankind* under?

The common opinion is, that it was a *free* and *voluntary* fubjection, with refpect to *fome* among them; and a *forced* one, with refpect to *all the reft*, at the great and general judgment, when they fhall be obliged, by the *fuperior* power of Chrift, to fubmit to him as their Lord. But this is evidently too low and reftrained an interpretation, and falls vaftly below the juft and full import of the apoftle's words. They are certainly capable, and without the help of any force to ftrain their fenfe, of being underftood to mean a *willing* fubjection with refpect to *all*, and not fome only. And this indeed is the fenfe that *firft* offers to the mind; and it is fo obvious and natural, that, perhaps, no other could have been thought of, had not previoufly received fyftems made it neceffary. When the apoftle fays, Chrift was exalted to regal

---

' *waters*. And fo the defign of the apoftle was to fhew, *that* ' *all the creation was to bow the knee at the name of Jefus.*' If this fhould be the true fenfe of thefe phrafes, the thought here defigned to be conveyed is the fame, for fubftance, with that in Eph. i. 9, 10, and Col. i. 19, 20; which we have before largely explained.

I   dignity

dignity and power, THAT *every knee might bow to him, and every tongue confess that he is Lord, to the glory of God the Father*, the just and full meaning of what he affirms is, " that he was thus highly exalted, not that he might, by superior power, *compel* mankind, who are *free agents*, to submit to his authority and government, owning him, by *constraint*, to be their Lord ; for there is no *moral worth* in such *forced submission :* But, that he might, being now qualified for it, use such means, in the execution of his regal trust, as should influence them *universally*, sooner or later, in a *rational moral* way, and as is befitting *free* and *intelligent agents*, to *bow* down before him, *practically* confessing him to be *Lord*, to the glory of the Father."

So far as Christ is now in the execution of this *power*, which was conferred on him, in *reward* of his humiliation, it is the truth of *fact*, that he is, in THIS WAY, endeavouring to reduce *mankind* under *obedience* to him, by approving themselves *faithful subjects* in that *kingdom of God* of which he has been constituted *head* and *Lord*. The first thing therefore we read of, after all power in heaven and earth had been given to him, is, the commission he gave his apostles to *go, and baptise all nations, teaching them to observe whatsoever he had commanded*, Matt. xxviii. 18. And the whole gospel dispensation, not only its ministers, but its doctrines, precepts, ordinances, rewards, and punishments, are evidently designed, and used, by
Christ,

Chrift, as *head* of the mediatorial kingdom, in order to bring men *univerfally* into that *obedient fubjection* to the laws of righteoufnefs, which is the grand fubjective qualification for rational and eternal happinefs.

'Tis true, he will not, in *this ftate*, prevail upon *all* willingly to bow down before him as their *Lord*. Multitudes, notwithftanding all the methods of his wifdom and grace, will ftand it out, *refufing to have this man to rule over them*. But fhall their prefent *obftinacy* defeat the glorioufly extenfive defign of his being exalted at the right hand of God in heaven? May he not, in the *next ftate*, reduce thofe under fubjection, whom he was not able effectually to work upon in *this*, in any of thofe *moral* ways, he might think proper, as their *moral* governor, to ufe with them? Where is the abfurdity of fuch a fuppofition? Why fhould it be thought unreafonable or incredible? There would be no difficulty at all in admitting, that Chrift might ufe *means* with finners, in the *next ftate*, in order to his making them *good fubjects* in the *moral* kingdom of God, and *fuch means* too as fhould be *effectual* to anfwer this end, were it not for the previoufly imbibed notion, that the *prefent ftate only* being intended for the *recovery* of men to *virtue*, thofe, who are not recovered *now*, muft be made *miferable* in the *next ftate*, which is a ftate of *endlefs torment*: Whereas, even the very *torments* of the *other* world may, in perfect confiftency both with *reafon* and *fcripture*, (as we fhall fee in
its

its proper place) be confidered as *means*, under the government of Chrift, in order to awaken the attention of the fubjects of them, bring them to confideration, and finally gain the *confent of their wills* to become the *willing people* of God. And if Chrift was exalted FOR THIS END, *that every knee fhould bow to him, and every tongue confefs his right of dominion, to the glory of the Father,* I fee not but he muft fail of accomplifhing this *end*, if mankind *univerfally*, fome time or other, in this ftate, or a future one, are not in *fact* reduced under a *willing* and *practical* fubjection to his government.

It will be of little avail to fay here, that the *end* of Chrift's exaltation will be anfwered, as, at the great and general judgment, the *faints* fhall be *rewarded* as his *good and faithful fervants*, and *finners* fent away to *hell* as his *fubdued enemies*. For the *genuflection* and *adoration*, here fpoken of, are evidently *voluntary* acts of *moral* agents, brought into an *obedient fubjection* to Chrift : Whereas the *damned in hell* do not thus bow before him in practical acknowledgments of his dominion, to the glory of the Father. The only fubmiffion indeed they are fuppofed to be brought to, is a *forced* one ; and confequently, they no otherwife *bow down to Chrift* than as *hardened* and *condemned malefactors*. And what a poor low kind of fubmiffion is *this*, in comparifon with *that* we are pleading for ! It is not worthy of being mentioned. A moft weighty confideration truly ! and may

very

very well be looked upon as a good argument in favour of the interpretation we have given of this paffage: Efpecially, if it be remembered, that the *reward* beftowed on Chrift for his humiliation in our flefh, was not *fimply* an exaltation to *dominion,* but to dominion iffuing in the *reduction of all under fubjection to him.* This reward therefore will be *great,* or comparatively *fmall,* according to the *fenfe* in which we underftand this *fubjection.* If *all men,* without limitation, are wrought upon, under his mediatory reign, fo as to become the *willing* and *obedient fubjects* of God's moral kingdom, his *reward* will be carried to the utmoft height of glory: whereas, if multitudes, the greater part of the human race (as the common thought is) will finally continue *rebels,* and, as fuch, be everlaft-ingly bound in chains of darknefs, his reward will be, comparatively, but *low* and *fmall.*

'Tis readily acknowledged, the glory of Chrift's power, as *head* of the government of God, will be illuftrioufly difplayed, if by *force* only he finally fubdues obftinate finners: But it muft, at the fame time, be faid, the glory will be *fmall, very fmall,* in comparifon with what it would be, if he fhould *univerfally* conquer their REBELLION, by fo working upon them as to difpofe and influence them, with the *freedom of moral agents,* eternally to adore before him as the *obedient fubjects* of God. There is no room for difpute here. The reduc-tion of one *rebel-finner* under a *voluntary fubjection* to the divine government, will reflect *more honour*

O

on *Chrift*, as feated at the head of God's kingdom, and tend *more* to the *glory* of the *Father*, than the *forcible* conqueft of multitudes by *fuperior power* only. And herein, it feems to me, lies the *fuperiority*, as well as *diftinguifhing glory*, of Chrift's dominion, that it will, under his wife, and righteous, and gracious management, prove *finally effectual* to the *reduction* of the *whole human race*, fo as to prepare them for a *happy immortality.* And how glorioufly heightened, in this view of the matter, is the *reward* of Chrift's humiliation to death, the death of the crofs ! The whole world of men, upon this fuppofition, will, with the *free* and *full confent* of their *wills*, bow down before him in chearful, thankful, humble adoration of his wifdom, and power, and grace, difplayed in the methods by which he has wrought upon them, as *moral agents*, reducing them under a *voluntary* fubjection to God, and, in this way, fitting them for final and everlafting happinefs : Whereas, according to the common interpretation, the greateft part of the human kind will no otherwife be ever prevailed upon to acknowledge him as *Lord*, than as *chained malefactors* fubmit to the *fuperior power* that confines them. There is certainly *more honour* done to *Chrift*, upon the *prefent* fcheme than the *common* one ; and the *reward* of his fufferings will turn out, beyond all comparifon, a *greater* as well as a *more eminently worthy gift*, from his infinitely benevolent God and Father. And this *voluntary* genuflection of the

whole

whole race of *Adam* before Chrift, as prime minifter in God's kingdom, may alfo, upon this interpretation, with a much greater emphafis, be faid
to be *to the glory of the Father.* Perhaps, the
thing hereby meant is, that it will be to *his glory,*
as it is that which will make way for the coming
on of that *eminently glorious difpenfation,* when *God,*
even the *Father,* fhall be ALL IN ALL. Compare
this *text* with what is faid upon the following one;
before I proceed to which, I would juft add,

That thefe words of the apoftle, we have been
confidering, if not a quotation from Ifaiah xlv. 23,
are, at leaft, an allufion to it. The whole paragraph, as it ftands in the prophecy is, " Look
" unto me, and be ye faved, all the ends of the
" earth: For I am God, and there is none elfe.
" I have fworn by myfelf, the word is gone out
" of my mouth in righteoufnefs, and fhall not
" return, that unto me every knee fhall bow, and
" every tongue fhall fwear. Surely, fhall one fay,
" in the Lord have I righteoufnefs and ftrength:
" Even to him fhall men come, and all that are
" incenfed againft him fhall be afhamed. In the
" Lord fhall all the feed of Ifrael be juftified, and
" fhall glory." I fhall, without any formal reafoning, from this paffage, leave it with every unbiaffed reader to judge, whether, by *all the ends of
the earth,* by *every knee,* and *every tongue,* it is not
more obvious to underftand the *whole world of
men,* than a *few* of them only ? As alfo, whether,
by their *bowing the knee,* it is not more natural to

O 2 underftand

underſtand a *voluntary*, than a *forced* ſubmiſſion ;
a ſubmiſſion of *freedom* and *love*, rather than of
conſtraint ?   And if ſo, whether this *prophecy* can
be juſtly ſaid to be accompliſhed, according to the
full ſenſe of the words in which it is delivered, but
in agreement with the doctrine we are proving:
Upon ſuppoſition of the truth of which, it may
have a moſt glorioully extenſive fulfilment.

I am not inſenſible, this prophecy of Iſaiah is
quoted by the apoſtle Paul with an immediate reference to the *general judgment.*   For having ſaid,
Rom. xiv. 10. " We ſhall all ſtand before the
" judgment-ſeat of Chriſt," he adds, in the words
that next follow, " For it is written," [that is, in
Iſa. xlv. 23] " As I live, ſaith the Lord, every knee
" ſhall bow to me, and every tongue ſhall confeſs
" to God."   But it can by no means be argued,
from this application of this prophecy, that it had
nothing in view beyond the *ſubmiſſive acknowledgments* that ſhould, at the day of judgment, be paid
to *Chriſt*, and herein to *God* ultimately, who conſtituted him judge of the world.   This was doubtleſs *one thing* intended in the *prophecy :* For which
reaſon it might pertinently be thus applied by the
apoſtle.   But then, his thus applying it is no argument, that it meant nothing more.   An inſtance
parallel to this, and a deciſive illuſtration of it, we
have in the ſecond chapter of the Acts, where
the apoſtle Peter applies that *prophecy* in Joel,
chap. ii. 28, 'which foretells that God would
" pour out his Spirit, in the laſt days, upon all
" fleſh,"

" flesh," to the *out-pouring of the Spirit* upon the
apoftles on the *day* of *Pentecoft*. This was, no
doubt, one thing intended to be pointed out by
this *prophecy*; and for this reafon, it was juftly
applied in this cafe. But it is certain, it was not
all that was meant by the *divine Spirit*. Nay, the
greater part of expofitors extend the meaning of
this prophecy beyond every thing that happened
in the apoftle's days; making it to look forward
to a more glorious *out-pouring of the Spirit* in times
yet to come. And herein, I am well perfuaded,
they fall in with the real mind of God in the
delivery of this *prophecy*. In like manner, this
prophecy of Ifaiah, though it includes a *bowing*
before Chrift at the *great day*, and is therefore juftly
applied by the apoftle in that fenfe, may yet have
a further meaning, and *look forward* to a far *more*
noble and *glorious fubjection*, fuch a fubjection of
mens wills to the *will of Jefus Chrift*, as fhall influence them *univerfally* to fall down before him in
voluntary, *humble*, and *grateful acknowledgments*,
that he " is Lord, to the glory of the Father."

The next portion of fcripture, in proof of the
propofition we are upon, I fhould efteem *decifive*
of itfelf, was there no other text in all the Bible
of the like import. It was this indeed that firft
opened to me the prefent fcheme, ferving as a
key to unlock the meaning of many paffages in
the facred writings, which before I could never
underftand. You will find it in the 1ft Epiftle to

the

the Corinthians, xvth chapter, from the 24th to the end of the 29th verse. And, as I lay great stress upon this important passage, and think that it will set this whole matter in a clear and strong point of light, I shall, to prepare the way for the *observations* I have to make upon it, present to the reader's view the *text* itself, together with a *paraphrase*, containing what I judge to be its true sense.

TEXT.	PARAPHRASE.
24 *Then cometh the end, when he shall have delivered up the kingdom to God, even the Father; when he shall have put down all rule, and all authority, and power.*	After that [the *resurrection* of the *saints* at Christ's *second coming*] shall be the *end*, when Christ shall have delivered up the *mediatorial* kingdom to God, even the Father ; when he shall have put down all principality, and authority, and power. Only, take care you do not mistake my meaning. I do not intend to insinuate, as though the *end* would come, that is, the scene of providence, with respect to the sons of Adam, be shut up, IMMEDIATELY after the advent of Christ to restore the saints to *happy life*. For observe, I have connected the *end*, not only with *Christ's*

TEXT.

PARAPHRASE.

Christ's delivery of the king-dom to the Father, but with his having also *put down all principality, and authority, and power :* And upon very good

25 *For he must reign till he hath put all enemies under his feet.*

reason; For he must still reign, and go on reigning, till he has totally subdued all enemies, and subjected them to his dominion, as *head* of God's kingdom; which may require a *long time,* God only knows how long, for its accomplishment. And let it be particularly

26 *The last enemy that shall be destroy-ed is death.*

observed, the last enemy that is to be destroyed, and that must and shall be destroyed, is DEATH, I mean, the SE-COND DEATH; that death which *wicked men must under-go,* before they can be made the *willing subjects* of Jesus Christ, and so fitted for an happy immortality : Nor let this seem any thing strange;

27 *For he hath put all things under his feet. But when he faith, All things are put*

For God hath purposed, that ALL THINGS shall be SUB-JECTED to his Son Jesus Christ. Only, when it is said,

O 4 ALL

TEXT.

put under him, it is manifeft, he is excepted which did put all things under him.

28 And when all things fhall be fubdued unto him, then fhall the Son alfo himfelf be fubject unto him that put all things under him, that God may be all in all.

PARAPHRASE.

ALL THINGS fhall be SUBJECTED to Chrift, it is obvious to perceive, that *that* glorious Being is to be excepted, who fubjected all things to him. And when all things fhall, in EVENT, or FACT, be reduced under *fubjection* to him, THEN, and NOT TILL THEN, however *long* a fpace of time it may require for its accomplifhment: THEN, I fay, fhall even the *Son himfelf* be fubject to him who put all things under him, THAT GOD MAY BE ALL IN ALL.

If I have, in the above paraphrafe, exhibited the *fenfe* the apoftle really intended to communicate to his readers, there is no room left for difpute, whether *all men fhall finally be faved.* It remains now to make it evident, that I have not, in any effential point, mifreprefented his meaning.

Only, before I come to this, it may not be improper to clear the *connection* of the words, and point out the *fpecial part* they bear in the difcourfe to which they are related. And here it may fuffice to obferve, that the apoftle having, in the *former part* of the *chapter,* largely proved the *certainty* of

9   a *refurrection*

a *resurrection from the dead*, from the *certainty* of this *fact*, namely, that " Chrift has rifen from the dead," whereby he became " the firft-fruits of them that " flept;" he goes on, in the 21ft and 22d verfes, fummarily to lead our thoughts up to the true *fources* both of *death*, and of *life after death*; deriving the *former* from *Adam*, the *latter* from *Chrift*. His words are thefe, " For fince by man came death, by man alfo " came the refurrection from the dead. For as in " Adam all die, even fo in Chrift fhall all be made " alive." It is, with me, beyond all controverfy evident, that the apoftle is fpeaking here, not of a *partial*, but *univerfal* refurrection ; not of the refurrection of the *righteous* only, but of the *whole race of Adam*. For he not only affirms, that *death came by Adam*, and the *refurrection by Chrift*; but that the SAME ALL who fuffer *death* through Adam, fhall through Chrift be *made alive*. The comparifon between the *damage* by *Adam*, and the *advantage* by *Chrift*, lies in this very thing. As by the *former* came *death*, fo by the *latter* comes *life*, and to the *fame perfons*. The particles ωσπερ and ουτω, *as* and *fo*, which point out a comparifon in the apoftle's words, and compleat it, neceffitate this fenfe. Only, it fhould be well regarded, the apoftle does but *briefly* and *fummarily* fpeak here of the *damage* by *Adam*, and the *advantage* by *Chrift*. And had he no where elfe opened his mind *more fully* and *particularly* upon this matter, the utmoft we could have argued, from his words, would have been, " that as all men die in Adam, fo in Chrift

they

they fhould all be delivered from this death by a refurrection to life." But as he has largely, and *ex profeffo*, treated of this fame point in his Epiftle to the Romans, we may explain, we ought to explain, we fhould deal unfairly if we did not explain, what he fays *here*, by what he has delivered *there*. And if we thus explain his words *here*, their amount will be this, " not *merely* that *all men* fhall be delivered from the *death* they fuffer in confequence of *Adam's lapfe*, but that they fhall be delivered from it, in confequence of the *obedience of Chrift*, with ABOUNDING ADVANTAGE, that is, fo as to *reign in life for ever*." See the interpretation we have given of Rom. v. 12, to the end. The apoftle, having fettled this point, and, as I imagine, in this fenfe, proceeds, in the following 23d verfe, to obferve, " But every man in his own " order ; Chrift the firft-fruits, afterwards they that " are Chrift's, at his coming." The thought he would fuggeft, perhaps, may be this, namely, " that God would obferve a *juft decorum*, keep to *rule* and *order* with refpect to *all men* (58), in the

(58) *Keep to rule and order with refpect to all men.*] This, it may be, is the true meaning of the phrafe εν τω ιδιω ταγμαli. The word ταγμα is no where elfe ufed in the New Teftament. But the fubftantive ταξις, another noun from τασσω, of like fignification, we feveral times meet with; particularly in 1 Cor. xiv. 46, where it is ufed in this fenfe : *Let all things be done* [ευσχημενως και καlα ταξιν] *decently and in order.* Agreeably to this fenfe, εν ταξει, δια ταξεως, are rendered, in Stephens's juftly entitled *Thefaurus Linguæ Græcæ, compofitè, concinnè, decorè, opportunè ;* as alfo, *non temerè, fed conftituta certaque ratione.*

great

great affair of *making them alive after death*, that is, so alive as to *reign in happy life*; for (as has been said) this is the *advantage by Christ*, that is opposite to the *disadvantage by Adam*, of which he had been speaking. Accordingly, that God might keep to *order*, observe a *proper decorum*, it is said *Christ is the first-fruits* from the dead, that is, the *first* that was raised from death to *immortal happy life*, having been previously *prepared* and *qualified* for it; and not only so, but his resurrection was an *earnest, pledge*, or *assurance* to ALL MEN, that they also should be raised to a *like immortality*, when it could be done in consistency with DUE ORDER. *After Christ, those that are his*, that is, believers in him, the true followers of him, such as have lived to him, and died in him, *shall be the next that are raised*, not *simply* to life, but to *immortal happy life*, as, by being *Christ's*, they are *fitted* for this life, and may be raised to it conformably to ORDER: And this their resurrection shall be effected *at his coming*, that is, his second coming, his coming at the end of the world, or of this *present state* of things. Or, perhaps, the apostle might intend to suggest, by the phrase, Εκαστος δε εν τω ιδιω ταγματι, that mankind will be hereafter raised, not *simply* to life, but to *happy life*; not *all at once*, but *successively*; not *all together*, but in *different ranks* or *companies*. And then his meaning, in this verse, will be, " *Christ is the first-fruits*, the *pledge* or *earnest* of a resurrection to *immortal happy life* with respect to ALL MEN; but *every man* shall be raised to *this life* IN HIS

OWN

OWN RANK, IN THAT COMPANY, UNDER THAT
STANDARD, to which he properly belongs (59).
                                        The

(59) *In his own rank, in that company, &c.*] The word
ταγμα, though uſed no where in the New Teſtament but in
this place, is yet ſeveral times uſed by the LXX, with
whom it ſeems to be a *military* term, as it often is with
the beſt Greek writers [ſee Stephens's Lexicon upon this
word, together with ταξις, and τασσω, from whence they are
both derived]. The LXX have uſed it once [2 Sam.
xxiii. 13] for the Hebrew word חַיָּה *caterva,* a troop. In the
other places, which are all in the *ſecond* and *tenth chapters* of
Numbers, it is the tranſlation of דֶּגֶל, which Buxtorf renders
vexillum, and our tranſlators a *ſtandard.* The verb דָּגַל,
which occurs in Canticles, Buxtorf tranſlates by *vexillum
erigere,* our tranſlators have the word *banner,* and the LXX
τασσω ; which verb, when applied to *military* affairs, (as it
very frequently is) ſignifies to *draw up troops in order of battle,*
or to *range them under their proper ſtandards,* or *banners.* The
paſſage before us may then, in ſtrict propriety, be rendered,
every man in his own rank, or, *in his own company,* or, *under his
own ſtandard,* or *banner.* The expreſſion naturally leads one
to think, that the whole body of mankind will be *ſucceſſively*
raiſed to *happy life* in *different* ταγμαλα, according as they
become qualified for it by *being Chriſt's,* by being formed
by him to a *meetneſs* for a *bleſſed immortality* ; for the *firſt*
ταγμα is to conſiſt of thoſe that *are Chriſt's at his coming,* that is,
thoſe who have been *prepared* by him, under the preſent adminiſtration of his kingdom, for a *reign in life* when he ſhall
appear the *ſecond time.* Perhaps the apoſtle John, in his book
of Revelation, might mean the ſame thing with *what* the
apoſtle Paul would here ſuggeſt, when he ſpeaks, chap. xx. 5,
of the FIRST RESURRECTION, that is, of the reſurrection
of the FIRST COMPANY of the ſons of Adam to a GLORIOUS
IMMORTALITY. Accordingly, this ſeems to be the explication
of its meaning in the following verſe ; for the partners in this
                                        reſurrection

The FIRST COMPANY that shall be raised to this happy life are *the saints, at Christ's second coming.*— And here, you observe, the apostle comes to a pause.—

resurrection are there pronounced *blessed**. And why? Not because their deliverance from death, simply in itself, PRE-CEDED *that* of others in point of *time*; but because the *second death should have no power over them*, as it would have over the wicked; and because they should be *kings and priests*, and *reign with Christ a thousand years*: Which thousand years are mentioned, not because they should *no longer* live and reign with Christ [for they are said, in the twenty-second chapter, 5th verse, to live and reign with him εις τους αιωνας των αιωνων, *for ages of ages*]; but because, during *this period*, no attempt should be made from any quarter to disturb their peace and happiness; as also because the *rest of the dead*, the wicked dead, though *raised to life* before the expiration of this *period*, could not, till it had run out, be *so raised* to it as to live without *dying again*, or to *reign with Christ as kings and priests*. The one only thing, as it appears to me, that can give force and emphasis to the epithet FIRST, here applied to the *resurrection*, is, its being the *first general resurrection of men*, not simply to life, but to *live happily in a glorious reign with Christ*; and the apostle John calls it *the first resurrection*, because it is the *first of this sort*; obviously insinuating, that it would, in God's way, and time, be succeeded with *others of the same kind*. It is true, he has said nothing in *particular* concerning any *following resurrection of this kind*; but, by speaking of a *first*, he has in the *general*, after the manner of the apostle Paul, in this place, given us reason to *hope* for still *others*; the manner, time, and circumstances of which, though hid from our knowledge at present, may, in after dispensations, be *revealed*, as shall best answer the purposes of divine grace. I have but mentioned this interpretation of the apostle John's FIRST RESURRECTION, because it would carry me too great a length

* See the *Appendix.*

paufe.—Inftead of particularly going on to fpeak of the *wicked's being raifed*, fo as that their refurrection fhould be an *advantage* ABOUNDING BEYOND

to offer what I have in readinefs for its fupport. So far as I am able to judge, the *three laft chapters* of the *Apocalypfe* cannot be fet in an intelligible confiftent light, but in conformity to *this fenfe* of *thefe words*; and thus explained, they exhibit a *noble*, and yet perfectly confiftent meaning.

I fhall only add, the expofition we have given of the 23d verfe of this fifteenth chapter of the fecond Epiftle to the Corinthians, is truly fignificant and grand; which cannot, as I conceive, be juftly faid of the *other* interpretations that are given of it. To explain the words, as moft do, of *mere order of time*; as though the apoftle had nothing more in view than this, namely, that Chrift, in point of *time*, was raifed *firft*; and next to him, in point of *time*, the *righteous* fhall be raifed; and then the *wicked*: I fay, to give this as the apoftle's meaning, is to make him, while fpeaking upon the moft interefting fubject, to deliver that which is of very little importance for any to know. *Every man in his own order*—are words that ought to be looked upon as carrying in them fome very *fignificant fenfe*; which they do not, in the common way of explaining them: Whereas, in the *fenfe* we have put upon them, they are *vaftly momentous*. For they are made to fuggeft, that the raifing men, not *fimply* to life, but to life that is *glorioufly immortal*, is not a thing that will be done *at random*, but conformably to RULE and ORDER. *Every man* fhall be *thus made alive by Chrift*; for this is the *advantage by him* that is oppofite to the *difadvantage by Adam*: But it fhall be done in DUE ORDER, confiftently with *fit, meet, wife, proper* conduct; that is, in one word, when they are previoufly *prepared* and *qualified* for this mercy of God in Jefus Chrift. Or, fhould the *other* fenfe we have given (which indeed *virtually* is the fame) be preferred, it would exhibit the like important meaning; as it leads us to think, that *mankind univerfally* fhall be raifed to *immortal happy life*, though *fucceffively*, and in *different* ταγματα, or *companies*, as they become *fit* for it.

the

the *difadvantage* they had fuffered through *Adam*, he interpofes, by way of *parenthefis*, the 24th, 25th, 26th, 27th, and 28th verfes; then refuming the fubject of the *refurrection*, but confining his dif- courfe about it to the *righteous*, without faying any thing of the *wicked*. And thus the *paffage* we are upon is introduced. It is this *ftop* in the run of the apoftle's argument; in which he has taken care to fuggeft feveral *very important truths*, proper to be thoroughly weighed, in their juft confe- quences, before we confider the *mediatory fcheme* as fhut up, or the *wicked* in circumftances to be *made alive by Chrift*, conformably to ORDER, in the mer- cifully ABOUNDING fenfe, in which *all that die in Adam* fhall, in the final refult of things, be *made alive by Chrift*.

If we critically compare the 23d verfe with the 29th and following verfes to the end of the chap- ter, and connect them together fo as to make out a coherent meaning, we fhall eafily perceive, that the *paragraph* under confideration is a *break* in the thread of the apoftle's difcourfe, not happening through careleffnefs, inattention, or confufion of thought, but made upon *exprefs defign*. This *pa- renthefis*, comprehended within the 24th and 29th verfes, was purpofely interpofed to bring us to a *paufe* in our thoughts, and give us opportunity and occafion to reflect upon, and duly confider, the *great truths* that are here *revealed*; purfuing them in their *juft tendency, neceffary connection*, and *final refult*: In the doing of which, we fhould our-

felves

felves *virtually* continue the difcourfe, and finifh it with refpect to the *wicked*, as the apoftle had done, in the *general*, with refpect to the *righteous*. This, as I imagine, will, upon the clofeft examination, be found to be the *part* the *paffage* before us bears in the apoftle's argument: Having obferved which, I now go on, as was propofed, to illuftrate and confirm the fenfe we have given to it. And here the following particulars fhould be heedfully attended to.

I. Though the apoftle, in this paragraph, turns our view to the END of the *mediatory fcheme*, the time when *Chrift fhall have delivered up the kingdom to the Father*, yet he has very evidently taken care to do it in *fuch a manner* as to guard againft the *error*, which expofitors, and Chriftian writers, have ftrangely run into, namely, that this fcheme will be *finifhed*, come to its intended period, upon the *fecond advent* of Chrift, by his then *finally* and *unalterably* fixing the ftates of men, whether *good* or *bad*: I fay, the apoftle, as though he had it in exprefs view, has taken all reafonable care to guard againft this *moft evident mifconftruction* of his meaning, by giving us very clearly and fully to underftand, that there is *a great deal to be done*, after the *fecond coming* of Chrift, for the doing of which *a long period of time* was abfolutely requifite, before the *plan* of God would be compleated, and the *whole* accomplifhed which he had entrufted his Son with the *mediatory kingdom*, in order to bring into *effect*. For,

II. It

II. It is moft peremptorily affirmed, that an *univerfal fubjection* to Chrift fhould YET be effected ; and the affirmation is expreffed in a variety of as ftrong and extenfive terms as could well have been ufed : As, by " putting down all " rule, and all authority and power ;" by " putting " all enemies under his feet;" by " putting all things " under his feet;" by " all things being fubdued to " him." All enemies then, yea, all things, muft be fubjected to Chrift, BEFORE he delivers up the kingdom to the Father. The meaning of *this part* of this fcripture is the *fame* with the two foregoing texts we have already confidered ; to which therefore I refer the reader, to prevent repetition.

III. It is worthy of fpecial notice, that, *before* Chrift's delivery of the mediatorial kingdom to the Father, and the *final fhutting* up the *falutary defign* of his being entrufted with it, *the laft enemy muft be deftroyed,* which is *death*; the SECOND DEATH, that *death* which thofe who die *wicked* men muft *fuffer,* BEFORE they can be reduced under *fubjection* to Jefus Chrift, as *head* of God's kingdom, and fitted for an *happy immortality.* So I have paraphrafed the apoftle's words, and, I think, for *weighty reafons.* They are thofe that follow.

1. It is evident, from the whole tenor of the New Teftament, that thofe who are not *Chrift's,* that is, the reft of mankind, the *wicked* and *impenitent,* thofe who have habitually indulged to fin while they lived, and then died in a finful

P   ftate :

ftate : I fay, 'tis evident, with refpect to thefe, that they muft fuffer a SECOND DEATH.   Hence *the wages of fin*, after the *firft death* has been fuffered, is faid, by the apoftle Paul, to be *death*.   And the apoftle John, fpeaking of the *wicked*, after their refurrection from the death they fuffered in Adam, declares, that they fhall be " caft into the " lake of fire," which, fays he, " is the SECOND " DEATH." And the " refurrection to damnation," the " going away into everlafting punifhment," the " being caft into the furnace of fire, where there " fhall be wailing and gnafhing of teeth," mean the fame thing, in the facred dialect, with the *fe-cond death*.

2. This *fecond death* may, with as much pro-priety, be called an *enemy*, as the firft death. Would the *firft death*, if not deftroyed, be an *enemy* to men's admiffion to a *glorious immortality*, an enemy fo as abfolutely to prevent it?   The fame may be faid of the *fecond death*, and with more *emphatical* truth.   And let any fenfe be af-figned, in which the *firft death* can properly be fpoken of as an *enemy*; and it will at once be eafy to make it appear, that the *fecond death* is, in the fame fenfe, as truly *an enemy*, and *much more fo*.   It is this indeed, if not deftroyed, that will prove the *bittereft enemy* to the happinefs of mankind ; and fuch an one as will be a vifible ftanding demonftration, that they are not AS YET reduced under *fubjection* to Jefus Chrift, as the *faithful* and *obedient fervants* of his kingdom.

3. This *fecond death*, ftrictly and properly fpeaking,

ing, is THE LAST ENEMY, and the ONLY ONE that
is ſo. For it is an enemy that has no exiſtence *till*
after the *firſt death* is ſo far deſtroyed, as that thoſe
who are under its power are again reſtored to *life*.
For it is *after* the *wicked* have been raiſed from
the dead, that they are *caſt into that lake of fire*,
which the ſcripture calls the *ſecond death*. As
therefore the *ſecond death*, or that which wicked
men will ſuffer in conſequence of their *own ſins*, is
a LATER ENEMY than the *firſt death*, or that death
they ſuffer in conſequence of *Adam's lapſe*, it
ſhould ſeem reaſonable, as it is obvious, when the
apoſtle ſays, " the laſt enemy, which is death, ſhall
" be deſtroyed," to underſtand him to mean by
death, the *ſecond death :* For this may, with the
ſtricteſt accuracy, be called the LAST ENEMY ;
whereas the *firſt death* cannot be ſo called, either
with *propriety* or *truth*, the *ſecond death* being
poſterior to it, and indeed having no exiſtence till
that has been ſo far deſtroyed as to allow of a
reſtoration to life. For theſe reaſons, which appear to me unanſwerably ſtrong, I take this to
be the meaning of the *death* here ſpoken of.

But ſhould we keep to the common interpretation, and underſtand by this death, the *firſt death*,
or the death that mankind ſuffer in conſequence
of *Adam's lapſe*, its *deſtruction* by Chriſt, underſtood as it ought to be, will, in reality of ſenſe,
amount to preciſely the *ſame thing* with what we
have been pleading for. For *ſimple reſtoration to
life* is not the thing the ſcripture means by *death*

deſtroyed.

deſtroyed. To be ſure, the apoſtle Paul had quite
another notion of it. And of this we have all the
evidence we can deſire, in the latter part of this
very *chapter*, where he is treating, *ex profeſſo*, of
death vanquiſhed, conquered, deſtroyed. For what is
the idea he leads us to entertain of it? Plainly,
not a *bare return to life*, but ſuch an one as is connected with a *glorious immortality.* His diſcourſe
upon this head is therefore thus:—" It is ſown in
" corruption; it is raiſed in incorruption: it is ſown
" in diſhonour; it is raiſed in glory: it is ſown in
" weakneſs; it is raiſed in power: it is ſown a
" natural body; it is raiſed a ſpiritual body."
And a little after come in thoſe remarkable words,
" So when this corruptible ſhall have put on in-
" corruption, and this mortal ſhall have put on
" immortality, THEN ſhall be brought to paſs the
" ſaying that is written, DEATH IS SWALLOWED
" UP IN VICTORY." And he cloſes all by putting
that ſong of triumph into the mouths of thoſe,
who have obtained this CONQUEST over death and
the grave, " Oh death, where is thy ſting? Oh
" grave, where is thy victory? The ſting of death
" is ſin, and the ſtrength of ſin is the law; but
" thanks be to God, which giveth us the victory,
" through our Lord Jeſus Chriſt."

It is eaſy to obſerve, and no attentive intelligent reader can well fail of making the obſervation, that the apoſtle's notion of *death ſwallowed
up in victory*, or, in other words, of death conſidered as a *conquered, deſtroyed enemy*, is this, and
only

only this—his being fo defpoiled of his power, as
that thofe, who were under it, are not *fimply raifed
to life*, but to *fuch a life* as fhall give juft occafion
for holy *triumph* in Jefus Chrift on account of
this victory; which cannot be, unlefs they are
raifed to an *immortality* that will be for their *advantage*. So that that if *death* is *deftroyed*, with
refpect to *wicked* men ; and deftroyed it muft be,
with refpect to them ALL, before Chrift's delivery
of the kingdom to the Father: I fay, if *death*, the
laft enemy, is *deftroyed*, the *whole human race* muft
not only be raifed from the dead, but fo raifed
therefrom as to *reign in life*, fooner or later, as the
reduced fubjects of Jefus Chrift. This is certainly
the apoftle's notion of *death deftroyed, fwallowed up
in victory*, in this *chapter*.

And it is remarkable, the idea he here gives of
death deftroyed perfectly coincides with that *abounding of the grace and gift through Chrift to all men*, of
which he fpeaks in the 5th chapter of his epiftle
to the Romans; which, over and above reverfing
the fentence of *death*, will finally inftate them all
in *eternal life*. For, as he there argues, [and his
argument refers to *mankind univerfally*, as I have,
I truft, fufficiently proved already] " If by the
" offence of one, death reigned by one ; MUCH
" MORE they who receive the abounding of grace,
" and of the gift of righteoufnefs, fhall REIGN IN
" LIFE by one, Jefus Chrift." And again, " That
" as fin hath reigned unto death ; even fo might

" grace

" grace reign through righteousnefs unto ETER-
" NAL LIFE, by Jefus Chrift our Lord."

IV. It is with a great deal of clearnefs and par-
ticularity afferted, in this fcripture, that *Chrift fhall
not give up his truft*, as *head* of the *mediatorial kingdom*, till he has, in EVENT and FACT, *fubdued all
enemies*. For it is declared in fo many words, " he
" muft reign till he hath put all enemies under
" his feet." And again, " WHEN all things fhall
" be fubdued, THEN," and not till then, " fhall
" the Son alfo himfelf be fubject to him that put
" all things under him." We were taught to
argue, in the before-explained, Heb. ii. 8, 9, that
all things would be fubjected to Chrift, fince he was
crowned with glory and honour. We are here explicitly given to underftand wherein the *true force*
of that argument confifts. It lies in this, that
Chrift, having been exalted to *regal dignity and
power*, fhall *continue vefted with it*, and *never lay it
afide*, till he has, IN FACT, brought ALL THINGS,
ALL ENEMIES, into *fubjection* to him. The apoftle
has left no room for debate upon this matter.
It is CERTAIN, if we may rely on his authority,
that Chrift will *continue* head of the kingdom of
God, and exercife his wifdom, and power, and
grace, in this capacity, till he has ACTUALLY SUB-
DUED ALL ENEMIES. Upon which I would afk,
Is SIN *an enemy* (60)? If it is, then it fhall be
deftroyed :

(60) It would be ftrange if any fhould queftion, whether
SIN may be called an *enemy*, or *one of thofe enemies* which are
to

deſtroyed : Nor will Chriſt deliver up his mediatory
kingdom, till he has, in EVENT and FACT, *deſtroyed*
it. Now, SIN can be DESTROYED in no poſſible
way but by reducing ſinners under *moral ſubjection*
to the government of God. See Heb. ii. 8, 9,
under which text this matter is argued. I would
aſk again, Is DEATH, the SECOND DEATH, *an*
enemy (61)? Then this enemy alſo ſhall be *de-*
ſtroyed; for Chriſt muſt deſtroy ALL ENEMIES, and
conſequently this: Nor can he, upon the plan of
God, deliver up the kingdom, till he has done
this. Now the *ſecond death* can be *deſtroyed* in

to be *deſtroyed.* For it is expreſsly ſpoken of [Rom. viii. 7.
and James iv. 4.] as *enmity to God,* and that which is *not ſub-*
ject to the law of God. And it was indeed SIN that at firſt
broke the *peace* between God and man ; and it has ever ſince
oppoſed the government of God, and is the *grand hindrance* to
that *moral ſubjection* to the divine authority, which all reaſonable creatures ought to be under to it. And it was PRINCI-
PALLY with a view to DESTROY THIS ENEMY IN PARTICU-
LAR, that Chriſt came into the world ; and it was to this end
PRINCIPALLY alſo, that he was exalted to the right hand of
God's power in heaven. SIN therefore is emphatically one of
THOSE THINGS, or ENEMIES, that muſt be *ſubdued, brought*
under ſubjection, before Chriſt's *delivery of the kingdom to the*
Father.

(61) Let not any ſay, that the SECOND DEATH is not an
enemy. For it may with as much propriety be ſo called as the
firſt death : Nor can the *firſt death* be ſaid to be *an enemy* in
any aſſignable ſenſe, but the *ſame* may be ſaid of the *ſecond*
death in the *ſame ſenſe.* Moſt certainly it is A THING capable,
in its own nature, of being *ſubdued :* And if ALL THINGS
abſolutely, God only excepted, ſhall be *ſubdued to Chriſt,* this
alſo muſt be *ſubdued.*

no way whatsoever, but by *putting an end to its power* over those who are the subjects of it. The arguing here appears to me strictly and absolutely conclusive.

There are two *texts* parallel to this, which I may properly mention here, as they tend to strengthen what I have been just saying. The *first* is Heb. x. 12, 13. " But this man, after he " had offered one sacrifice for him, for ever sat " down at the right hand of God, from hence- " forth expecting till his enemies be made his " footstool." The *perfect* and *entire* reduction of *all enemies* is what Christ is here represented as *looking*, or *waiting for*, as the *effect* of his *exaltation*, in reward of his *sufferings* and *death*. And surely, he ought to be supposed to *expect this*, upon *good grounds*; such as would not, in the end, *disappoint* and make him *ashamed.*——The *other* text is Psalm cx. 1. " The Lord said unto my Lord, Sit thou " at my right hand, until I make thine enemies " thy footstool." It is remarkable, this passage is no less than five times applied to Christ, by the writers of the New Testament; as in Matt. xxii. 44. Mark xii. 36. Luke xx. 42. Acts ii. 34. Heb. i. 13. And the plain meaning of it is, that Christ was seated at God's right hand in heaven, to *continue* there as *Head* and *Lord* of the mediatorial king- dom, till *all enemies* should be *perfectly* and *abso- lutely subjected* to him ; which means the same thing with what is declared in the passage we are upon, namely, that he shall *go on reigning*, and

not

not give up the kingdom, till he has ſubdued all enemies.

V. In the laſt place, it readily falls in with the obſervation of every attentive reader of this paragraph, that the *reign of Chriſt*, in his mediatory kingdom, is to make way for GOD'S BEING ALL IN ALL; and will accordingly *laſt*, till he has *ripened* and *prepared* things for the *commencement* of this *glorious period*. As the *mediatory kingdom* was put into the hands of *Chriſt* for the *reduction* of *all enemies*, he will be *all in all* till he has accompliſhed this end; that is, the adminiſtration of government, till this time, will be *wholly* in his hands. He will be head over all; he will govern all; he will be all unto all. But when he has diſcharged his *mediatorial truſt*, by having reduced all enemies under ſubjection to the divine government, THEN will he deliver up the kingdom to God, even the Father, when GOD SHALL BE ALL IN ALL, that is, ſhall govern all, influence all, make communications to all, IMMEDIATELY, and NOT THROUGH THE HANDS OF A MEDIATOR. *Now*, and *as long* as the mediatory kingdom laſts, nothing is done but THROUGH THE INTERVENTION OF CHRIST; but THEN, all things ſhall be DIRECTLY GOVERNED BY GOD HIMSELF. All duty will be IMMEDIATELY tendered to him, and all favours and rewards IMMEDIATELY communicated from him.

It is eaſy to diſtinguiſh between theſe *two periods*, THAT wherein the mediatory kingdom is in the hands

hands of Jefus Chrift; and THAT which will afterwards commence, when God, as King, will be
IMMEDIATELY ALL IN ALL. Thefe are certainly
periods *quite diftinct* from each other. The juft
difference between them has not, I believe, been
fufficiently attended to : Whereas, if it had been
clearly ftated, it might have ferved as a *key* to
open the true fenfe of a great many texts of fcripture, I mean, thofe in particular which relate to
the *future exiftence* of the race of Adam.

I fhall endeavour, as briefly as I can with per-
fpicuity, to point out the *difference* between thefe
periods, or *difpenfations*.

As to the *firft*, the *reign of Chrift in his mediatorial kingdom* ;—this takes in the whole fpace of
time, from his exaltation to this dignity and truft,
till *all enemies, all rebel-men*, the *whole human kind*,
fhall be recovered from their apoftacy, and reduced under *due fubjection* to God. And whatever
is done, within this fpace, whether to *good* men,
or *wicked* men ; in a way of *reward*, or *punifhment*;
in the *prefent* ftate, or the *future* one, it is all to be
confidered as the refult of Chrift's *adminiftration in
the kingdom of grace*, and in order to *prepare* the
way for the coming on of the *other grand period*,
the time when GOD SHALL BE ALL IN ALL.

This fpace of time, the time, I mean, of *Chrift's
reign* in his mediatorial kingdom, may be divided
into *two general periods*. The *one* takes in this
prefent ftate of exiftence ; as to which we are all
ready enough to acknowledge, that Chrift reigns

at

at the head of *God's kingdom of grace*, and that *one effect* thereof will be the *reduction* of a number of the fons of Adam under *fuch obedience* to God, as that they will be fitted for a *glorious immortality* in the next ftate. The *other period* of Chrift's reign is THAT which *intervenes between the general refurrection and judgment*, and *the time when God fhall be all in all*. There is, as I imagine, a juft foundation to fpeak of *fuch a period* as this ; and it is, if I miftake not, a period of *very great importance* : Upon which therefore I fhall be a little particular in explaining myfelf.

It has been commonly fuppofed, that, at the fecond coming of Chrift, and the general refurrection and judgment, the *faints* fhall be received to *heaven*, and the *wicked* fent to *hell*; and that now the fcene of Providence will be clofed, the *final ftates* of men being abfolutely fixed : Whereas, it is very evident, from this paragraph of facred writ, that a *fecond period* of the reign of Chrift will *commence* at the *general refurrection*, when, as *head* of the kingdom of God, he will open a *new difpenfation*, with refpect to both the *righteous* and the *wicked*.

As to the *righteous*, whom he has *already*, or in the *firft period* of his mediatory reign, reduced under *fubjection* to the *moral* government of God, he will, at his *fecond coming*, beftow upon them the *reward* of good and faithful fervants : Not giving up the kingdom to the Father, upon having done this, as is commonly fuppofed ; but ftill reigning

at

at its head, under a *new* and *more glorious* adminiftration, and going on to do fo, NOT FOR EVER,
but till the time is come when GOD SHALL BE
ALL IN ALL : Upon which will commence a ftill
new, and ftill *more glorious* difpenfation.

And as to the *wicked*, who would not be perfuaded, by any of the methods that were ufed
with them, in this *prefent ftate*, to fubmit to the
divine government, *they*, while the *righteous* are
reigning in life and glory, fhall be fent, by the Lord
Jefus Chrift, in execution of his mediatory truft,
to the place of *weeping*, *and wailing*, *and gnafhing*
of teeth ; not to continue there *always*, but till the
rebellion of their hearts is fubdued, and they are
wrought upon to become the *willing* and *obedient*
fubjects of God.   For 'tis plain, from this text,
that Chrift, after the refurrection of the faints, at
his fecond coming, and their being crowned with
immortality and life, will ftill *continue* at the *head*
of the kingdom of God, yea, and go on exercifing
his wifdom, and power, and grace, in his kingly
office, till he has *conquered all enemies* ABSOLUTELY
and WITHOUT EXCEPTION.   Poffibly, it may be a
long feries of time before they will *all* be *willing* to
fubmit, fo as that they may be *prepared* for *mercy* :
But yet, they will *all*, fooner or later, and fome
of them, probably, much fooner than others, be
brought to fubmit with freedom and pleafure
too.

The idea, in fhort, I would convey of the matter is this ;—that the *ftate*, between the *general*
refurrection,

refurrection, and *God's being all in all*, may contain
a duration of *long continuance*, fo long as to anfwer
to that fcripture phrafe, εις τους αιωνας των αιωνων,
for ever and ever, or, as it might more properly
be rendered, *for ages of ages*; and that, during
the whole of this ftate, the *righteous* fhall be *happy*,
under the government of Chrift, and the *wicked
miferable* [at leaft fuch of them as are moft *obdurate*. See what is afterwards faid upon this phrafe
in the Revelation, *for ever and ever*]: Not with a
view to their continuing fo *finally*, and *eternally*;
but as a *mean*, under the conduct and influence
of Chrift, ftill at the *head* of God's kingdom of
grace, to deftroy the *enmity* of their hearts, and
make them his *willing* and *obedient people*: Which,
when accomplifhed, the *grand period* fhall come
on, when God fhall be himfelf IMMEDIATELY
ALL IN ALL.

And the *difference* between *this period*, and *that*
we have been defcribing, feems to me to lie in
thefe things:—The *one* has *Chrift* reigning at its
head; which reign will be for *a time only*, though
it may be a *long time*: During which time a
part only of mankind, having been previoufly prepared for it, fhall be inftated in the poffeffion of
immortality and happinefs; while the reft fhall
have their portion in the place of *blacknefs of
darknefs*, as a fuitable and neceffary *difcipline*,
under the government of Chrift, in order to their
being reduced under *moral fubjection* to him:
Which being accomplifhed, *this period* will now

have

have an *end*, and the *other* be uſhered in, the *diſtinctive characteriſtic* of which is, that GOD WILL BE ALL IN ALL ; that is to ſay, the adminiſtration will be now in *his hands*, not in the hands of *Jeſus Chriſt*, for he alſo will be *ſubject to the Father.* And *mankind univerſally*, having been cured of their *enmity*, and formed to a readineſs to be in *ſubjection* to God, ſhall be the objects of his merciful care. He will now be a God to them ALL, and IN ALL THINGS, IMMEDIATELY concerning himſelf for their welfare, ſo as that they ſhall be *happy beyond conception*, and *without end.*

I would here remark, upon what has been above offered, that the *reward* promiſed, under the adminiſtration of Chriſt's kingdom, in this *preſent ſtate*, in order to perſuade men to become his good and faithful ſubjects, is not the *final happineſs God intends to beſtow upon them*, but the happineſs of THAT STATE which intervenes between the *reſurrection* and *God's being all in all.* And the ſcripture account of this reward ſurpriſingly agrees with this ſentiment. It is frequently ſpoken of under the notion of happy enjoyment IN THE KINGDOM OF CHRIST ; which directly points our thoughts to a *period*, *diſpenſation*, or *œconomy*, that has *Chriſt* for its *Head* and *Lord.* And, in truth, *that kingdom*, in which Chriſt is ſaid to *reign for ever*, muſt have a comparatively low ſenſe put upon it, if it continues no longer than the *end* of this *preſent world*: Whereas, it will have a very ſignificant meaning, if *Chriſt is to reign king of the ſaints,*

ſaints, in that *glorious ſtate* that will be erected at his *ſecond coming*.—This *reward* alſo is deſcribed by the ſaints *ſitting down with Chriſt in his throne, as he is ſet down with the Father in his throne* ; and by *their living and reigning with him* : Both which repreſentations obviouſly ſuppoſe, that *He* is yet at the *head* of his mediatorial kingdom ; the time not being come, when God even the Father is *immediate Lord* and *Sovereign*. And it is obſervable, the promiſe of this *reward* is expreſſed, Rev. v. 10, by *their reigning on earth* ; which, by the way, is a plain intimation, that it will be beſtowed on them in *the new heavens*, and *the new earth*, which will ſucceed the *diſſolution* of the *preſent form* of this lower world by *fire*. HERE the ſaints, in their *reſurrection-ſtate*, ſhall live under the *reign of Chriſt*, who will be *all in all to them*, till the *period* commences, when the adminiſtration ſhall change hands, and God be himſelf IMMEDIATE *king* and *ſovereign*.—But I have room only to ſuggeſt this thought. To ſet it in a full light would carry me too far beſide my preſent deſign.

It is likewiſe an obvious and natural deduction from what has been ſaid, that the *puniſhment threat-ened*, under the *preſent reign* of Chriſt in God's king-dom, to diſcourage our rebellion againſt the *moral government* of Heaven, and to promote our *ſubjection* to it, is the *miſery of the* SAME INTERMEDIATE STATE, and not miſery that will have NO END. And with this remark, the ſcripture alſo admirably well agrees. Hence the *future puniſhment* is moſt

frequently

frequently fpoken of in terms, that evidently convey the idea of a *difpenfation, age,* or *period of duration.* This is plainly the meaning of that fa-
mous text, in which this mifery, as is commonly
fuppofed, is faid to be εις τους αιωνας των αιωνων,
for ages of ages; and of thofe texts which call it
κολασιν αιωνιον, το πυρ το αιωνιον, ολεθρον αιωνιον, *everlafting punifhment, everlafting fire, everlafting deftruction:* So the words are rendered in our Englifh Bibles ; but we are very obvioufly led to underftand by them, *mifery* that muft be fuffered for
a *certain period, age,* or *difpenfation*; for that is the
proper meaning of the word αιων. It is *moft commonly* ufed in this fenfe throughout both the Old
and New Teftament; as we fhall have occafion
particularly and largely to fhew afterwards.

Conformably to the above remarks, the *great
difference* between thofe, who go out of this *prefent
ftate* God's *obedient fubjects,* and others who die
rebels againft him, will lie in this, not that the
former will enter upon *final happinefs,* or the *latter*
upon *final mifery*; but that the *one* fhall be admitted, at Chrift's *fecond coming,* to dwell with him
in his *kingdom of glory* for a *certain period of duration,* while the *other* fhall be banifhed his prefence,
to dwell in *unfpeakable torment* till they are
wrought upon to fee their folly, repent of it, and
willingly yield themfelves up to God as his *obedient
fervants.* And, in this view of the matter, full
fcope is allowed for an adjuftment of that *inverted
conduct* of Providence, in this *prefent ftate,* according

ing to which it has *happened to the righteous accord-ing to the work of the wicked, and to the wicked according to the work of the righteous*; and not only fo, but opportunity is given alfo, by means of this *different* treatment of the *righteous* and *wicked*, to prepare them both, no doubt, in the wifeft and beft-adapted manner, for that NEW and GRAND DISPENSATION, which is yet to take place. And now the *fcheme* of God, fo far as it was put into the hands of *Chrift* to be carried into *execu-tion*, under his *mediatory* management, is FINISHED. For the whole conduct of Providence, under his adminiftration, having been adjufted, and the *whole human race*, at the fame time, reduced under *moral fubjection* to the divine government, *He* will now give up his *mediatory kingdom to the Father*, who will, from this time, *reign* IMMEDIATELY *himfelf*; making the moft glorious manifeftations of his being a *God*, and *Father*, and *Friend to all, in all things, without end.*

I need not now fay, what a poor, low, lean idea the *common explanation* of this fcripture gives us of the FINAL EFFECT of *Chrift's reign* in his media-tory kingdom, in comparifon with *that*, the *above interpretation* lets us into. According to *this*, SIN, SATAN, and DEATH, the SECOND as well as FIRST DEATH, fhall be TOTALLY and ABSOLUTELY DE-STROYED, and the WHOLE HUMAN RACE reduced under a *free*, and yet *full*, fubjection to the govern-ment of God, fo as to be the *meet objects* of his *mercy*, when he fhall *finally* take the *kingdom into*

Q   *his*

his own hands: Whereas, according to the *other*, myriads of the ſons of *Adam* will be EVERLAST-INGLY CONFINED IN HELL, as REBELS againſt the government of God, that is, as the MORAL ENE-MIES of his kingdom; notwithſtanding it is here moſt peremptorily affirmed, that *all enemies ſhall be ſubdued,* yea, that *all things ſhall be put under the feet of Chriſt;* and that *he ſhall not deliver up the kingdom to the Father* TILL ALL THIS IS ACTUALLY CARRIED INTO FACT.

No wonder this has been reckoned among the dark and difficult texts in the apoſtle Paul's writings, while men have endeavoured to faſten a *ſenſe* upon it, that really ſets it at variance with itſelf, beyond the poſſibility of a reconciliation by any human ſkill: Whereas, according to the *ſenſe here given,* the apoſtle's meaning is quite eaſy, and yet con-ſiſtent. And it is indeed a circumſtance much fa-vouring the *interpretation* we have gone into, that it is not the reſult of nice and laboured *criticiſm* upon the words here uſed, but obviouſly ariſes from the juſt import of them, in their moſt *ſimple* and *natural* conſtruction, without the help of *art,* or the ſhow of any *extraordinary underſtanding* in the force of language.

Before I proceed to another text, I would in-terpoſe an obſervation here, which, as I apprehend, will not be wholly uſeleſs. It is this:—Upon ſup-poſition of the truth of the above explication of this ſcripture paſſage, it is obvious, at the firſt glance, that *ſome* among the ſons of men will be ſo

wrought

wrought upon, in this *prefent ftate,* under the adminiftration of God's kingdom by Jefus Chrift, as
to be *prepared* for an *immediate reign* with him in
life and *glory* at his *fecond coming*; while *others*
will ftand it out againft all the methods of wifdom
and grace, he fees fit, as a *moral* governor, to ufe
with them, and will not be perfuaded to become
his *willing people,* till they have firft known by experience what the *torments of hell* mean. And
may it not be with a view to *this difference,* which
God knew, before all worlds, there would be
among men, that the *language* of many texts of
fcripture is *formed?* And if this thought were duly
attended to, in their *explication,* might it not give
a *clear* and *unexceptionable* meaning to them? I
fhall not think it a needlefs digreffion to explain
myfelf here by coming to inftances. Thus, when
it is faid, 1 Tim. iv. 10, " God is the Saviour of
" all men; efpecially of them that believe," are
we not herefrom at once enabled to put upon the
words an eafy and fignificant fenfe? For God may
properly be called *the Saviour of all men,* as they
fhall *all,* in the *final iffue* of things, partake of
the *falvation by Jefus Chrift*; and yet, he may
eminently be faid to be *the Saviour of them that believe,* as, by their being *believers,* they are *prepared* for an entrance upon *an happy immortality,*
and *fhall enter upon it* IMMEDIATELY at *Chrift's
coming,* without firft paffing through the *fecond
death.* So when our Saviour fays, John x. 14, " I
" am the good fhepherd, and know my fheep, and

Q 2

" I am

" I am known of mine ;" and again, in the 15th
verfe, " I lay down my life for the fheep ;" and
yet again, in the 27th, 28th, and 29th verfes,
" My fheep hear my voice, and I know them, and
" they follow me. And I give unto them eternal
" life, and they fhall never perifh, neither fhall
" any pluck them out of my hand. My Father,
" which gave them me, is greater than all ; and
" none is able to pluck them out of my Father's
" hand:" I fay, by the help of the above thought,
may it not be eafy to give a plain and confiftent
meaning to his words ? By *thefe fheep* which the
Father hath given to Chrift, for whom *Chrift laid
down his life,* to whom he will *give eternal life,* and
who both *know him* and are *known of him,* may we
not fairly underftand *that part* of mankind who
are of *fuch a temper of mind* as to be perfuaded to
fubmit to Chrift, as their *fhepherd* and *guide,* in
confequence of the *means* that are proper to be
ufed with men in this *prefent ftate* of the kingdom
of God ? And as God knew who *thefe* were, he
might *give them to Chrift* to be fitted by him to
reign in life a *certain age, difpenfation,* or *period of
duration,* to commence IMMEDIATELY upon his
fecond coming ; and he will certainly *prepare* them
for this reign in life, and bring them to it, and
nothing fhall be ever able to prevent the *execution*
of this *purpofe of God's mercy* concerning them. But
then, it ought to be remembered, and particularly
confidered, thefe are not *Chrift's fheep,* neither did
God *give them to him* to bring them to *eternal life,*

to the *final exclusion* of the *rest* of mankind. For
he says, in this very chapter, ver. 16th, " And
" other sheep I have, which are not of this fold:
" Them also must I bring; and they shall hear my
" voice, and there shall be ONE FOLD, and ONE
" SHEPHERD." Other interpretations may be
given of these words; but may not the *true meaning* of them be this—that the *rest of mankind* are the
sheep of Christ, have been *given to him* by the Father, and shall, in the time laid out for it in
the scheme of God, certainly *hear his voice*, so as
that the *whole human race* shall make *one fold* and
have *one shepherd?* And may we not understand
in the same sense, what has sometimes been called,
the golden chain of salvation, Rom. viii. 29, 30?
" For whom he did foreknow, he also did pre-
" destinate to be conformed to the image of his
" Son, that he might be the first-born among
" many brethren. Moreover, whom he did pre-
" destinate, them he also called; and whom he
" called, them he also justified; and whom he
" justified, them he also glorified." As if the
apostle had said, " Whom God, in his infinite pre-
science, knew to be of a *disposition* to be wrought
upon, under the administration of his kingdom
of grace, in this *present state*, them he *destinated*,
or *determined*, before all worlds, should be conformed to the *image of his Son* in the glories of the
next state, that he, that is, the Son of God, might
have *many brethren*, and be *the first-born*, that is,
the *chief* and *head* among them in *that state.* And

Q 3   whom

whom he thus deftinated, or determined, fhould enter upon the joys of the *next ftate,* them he pur- pofed to *call,* or *invite,* into the *gofpel-kingdom,* by the preaching of Chrift, or his apoftles, or their fucceffors ; and whom he thus invited into this kingdom, them he purpofed to *juftify,* upon their becoming the qualified objects of this favour ; and whom he juftified, them he alfo purpofed to *admit* to the glories of the *refurrection-ftate.*" Not that it was the defign of the apoftle, in this text, to leave the *reft of mankind* to *perifh* without hope, or mercy : For he elfewhere fays, in this very Epiftle, that they fhall *all reign in life through Jefus Chrift.* But he is here fpeaking of thofe who are the perfons that fhall be *glorified,* according to the fcheme of God, in the *ftate that follows next upon this.* God knew who, among the fons of Adam, would be fo difpofed as that they might, in con- fiftency with their *liberty* as *free agents,* be wrought upon to become his *obedient fubjects,* in confe- quence of the *means* his wifdom thought proper to ufe with men in this *prefent ftate* ; and *them,* in the manner before defcribed, he *determined* fhould be *glorified* in the *refurrection-ftate.*——In the fame fenfe ftill may we not underftand thofe texts, in which *particular perfons* are fpoken of as the *elect,* or *chofen* of God ? I am fully fatisfied, that the terms *Elect, Chofen,* are often ufed, in the New Teftament, with refpect to the *whole body* of Chriftians, as fignifying nothing more than their being felected from the reft of the world, and ad- mitted

mitted into the *viſible kingdom* of God, in order
to their being under *peculiar advantages* that they
may be fitted for *eternal life.* But this notwithſtanding, I think it certain, that they are ſometimes uſed otherwiſe, and ſtand to ſignify *particular
perſons infallibly ſelected for ſalvation.* Thus the
term *choſen* is uſed by our Saviour, in that obſervable paſſage, Matt. xix. 30, " Many are called,
" but few are choſen;" which is repeated again,
chap. xxii. 14. And in the ſame ſenſe the word
elect is taken, as I apprehend, in Rom. viii. 33 :
" Who ſhall lay any thing to the charge of God's
" elect ? It is God that juſtifieth— ;" and in other
places that might be mentioned. But whenever,
by *elect*, or *choſen*, the ſcripture means *particular
perſons certainly ſelected for ſalvation*, why may we
not underſtand by them *thoſe*, whom God knew
would be *wrought upon*, in this *preſent ſtate*, under
the government of Jeſus Chriſt, and therefore fixed
upon them as the *perſons* that ſhould, in the *next
ſtate*, be *glorified* by him ? though not to the *ex-
cluſion* of *others* ; as has been already ſaid, and need
not be again repeated. And whatever other texts
there are of the like import with thoſe above-
mentioned, may they not *all*, in *this way*, have an
eaſy ſenſe put upon them, and *ſuch an one* as is
conſiſtent with the *univerſal benevolence* of God,
and the *univerſal efficacy* of Chriſt's power, as
ſeated at the *head* of God's kingdom of grace,
in order to *prepare mankind* for the bleſſed time,
when *God ſhall be all in all?*—I have not yet had

leiſure

leiſure ſo thoroughly to examine all the texts of *this ſort*, as to ſay, that they certainly ought to be thus interpreted ; but I know of no valid objection to the contrary, and cannot but think it well worthy of conſideration, whether this may not be the real truth of the caſe : Which, if it ſhould prove to be ſo, would at once put an end to *ſome controverſies*, which are thought to be important.

I ſhall now cloſe the *proof* of this propoſition I have been ſo long upon, becauſe an *important* one, and that indeed on which the preſent cauſe entirely reſts, by turning your thoughts awhile to one of the *firſt texts* in the Bible, and the *very firſt* that *reveals* the *promiſe* of a *Saviour* ; and I would the rather bring *this text* into view, as it *ſummarily* comprehends *the whole* of what we have been ſaying concerning the *reduction* of mankind *univerſally* to an *obedient ſubmiſſion* to the governing will of God. The text I have in my eye is Gen. iii. 15, " And I will put enmity between thee and " the woman, and between thy ſeed and her ſeed ; " it ſhall bruiſe thy head, and thou ſhalt bruiſe his " heel." Expoſitors ſeem univerſally agreed, that *Chriſt*, who was *born of a woman*, is the *ſeed* here principally intended. And when it is affirmed of him, that he ſhall *bruiſe the ſerpent's head*, the thought deſigned to be conveyed is, the *compleat victory* which he ſhould gain over the *Devil*, here ſpoken of under the emblem of a *ſerpent.* For the words are evidently an alluſion to the way of *killing ſerpents*, by ſtriking at their head. To
bruiſe

bruise a serpent's head, is a phrase expressive of one
and the same thing with *killing a serpent*. Consequently, when it is said of Christ, that he shall
bruise the serpent's head, the idea naturally and obviously communicated by the words is, that he
shall *destroy the Devil*; not *his being*, but *that kingdom of sin*, which, by his *means*, as a *tempter*, he had
introduced into the world, accompanied with
sorrow and *death*. If interpreters have been right,
as I judge they have (62), in understanding these
words

(62) It would be needless, in a work of this nature, to
enter upon a laboured proof of the propriety of this interpretation. The reader who needs, and desires, satisfaction herein, may meet with it in Bishop Sherlock's *Use and Intent of
Prophecy*, or in Dr. Shuckford's *History of the Creation and
Fall of Man*. I would only observe, it would be treating *Moses*
with great dishonour, to make him speak, in this text, as some
are pleased to do, of a *mere contest* between the *race of men*, and
the *race of serpents*; as though he intended only to suggest
this, " that serpents would be apt to bite men's heels, and
that men would be apt, in return, to strike their heads." This
is too trifling a business to be introduced, with so much so-
lemnity, by any valuable writer, much less so grave, serious,
and judicious an one as *Moses*, considering him only in his
ordinary character. Besides, it ought to be remembered,
' *Moses* does not here say [to use the words of the *last* of the
' above-mentioned authors], that *mankind* and *serpents* should
' have a general enmity at each other; but the *Hebrew* words,
' if truly interpreted, denote, that some ONE PERSON should
' descend from the woman, who should *capitally* conquer and
' subdue the *great enemy of mankind*.' The words, *Hua Je-
supbka rosh*, as this writer largely shews, ' cannot mean IT,
' *her seed, shall bruise thee in the head*, taking the word *seed*, as
' a noun

words of Chrift, and his *victorious conqueft* of the *Devil*, that is, his *works*, that *fin* and *wickednefs*, he has all along, from the beginning, been the encourager of, by his *temptations*; I fee not but this *firft promife* of God fairly leads us to look for the time, when SIN fhall be TOTALLY and ABSOLUTELY DESTROYED by him, who was *born of a woman*. This is certainly the moft fimple, plain con-

‘ a noun of *multitude*, to mean *many*; for, in fuch cafe, the
‘ Hebrew language would have been, *they fhall bruife thee in*
‘ *the head*: But it ought to be tranflated; HE HIMSELF, in-
‘ tending *one perfon*, and no more, *fhall bruife thy head*.’ And
it is obfervable, as this author further remarks, ‘ the tranf-
‘ lators of the *Septuagint* have thus rendered the place with-
‘ out *infpiration*, and before any *prophet*, or *apoftle*, had directed
‘ any fuch interpretation, by being only true mafters of the
‘ Hebrew tongue, fo as not to lofe, or vary from, the *precife*
‘ *meaning* of a very fignificant expreffion in it.’—Having faid,
the *Septuagint* verfion runs thus, “ And I will put enmity be-
“ tween thee and the woman; and between thy feed and the
“ feed of her : HE [ΑΥΤΟΣ] fhall bruife thy head, and thou
“ fhalt bruife his heel ;” he proceeds to fay, ‘ the point to be
‘ obferved in this tranflation is, that it does not fay IT fhall
‘ bruife thy head. The pronoun does not refer to the word
‘ *feed*, but it is, HE fhall bruife the head of the enemy here
‘ fpoken of. Had the Greek interpreters thought the text to
‘ mean, that the woman’s feed or offspring in the *general* were
‘ here intended, they would have faid αυτο, to agree with
‘ σπερμα, as we fay IT in our Englifh : But they more cor-
‘ rectly rendered the place αυτος, HE ; apprehending fome *one*
‘ *particular perfon* to be here intended, and not the offspring of
‘ the woman in the *general*.’ This fame author largely fhews
this to be the true meaning of the Hebrew likewife, *Hiftory*
of the Creation and Fall of Man, page 240, and onwards.

ftruction

ſtruction that can be put upon the words (63), if
they have any reference to *Chriſt*, and his *conqueſt*
of

(63) When I ſpeak of this as an eaſy plain conſtruction of
the words, I would be underſtood to mean with reſpect to us,
who are acquainted with *after ſimilar*, but *more explicit*, promiſes and predictions, together with the *explanation* of them
by their accompliſhment (in part) in the *incarnation, life,
death, reſurrection*, and *exaltation*, of our Saviour Jeſus Chriſt,
and what we are directly told will be *conſequent thereupon*. To
us, in this ſituation, under theſe circumſtances, *this promiſe*
very evidently appears to contain the *meaning* we have put
upon it. I do not ſay, that it appeared to Adam, or to his
poſterity in *former ages*, in this light; or that God intended it
ſhould. Perhaps, it would not have conſiſted with the *intermediate ſteps* in the accompliſhment of this promiſe, to have
delivered it in a manner *ſo explicit* as that they might have
thus underſtood it. But this is no argument, that it did not
really contain this *meaning*, or that we may not be rationally
convinced that it did, conſidering it in *connection* with the
ſcheme of Providence, as it has *ſince been opened*, more eſpecially in the *revelations* of God by his Son *Jeſus Chriſt* to the
apoſtles and *prophets*, and through them to us. We may, in
conſequence of theſe advantages, be able very eaſily and obviouſly to perceive, that this was the *real intention* of God in
his *promiſe* to *Adam*, and that the words, in which the promiſe
is delivered, are not only capable of *this ſenſe*, but as *clearly*
and *fully* expreſſive of it as words *ſummarily* could be. And,
in truth, it is with me one of the *ſtrongeſt evidences* of the *divinity* of the *ſcriptures*, that *this*, and *other* ancient promiſes and
predictions, are *ſo worded*, as that the ſcheme of ſalvation, as
it has been gradually unfolding till theſe laſt days, is *very obviouſly*, however *ſummarily*, pointed out in them ; inſomuch
that a ſober enquirer can ſcarce fail of perceiving, that *one*
and the *ſame ſcheme* has been in proſecution even from the days
of *Adam* ; which ſcheme, however *dark* to *former ages*, is *now,*
in

of the *Devil*, that is, of the *kingdom of fin* which he had been an *inftrument* in introducing into the world. So that the *whole* of what we have done, in this effay, is nothing more than an enlargement upon that which was *fummarily*, and in a few ftrong and expreffive words, delivered as the *grand intention* of God, in conftituting his Son Jefus Chrift the Saviour of men. And I fee not, I confefs, if the time does not come, before Chrift's *delivery of the kingdom to the Father*, when it fhall be true, in EVENT and FACT, that SIN IS TOTALLY DESTROYED, by a reduction of ALL MEN UNDER MORAL SUB-JECTION TO GOD, but that it ought fairly and honeftly to be owned, that *he has not bruifed the ferpent's head*, as it is here declared that he fhould. How can it be, that the *Devil*, that is, *his kingdom*, which *effentially* confifts in the *reign of fin and luft*, fhould be *deftroyed by Chrift*, in any propriety of fenfe, while thoufands and millions of the fons of *Adam*, not only in the *prefent ftate*, but *throughout all eternity*, (as the commonly-received opinion is) will live IN ENMITY WITH GOD, retaining their character as REBELS AGAINST HIM, but SUBJECTS IN THE DEVIL's kingdom? I know not in what light the above evidence, in favour of a *univerfal reduction* of mankind, may appear to others; but

in the times of the Gofpel, made *fufficiently* manifeft to all men: Though the *evidence* is not fo *full* as it will be, when *mankind* are got ftill further into the *accomplifhment* of the *grand purpofe* of God, generally declared in this *original promife* to *Adam*.

to

to me it is fo glaring, that I cannot but wonder it
has been fo generally unperceived in the Chriftian
world, all along to the prefent day ; and that even
ftill multitudes are fo blind as not to fee it. It
cannot eafily be accounted for from any other
caufe, than that ftrong bias there has been upon
the minds of men, even from children, in favour
of contrary doctrines.

PROPOSITION VI.

" The fcripture language, concerning the RE-
" DUCED, or RESTORED, in confequence of the
" mediatory interpofition of Jefus Chrift, is fuch
" as to lead us into the thought, that THEY are
" comprehenfive of MANKIND UNIVERSALLY.

There is *one text*, at leaft, expreffed in fuch
terms as render it incapable of being underftood
in any *other fenfe*, and feveral *others* that may naturally and reafonably be interpreted to carry *this
meaning*; efpecially if compared with the texts
that have been already explained.

The *text* that I will venture to fay is clearly and
fully expreffive of this idea, namely, *that the redeemed by Chrift are comprehenfive of mankind univerfally*, is in the *book* of the Revelation. I fhall
introduce what I have to fay upon it with this fhort
previous remark, namely,

That as the apoftle John, or rather the Divine
Spirit who fpake by him, had it in defign to
exhibit

exhibit a *prophetic* reprefentation of the *feveral fucceffive ftates* of the Chriftian church, before the
fecond coming of Jefus Chrift ; and of *that ftate* alfo,
which will intervene between his fecond coming
and the *finifhing* of the fcheme of God, with reference to men, as *managed* by him ; he was led, in
purfuance of it, to open to our view *that period
under Anti-Chrift*, which would give occafion for
tremendous judgments in the conduct of Providence.
And, while he was upon this dark and terrible
fcene of things, for the relief of the apoftle's mind,
and for the encouragement and fupport of the
people of God, he has now and then *interpofed a
vifion*, in which he had a fight of the *victorious efficacy* of Chrift's dominion, as *head* of the kingdom
of God, the glory whereof he heard afcribed to
him by the *holy angels* above, as well as the *happy
fubjects* of it.   And, in one of thefe interpofed
vifions, the text I lay this ftrefs upon, in proof of
the prefent propofition, has a place.

It is, Rev. v. 13, " And every creature which
" is in heaven, and on the earth, and under the
" earth, and fuch as are in the fea, and all that are
" in them, heard I, faying, Bleffing, and honour,
" and glory, and power, be unto him that fitteth
" upon the throne, and unto the Lamb, for ever
" and ever."   Thefe words evidently look forward
to the COMPLETION of the fcheme of God with
reference to mankind, or to the *time* of God's
being *all in all* ; bringing in the *finlefs intelligences
above*, as uniting with *the whole race of Adam*, in
giving

giving the glory of their RESTITUTION, or RE-
DEMPTION, to *God* who *contrived* the plan of it,
and to *Chrift* who was the perfon, under God, that
carried it into *execution*. And that *mankind univerfally* are the perfons finging this hymn of praife,
in concert with the holy *angels* of heaven, is
evident, as I imagine, beyond all reafonable difpute, from the *enumeration* here made, which is in
the *fulleft* and *moft extenfive* terms. For not only
the creatures which are *in heaven,* but thofe alfo
which *are on earth,* and *under the earth,* and *in
the fea,* are the creatures whom the apoftle John
faw bowing down in *voluntary acts* of homage, and
thankful adoration, before *God,* and the *Lord
Jefus Chrift,* for the great benefit of *redemption,* or
falvation. And, as though fufficiently *extenfive* language had not as yet been ufed, in the above
enumeration, it is further added, *And all things in
them.* If the apoftle had really intended to have
introduced *the whole human kind,* together with the
angels, as afcribing thankfgiving, and bleffing, and
honour, to *God* and the *Lamb,* for their *reftoration,
reduction,* or *falvation,* how could he have done it
in words that more eafily and certainly convey
this fenfe ? For *the whole human kind* are to be
found in the *places here fpecified;* and the *fpecification*
of thefe places, which contain them *all,* is a fure
argument that he intended to comprehend them
all. Why elfe fhould he be thus particular in
fpecifying them ? It is obfervable, when this fame
apoftle, in the 20th chapter of this *book,* would

5   ranfack

ranfack the whole creation, in order to bring *all the individuals of the human race* before the throne of Chrift's judgment, his language is, " And the fea " gave up the dead that were in it; and death and " the grave" [fo I fhould tranflate the word ᾁδης, in this place, and not *hell*] " delivered up the dead " that were in them." Now, the *creatures* fpoken of, in the foregoing 5th chapter, as *under the earth*, are thofe very ones concerning whom it is faid, in the 20th chapter, that " death and the grave de-" livered up the dead that were in them :" In like manner, the *creatures* that are *there* faid to be *in the fea*, are *the dead* that *the fea* is *here* faid *to give up*. So that if *mankind univerfally* are included in the terms ufed in the 20th chapter, they ought alfo to be included in thofe that are ufed in the 5th chapter. And there is indeed *greater reafon* to interpret the language in the 5th chapter, as including *mankind univerfally*, than in the 20th ; becaufe the enumeration *there* is more *full* and *compleat :* For it takes in *all on the earth*, as well as *under it*, and *in the fea* ; that is, it takes in both *the quick* and *the dead*, which are terms, in the facred dialect, comprehenfive of *all the individuals of the human kind*. In fhort, *the creatures*, the apoftle John faw paying their thankful acknowledgments before the throne of God, in concert with the angels of heaven, for the *falvation* by Jefus Chrift, were the *whole pofterity of Adam*, mankind without exception : And left we fhould be led to think other-wife, he has ufed language that comprehends *all*

that

that live on the earth ; *all that ever died on it, and
were buried under it* ; *and all that ever died on the
fea, and were thrown into it.* And if EVERY CREA-
TURE that *lives on the earth,* and EVERY CREATURE
that is in *the ftate of the dead,* does not comprehend
mankind univerfally, it is difficult to find words
that can do it. I am pretty confident, no other
fenfe than *that* we have given this text can be put
upon it, allowing the words in which it is expreffed their natural due force, and, at the fame
time, a confiftent meaning.

There are ftill other texts, though perhaps not
conclufive in themfelves fimply confidered, yet of
confiderable weight, and well worthy of notice, if
explained by the *fcriptures* we have already offered
to view.

Such are thofe, Gen. xii. 3, " In thee fhall all
" families of the earth be bleffed." And, chap.
xviii. 18, " In thee fhall all nations of the earth
" be bleffed." And chap. xxii. 18, " In thy
" feed fhall all the nations of the earth be blef-
" fed." That thefe paffages refer to *Chrift,* and
the *fpiritual falvation* wherewith *all families,* and
all nations, in the earth, fhould be *bleffed in his
day,* will be beyond difpute with thofe who will
pleafe to compare them with Acts iii. 25, 26,
where the apoftle, having quoted the words " in
" thy feed fhall all the kindreds of the earth be blef-
" fed," adds thereupon, " Unto you hath God
" fent his fon Jefus, to blefs you, in turning away
" every one of you from his iniquities ;" or with
Gal. iii. 8, where it is faid, that " the fcripture

R   " forefeeing,

" foreseeing, that God would juftify the heathen
" through faith, preached before the gofpel unto
" Abraham, faying, *In thee fhall all nations be blef-*
" *fed.*" And in what better fenfe; in what fenfe
more honourable to God, or to his fon Jefus Chrift,
can thefe words be interpreted, than in *that* which
makes them to mean, that *mankind,* however divided into a great number of *nations,* and into a
ftill vaftly greater number of *families,* fhall yet *all*
be *fpiritually bleffed* by Jefus Chrift, *fo bleffed,* as,
fooner or later, to be *turned from their iniquities,*
and formed to a *meetnefs* for *eternal life,* that they
may be crowned therewith? The words are certainly capable of being conftrued in this fenfe:
Nor need they be at all tortured to make them
fpeak it out. *All nations,* and *all families, of the
earth,* are phrafes naturally expreffive of *mankind
univerfally*; and the facred writings often ufe them
to convey this idea. Confequently, when Chrift is
promifed to *blefs all nations,* and *all families, of the
earth,* the words confidered in themfelves, much
more if confidered in connection with the foregoing
texts, very readily offer the *fenfe* I have put upon
them, far more readily than *that* which makes a
few only of mankind *finally bleffed by Chrift*; leaving
the *reft* to be *curfed by him* in *event* and *fact,* and
this to *all eternity.* A ftrange fenfe this, however
generally received for the true one: And a fenfe
it is, I believe, that never could have been thought
on, had interpreters known how, in confiftency
with *other fcriptures,* to have fixed upon a more
fignificantly benevolent meaning. This we are

I   enabled

enabled to do, by what has been diſcourſed in the foregoing pages: For which reaſon, I ſee not but we may explain theſe phraſes, as they are fairly capable of it, in the glorioully high and extenſive ſenſe we have given them.

Another text of the like import, and the only remaining one to be mentioned under this head, is that in Gen. xv. 5, where, upon God's having brought forth Abraham abroad, he ſaid to him, " Look now toward heaven, and tell the ſtars, if " thou art able to number them : SO SHALL THY " SEED BE." If any will be at the pains carefully to compare this promiſe of God with Rom. iv. from the 11th to the 17th, and with Gal. iii. 7th, 8th, they muſt be convinced, if they can depend upon the authority of the apoſtle Paul, that it includes the *ſpiritual*, as well as *natural, ſeed* of *Abraham*, that is, thoſe who ſhould be his *children* by a reſemblance of him in his *moral temper*, as well as thoſe who ſhould deſcend from him by *ordinary generation*. It is readily owned, the promiſe, taken even in this ſenſe, does not, in itſelf ſimply conſidered, convey any other idea than this general one, namely, that the *children* of *Abraham*, by a participation of his *moral likeneſs*, ſhould be *vaſtly numerous*, a multitude ſo great as that, like the *ſtars of heaven*, they *could not be numbered*. But ſtill, if we conſider this promiſe in connection with the *other ſcriptures* we have brought to view, we may fairly and reaſonably fix it to a more *particular* and *determinate* ſenſe; ſuppoſing that God, when

R 2 he

he made it, really meant by it an engagement that *mankind univerfally* fhould, in due time, fo far *refemble Abraham*, in his *moral temper*, as that they fhould be his *fpiritual children* : Which, in true fenfe, is one and the fame thing with their being *bleffed in Chrift*, or with their being *reduced by him under moral fubjection to the government of God*; as the matter is expreffed in the above texts. And it is certain, this promife to Abraham is fo worded as to be very obvioufly capable of this extenfive meaning : Nor will any meaning that has ever yet been put upon it, fo fully anfwer the *proper natural force* of the words here ufed, as this we have of-fered. The *common* one falls vaftly fhort of their juft import : Whereas, *this* happily comes up to it ; giving them a full and extenfive fenfe, and hereby making the promife glorioufly fignificant in itfelf, as well as an eminently worthy engagement from him who is the God and Father of all.

There are many *other texts*, though not men-tioned under either of the foregoing *propofitions*, becaufe not relied on as their *main proof*, that yet evidently favour the *fcheme* we have been endea-vouring to illuftrate and confirm : At leaft, they are capable of a *much higher* and *more fignificant* fenfe, and would appear in a *much more advantage-ous* light, upon fuppofition of its *truth*, than the contrary. I fhall not think it a needlefs digreffion to fubjoin a few thoughts upon them, by way of *appendix* to what has been already offered ; though I fhall do this in a curfory manner only, and with-

3

out

out any other order than *that* in which *these texts*
may come into my mind. For, inftead of depend-
ing on them as *proofs*, I have it rather in view to
fhow, how *much better accommodated* they are to the
prefent doctrine, than *that* which is *contrary* to it.

The firft of thefe texts is, Pfalm lxviii. 18,
" Thou haft afcended on high, thou haft led cap-
" tivity captive, thou haft received gifts for men,
" yea, for the rebellious alfo, that the Lord God
" might dwell among them." Here evidently
feems to be a diftinction between *men*, and *the
rebellious*, for both of whom our Saviour is faid
to *have received gifts*. But who are meant by *men*,
and by *the rebellious alfo*? Why may we not fay
lapfed mankind, confidered in all the *difference* there
is between them by means of their *contracted obftinacy* and *rebellion*? And why may we not fuppofe, that our Saviour, when *he afcended on high*,
received SUCH GIFTS for the fons of lapfed Adam
as were fuited to their *refpective different characters*,
and to this end, that he might, in *due time*, and by
proper means, prepare them *all* for *God's dwelling
with them*? It may, perhaps, give countenance
to this interpretation, if it be remembered, that
the apoftle Paul had this text, in the Pfalms, in his
eye, when he faid of Chrift, Eph. iv. 10, that he
" afcended up far above all heavens, that he might
" fill all things;" that is, that he might fo difpenfe
thofe gifts, which he had *received* upon *his afcenfion*,
as that, in the time laid out for it in the fcheme
of God, he might FILL ALL THE SONS OF LAPSED

ADAM,

ADAM, however *obdurate* and *rebellious*, with that *spiritual fullness* which would *prepare* them for *God to dwell with them.*—Can it be truly said of Christ, that he hath accomplished *that*, which is here said to be the *end of his ascension*, namely, THE FILLING ALL THINGS, if the greater part of mankind, especially of the *more rebellious* among them, are left finally and everlastingly *empty* both of his *sanctifying* and *saving* gifts?—See the illustrations on Col. i. 19.

Another text in this class is, John xii. 32, " And I, if I be lifted up from the earth, will " draw all men to me." Here is no exception of *any individual* of the human race. And what right has any one to *limit* these gloriously extensive words of our Saviour Jesus Christ, in describing the *merciful effect* of his *death on the cross?* Especially, as we have seen the way pointed out, from the *scriptures* themselves, in which *all men*, according to the strictness of the letter, may certainly be *drawn to Christ.*

Parallel to the former text, is John xvii. 2, " As " thou hast given him power over all flesh, that " he might give eternal life to as many as thou " hast given him." It is in the original, παν ὁ δεδωκας αυτω, *to all thou hast given him*. There is some difficulty as to the grammatical propriety of the word παν in this place. Erasmus, Beza, Grotius, and many others, consider it as an Hebraism for παντι. L. de Dieu, in Pool, construes it as a *nominative case* used *absolutely*. Wolfius construes

it

it the fame way, and produces instances of the like conftruction, both out of the New Teftament and other Greek writings. Vid. Wolf. Cur. Philolog. in loc. But however the *grammatical* propriety of this word be accounted for, the plain fenfe of the text is, " that the Father had given Chrift power over all men, THAT, or TO THE END THAT, he might give *eternal life* to THESE ALL MEN he had fubjected to him."

In like manner, when our Saviour, in Matt. xix. 28. ufes thefe words, εν τη παλιγγενεσια, *in the regeneration*, he would very evidently hereby lead us to think, that the time was coming, when this *whole* lower world fhould be, as it were, *born again*, formed into a *new* and *better ftate* of exiftence: Which fame thought is fuggefted by the apoftle Peter, in Acts iii. 21, under that mode of expreffion, αχρι χρονων αποκαταστασεως παντων, *until the times of the reftitution of all things.*

Perhaps, thofe words, in Rom. xi. 32. may properly come in here, " God hath concluded " them all in unbelief, that he might have " mercy upon all." I will not fay, that *God's having mercy upon all*, has no reference to a *more full* admiffion both of Jews and Gentiles, confidered in the *collective* fenfe, to the *vifible privileges* of Chrift's kingdom here on earth ; but this may not be the *principal* meaning of the words. They are obvioufly capable of a *much larger* and *more extenfive* fenfe: And thus much is certain, if we *extend* their fenfe to *mankind univerfally*, in the

R 4 *final*

final iffue of things, the exclamation of the apoftle, in the words that immediately follow, will be much more emphatical, " Oh the depth of the " riches both of the wifdom and knowledge of " God! How unfearchable are his judgments, " and his ways paft finding out!" And there will be a far *more noble fignificancy* alfo in the afcription to God, which concludes his difcourfe upon this head, " For of him, and through him, " and to him, are all things ; to whom be glory " for ever. Amen."

In the like fenfe may we take that paffage of this fame apoftle, Tit. ii. 11, " For the grace of God, " that bringeth falvation, hath appeared to all " men." So the words are in our Englifh Bibles ; but the original has it, επεφανη γαρ η χαρις του Θεου η σωτηριος πασιν ανθρωποις, that is, *the grace of God, which bringeth falvation to all men, hath appeared.* —It is known to thofe acquainted with Greek, that the words *may* be thus tranflated ; and it feems to me that it is the moft obvious and grammatical conftruction of them, if read without *artificial ftops,* as they ought to be, becaufe they are without them in the *manufcript* from whence they were taken. And in what fo fignificant a fenfe can the *grace of God* be affirmed to be *falutiferous,* or *faving,* to *all men,* as in *that* we are pleading for?

And when the *birth* of *Chrift,* the *Saviour,* is fpoken of, Luke ii. 10, as " good tidings of great " joy to all people," the moft vulgar underftand-ing muft perceive, that the words are capable of a

more

more literal, and a *more exalted* fenfe, upon the above fcheme than any other. According to the *common* doctrine, it is not indeed *true,* that Chrift's coming into the world, in the quality of a *Saviour, is good tidings of great joy to all people,* unlefs, by *all people,* we underftand, by the affiftance of a very ftrong figure, a *very few people*; for as to the *greater part* of the human race by far, they have either never heard of the name of Chrift, or will be *eventually,* or in *fact,* much the *worfe* for having heard of him. To be fhort, it is comparatively but a poor low fenfe that can be put upon this text, according to the *common* fcheme : Whereas, if we interpret it agreeably to the *doctrine* explained in thefe papers, we may allow the words their juft and full import, and take them in their *greateft latitude*; that is, we may underftand them in a fenfe that is *highly honourable* to *God,* and *Chrift,* and *univerfally joyful to men.*

Thofe texts likewife deferve a place here, which fpeak of God as *not keeping anger for ever*; as *not contending for ever*; as *not chiding always,* and *not being always wroth.* Can thefe expreffions be *fo fully,* and *fignificantly,* applied to God, upon any hypothefis as that we have here advanced ? Does not this fet thefe phrafes in a *ftronger* and far *more glorious* point of light, than the common interpretation, which is founded on the thought, that God not only *may,* but that he actually *will,* abandon the *greateft part* of the human fpecies to *final* and *everlafting damnation ?*

The

The same may be said of those numerous passages, which represent the blessed God as *tender in mercy*; *plenteous in mercy*; *abundant in mercy*; as *the Lord that hath mercy*; *the Lord to whom mercy belongeth*; *the Lord that delighteth in mercy.* It would be an affront to the underftandings of men to go about to prove, that thefe defcriptions of the infinitely merciful God are capable of a *much more fublime* and *honourable* meaning, upon the plan of *univerfal falvation*, than the *oppofite* fcheme.

And this is emphatically true of the many texts, which characterife the Deity as a Being whofe *mercy endureth for ever*; whofe *mercy is everlafting*; whofe *mercy is from everlafting to everlafting*; yea, whofe *mercy*, whofe *tender mercy, extendeth over all the works of his hands.* A far more emphatically *great* and *benevolent* fenfe is certainly given to thefe expreffions, upon the *doctrine* we are fetting forth, than the *common* one : Nay, upon the *common* one, they can fcarce have any meaning at all, without the help of art to qualify, and bring down, the *fenfe* they *naturally* and *obviously* carry in them ; and, even with the help of a figure, it cannot be faid of God, unlefs in a comparatively low fenfe, that his *mercies endure for ever*, and are *over all his works*, if, as the generally-received opinion fays, they are confined to a *few only* of the race of men, while *all the reft*, inftead of *feeling the advantage* of his *mercies for ever*, are *for ever fuffering* the effects of his *anger* and *wrath*.

In

In fine, there are a great many *prophecies* scattered all over the sacred books of revelation, concerning the *times of Christ*, and the *great things* that should be accomplished, under his administration at the *head* of God's kingdom, which cannot be understood, upon any scheme, in a sense so *honourable* to *God*, and his Son *Jesus Christ*, and that so well answers the natural import of the words in which they are delivered, as this we have been opening. Instead of *particularly* quoting these prophecies (which would carry me too great a length), I would rather say in *general*, the *partial events*, to which they are commonly applied, and which leave the *greatest part* of the posterity of lapsed Adam in a state of *degeneracy* and *misery*, do, by no means, come up to the *full meaning* of those *strong* and *extensively benevolent* terms in which they are expressed. And it deserves serious consideration, whether there is not danger left the *oracles of God* should be exposed to *contempt*, while they are represented as speaking in a strain that is plainly too *hyperbolical* and *exaggerating?* And will not this be the real truth, if we confine the *sense* of those *prophecies*, which are delivered in the *most grand* and *universal language*, to *partial* and comparatively *small events*, such as are no ways answerable to the ideas we have of the *infinite greatness*, and *wisdom*, and *knowledge*, and *power*, and *benevolence* of God?

I have now collected, and put together, in the most intelligible manner I could, the *direct evidence* in favour of the important point I undertook to reprefent as a *fcripture truth.* The *proofs* I have refted the caufe on are not *fingle independent fentences,* detached from this and the other part of the Bible, merely for the fake of their *found*; but *paragraphs* of facred writ, and fome of them *large* ones too, and taken in *connection,* and as falling in with the *principal defign* of the infpired authors in inferting them in the places where they are found. After all, I may be miftaken. If any fhould perceive that I am, and would be at the pains, in a candid and Chriftian way, to fhew me particularly wherein, I fhould efteem it a kindnefs, and hold myfelf greatly obliged to them ; for I have really nothing in view but the *good of mankind,* as grounded on *the truth as it is in Jefus.* Or fhould any think, that the *evidence* the *above texts* are capable of yielding is *fufficient,* though I have not been able to reprefent it *as fuch*; if what I have done fhould prove a motive to ftir them up to place this evidence in a *ftill clearer* and *ftronger* point of light, inftead of envying their *fuperior abilities,* and *greater merit,* I fhall heartily join in giving them their juft praife ; efteeming my pains (in which I have not been wanting) well-fpent labour, fhould this only be the effect.

I have only this to fay further, that, as our *more immediate* concern, in this prefent ftate, is to fecure our *well-being* in the *next,* it is not a matter of wonder, that no more is faid, in the *revelations* of God, either by the *ancient prophets,* or his Son

Jefus

Jesus Christ and his *apostles*, with reference to the *state* which is still *beyond that*; at least, in *plain* and *explicit* language (64), leaving no room for doubt. It is indeed no other than might reasonably be expected, that the inspired writers should *largely* and *particularly* treat of the *joys* and *miseries* of the *resurrection-state*, and but *sparingly* and *generally* of *that* which will commence *afterwards*. And this is the

(64) It was doubtless best, and God might know it was so, to speak upon this matter *so as that* it should not be clearly understood, till the *time came* when *such knowledge* might be *fit* and *proper* for the world. Possibly, as a very considerable author expresses it [*Hartley on Man*, vol. ii. pag. 435], ' the writers ' of the Old and New Testaments did not see the full mean- ' ing of the glorious declarations, which the Holy Spirit has ' delivered to us by their means ; just as Daniel, and the *other* ' *prophets*, were ignorant of the full and precise import of their ' *prophecies*, relating to Christ. Or perhaps they did; but ' thought it expedient, or were commanded, not to be *more* ' *explicit*. The Christian religion, in converting the various ' Pagan nations of the world, was to be corrupted by them ; ' and the *superstitious fear* of God, which is one of those cor- ' ruptions, may have been necessary hitherto on account of ' the *rest*. But now the corruptions of the true religion begin ' to be discovered, and removed, by the earnest endeavours ' of good men of all nations, and sects, in these *latter times*, ' by their *comparing spiritual things with spiritual*.' And as knowledge, in other respects, has been greatly increased, it may *now* be *proper* that *more* should be understood with refe- rence to the *extensive benevolence* of God towards mankind through Jesus Christ, than was necessary in *former ages*. The *support of Christianity* may be connected herewith. Perhaps, the amiable light in which it is placed, by the above represen- tation of it, is the *most effectual* antidote against *infidelity*.

truth

truth of *fact*. They have *mostly* laid out their endeavours to promote our *welfare*, in the *state that will succeed next after this*; while, at the same time, they have interposed enough to lead an impartial and attentive enquirer into the thought, that the *final result* of the *scheme* of God, conducted by his Son *Jesus Christ*, will be the HAPPINESS of MANKIND UNIVERSALLY. when *God shall be all in all*; as has, I trust, been sufficiently evinced in these papers.

CHAPTER

CHAPTER III.

Stating and answering Objections.

NOTWITHSTANDING all that has been offered in proof, that the *final salvation* of *all men* is a doctrine of the *Bible*, it ought not, it is freely acknowledged, to be received as such, unless the *contrary evidence* can be fairly invalidated. This makes it necessary to examine the *objections* that lie against the truth of the foregoing scheme: In the doing of which, I shall propose them in their full strength, so far as I am able; for if they will not, viewed in this light, admit of a clear and satisfactory answer, they will remain *objections* still, and ought, in true reason, to restrain us from embracing the above system, however plausible the arguments in its favour may appear, considered separately from *those difficulties* that lie against it.

I know of no *objections* to the *final salvation* of *all men* from *natural reason*, in the sense we have explained it. *This* seems to speak rather *for*, than *against* it. Or if, on the one hand, it should not give any *positive grounds* to expect a *final* and *universal restoration*; neither, on the other hand,

hand, does it offer any *objections* against it : To be sure, not against the *possibility* of it. Does it contradict any dictate of true reason to say, that the infinitely benevolent God *may*, if he so pleases, make the *whole human race finally happy?* None will pretend to affirm such a thing. And if a good God *may* make them happy, he may open his mind upon this matter ; declaring that he certainly and actually will : Upon the supposition of which, *reason* would rather approve of the revelation as worthy of him, than cavil at its meaning as reflecting dishonour upon him. We have therefore no concern, in the present debate, with any *objections* that are *purely rational.*

The only difficulties, thrown in our way, are fetched from the *scriptures*. And the difficulties from this quarter, it is confessed, are not without their weight. We shall give them a distinct and particular consideration.

OBJECTION I.

" *Endless never-ceasing misery* is, according to the " *scriptures*, the portion of *wicked* men beyond the " grave ; and consequently the *whole* human kind " cannot be *finally happy.*"

This consequence, I readily own, is unavoidable, if *never-ceasing misery*, with respect to wicked men, is a doctrine of the *Bible*. The *objection* says it is. My business shall be to show, that it is not.

The

The *evidence*, the *objection* would bring, in fupport of the doctrine of *endlefs mifery*, may be fet in the following light :—The *mifery* of wicked men, in the future ftate, is frequently faid, in the *fcriptures*, to be *everlafting :* And this fame word *everlafting*, which is joined with the *mifery* of the *wicked*, is joined alfo with the *happinefs* of the *righteous* ; fo that if the *one* is *endlefs*, the *other* muft be fo too : Nay, the *righteous* and *wicked* are fpoken of in the *fame fentence*, and it is affirmed of the *wicked*, in the fame peremptory manner, *that they fhall go away into everlafting punifhment*, as it is of the *righteous*, that they *fhall go away into* ETERNAL *life :* Yea, this fame word, *everlafting*, which is ufed to point out the *duration* of the *future torments*, is the very word that is often ufed to point out the *ftrict abfolute eternity of God.* Befides all which, the mifery of the *wicked* is faid to be *for ever ;* and, as though this was not fufficiently expreffive of its *endlefs continuance*, it is further declared to be *for ever and ever*, the ftrongeft phrafe ufed, in fcripture, to defcribe the *proper eternity* of the Supreme Being. And further ftill, our Saviour, as if it had been his view to put this matter beyond all controverfy, has *thrice*, in the fame difcourfe, moft folemnly repeated thofe emphatically ftrong words, with refpect to *wicked* men, in the coming ftate, " WHERE THEIR WORM DIETH NOT, AND THEIR " FIRE IS NOT QUENCHED." Upon which it is added, In what more clear and decifive language, could the *endlefs never-ceafing mifery* of the *wicked*

S have

have been revealed? No words could have been chosen, the language in which the scriptures were wrote afford none, that more easily, obviously, and strongly, convey this idea.

This is the *objection*, and, I think, in its *full force*. I know of nothing that has been offered, in defence of the doctrine of *endless misery*, that is left out of the plea, as above summarily stated. If I could make it stronger, I would willingly do so.

It begins, The punishment of wicked men is frequently said, in the scriptures, to be *eternal*, or *everlasting*. The texts in proof of this are as follow: Matt. xviii. 8, " Wherefore, if thy hand " or foot offend thee, cut them off, and cast them " from thee: It is better for thee to enter into " life halt, or maimed, rather than having two " hands, or two feet, to be cast into EVERLASTING " fire."—xxv. 41, " Then shall he say to them " on the left hand, Depart from me, ye cursed, " into EVERLASTING fire, prepared for the Devil " and his angels."—46th verse, " And these shall " go away into EVERLASTING punishment."— Mark iii. 29, " But he that blasphemeth against " the Holy Ghost,—is in danger of ETERNAL " damnation."—2 Thess. i. 9, " Who shall be " punished with EVERLASTING destruction from " the presence of the Lord, and the glory of his " power."

These *five* texts are the only ones, in all the New Testament, in which the misery of the wicked is said to be *eternal*, or *everlasting*; unless we take

in

in thofe words of Jude, which are fpoken of the Sodomites, " fuffering the vengeance of ETERNAL " fire." Upon which I cannot help making a paufe, before I proceed, to exprefs my furprize to find the facred writers fo very fparing in their ufe of this word *eternal,* or *everlafting,* as referring to the *future torments,* upon which fuch vaft ftrefs is laid in the prefent controverfy. I muft needs fay, I expeded, when I began to colled *this part* of the evidence, to fet before the reader's view, to have feen the word *everlafting,* conneded with the *mifery* of the *next ftate,* at leaft, in *every book* of the New Teftament, if not *feveral times* in each book : Whereas, upon examination, it appears, that by far the *greater part* of the infpired writers have never ufed this word, nor any other word allied to it in fenfe and meaning, with reference to the *future torments* ; while thofe who have ufed it, have very rarely done fo. It is ufed but *thrice* by the evangelift Matthew ; but *once* by the evangelift Mark, and this in a *fpecial cafe only* ; and but *once* likewife by the apoftle Paul, though his epiftles make fo confiderable a part of the New Teftament. It is not to be met with in the gofpels either of Luke or John ; nor in either of the three epiftles of John. It no where occurs in the epiftles of Peter or James. And, what is very remarkable, in the account we have of the preaching of the apoftles, from place to place, throughout the world, in the book of Ads, there is a *total filence* as to their ever having ufed *this word,* or any other importing

S 2 that

that the mifery of the wicked is *endlefs* and *never-ceafing*. All which is very extraordinary, if this is a doctrine of *Chriftianity*. For, if it really be fo, it is a moft important one; and it cannot eafily be accounted for, that the infpired writers fhould have fo ftrangely paffed it over with neglect. It might rather have been expected, that they fhould perpetually have infifted on it, and with great folemnity too, and in a great variety of plain and indifputable terms. And their omiffions, upon this head, are a ftrong prefumptive argument, that they knew nothing of this doctrine, which has been fo vehemently pleaded for in thefe latter days.—But to return to a more direct and particular anfwer to the *objection*, in this branch of it. And,

I. It is obvious to remark, that the fubftantive αιων, and its derivative αιωνιος, commonly tranflated in the Bible *eternity, eternal,* or *everlafting,* MAY fignify a *limited duration.* None acquainted with Greek will deny this, becaufe they know, or eafily may know whenever they pleafe, that they are in fact often ufed in this fenfe, in the facred writings. We fhall have occafion prefently to produce a large number of inftances to this purpofe.

Now, from this remark only, had we nothing further to fay, it follows, that the preceding evidence, in favour of *univerfal falvation,* remains ftrong and valid, notwithftanding the *fcripture* has joined the word αιωνιος, tranflated *everlafting,* with the *punifhment* of wicked men, in the future world;

becaufe

becaufe this fame word is often ufed, in the *fcrip-ture itfelf*, to fignify a *limited* duration only. Though therefore it is true, not only that the wicked fhall be bid, at the great day, *to depart away*, εις το πυρ το αιωνιον, *into everlafting fire*; but that they fhall likewife, in confequence of this doom, actually *go away*, εις κολασιν αιωνιον, *into everlafting punifhment:* Yet it MAY notwithftand-ing be as true, that they fhall, in the final iffue of things, be made *happy*; becaufe the fcriptures have informed us, in numerous places, that the word αιωνιος MAY mean nothing more than a *limited period of duration*. All I infift upon, in confequence of the prefent remark, is only this, that the word αιωνιος, tranflated *everlafting*, MAY fignify a *period of time only*; and if it MAY be conftrued in this fenfe, there is not the fhadow of an interference be-tween its connection with the *punifhment* of wicked men, and their being *finally faved*. In order to deftroy the above evidence, in a way of ftrict and conclufive reafoning from this word, it muft be fhown, that it not only means an *endlefs duration*, but that it cannot be underftood in any other fenfe; which every one, that knows any thing of Greek, knows to be befide the truth of fact.

II. Thefe words, αιων and αιωνιος, are evidently more *loofe* and *general* in their meaning, than the Englifh words *eternity*, *everlafting*, by which they are commonly rendered in our Bibles. If it were not fo, how comes it to pafs, that αιων and αιωνιος will not always bear being tranflated *eternity, ever-*

lafting?

lasting? It would many times sound quite harsh to call that, in English, *eternal* or *everlasting*, which yet, with great propriety, might have the word αιωνιος joined with it. A few examples will bring this down to the lowest understanding. *Before the eternal times* is an impropriety in English ; but πρα χρονων αιωνιων is a beautiful Greek phrase, putting us upon looking back beyond *former ages:* The translators of the New Testament have accordingly rendered it, Tit. i. 2, *Before the world began.* So when our Saviour says to his apostles, and to their successors, for their encouragement in their work, " Lo, I am with you alway," εως της συντελειας του αιωνος; the words are a promise very easily and naturally assuring them of his presence, *through the whole time of the gospel-dispensation.* It is accordingly rendered, in our Bibles, " even to the " end of the world :" But the natural force of the English word *eternal* would not allow of its being translated, *to the end of eternity.* In like manner, when the evangelist Luke speaks of *holy prophets which have been* απ' αιωνος, it is translated, *since the world began:* But the rendering would have been uncouth, *from eternity ;* nor would such a translation have conveyed a right meaning. In fine, for I would not needlesly multiply instances, when the apostle Paul speaks of *the mystery which hath been hid,* απο των αιωνων, it is very justly translated, *from ages that are passed:* But it would have been a solecism in English to have said, *from past eternities.*

I may

I may not impertinently remark yet further here, the particles, ετι and επεκεινα, are sometimes added, in the Septuagint version of the Old Testament, to the word αιων, to give it the greater emphasis: Whereas, should we add the English words, answerable to those Greek particles, to the term *eternity*, it would make evident nonsense; as any one may readily perceive upon trial. Thus, Exod. xv. 18, *The Lord shall reign,* τον αιωνα, και επ αιωνα, και ετι, *for ever and ever, and farther.* —Dan. xii. 3, *They shall shine as the stars,* εις τον αιωνα, και ετι, *for ever and farther.*—Mic. iv. 5, *We will walk in the name of the Lord our God,* εις τον αιωνα, και επεκεινα, *for ever and beyond it.*

The plain truth is, these Greek words have a different natural force from the English ones, by which they are mostly rendered in the Bible; being more *loose* in their meaning, and not so certainly signifying *duration without bounds or limits:* Otherwise they might, without impropriety in sense, or indeed any harshness in sound, be always translated by them, or used with like additions to them; which we have seen they cannot.

Now, from this remark, it is obvious, that the *sacred writers* ought not to be looked upon as having in their minds the *same idea,* when they apply the words αιων and αιωνιος to the *future torments,* pointing out their continuance, which *we* are naturally led to have, when we connect with them the words *eternity, everlasting.* Those

S 4   acquainted

acquainted with the Englifh language only, having
been ufed, from their childhood, to join the idea
of *endlefs duration* with the words *eternity, everlafting*, are apt at once to put this fenfe upon them,
whenever they fee them, in the fcriptures, applied
to the *hereafter punifhment* of the wicked. But it
is far from being certain, or indeed fo much as
probable, that the *facred penmen* were, in the fame
manner, ready, when they ufed the *original* words,
to which thefe *tranflated* ones are made to anfwer, to underftand them in the *fame fenfe*. We
have feen they have a *different force*; and confequently the idea *they* applied to them muft be
proportionably different, that is, not fo determi-
nately fignificative of *continuance beyond all bounds
or limits*.

III. The word αιων, and its derivative αιωνιος,
are fo far from being confined in their meaning to
endlefs duration, that they really fignify nothing
more than an *age, difpenfation, period of continuance,*
either longer or fhorter. It is certain, this is the
fenfe in which they are commonly, if not always,
ufed in the facred pages. The texts in proof of
this are almoft numberlefs. I fhall mention a
few at large, and more generally point out a
great many more, both in the Septuagint tranflation of the Old Teftament, and in the writings
of the New.

To begin with the Old Teftament.—Gen. vi. 4.
" There were giants in the earth in thofe days,—
" mighty men which were of old, απ' αιωνος."—

9   ix. 12.

ix. 12, "This (the rainbow) is tne token of
"the covenant which I make between me and
"thee, and every living creature, for perpetual ge-
"nerations, εις γενεας αιωνιους."—16. "And the bow
"fhall be in the cloud, and I will look upon it,
"that I may remember the everlafting covenant,
"διαθηκην αιωνιον, between God and every living
"creature."—xiii. 15. "All the land which
"thou feeft, to thee will I give it, and to thy feed
"for ever, εως αιωνος."—xvii. 8. "I will give
"unto thee, and unto thy feed,—all the land of
"Canaan for an everlafting poffeffion, εις κατασχε-
"σιν αιωνιον."—13. "He that is born in thy houfe
"—muft needs be circumcifed,—and my covenant
"fhall be in your flefh for an everlafting cove-
"nant, εις διαθηκην αιωνιον."—Exod. xii. 14. "And
"you fhall keep it (the paffover) throughout your
"generations : You fhall keep it a feaft by an or-
"dinance for ever, νομιμον αιωνιον."—24. "And ye
"fhall obferve this thing (the paffover) for an or-
"dinance to thee, and to thy fons, for ever, εως
"αιωνος."—Numb. xxv. 13. "And he (Phinehas)
"fhall have it, and his feed after him, even the
"covenant of an everlafting priefthood, διαθηκη
"ιερατειας αιωνια." In like manner, the Jewifh
ftatutes and ordinances are ftiled αιωνιοι, and faid
to be εις τον αιωνα, in the following places, as
they are enumerated by Mr. Whifton.——Exod.
xxvii. 21.— xxviii. 43.— xxix. 28.—xxx. 21.
— xxxi. 16.——Levit. vi. 18, 22.— vii. 24,
26.—x. 15.—xvi. 29, 31.—xvii. 7.—xxiii. 14,

31, 41.—xxiv. 3, 8, 9.——Numb. x. 8.—xv. 15.
—xviii. 8, 19, 24.—xix. 10.—xxv. 13. Upon
which he adds, with great truth and propriety, ' There is no end of citing more *ordinances,*
' or *statutes,* or *grants,* which were to be *eternal,* or
' *everlasting,* or to *last for ever,* in our modern way of
' interpreting those Greek words : Which yet were
' to last no longer, at the utmost, than the Mosaic
' œconomy itself ; and have many, very many, of
' them ceased, or at least have been intermitted
' above sixteen hundred years together *.'

And the same use of these words is retained in
the New Testament ; as may be seen by the following texts.—Matt. xxviii. 20. " Lo, I am with
" you alway, even to the end of the world," του
αιωνος, the gospel age, or dispensation.—Luke xvi. 8.
" The children of this world," του αιωνος τουτου, *of
this age,* " are wiser in their generation, than the
" children of light."—xx. 34. " The children of
" this world," του αιωνος τουτου, *of this age,* " marry,
" and are given in marriage."—1 Cor. i. 20.
" Where is the wise ? Where is the scribe ? Where
" is the disputer of this world," του αιωνος τουτου,
of this age ?—x. 11. " All these things happened
" unto them for ensamples, and they are written
" for our admonition, upon whom the ends of the
" world," των αιωνων, *of the ages,* " are come."
Gal. i. 4. " Who gave himself for our sins, that
" he might deliver us from this present evil world,"

* Eternity of Hell Torments considered, page 21.

εκ του ενεστωτος αιωνος πονερου, *from this present evil age.*—Eph. ii. 7. " That he might shew in " ages to come, εν τοις αιωσι επερχομενοις, " the ex- " ceeding riches of his grace."—iii. 9. " And to " make all men see what is the fellowship of the " mystery, which from the beginning of the " world," απο των αιωνων, *from ages,* " hath been " hid in God."—Col. i. 26. " The mystery which " hath been hid," απο των αιωνων, " from ages, " and generations."—But I am weary of citing particularly any more texts, and shall content my-self with desiring the reader to turn to the follow-ing ones, as they are to be seen in the Greek Testament.—Matt. xii. 32.—xiii. 22, 39, 40, 49.— xxiv. 3.—Mark iv. 19.—Luke i. 55.—xviii. 30.— John viii. 35.—ix. 32.—Acts iii. 21.—Rom. xii. 2. —xvi. 25.—1 Cor. ii. 6, 7, 8.—iii. 18.—viii. 13. —2 Cor. iv. 4.—Eph. i. 21.—1 Tim. vi. 17.— 2 Tim. iv. 10.—Tit. ii. 12.—Heb. i. 2.—iv. 26, with several others, which I may have passed over; for I pretend not to have exhibited a com-plete list.

From this frequent, and almost perpetual, use of the words αιων and αιωνιος, it is, I think, beyond all reasonable dispute, evident, that their *proper meaning*, at least, as used in the sacred writings, is an *age, œconomy,* or *period of duration*, whether *long* or *short*.

It will, perhaps, be said here, the words αιων and αιωνιος, whatever they may be supposed to signify in strict propriety of speech, are certainly used,

uſed, in ſcripture, to mean ſometimes *duration* WITHOUT *bounds, as well as* WITH. To which I anſwer, As αιων properly ſignifies *an age,* or *period of duration,* the circumſtance of *longer* or *ſhorter, definite* or *indefinite,* does not depend on the nature of the *word,* but *other things,* which ſhould be conſidered, in order to aſcertain its *preciſe ſenſe* in this reſpect. From whence I freely allow the following obſervation to be a juſt and true one, namely,

That the *preciſe duration,* intended by the words αιων and αιωνιος, in any particular place, cannot, with certainty, be collected from the force of the words, in themſelves ſimply conſidered ; but muſt be determined, either by the *nature* of the thing ſpoken of, or other paſſages of ſcripture that explain it. As, to illuſtrate this in a few inſtances, when it is ſaid of *God,* as in Rom. xvi. 26, that he is Θεος αιωνιος, we cannot argue that his duration is *boundleſs* and *unlimited,* merely becauſe this *epithet* is applied to him : But yet, we may reaſonably conſtrue it in this ſenſe, becauſe he is *previouſly known* to be a *ſubject* capable of this kind of duration, and the word αιων allows of the conſtruction, as it naturally ſignifies *an age,* or *period of duration in general,* leaving the circumſtance of *longer* or *ſhorter, definite* or *indefinite,* to be ſettled by the *nature* of the ſubject with which it is connected. In like manner, when it is ſaid of the *holy prophets,* that they *have been* απ᾽αιωνος ; we do not interpret this of a *duration* within ſuch and ſuch certain

bounds,

bounds, merely from the *force* of the *word,* but from the *nature* of the *subject* to which it is related. And the fame may be faid, with refpect to the *happinefs* of the *righteous,* and the *mifery* of the *wicked;* they can neither of them be certainly fixed to *this* or *that precife duration,* whether *longer* or *fhorter,* *limited* or *unlimited,* MERELY from the joining the word αιωνιος with them; becaufe this word properly fignifies a *period of duration,* without taking into its meaning, its *precife length,* or determining whether it is *bounded,* or *unbounded.* In order therefore to fix the *true duration* intended by this *epithet,* thus applied, we muft recur to the *nature* of the *subject,* or what may be faid with reference to it in *other texts;* nor can it, with any manner of certainty, be done in any other way: Though I would obferve here, and the obfervation may be worthy of fpecial notice; if we will confine ourfelves to the *mere force* of the *word itfelf,* it more probably means a *limited,* than an *endlefs,* duration; and for this very good reafon, becaufe *this* is, by far, the moft *frequent* ufe of it in the facred writings; as any one may foon fatisfy himfelf by the help of a Greek Concordance.

And from hence it appears, at once, that the fcripture account of the *future mifery* as *everlafting,* is no ways inconfiftent with the foregoing fcheme of *univerfal falvation:* Nay, from the proof above offered, that mankind *univerfally* fhall be *faved,* we are clearly and certainly taught how to underftand

stand the word αιωνιος, when joined with the *future misery*, namely, as meaning, not an *unlimited*, but *limited* duration. For, as this word is evidently found, in fact, to be capable of being understood in either of these senses, it is now put out of all doubt, in which of them it is to be understood, namely, in the *limited* sense. To illustrate this by an example. It is said of Christ, Dan. vii. 14, that " his dominion is an everlasting do- " minion;" and again, Mic. iv. 7, that " he " shall reign in Mount Zion from henceforth " even for ever." The words, αιωνιος, and εις τον αιωνα, in the Septuagint, in themselves simply considered, do not absolutely determine, whe- ther the reign of Christ shall be *endless*, or for a *period*, or *dispensation* only: But when an inspired apostle expresly declares, that, after the reduction of all enemies, Christ " shall deliver up the king- " dom to the Father, and be himself subject to " him, that God may be all in all," the precise meaning of these words is *now fixed*, and we are no longer at a loss to say, that they are to be un- derstood of a *limited* duration, though a long one. So, when it is affirmed of the wicked, that they *shall go away*, εις κολασιν αιωνιον, *into everlasting pu- nishment*, the certain meaning of this word, αιωνιον, *everlasting*, is clearly and fully settled by the above proof of the *final salvation of all men*. We are no longer left in suspense, but may assuredly say, it is to be understood in the *limited* sense.

But, to give the present objection the utmost possible

poffible advantage, I will fuppofe, what has never yet been proved, nor can be proved, *viz.* that the word αιωνιος *properly* and *ftrictly* fignifies *duration without end*; and that, whenever it is ufed in the *limited* fenfe, it is in a *lax* and *lefs proper* way of fpeaking. And, even upon this large fuppofition, the above evidence, in favour of *univerfal falvation*, is not overthrown. For, as the fcripture itfelf has taught us this *lax* and *lefs proper* fenfe of the word, by ufing it in this fenfe, and more frequently too than in its fuppofed *proper* one, it cannot be thought hard, or unreafonable, to put this fenfe upon it, when plain proof is offered, from the fcriptures themfelves, that men fhall be *univerfally faved at laft*. So that if the proof we have given of the doctrine of *univerfal falvation* is good, in itfelf, it remains good, notwithftanding this *objection*; becaufe the *future mifery*, the thing *objected*, is eafily capable, upon this ftrongeft fuppofition, of being reconciled with it.

I have now faid enough to free the foregoing difcourfe from any difficulty, arifing from the connection of the word αιωνιος, tranflated *everlafting*, with the *mifery* of wicked men in the future ftate; and might therefore content myfelf without adding any thing further. But, as the doctrine of *endlefs torments* is ftrenuoufly pleaded for by a great many, and reprefented as an *effential* truth of the *Chriftian revelation*, while yet, in my opinion, it has no real foundation in the facred books of the *New Teftament*, I fhall, though I do not think it needful, in

10 vindication

vindication of the preceding fyftem, go on, and fay,

IV. It is fufficiently evident, even from the very *texts* that are brought to prove the *ftrict eternity of bell torments*, that they contain no fuch doctrine ; and much more is this evident from *other texts* which fpeak of the fame torments.

If we attend to the *produced texts*, we fhall find, that the *exiftence of wicked men in mifery without end* is rather a *confequence* deduced from, than *the thing itfelf* affirmed in, them. For, let it be obferved, in two of the above five texts [Matt. xviii. 8. and xxv. 41.] it is only faid of the *fire* wherewith the wicked fhall be punifhed, that it is *everlafting.* And ' could it be proved, (as a late valuable
' writer expreffes it *) that the *fire* itfelf will be ab-
' folutely *without end*, it will not neceffarily follow
' from thence, that *every individual fubject*, which
' is caft into it, muft be fo too : Becaufe God may
' either think fit to *continue* this *fire* in being, as a
' *perpetual* monument of his juftice ; or, becaufe,
' in fo large a fyftem of rational beings as the
' *univerfe* contains, there may be, as well in *future*
' ages, as in the *prefent*, beings that abufe their
' moral agency, and become proper fubjects to be
' punifhed in it. I fay, either of thefe propo-
' fitions may be true, and, as fuch, fufficiently
' account for this phrafeology (if underftood in
' its utmoft rigour), and yet no neceffity of infer-

* Mr. Nichol Scot.

' ring,

' ring, that *every individual subject*, that is cast
' into this fire, shall be *continued alive in it without*
' *end*.'—But not to insist upon this, which yet I
think well worthy of notice.

It may be of more importance to remark, that
there is no good reason to suppose, that the word
αιωνιον, *everlasting*, here joined with the *fire of hell*,
is to be understood, as pointing out a strictly and
absolutely *endless duration*. And, I believe, nothing but mere custom prevents our perceiving,
at once, the absurdity of such an interpretation.
No one ever imagined himself obliged to think,
that this *earth* will continue, strictly speaking,
to all *eternity*, because it is said, in scripture,
to *abide for ever*. No one ever supposed the *hills*
and *mountains* to be absolutely *endless in duration*,
because the term *everlasting*, is applied to them by
the sacred writers. And, in fine, no one ever
imagined there had been an *eternal succession of*
prophets, because the scripture speaks of *prophets*,
απ' αιωνος, *from eternity*. Common reason, in these
cases, readily understands the word *eternal* in the
limited sense. And the same reason, one would
think, if not under some previous bias, would as
readily understand the *same word*, in the *same sense*,
in the *present case*. For it is, perhaps, as great
an absurdity to suppose *fire* to be *strictly* and *ab-*
solutely eternal, as to suppose the *earth*, or *mountains*,
or *prophets in succession*, to be so. *Fire*, as such,
naturally tends to an *end*, and will, in time, actually
come to an *end*; and it is impossible, according to

T   the

the eftablifhed laws of nature, but that it fhould certainly do fo. The *nature* of the *fubject* there-fore obliges us to put a *limitation* on the word αιωνιον, *everlafting*, when joined with *fire*. And this is fo often the *fenfe* of this *fame word*, in like cafes, even in the fcriptures themfelves, that it is ftrange any fhould be at a lofs in this matter. A *reftrained* interpretation of the *word*, when connect-ed with *fire*, is certainly the moft natural, as well as rational. And I fee not but an *age*, *difpenfation*, or *period*, for the *continuance* of this *fire*, will very well anfwer the full import of the word αιωνιον, *everlafting*; especially, if we fuppofe this *age* to *laft*, till the *fire* has accomplifhed the *end* for which it was enkindled. And we may the rather reft fatisfied with this interpretation, which reafon fug-gefts, by calling to mind the language of fcrip-ture, with reference to the cities of Sodom and Gomorrah, which is, that " they are fet forth for an " example, fuffering the vengeance of eternal fire." Surely, we have no need, in order to do juftice to the fcripture, to fuppofe, that thofe *cities* are *now* in flames, and will be fo to *all eternity*. The words, interpreted as they eafily and naturally may be, import no more than this, that this fire *lafted*, till it had accomplifhed the *defign of Heaven in the de-ftruction of thofe cities, for a ftanding public example of the divine vengeance to after ages.* And the *fire* of *hell* is doubtlefs called *everlafting* for the like reafon.

And if by το πυρ το αιωνιον, *everlafting fire*, we
are

are to underſtand a fire that will laſt, not *always*, but an *age*, or *diſpenſation*, there is no difficulty in fixing the meaning of the ſame word αιωνιος, *ever-laſting*, in the *other three texts.* In that [Matt. xxv. 46.] where the phraſe is *everlaſting puniſhment*, it is evident, the epithet *everlaſting*, is joined with *puniſhment* on account of the *fire* that will occaſion it. For the wicked's going into this everlaſting puniſhment is expreſsly mentioned as the *execution* of the *ſentence* in the foregoing words, " Depart, ye " curſed, into everlaſting fire." Conſequently, the *duration* of this puniſhment cannot be *longer* than the *duration* of the *fire* that cauſes it. If *that*, from the *nature* of *the thing*, *muſt* have a *limited* ſenſe put upon it, the *ſame limitation* muſt be put alſo upon the *puniſhment* that is the *effect* of it. So, in Mark iii. 29, where they who blaſpheme againſt the Holy Ghoſt are ſaid to be in danger, αιωνιου κρισεως, *of eternal judgment*, it is evident this judg-ment is called *eternal*, becauſe the *effect* of it will be their *departing into eternal* or *everlaſting fire* ; for that is the *judicial ſentence* itſelf, as we have ſeen, Matt. xxv. 41. In like manner, when the apoſ-tle Paul, in the laſt of thoſe texts, ſpeaks of " ever-" laſting deſtruction from the preſence of the Lord," 2 Theſſ. i. 9 ; he very evidently uſes this term *ever-laſting*, on account of the *fire* that is to bring on this deſtruction. The connection of the words puts this beyond all diſpute. It is thus : " When " the Lord Jeſus ſhall be revealed from heaven, " with his migh y angels, IN FLAMING FIRE,

T 2 " taking

" taking vengeance on them that know not God,
" and that obey not the gospel of our Lord Jesus
" Christ, who shall be punished with EVERLAST-
" ING DESTRUCTION." Their destruction is
plainly spoken of as *everlasting*, because it will be
the effect of FLAMING FIRE, which *fire* is called
by our Saviour himself *everlasting*, in the very sentence which dooms wicked men to this destruction.
So that the true sense of the word *everlasting*, in
these *three last texts*, appears to be the *same* with
that in which it is used in the *two former*; where,
being joined with *fire*, the *nature* of the *subject*
obviously fixes it, as we have seen, to a *limited
duration* only.

I may pertinently add to what has been said
above, that *fire*, being a destructive element, powerfully tending, according to the stated laws of
nature, to bring on a solution of continuity in those
bodies that are cast into it ; this alone, one would
think, might be sufficient to satisfy a considerate
reader, that wicked men would not suffer, in the
never-ceasing sense, by the *fire* that is called *everlasting*. We know of no substances that will endure
the force of fire without *dissolution*, in time. And
as *fire* is that by which, in *those texts*, the *punishment* of the wicked is said to be effected, the *nature*
of the *subject* obviously, and, I think, necessarily,
leads us to conceive of this punishment as *everlasting*, not in the sense in which the scripture says
that *God* is *everlasting* ; but in the sense in which
it says the *hills* are *everlasting*, and the *prophets have*
                                                    been

been for everlaſting, that is, for a *limited duration only*. It ſhould ſeem evident, were we confined to theſe texts alone, that there is enough contained in them clearly and fully to ſatisfy an impartial attentive reader, that there is no good reaſon to think, either that the *fire* of hell is *endleſs*, or that the *miſery* of the wicked there will be ſo.

But there will not be left much room for diſpute, upon this head, if we go on, and conſider the *other texts* which ſpeak of the *future miſery.* And here it ought to be particularly remembered, it is not ſaid in any of them, either that the wicked ſhall ALWAYS LIVE IN TORMENT WITHOUT DYING; or that their *bodies*, at the *reſurrection*, ſhall be IMMORTAL, or INCORRUPTIBLE, or INDISSOLUBLE: No; but, on the contrary, it is expreſsly declared, in theſe texts, that the wicked *ſhall reap* CORRUPTION *(a)*; that they *ſhall be* DESTROYED *(b)*; that they *ſhall* PERISH *(c)*; that they ſhall undergo DEATH *(d)*: And this *death*, which they ſhall ſuffer, is ſaid to be the SECOND DEATH *(e)*. And it is remarkable, this *ſecond death* is ſpoken of as that, which ſhall be effected by the *fire* of *hell.* Hence the *ſecond death*, which wicked men ſhall

(a) Gal. vi. 8.   *(b)* Matt. vii. 13. — x. 28.—2 Theſ. i. 9. — 1 Tim. vi. 9. — James iv. 12. — 2 Pet. iii. 16. *(c)* John x. 28.—Luke xiii. 3, 5.—1 Cor. i. 18.—2 Cor. ii. 15.—2 Theſ. ii. 10.—2 Pet. iii. 9.   *(d)* John viii. 51. —Rom. vi. 21, 23.—viii. 13.—2 Cor. ii. 16.—1 John iii. 14. —v. 16.   *(e)* Rev. ii. 11.—xx. 14.—xxi. 8.

paſs

pass through, and their being *caft into the lake of fire*, mean, in the *book* of the Revelation of John, precifely *one* and the *fame thing*; as may be feen in the 20th chapter. Accordingly, in conformity to this reprefentation of their *dying*, and this by *fire*, they are often compared, not to things (if any fuch there be) which will bear the action of *fire*, without being *confumed*; but to CHAFF, and TARES, and WITHERED BRANCHES *(a)*, which, when caft into the fire, muft, without a continued miracle, be *deftroyed*. And in allufion, doubtlefs, to this idea of the *fire of hell*, God is called, not a *perpetual tormenting*, but *confuming*, *fire (b)*. And the *deftruction* of wicked men is connected, by the apoftle Paul, with Chrift's appearing *in flaming fire to take vengeance on them (c)*. This deftruction, it is true, is called an *everlafting deftruction*; but for this reafon, as has been faid, becaufe it will be effected by *fire* that will *laft an age*, or *difpenfation*, during which period *it* fhall certainly and fully be accomplifhed.

It cannot, perhaps, be determined, with any certainty, whether the *fire* of *hell* is to be underftood *literally*, or *figuratively*; but whether we take it in the *former* or *latter* fenfe, it is plain, from the above texts, that the *torments* fignified thereby, inftead of rendering wicked men *never-ceafingly miferable*, will, fooner or later, bring on their *dif-*

(a) Matt. iii. 12.—xiii. 30, 40, 42.—Luke iii. 17.—John xv. 6.　*(b)* Heb. xii. 29.　*(c)* 2 Thef. i. 8.

folution,

folution, deſtruction, or *death.* This is the idea, they very clearly and ſtrongly convey to our minds: Which makes it quite eaſy to fix the ſenſe of the word αιωνιος, *everlaſting,* when joined with the *future miſery*; underſtanding by it, not an *endleſs,* but a *limited,* duration : Which *limited* ſenſe of the word will not appear in the leaſt *ſtrained* or *forced,* if theſe two undoubted facts are attended to. *Firſt,* that this is the very ſenſe in which this word is MOST FREQUENTLY USED throughout the *New Teſtament.* *Secondly,* that the *texts* which join the word αιωνιος, *everlaſting,* with the *miſery* of the wicked, are VERY FEW, in compariſon with thoſe which join with it a *diſſolution, deſtruction,* or *death.*

Nor need we be at any loſs to know, in general, what is ſignified by this *deſtruction,* or *death.* A juſt idea of the *firſt death* will lead us into a right conception of the thing meant by the *ſecond death.*

The *firſt death* was never intended to put an end to our *exiſtence,* but only its *preſent mode,* with all its *connections* and *dependencies.* The *human ſyſtem* is a moſt curious piece of divine workmanſhip. It is compounded of a *material body,* conſiſting of numberleſs parts, admirably put together, and *organiſed,* ſo as to be capable of ſerving a vaſt variety of uſeful purpoſes ; and a *ſpiritual ſubſtance,* or *ſoul,* endued with noble powers, the ſource of thought, ſelf-determining, ſelf-conſcious, and ſuſceptible of pleaſure and pain, indefinitely

T 4 diverſified,

diverfified, both in kind and degree. Between thefe two, though thus different in their natures, the God of heaven has formed a moſt *intimate relation*, or *cloſe union*, in confequence of which, fuch is their dependence on each other, that the *body* is a *mere uſeleſs machine*, only as it is actuated by the *foul:* Neither can the *foul* actuate it, to any of the valuable purpofes of life, till, by the organs of fenfation, it is furniſhed with the materials of knowledge; Nor, when furniſhed, can it exert itfelf but by the *body*, as its *inſtrument.* This is our frame. Thus are we conſtituted *living active agents*, and become fitted for thoſe various employments and enjoyments, whether *bodily* or *mental*, *fecular* or *religious*, wherein confiſts the benefit of life, and in the due proportioning of which lies its perfection and glory in this prefent world, and its preparation for the coming one. Now, *death* puts an *end*, not to the *exiſtence* either of our *bodies* or *fouls*; but to the *relation*, or *union*, there is between them, and their *confequent fubferviency* to each other, and every thing dependent thereon. No more ideas, either *pleafurable* or *painful*, are let into the mind by the *bodily fenfes*; neither can the *mind* itſelf any more exert any of its powers, in the ufual way, in its prefent ſtate. And there is now, in a word, a total period put to all communication with the world; infomuch, that we have no more to do with it, and are no more capable of receiving *pleafure*, or *pain*, from it, than if we had never been brought into exiſtence.

Now,

Now, this notion of the *first death* will lead us into just sentiments, in the general, concerning the *second death*. It is evident, from the scriptures, that the *respective souls* of wicked men will, at the *resurrection*, be again *related*, or *united*, to *particular systems of matter*, somehow or other adapted, by the wisdom of God, to render them capable of *communication* with the *world* they shall then be placed in. Ideas will be let into their minds by the *mediation* of their *bodies*; though the manner, to us, at present, may be inexplicable. And, in the same way, they will become fitted for *sensations* of *pain*, vastly more *various* in *kind*, and *greater* in *degree*, than at present; which yet they will be able to endure for a *much longer continuance*. But, in time, the *torments*, they must suffer, will *end* in their *death*, that is, the *dissolution* of the *union* between their *souls* and *bodies*; upon which, they will have no more concern with *that world*, than they have with *this* upon the coming on of the *first death*.

Should any enquire here, what becomes of wicked men after the *second death?* The answer is easy, upon the foregoing scheme. They are no more turned out of *existence*, than when they died the *first death*; but their *souls*, in God's time, shall be *united again* to their respective *bodies:* And if, by means of the *torments of hell*, they have been *humbled*, and so brought into *subjection* to the government of God, as that they are *meet* for his mercy in Jesus Christ, the *bodies* they shall be re-

lated

lated to fhall, by the divine wifdom and power, be fitted for that *glorious difpenfation,* when *God fhall be all in all.* Or, if any of them fhould be fo fixed in their *obftinacy,* as not to be wrought upon, by the *torments* of the *next ftate,* to yield themfelves up to God as his *willing fubjects,* they fhall *again,* in fome *other form* of exiftence, be put into a ftate of *fuffering* and *difcipline,* till, at length, they are, in a wife and rational way, prepared for *final* and *everlafting happinefs.*

But if the foregoing fcheme fhould be found to have no truth in it, and the wicked are fent to *hell* as fo many *abfolute incurables,* the *fecond death* ought to be confidered as that which will put an *end* to their *exiftence,* both in *foul* and *body,* fo as that they fhall be NO MORE in the creation of God.

The *objection* proceeds :—The fame word, *ever-lafting,* which is joined with the *mifery* of the *wicked,* is joined alfo with the *happinefs* of the *righteous* ; fo that if the *one* is *endlefs,* the *other* muft be fo too : Nay, to fatisfy us of this, it is affirmed of the wicked, " that they fhall go away into ever-" lafting punifhment," in the *fame text* in which it is faid of the righteous, that " they fhall go into " everlafting life."

I anfwer;—If we may fuppofe the foregoing fcheme to have been well fupported, this difficulty is happily and entirely fuperfeded. For, according to the difcovery there made, the *next ftate* will not laft *for ever,* either with refpect to the *righteous,*

teous, or the *wicked*; but for *an age*, or *ages* only : Upon which, the *difpenfation* will come on, when *God* will be himfelf *immediately all in all.* See before.

The *righteous*, it is true, will pafs into this *final difpenfation*, not by *dying again*, but probably in fome way analogous to *that*, in which the believers that are *alive* on the earth, at Chrift's fecond coming, fhall pafs into the *refurrettion-ftate:* Upon which account, their life and happinefs may properly be faid *never to have an end.* But ftill, the *next ftate* they will be in, and, I believe, their *next mode* of exiftence, with all its *connettions* and *dependencies*, will come to a *period*, and, by a quick and pleafing tranfmutation, be fwallowed up in that *grand œconomy*, of which *God* will be *immediate head* and *fovereign.* So that the whole difficulty, arifing from the application of the word αιωνιος, *everlafting*, to the *next ftate* of the *wicked*, as well as of the *righteous*, and in the *fame verfe* too, is entirely fuperfeded; becaufe it means the fame thing, with refpect to them both, namely, a *limited duration only.* This I take to be the true, and beft anfwer to this *difficulty* ; and it abfolutely removes away, even the very foundation upon which it is built.

But if we fhould fuppofe the foregoing fyftem to have no truth in it, and that the *next ftate*, agreeably to the common opinion, is FINAL with refpect both to the *righteous* and the *wicked:* I fay, if we fhould fuppofe this, it will not follow,

I   that

that the *wicked* muſt be *miſerable without end*, becauſe the *righteous* are *thus happy* ; though the ſame
word, αιωνιος, *everlaſting*, is joined both with
the *puniſhment* of the *one*, and the *happineſs* of the
other. And for theſe reaſons :

1. There is an obſervable difference between
the application of the word αιωνιος, *everlaſting*, to
the *righteous*, and to the *wicked*. It is but *five
times* applied to the *future ſtate* of the *wicked*
throughout the *New Teſtament* : Whereas it is applied to the *future ſtate* of the *righteous* more than
forty ; which I do but mention *in tranſitu*. It is
of more importance to remark here, *this word*,
when applied to the *righteous*, is moſtly joined
with the word LIFE, ſo as that, if it is underſtood
in the *endleſs* ſenſe, we muſt ſuppoſe they ſhall live
in happineſs *without ever dying again :* Whereas
this word, when applied to the *wicked*, is never
once connected with their LIFE, but always with
the *fire* they ſhall depart into, or with that *damnation, puniſhment*, or *deſtruction*, which ſhall be effected by means of this *fire*. Now, ſhould the *fire*
of *hell* be *everlaſting*, in the *never-ceaſing* ſenſe of
the word, there is not the *ſame reaſon* to ſuppoſe
that the *wicked* ſhall *live without end* in this *fire*,
as that the *righteous* ſhall *live without end* in *happineſs* ; becauſe the word, *everlaſting*, is joined
with the LIFE of the *righteous*, while it is joined
only with the *fire* the *wicked* ſhall go into, or with
their *puniſhment*, or *deſtruction*, that is hereby effected. And it is a ſuppoſeable caſe, at leaſt,
that

that the *fire* of *hell* may be *endless*, and not the LIFE
of the *wicked*. And if this *fire* may be *endless*,
while the LIFE of the wicked is not so ; their *damnation*, *punishment*, or *destruction*, may be called
everlasting, on account of this *endless fire*, and not
with a view to the *duration* of their LIFE in it.
This, I am sure, is a possible supposition ; which
is enough to show, that the *wicked* MAY NOT endure *never-ceasing misery*, while the *righteous* MAY
enjoy *never-ending happiness* ; though the same
word, *everlasting*, is used in both their cases.

2. There is a very *wide difference* between *happiness* and *misery*, *reward* and *punishment* ; which
may make it proper to understand the word *everlasting* in a *different sense* with respect to these *different subjects*. Common reason, as has been observed, teaches us to explain this term, which is
capable of being understood, either of *limited* or
unlimited duration, by the *different natures* of the
subjects to which it is applied. And as the *subjects*,
in the present case, are *widely different*, this ought
to be the rule of interpretation here ; which, if it
is, a *different* construction of the word may reasonably be admitted. It perfectly falls in with the
notions mankind universally entertain of the *infinite benevolence* of the Deity, to interpret the word
everlasting, in the *endless* sense, when joined with
a *reward*, which is the gift of grace ; to be sure,
there is nothing in such a construction, that carries
in it the least repugnancy to the ideas we have of
the attributes, and government, of God. But will
any

any fay, that there is the *like reafon* to underftand
the word *everlafting*, in the *fame fenfe*, when joined
with *punifhment*, which is God's *ftrange work*, and
what he takes *no pleafure in?* Does the doctrine
of *never-ending torments* agree fo well with the idea
of *infinite mercy*, an allowed effential attribute of
the *only good God*, as that of *never-ending happinefs?*
Does not the *one*, at once, approve itfelf to the
univerfal reafon of men, while the *other* cannot,
without great difficulty, if at all, be made to confift with it? As thefe *fubjects* are thus vaftly *different* in their *natures*, why fhould not the *duration*,
fignified by the term *everlafting*, be fo too? Why
may we not, yea, why ought we not, to *limit* the
word, with refpect to the *one* ; while we *extend* it,
with refpect to the *other*, as far as it will bear.
But,

3. It is moft of all worthy of confideration, that
we are naturally and obvioufly led to interpret the
word αιωνιος, *everlafting*, when joined with the
happinefs of the *righteous*, in the *endlefs* fenfe, from
other texts which determine *this* to be its *meaning :*
Whereas we have not the *like reafon* to underftand
the *fame word* in the *fame fenfe*, when joined with
the *mifery* of the *wicked*. The citing here a few
texts of fcripture will fully illuftrate the propriety
and force of this remark. Luke xx. 36, Ουτε απο-
θανειν ετι δυναντ]αι " NEITHER CAN THEY DIE ANY
" MORE, for they are equal unto the angels, and
" are the children of God, being the children of
" the refurrection."—1 Cor. ix. 25, " They do it
" to

" to obtain a corruptible crown; but we, αφθαρ⸃ον,
" AN INCORRUPTIBLE."—Chap. xv. 42, " So alſo
" is the reſurrection of the dead; it is ſown in
" corruption, it is raiſed, εν αφθαρσια, IN INCOR-
" RUPTION."—52d verſe, " The dead ſhall be
" raiſed, αφθαρ⸃οι, INCORRUPTIBLE."—53d verſe,
" This corruptible muſt put on, αφθαρσιαν, INCOR-
" RUPTION; and this mortal muſt put on, αθα-
" νασιαν, IMMORTALITY."—54th verſe, " When
" this corruptible ſhall have put on, αφθαρσιαν, IN-
" CORRUPTION; and this mortal ſhall have put on
" αθανασιαν, IMMORTALITY."—1 Theſ. iv. 17,
" So ſhall we be, παντοτε, ever with the Lord."—
2 Tim. i. 10, " Jeſus Chriſt, who hath aboliſhed
" death, and brought LIFE and IMMORTALITY,
" ζωην και αφθαρσιαν, to light, through the goſpel."
—Heb. xii. 28, " We receiving a kingdom that
" CANNOT BE MOVED, ασαλευ⸃ον."—1 Pet. i. 4,
" He hath begotten us—to an inheritance, αφθαρ-
" τον και αμιαν⸃ον και αμαραν⸃ον, INCORRUPTIBLE,
" UNDEFILED, and that FADETH NOT AWAY."
—Rev. ii. 11, " He that overcometh ſhall not be
" hurt, εκ του θαναʃου δευʃερου of the SECOND DEATH."
—Chap. xxi. 4, " God ſhall wipe away all tears
" from their eyes, and, ο θαναʃος ουχ εσʃαι ετι,
" THERE SHALL BE NO MORE DEATH."

Now, as the above ſcriptures expreſsly affirm,
that the *righteous*, at the *reſurrection*, ſhall be made
INCORRUPTIBLE, IMMORTAL, and that they SHALL
NOT DIE ANY MORE, we are abſolutely obliged (if
the *next* ſtate is *final*, the ſuppoſition I am now
arguing

arguing upon), as we would not set the scripture at odds with itself, to understand the word αιωνιος, *everlasting*, when joined with the *life* of the *righteous*, in the *endless sense*. And could the *like texts* be produced, wherein it is affirmed of the *wicked*, that they shall be IMMORTAL, or INCORRUPTIBLE, or that they SHALL NOT DIE AGAIN, after the *general resurrection*, we should be obliged to put the like *endless* sense upon the word *everlasting*, when joined with the *torments* they must suffer. But, instead of their being ever represented as IMMORTAL, or INCORRUPTIBLE, or NOT AGAIN SUBJECTED TO DIE, it is most peremptorily affirmed that they shall REAP CORRUPTION, PERISH, be DE-STROYED, and DIE A SECOND TIME; which fixes the sense of the word *everlasting*, when joined with the *misery* they shall be doomed to undergo, *limit-ing* its meaning to *an age*, or *period of duration* only. This I call a decisive answer to *this branch* of the *objection*, upon supposition that the *next* is the *final* state of men.

And whereas it is said, that the *same word* is used, in the *same verse*, to point out the *duration* both of the *future misery*, and of the *future happi-ness* ; and that it would be unreasonable and ab-surd to interpret the *same word*, in the *same sen-tence*, in two *different* senses : I answer, the fact contained in this plea is readily allowed to be true ; for, in Matt. xxv. 46, αιωνιος, *everlasting*, is the *word* that is joined both with the *punishment* of the *wicked*, and with the *happy life* of the *righteous*.

But,

But, inftead of its being *unreasonable* or *absurd*, it is highly *fit* and *proper*, that we fhould underftand *this word* as applied to the *righteous* in *one fense*, and as applied to the *wicked* in *another*; that is, if the *next* is the *final* ftate of men, the fuppofition we are now arguing upon. The *reasons* given in anfwer to the foregoing branch of this *objection* are equally pertinent here, and make it neceffary to put a *different fense* upon the word *everlasting*, according to the *different nature* of the *subjects* treated of in this *verse*. But I have one thing to offer further, which, if attended to, will, I believe, fufficiently fhew, that it is no fuch *absurdity*, as is pretended, the *objectors themselves* being judges, to interpret this *same word differently*, even in the *same fentence*. It is this:

There are two other fentences, in the New Tef- tament, in each of which this word αιωνιος, *ever- lasting*, is *twice used*, but, in the opinion of *these objectors*, in a *different fense*. As in Rom. xvi. part of the 25th and part of the 26th verfes, "According "to the myftery which was kept fecret [χρονοις "αιωνιοις] fince the world began; but is now made "manifeft—according to the commandment [του "αιωνιου Θεου] of the everlafting God." And, in Tit. i. 2, "In hope [ζωης αιωνιου] of eternal life, "which God, that cannot lie, promifed [προ χρονων "αιωνιων] before the world began." In both thefe fcripture fentences, the word αιωνιος is *twice* ufed, but, upon the principles of the *objectors*, in a *different fense*. In the *one*, αιωνιος, as joined with Θεος, is

U   taken

taken in the *endless* senfe ; whereas, as joined with χρονος, it can mean only *an age*, or *period of duration:* And it is accordingly fo tranflated in our Bibles. In the other, αιωνιου, joined with ζωης, muft, in the fenfe of the *objection*, be underftood of a *never-ending duration*; whereas it can mean nothing more than *an age*, or *difpenfation*, as joined with χρονου : And it is accordingly fo rendered by the tranflators of the New Teftament. It is evident then, in point of fact, and by the *practical* acknowledgment even of the *objectors* themfelves, that the word αιωνιος, *everlafting*, may be ufed in a *different fenfe*, and the *very one* we are pleading for, and in the *fame fentence* too. So that they cannot complain of us for being either arbitrary, or abfurd, in the interpretation we put upon Matt. xxv. 46, without condemning themfelves for the fenfe they put upon the above-quoted texts.

It will, perhaps, be pleaded here, *common reafon*, in the produced cafes, eafily difcerns a *neceffity*, from the things fpoken of, to interpret the word αιωνιος *differently*, according to their *different natures.* The fame may be faid in the prefent cafe. For *reafon* difcovers a *wide difference* between the *fubjects* here treated of. Befides which, the fcripture exprefsly declares, concerning the *righteous*, on the one hand, THAT THEY SHALL NEVER DIE ANY MORE; and as exprefsly, on the other hand, concerning the *wicked*, that THEY SHALL DIE A SECOND TIME: Which is enough, one would think, to make a confiderate reader underftand the word

everlafting

everlasting in a *corresponding sense* with respect to them both, that is, in the *endless* sense, with respect to the *former*; and the *limited one*, with respect to the *latter*.

This *branch* of the objection is still further enforced by the following remark, namely, that the word αιωνιος, which is used to point out the *duration* of the *future torments*, is the *very word* which is used also to point out the *absolute eternity of God*. But this criticism I take to be of very little weight; insomuch that I should not have mentioned it, but that I have often heard, and seen, it urged in the present controversy. It might indeed be mentioned to good purpose, could it be shown, that the word αιωνιος is joined, in scripture, with nothing but what is *strictly eternal*: But, as it is otherwise in fact, this remark can be of no real importance; because, if it proves any thing, it proves a great deal too much. If the *punishment* of the wicked must be *never-ending*, MERELY because the word αιωνιος, which is sometimes joined with the word *God*, is joined with *that* also; it will follow, as this same word is joined with the *earth*, and *hills*, and *generations*, and *prophets*, that they must all of them be *strictly* and *absolutely eternal*; the absurdity of which is too glaring not to be, at once, perceived. The plain truth is, the *nature* of the *subject* treated of, together with *other scriptures*, must always be taken into consideration, in order to fix the *precise meaning* of this word, with any degree of certainty. Nay, the *eternity*

U 2   even

even of God himfelf is not to be collected *merely* from the *force* of this *word*; but from the *previ-oufly known nature* of the *fubject*, and the *word*'s being capable of this *unlimited* conftruction; as has been obferved already.

The *objection* goes on;—The *mifery* of the wicked is not only faid to be *everlafting*, but FOR EVER; and, as though this was not fufficiently expreffive of its *endlefs continuance*, it is further declared to be FOR EVER AND EVER, the ftrongeft phrafe ufed, in fcripture, to defcribe the *proper eternity* of the Supreme Being.

The texts, in which the *mifery* of the wicked is faid to be FOR EVER, are only *two*.—2 Pet. ii. 17, " To whom the mift of darknefs is referved " FOR EVER."—And verfe the 12th of Jude's Epiftle, " To whom is referved the blacknefs of " darknefs FOR EVER." But as the word αιων differs from the word αιωνιος, no otherwife than *eternity* differs from *eternal*, the *one* being a *fubftantive*, the *other* an *adjective*, as the grammarians fpeak; I have nothing to do here but to refer the reader to what has been faid, in the preceding pages, upon the word *eternal*, or *everlafting*.

The texts, which reprefent the *mifery* of the wicked as what will be FOR EVER AND EVER, are *three*, and no more.—Rev. xiv. 9, 10, 11, " If " any man worfhip the beaft, and his image, and " receive his mark in his forehead, or in his hand, " the fame fhall drink of the wrath of God, which " is poured out, without mixture into the cup of
" his

" his indignation: And he fhall be tormented with
" fire and brimftone in the prefence of the holy
" angels, and in the prefence of the Lamb. And
" THE SMOKE OF THEIR TORMENT ASCENDETH UP
" BEFORE GOD FOR EVER AND EVER, and they
" have no reft day nor night."—Chap. xix. 1, 2, 3,
" And after thefe things I heard a great voice of
" much people in heaven, faying, Alleluja; fal-
" vation, and glory, and honour, and power, unto
" the Lord our God: For true and righteous are
" his judgments; for he hath judged the great
" whore which did corrupt the earth with her forni-
" cation, and hath avenged the blood of his fervants
" at her hand. And again they faid, Alleluja;
" and HER SMOKE ROSE UP FOR EVER AND EVER."
—Chap. xx. 7, 8, 9, 10, " And when the thoufand
" years are expired, Satan fhall be loofed out of
" his prifon, and fhall go out to deceive the na-
" tions, which are in the four quarters of the
" earth, Gog and Magog, to gather them toge-
" ther to battle; the number of them is as the
" fand of the fea. And they went upon the
" breadth of the earth, and compaffed the camp
" of the faints about, and the beloved city; and
" fire came down from God out of heaven,
" and devoured them. And the Devil that de-
" ceived them was caft into the lake of fire and
" brimftone, where the beaft and falfe prophet
" are, and SHALL BE TORMENTED DAY AND NIGHT
" FOR EVER AND EVER."

The reader is defired carefully to confider thefe

U 3   paffages,

paffages, which I have thus tranfcribed at large, that he may be the better able to judge, whether they refer, as is pleaded, to the *torments* which wicked men will endure, in the *refurrection-ftate*, for the fins they committed in this. It does not appear certain to me, that they have this reference ; and much might eafily be faid to fhow the contrary : But fhould it be allowed, that they have this reference, they are fo far from fpeaking of the torments of *finners in common*, that the *two former* relate only to the *worfhippers of the beaft* ; and the *latter*, to the *Devil*, and a *rabble-rout of men*, whom he will be permitted to deceive, after the *millennium* is over, with *the beaft* and *falfe prophet* *: And confequently, thefe finners, which include, comparatively fpeaking, but a very fmall part of the *wicked*

---

* It cannot, perhaps, be certainly determined, of whom it is here faid, *And* [βασανισθησονται] *they fhall be tormented.* I have gone upon the largeft fuppofition, taking in the *beaft* and *falfe prophet*, as well as the *Devil* and *Gog* and *Magog*. Mr. Whifton [The Eternity of Hell Torments confidered, page 50] conftrues the words thus, ' *And they* [*Gog* and *Magog*, ' with the *Devil* himfelf] *fhall be tormented*;' obferving, that ' it ' is not directly faid here, that *the beaft and the falfe prophet*, ' but only the *Devil*, with *Gog* and *Magog*, fhall be *fo long* ' *tormented*.' And if the *Devil* be confidered as a *collective noun*, by which we are to underftand the *evil angels*, I fee not but the *Devil* only may be the *antecedent* to βασανισθησονται. In the preceding verfe, *Gog* and *Magog* are fpoken of as *punifhed* by *immediate infliction* from God. In this, as I imagine, the *evil angels*, who DECEIVED *Gog* and *Magog*, and FOR deceiving them, are fpoken of as *punifhed* likewife, and in the *place* where

wicked there have been among men, in all fucceffive ages, from the beginning of the world, are the *only ones*, with whofe *torment* we have a right to conneƈt the *duration*, whatever it is, that is pointed out by the phrafe, ɛıς τους αıωνας των αıωνων, tranf-lated, in our Bibles, FOR EVER AND EVER.

But, to give the *objeƈtion* all the advantage that can be defired, let it be fuppofed, that thefe paf-fages relate, not only to the *future torments*, but to thofe torments as they will be fuffered by *wicked men in common.* And what is the confequence herefrom? Not that they will fuffer them in the *never-ending fenfe:* And for this very good reafon, becaufe the *above phrafe* is obvioufly capable of being underftood of a *limited,* as well as *endlefs,* duration; and may, to fay the leaft, be as properly rendered *for ages of ages,* as *for ever and ever.* We have already feen, that the word αıων, in the *fingu-lar* number, almoft perpetually fignifies *an age*; and it would be very ftrange, if its being ufed in the *plural* fhould effentially alter its meaning. It is certain it does not. For it is remarkable, though

where the *beaft* and *falfe prophet* were punifhed, for which reafon *they* are here brought in, and not becaufe they are to be looked upon as *partners* in this *punifhment*, as they were not partners in the fin that occafioned it. But however this be, it is worthy of our particular remark, that, excepting *this*, and the *two* foregoing places, which yet do not relate to *finners in general,* but to finners in the *times of Antichrift,* and in *the days of Gog* and *Magog,* the *duration* conneƈted with the *mifery* the wicked fhall undergo, in the refurreƈtion, is no where in *all the Bible* faid to be ɛıς τους αıωνας των αıωνων; no, nor ɛıς τους αıωνας, fimply in the *plural,* without a *reduplica-tion.*

it

it is to be met with, in the *Septuagint,* in *several*
places, it is used in *them all* to signify nothing
more than the *plural* of *an age,* that is, a duration
that is considered as made up of *more ages* or *periods
than one.* Such are the texts that follow.—2 Chron.
vi. 2. " I have built an house of habitation for thee,
" and a place for thy dwelling for ever," εις τους
αιωνας, *for ages.*—Psalm xlviii. 14. " He will be our
" guide even to death," εις τους αιωνας, *through the
several ages or periods of life:* So the *Seventy* render
the original words על מות, which, in our English
Bibles, are more literally translated *even to death.*—
Psalm lxi. 4. " I will abide in thy tabernacle for
" ever," εις τους αιωνας, *for ages.*—Psalm lxxii. 17.
" His name" [that is, his kingdom, his regal admi-
nistration] " shall endure for ever," εις τους αιωνας, *for
ages.* Whether these words are spoken of *David,* or
Christ, the *son* of *David,* they mean nothing more. See
the next text but two.—Psalm cxlv. 13. " Thy king-
" dom is an everlasting kingdom," βασιλεια παντων
των αιωνων, *a kingdom over all ages.*—Dan. ii. 4. " Then
" spake the Chaldeans,—O king, live for ever," εις
τους αιωνας, *for many days, long periods of time.*—
Ver. 44. " And in the days of these kings shall the God
" of heaven set up a kingdom,—and it shall stand,
" εις τους αιωνας, for ever." The meaning of this *for
ever* is punctually ascertained by the apostle *Paul,*
who says, 1 Cor. xv. 28, that " when all enemies
" shall be subdued, Christ himself shall be subject to
" him who put all things under him, that God may
" be all in all." It is, in like manner, observable,
the *plural* of this αιων is most commonly, if not
always,

always, ufed, in the New Teftament, to point out a *duration*, confifting of *ages, difpenfations*, or *periods*; as may be feen by taking a view of the following texts.—Luke i. 33. " And he fhall reign " over the houfe of Jacob, εις τους αιωνας, for ever;" the meaning of which *for ever* has been above explained from the apoftle Paul.—1 Cor. ii. 7. " The " hidden wifdom which God ordained before the " world," προ των αιωνων, *before the ages*, " to our " glory."—Chap. x. 11. " All thefe things are writ- " ten for our admonition, upon whom the ends of " the world," των αιωνων, *of the ages*, " are come." —Eph. ii. 7. " That, in ages to come, εν τοις αιωσι " απερχομενοις, he might fhew the exceeding riches " of his grace."—Chap. iii. 9. " The myftery which " from the beginning of the world," απο των αιωνων, *from former ages*, "hath been hid in God."—Col. i. 26. " The myftery which hath been hid, απο των αιωνων, " from ages, and from generations."—Heb. i. 2. " By whom alfo he made the worlds, τους αιωνας." —ix. 26. " Now once in the end of the world," επι συντελεια των αιωνων, *at the clofe of the ages*, " he ap- " peared to put away fin."—xi. 3. " By faith we " underftand that the worlds, τους αιωνας, were made " by the word of God." Now, if αιωνες, in the plural, is thus frequently ufed to fignify a duration that confifts of *more ages* or *periods than one*, its being *doub- led* cannot make it improper to underftand it in the fame general fenfe ftill; but is rather a good reafon why we ought fo to underftand it. For a *dura- tion* containing in it a *collection of ages* is, at once, intelligible; but a duration *for eternities of eter- nities*

nities. is, to fay the leaft, a very uncouth mode of expreffion, and would found as harfh in Greek, as it does in Englifh, if the natural force of the Greek word, αιων, was the *fame* with the Englifh word, *eternity.* It is therefore very clear to me, that the *plural* of αιων, even when *doubled,* as in the phrafe, εις τους αιωνας των αιωνων, *may* always be underftood in this fenfe, and perhaps *ought* always to be fo. This is certainly its meaning in Rev. xi. 15, " The kingdoms of this world are become " the kingdoms of our Lord, and of his Chrift; and " he fhall reign," εις τους αιωναι των αιωνων, *for ages of ages.* This fenfe an infpired apoftle has virtually or conftructively put upon this phrafe, by affuring us, 1 Cor. xv. 24—28, that the time will come, when Chrift fhall *deliver up his kingdom,* and be himfelf *a fubject* in *another kingdom* that will *fucceed in its room,* having the *Father* at its head, as its *immediate King* and *Sovereign.* This alfo is its meaning, Eph. iii. 21, where the *doxology* to God is expreffed in thefe words, " Unto him be " glory in the church, by Jefus Chrift," εις πασας τας γενεας του αιωνος των αιωνων, *through all fucceffions of future ages,* or literally, *to all generations of the age of ages.*

It ought to be well regarded here, the phrafe we are examining is to be met with, for the moft part, in the *New Teftament doxologies* to *God* or *Chrift.* And there is no manner of need to fuppofe, that the facred penmen, when they *thus* ufed this phrafe, had it in their view to fpeak *metaphyfically* of a *ftrict* and *proper eternity.* It will every whit as

well

well anfwer all the ends of piety and devotion, if
we underftand them as fpeaking in a *popular* way
only, and meaning by thefe *afcriptions of glory*, in
regard of *duration*, the fame thing that is meant
in Eph. iii. 21, which we juft now quoted. And
there will be the more reafon to think thus, if
we compare the *doxologies* in the *New Teftament*,
with thofe in the *Old*. The *latter* are expreffed
[1 Chron. xvi. 36. — xxix. 10. — Pfalm xli. 13.
—cvi. 48.—Dan. ii. 20.] in that form, " Bleffed
" be the Lord, the Lord God of Ifrael," απο του
αιωνος και εως του αιωνος ; that is, in the Englifh tranflation, " from everlafting to everlafting:" But not
with fo much propriety as if it had been rendered,
from age even to age. To ufe here the words of
Mr. Hallett, in his *note* upon Pfalm xli. 13,
" Bleffed be the Lord God of Ifrael, from ever-
" lafting, and to everlafting ! Amen, and Amen."
' I am apt to think,' fays he, ' that many Eng-
' lifh readers fuppofe, that the words, *from ever-*
' *lafting*, fignify a duration that was *paft* in the
' days of the Pfalmift. But, upon fecond thoughts,
' the Englifh reader will perceive, that this can-
' not poffibly be. The Pfalmift here expreffes
' his defire, that *God may be bleffed*. But it is im-
' poffible to defire, that God may be bleffed *here-*
' *tofore*. To fay, *Bleffed be God in paft ages*, would
' be ridiculous.—The *text* then muft be rendered,
' *Bleffed be the Lord God of Ifrael* FROM AGE TO
' AGE ! that is, from this time forth, throughout
' all ages. Every one will allow that the Hebrew
' word, *Olam*, here rendered, *everlafting*, does fre-
' quently

' quently fignify *an age*, or *generation*. Nor will
' any one object to this interpretation the word
' AND ; *from everlafting* AND *to everlafting*, as if
' this would hinder us from rendering the ex-
' preffion, *from age to age* ; when he fhall confider,
' that the word, *and*, in fuch like expreffions, is
' redundant, or fuperfluous, in our language, what-
' ever grace it adds to the Hebrew phrafe. Thus
' the Hebrew expreffion, 2 Chron. ix. 26, is lite-
' rally to be rendered,—*from the river* and *unto*
' *the land of the Philiftines*. Our tranflators have
' rendered the Hebrew particle by, *even*;—*from*
' *the river* even *unto the land of the Plilifines*. It
' would have been as well if they had dropt it
' quite, and had faid, *from the river to the land*
' *of the Philiftines*. See alfo 2 Chron. xxx. 5.
' So the paffage of the Pfalm now under con-
' fideration may be rendered, *Bleffed be God, from*
' *age even to age*, or, more fimply, *from age to age*.
' In the fame fenfe the expreffion is to be under-
' ftood, Pfalm ciii. 17. *The mercy of the Lord is*
' *from everlafting to everlafting*, or rather, *from*
' *age to age*, that is, from this age to the next,
' and fo on throughout all future ages.' *Notes on*
peculiar texts, pag. 75, 76.——In the fame fenfe
ftill, I would add, we muft interpret, Jer. vii. 7.
and xxv. 5, " The land that I gave to you, and to
" your fathers, for ever and ever, απ' αιωνος και εως
αιωνος, *from age to age*. And this is the fenfe alfo
in which, as it feems to me, we are to underftand
the *doxologies* in the *New Teftament*. It is plain,
they *may* be thus underftood : Nor is there any
neceffity

neceſſity to give the *duration* ſignified by them an higher meaning. And we may the rather be ſatisfied of this, if we conſider ſtill further, that, in the *Septuagint*, the phraſe, εις αιωνα αιωνος, in our Engliſh Bibles uſually *for ever*, and the yet ſtronger one, εις τον αιωνα και εις τον αιωνα του αιωνος, in the ſame Bibles *for ever and ever*, are frequently to be met with, and always, as I think, to be underſtood in *this ſenſe*. To be ſure, they are uſed, in a variety of places, ſo as not to be eaſily capable of an *higher* meaning. We ſhall give inſtances with reſpeĉt to them both.

The *firſt* of theſe phraſes cannot well be taken in any *other ſenſe* in the following texts.—Pſalm xxxvii. 28, 29. " The ſeed of the wicked ſhall " be cut off. The righteous ſhall inherit the " land, and dwell therein for ever," εις αιωνα αιωνος, *from generation to generation.*—Pſalm lxi. 8. " So will I ſing praiſe to thy name for " ever," εις αιωνα αιωνος, *from one age or period af my life to another*; for the following words are, " that I may daily perform my vows."—Pſalm cxii. 9. " He hath diſperſed, he hath given to " the poor, his righteouſneſs endureth for ever," η δικαιοσυνη αυτου μενει εις τον αιωνα του αιωνος, *he is a merciful man through the ſeveral periods or ages of his life.*—Pſalm cxxxii. 13, 14. " The " Lord hath choſen Zion, he hath deſired it for " his habitation; this is my reſt for ever," εις αιωνα αιωνος, *from age to age.*

The *other* mentioned *ſtronger* phraſe is uſed, in the like ſenſe, in the following places.—Pſalm

xlvii. 13, 14. " Mark ye well her bulwarks, con-
" fider her palaces, that ye may tell it to the ge-
" neration following; for this God is our God for
" ever and ever," εις τον αιωνα και εις τον αιωνα του
αιωνος. It is plain, the *duration* fignified by this
phrafe, in this place, can mean no more than
one age upon another ; becaufe it is the truth of
fact, that God has long fince ceafed to be the *God
of the Jews*, in the fenfe here fpoken of.—Pfalm
cxix. 44. " So fhall I keep thy law continually for
" ever and ever," εις τον αιωνα και εις τον αιωνα του
αιωνος, *as long as I have a being, through the feveral
ages or periods of my life on earth.*—Pfalm cxlv. 2.
" Every day will I blefs thee, and I will praife thy
" name for ever and ever," εις τον αιωνα, &c.
through every period of my life.—Verfe 21. " Let
" all flefh blefs his holy name for ever and ever,"
εις τον αιωνα, &c. *from age to age, and through
every age.*—Pfalm cxlviii. 6. " He hath eftablifh-
" ed them" [the fun, and moon, and heavens]
" for ever and ever," εις τον αιωνα, &c. *throughout
all ages.*

It is, I would hope, abundantly evident, by this
time, that the phrafe, εις τους αιωνας των αιωνων,
ought to be conftrued, *for ages of ages.* Thus
much, at leaft, is indifputably clear, that it *may*,
without impropriety, be thus interpreted; and for
this very good reafon, becaufe the *Bible* itfelf has
taught us this ufe of it. From whence the conclufion
is, that the *future torments* cannot be proved to be
abfolutely endlefs, MERELY from the joining of this
ph rafe with them. The *nature* of the *thing*, or

I　　　　　　　　　　　　　　　　　　　　　*other*

other texts of fcripture, muft be taken into confideration. And if fo, the greater part of what
has been offered to fhew the *reafonablenefs*, and
neceffity, of underftanding the word, *everlafting*,
not in the *endlefs*, but *limited* fenfe, is equally pertinent here, and will as ftrongly evince, that *this
phrafe* alfo muft have the like meaning.

Nor is it of any fignificancy, in point of argument, that *this phrafe* is fometimes applied to *God*.
For if, from the *force* of it, fimply confidered, the
abfolute eternity of God could be argued, we might
as well argue the *abfolute eternity* of the *land* of
Canaan, and of the *fucceffive generations of men*, becaufe this phrafe, or one equivalent, is joined with
each of them, as well as with *God*. ' Reafon affures
us, that God is a Being whofe *duration* will have
no *end*; and it is from this *previoufly known nature*
of God, and not fimply from the *force* of this
phrafe, that we interpret it, when applied to God,
as meaning a *duration without end.* And when we
can, upon as good a foundation, interpret the *fame
phrafe*, in the *fame* fenfe, when applied to the *future
mifery*, then fuch a conftruction may reafonably be
admitted ; but not till then. The plain truth is,
it muft be faid of the *phrafe,* εις τους αιωνας των
αιωνων, as of the *word* αιωνιος, that the *duration,* intended to be pointed out by it, cannot be determined by the *naked force* of the *phrafe itfelf* ; but
the *fubjeft* with which it is connected muft be
taken into confideration, as alfo *other texts* which
fpeak of the fame thing. And, in this view of
the

the matter, it is as certain, that it ought to be conftrued *for ages of ages*, and in this fenfe only, as that the *wicked*, in the *refurrection-ftate*, will not be INCORRUPTIBLE, but *fhall* DIE A SECOND TIME; in declaring of which the fcripture is very peremptory and exprefs, as has been proved.

I may pertinently fubjoin to what has been faid, that it is not certain, that *every individual finner*, in the future ftate, fhall be *tormented* the *whole duration*, pointed out by the phrafe εις τους αιωναι των αιωνων, though it fhould be allowed to fignify no more than *for ages of ages*. For, as is obferved by Mr. Nichol Scot, ' It fhould not be fuppofed, ' that, as by the *beaft* and *falfe prophet* [in the laft ' of the above texts] are meant, not *two fingle per-* ' *fons*, but *collective bodies* of men, fo by the *Devil's* ' being *caft into this lake* (if it relate to the future ' judgment) may be intended, not merely that ' the *individual perfon*, fo called, was caft therein, ' but the *Devil* and *his angels* inclufive; for it is a ' *fire prepared for the Devil and his angels:* And, if ' thofe *collective bodies* are intended, it may be ' ftrictly true, that, as *collective bodies*, their tor- ' ture may laft for *many ages*, without any neceffity ' of inferring from hence, the *fame duration* of tor- ' ture holds true of *any*, much lefs *every individual*, ' that belongs to them ; for as the *future judgment*, ' from the nature of the thing, muft be a work ' of very confiderable time, fo as that the indivi- ' duals, of which thofe *bodies* are compofed, may ' be *fucceffively* tried and condemned, and *fucces-*

5

' *fively*

' *fively* caft into this *lake of fire*, in order to be *con-*
' *fumed* there : And confequently, how true foever
' it is, that the *fum total* of this judiciary proceed-
' ing may be *for ages of ages*, it will not neceffarily
' follow, that the *torture of any*, much lefs of *every*
' *individual*, fhould continue for that length of
' time. Nor fhould it be overlooked, that, as
' this diftinction has its foundation in the *nature*
' of the *thing*, fo it feems to have been favoured
' by as remarkable a variation in the *fcripture ftyle* ;
' for, after having faid [in the former of the above
' texts], " If any one worfhip the beaft, the fame
" [και αυτος, *he alfo*] drinketh of the wine of the
" wrath of God, and he fhall be tormented with
" fire and brimftone," it is not fubjoined, *and the*
' *fmoke of* HIS *torment*, in the fingular number,
' which might feem to have determined the pro-
' pofition to *individuals* ; but " the fmoke of THEIR
" [αυτων] torment," in the plural, and which, con-
' fequently, may relate to *collective bodies* ; which
' laft propofition may be very true, without any
' neceffity of inferring, that *any*, much lefs *every*
' *individual*, that belongs to thofe *collective bodies*,
' fhall be tormented for fuch a length of time.'

' And what renders this criticifm the more pro-
' bable is, that we find terms of much the fame
' import ufed by the *prophetic fpirit*, in that cafe,
' where a long feries of *national* calamities are
' defcribed, that is, in a cafe where, from the
' *nature* of the *thing*, there is, indeed, an *uninter-*
' *rupted* fuffering of the *collective* body, but withal

X

' only

" only a *succeſſive* suffering of *individuals.* " My
" sword (says the prophet Isaiah, chapter xxxiv.)
" shall come down upon Idumea, — and the dust
" thereof shall be turned into brimstone, and the
" land thereof shall become burning pitch; it
" shall not be quenched night nor day, the
" smoke thereof shall go up for ever : from gene-
" ration to generation it shall lie waste, none shall
" pass through it for ever and ever."

This excellent writer may, perhaps, be mistaken,
when he suggests, that the *individuals,* of which
the *collective body* of the wicked is made up, may
be *succeſſively condemned,* and *caſt into the fire of hell*;
and that they may be spoken of as tormented in
this fire *for ages of ages,* not because this will hold
true of *any* of the *individuals,* but because, being
succeſſively condemned, and thrown into *the lake of
fire,* it may take up the *duration* signified by the
phrase, *for ages of ages,* before they will *all* be *deſtroyed,* or *confumed,* in this fire : In this, I say, the
above author is probably mistaken. For it is not
intimated in any of the descriptions we have of the
future judgment, as though the *wicked* would be
succeſſively, that is, *individually, one by one,* condemned, and sent into the place of coming torment : But, on the contrary, they are all, as a *collective body,* represented by our Saviour (particularly in Matt. xxv.) as standing before his *judgment-
feat*; and the *judicial fentence* is pronounced, not
against the *individuals,* in *fucceſſion*; but the *whole
body,* at one and the same time : And they are
                                          accordingly

accordingly ſpoken of as *going away,* in conſequence of this ſentence, *into everlaſting puniſhment,*
not *ſucceſſively,* but *all at once.*

It muſt therefore (according to this account of
the *future judgment*) hold true of *ſome* of the *individuals,* conſtituting the *collective body* of the *wicked,*
that they ſhall be *tormented for ages of ages:*
Though I ſo far agree with this very good writer
as to think, that there is no neceſſity this ſhould
be the truth with reſpect to them *all*; becauſe, if
a *duration,* conſiſting of *ages of ages,* actually runs
out before the torments of *all* the miſerable wicked
come to an *end,* it will be ſtrictly true, in the *collective* ſenſe, that they will be *tormented for ages of
ages*; though *ſome* of them *only* ſhould be tormented through the *whole* of this period, and the
reſt *variouſly,* as to *time,* in proportion to their de-
ſerts.

And this interpretation, it is obvious, very naturally makes way for an *indefinitely various puniſhment* of wicked men, according to the *indefinitely
various degrees* of that *moral depravity* they have
contracted in this *preſent ſtate*; and in a *manner*
too that is perfectly analogous to what takes place,
in fact, here upon earth. The *firſt death,* we find,
by daily obſervation, is brought on with *great variety,* both in reſpect of *time,* and the *cruciating
pains* that accompany it. And this, according to
the preſent explication, may be the real truth,
with reſpect to the *ſecond death.* The *reſurrection-
bodies* of the wicked may, by the wiſdom of God,

be

be *variously* fitted, both for the *sensations* of *torment,* and a *continuance* under the pressure of them. Thus it is in the *present state.* Some, from the very formation of their bodies, are capable of suffering *keener pain* than others ; and they can bear it a *great while longer,* without giving up the ghost. And why may it not be reasonably supposed, that it shall be thus also in the coming state of " weeping, and wailing, and gnashing of " teeth ?"

It is true, there is awful reason to think, with respect to *all* the wicked, that their *resurrection-bodies* will be formed for a *much longer duration,* than they are capable of existing at *present* ; and that they must pass through *much more intense,* and, it may be, *various, pain,* before their *dissolution* will be effected. But this is no objection against the supposition, that they may *die, some* of them at *one time,* and *others* at *another* ; and *some* of them, not till their torments have lasted *for ages of ages.* If they must finally undergo a *second death,* as the scripture declares that they must, it is rather agreeable, than contrary, to *reason,* to think, that their *dissolution* will be thus *variously* effected, by the *pains* which they will suffer.

And it is certain, there will be full scope, upon this supposition, for *proportioning* men's torments to all the *various degrees* of their contracted stupidity, stubbornness, and moral degeneracy, in every conceivable shape and form. And it deserves consideration, ' Whether this important truth can

‘ be

' be fo well fecured, upon the contrary fuppofition?
' For an *eternity* of mifery fwallows up all propor-
' tion: Or, though there fhould be *fome difference*
' in the *degree* of pain, it is fuch a difference, I fear,
' as will be fcarce thought worthy of being brought
' into the account, when the circumftance of *endlefs*
' *duration* is annexed to it.'

But there is another fenfe ftill, in which we may
take this phrafe, *they fhall be tormented for ages of*
ages; underftanding it yet as fpoken of the *collec-*
tive body of wicked men, and not of *every individual*
that goes to conftitute this body. It may be intended to lead us into the thought, that it will take
up, not only a *long period* of duration, but a period
that will confift of *many difpenfations, ages,* or *ftates,*
varioufly adapted for the *difcipline* of *ftubborn* and
rebellious creatures, before they will ALL, in a wife
and rational way, be fitted, agreeably to the foregoing fcheme, for *final happinefs.* To explain myfelf more particularly. They may *all,* in one *col-*
lective body, be doomed, at the great day of *judg-*
ment, to a *ftate of mifery* which will laft *an age:*
In which ftate, *fome,* under the miniftration of
Jefus Chrift, as *head* of this ftate, may be wrought
upon to fubmit themfelves to God as his *willing*
and *obedient fubjects*; upon which, in God's time
and way, they fhall be made *happy. Others* may
die in this ftate *ftupid* and *ftubborn,* notwithftanding
all the *torments* of it for a *whole age:* And thofe
who thus *died* in their *obftinacy* may again, in fome
other form of exiftence, be put into a place of fuf-

fering·

fering for *another age* ; in which *some* may be reduced under *moral subjection* to God, and *others*
ſtand it out *ſtill.* And *theſe others* may, in yet
another form of exiſtence, be ſent into a place of
diſcipline for *another age*; and ſo on, till there has
been *torment for ages of ages,* before the *whole collective body* of rebellious men are prepared for the
FINAL DISPENSATION, when God ſhall be ALL IN
ALL TO THEM ALL.

In either of the foregoing ſenſes, wicked men,
as a *collective body,* may be tormented *for ages of
ages,* without ſuppoſing that this ſhall be the caſe
with reſpect to *every individual.* And it is highly
probable, if not certain, that the *duration* of this
torment is to be interpreted in *one* or *other* of theſe
ſenſes.

But if it ſhould be allowed, that there is no juſt
foundation for this *criticiſm,* and that *every individual* wicked man ſhall be *tormented,* in conſequence of the *future judgment,* εις τους αιωνας των
αιωνων, it is abundantly evident, from what has
been above offered, not only that this phraſe MAY
mean a *limited duration,* though a long one ; but
that *this* is the *ſenſe* in which it OUGHT to be underſtood ; which is a ſufficient anſwer to the *objection :—*

The *ſtrongeſt enforcement* of which, in the opinion
of ſome, is ſtill behind. It is this. Our Saviour
himſelf has *thrice,* in the ſame diſcourſe, moſt ſo-
lemnly uſed theſe forcible words, with reſpect to
wicked men, in the *future* ſtate, " WHERE THEIR
" WORM

" WORM DIETH NOT, AND THE FIRE IS NOT
" QUENCHED." Mark ix. 44, 46, 48.

In anfwer whereto, it is obvious to remark, it
may be *literally* and *ftriƈtly* true, that, in *hell,* the
worm dieth not, and the *fire is not quenched*; while
yet, it *may* be as true, that wicked men may *die* in
hell, and be no more capable of the *fenfations* of
pain, either from *this worm,* or *this fire.* If, by the
worm that dieth not, we underftand, even according to the common opinion, *remorfe, horror,*
and *agony* of *confcience,* this may not ceafe, while
the wicked are in *hell*; but it does not certainly
follow from hence, that they fhall *live eternally* in
this place. And if, by *the fire that is not quenched,*
we underftand the *lake of fire* the wicked fhall be
caft into, even this may be *unquenchable,* while
yet the wicked may not *live eternally* in it. The
plain truth is, thefe words, in point of ftriƈt argument, can prove no more than this, that the *torments* of the wicked fhall laft *as long as their next
ftate of exiftence lafts,* without determining *how long*
this fhall be, whether for *a period only,* or *for ever.*
If their *worm* preys upon them, without ceafing,
as long as they are in hell, it is, to them, ftriƈtly and
rigidly fpeaking, *a worm that does not die:* So if
the *fire* torments them *as long as they exiſt in the
next ftate,* it is, to them, an *unquenchable fire,* though
their exiftence, in that ftate, fhould not be *abfolutely eternal.*

But the moft fimple, eafy, and fatisfaƈtory anfwer is, that *thefe words* are taken from the book
of

of Isaiah's prophecy, and allude to the *punishment*
of those, whose bodies were either *burnt* in the
valley of Hinnom, or permitted to lie upon the
ground, in the form of *dead carcases*, to be fed
upon by *worms* that delight in putrefaction.   And
consequently, as the *fire* which burnt these bodies,
and the *worms* which fed upon them, can, in no
other sense, be said *not to be quenched*, and *not to die*,
than this, that they *continued till these carcases were
entirely consumed :* So may it be said of the *worm*
that preys upon the wicked in *hell*, and of the *fire*
that torments them, that the *one dieth not*, and the
other is not quenched, till they have certainly and
universally effected the *dissolution*, *destruction*, or
death, of wicked men, in the future state.   And it
is observable, this interpretation perfectly coincides
with the other scriptures which speak of this matter; as has been largely shown in the preceding
pages.

I have no where seen this text set in so clear
and full a point of light, as in the discourses of the
last-quoted author, upon the *future torments :* For
which reason I shall be at the pains, in order further
to satisfy the reader, to transcribe his words at
large. — ' It should be here observed,' says he,
' that *these words* of Christ are taken from the *last*
' *verse* of the *prophecy* of Isaiah : " They shall go
" forth, and look upon the carcases of the men
" that transgressed against me ; for their worm
" shall not die, neither shall their fire be quenched,
" and they shall be an abhorring to all flesh."
                                                ' Now,

' Now, as this proposition is most evidently affirm-
' ed, with reference to *carcases* [see also ver. 16
' of the same chapter of Isaiah], or *bodies deprived*
' *of life*, and consequently no longer in a state of
' *sensation*, whatever is intended by it, this cannot,
' with any consistency, be intended, that *these bodies*
' themselves should be *continued* in a state of *never-*
' *ending misery*.

' It is affirmed, indeed, of the *worm* that preys
' upon these carcases, that *it dieth not*, and of *the*
' *fire*, by which, I suppose, their *life* [they are said
' expressly in the 16th verse to be the slain of
' the Lord. See also Rev. xx. 9.] was *destroyed*,
' that *it is not quenched*: Both which may be very
' true, and true, if taken in the most strict and
' rigorous sense of the words ; and yet no necessity
' of drawing so strange a conclusion from hence,
' as though the *carcases themselves* should be *con-*
' *tinued* in a state of *misery*, when described as
' *carcases*, that is, as *bodies deprived of life*, and,
' with that, of all *sensation*.

' As to that construction, which some modern
' writers have put upon this *worm*, as though it
' should relate to the *remorse of conscience*, it re-
' quires no other reply than this, that it is a mere
' arbitrary interpretation, that has no proof, or
' warrant, from the *scripture use* of this phrase.
' And, indeed, whoever consults the passage of
' Isaiah, from whence this citation is made, will
' find the *worm* is something that relates, not to
' *sensation*, or *perception*, but *corruption*. " By fire,
" and

" and by his fword, will the Lord plead with all
" flefh, and the flain of the Lord fhall be many.—
" They fhall go forth, and look upon the carcafes
" (or dead bodies) of the men that tranfgreffed
" againft me; for their worm dieth not." And
' whereas it is fubjoined, that " their fire fhall not
" be quenched," by *their fire* may be meant (as I
' have fhewn) the *fire* by which they were *deftroyed.*
' And this *fire* may be faid, *not to be quenched*, either
' to imply, that it is fuch a fire as *cannot be put out*,
' but, on the contrary, *fubdues* and *deftroys* whatever
' is caft into it; or, poffibly, that this very inftru-
' ment of divine vengeance may be *continued* as an
' awful memorial to *after-times :* Either of which
' propofitions may be very true, and yet lay us
' under no neceffity of fuppofing, in direct con-
' tradiction to the fcripture account (for they are
' reprefented as *carcafes,* or *bodies deprived of life)*
' that the *fubjects* that were *killed* by this *fire*, muft
' be preferved *alive*, in a ftate of *never-ending*
' *mifery.*

' As to that claufe, which immediately follows
' this paffage in St. Mark, " For every one fhall
" be falted with fire ;" though it will admit of
' fome debate, whether this claufe fhould be con-
' nected with the immediately foregoing verfe,
' and not rather with the whole preceding para-
' graph, in which our Saviour inculcates upon his
' difciples, in common, the great duty of felf-
' denial, and fuffering, for the fake of religion and
' virtue : Yet (to give our *objector* all the advan-

5   ' tage

' tage that his heart defires) let it be fuppofed,
' that *this claufe* fhould be underftood of the *future*
' *mifery*: And here, I fay, that whoever infers
' from hence, that, becaufe the *fire* is reprefented as
' performing the office of *falt*, and becaufe the
' ufe of falt is to *preferve from corruption*, that
' therefore the *bodies* of the wicked fhall be *pre-*
' *ferved incorruptible*, and confequently *alive* by the
' *fire*; he does, in the firft place, by this conftruc-
' tion, introduce the moft prepofterous confufion of
' images, by reprefenting the fire, which is a *de-*
' *ftructive* element, and which rends afunder what-
' ever is caft into it, as a means of *preferving*
' from *diffolution*, and this too in direct contra-
' diction to the exprefs affertions of fcripture, with
' reference to this very affair; for the fcripture
' affirms, they fhall *reap corruption*, or *diffolution of*
' *parts*; and, in this very context, it is obferved,
' that *their worm* (which is an emblem of corrup-
' tion) *dieth not.*

' Thefe confiderations, one would think, are
' fufficient to put any unbiaffed mind upon the
' enquiry, whether the ancients did not confider
' this metaphor in more views than one? Or,
' whether the genius of the oriental languages will
' not admit of a different interpretation? In Ifaiah
' li. 6, we are told, that " the heavens fhall vanifh
" away like fmoke, and the earth wax old," or be
' fretted, or worn out, " like a garment." Here,
' therefore, the ideas of *confumption*, or *diffolution*, are
' manifeftly intended; and what we render, *fhall*
' *vanifh*

' *vanish away*, is expreſſed, in the original, by a
' verb which exactly anſwers to this in the text;
' *the heavens ſhall be ſalted*, that is, as Buxtorf ex-
' plains it, *be diſſolved*. It is a well-known maxim
' in *chemiſtry*, that *bodies are deſtroyed by ſalts* * :
' And, becauſe things, which are grown old and
' putrid, are eaſily pulled aſunder, hence we find a
' word of the ſame derivation, in Jer. xxxviii. 11,
' applied to *putrid rags*, or, as our tranſlators ren-
' der it, " and he took the rotten rags, and let
" them down by cords into the dungeon."

' Now, whether our Saviour refers to this ancient
' uſe of this word, or, whether he intended by it,
' that the *fire* ſhould not merely ſcorch the *external*
' ſurfaces of bodies, but penetrate (like ſo much
' *ſalt* or *brine*) into their *inmoſt* parts, is not ne-
' ceſſary to my preſent argument to determine ;
' but, conſidering in what different points of view
' a *figurative* mode of ſpeech may be taken, I may
' appeal to any candid impartial enquirer, whether
' a word, confeſſed on all hands to be uſed in a
' *figurative* ſenſe, ſhould be underſtood in *that*
' *ſenſe* which ſuits, or in *that* which contradicts,
' the *nature* of the ſubject to which it is applied ?

' Had the ſcripture never told us, that the *ſub-*
' *jects*, which are caſt into this fire, ſhall reap
' *corruption*, or *diſſolution*, ſtill, as fire, from the

---

* Alia corpora deſtruunt; hoc confirmat calcinationes
cum ſalibus, cœmentationes, et corroſiones, immò ipſorum
metallorum intimæ et radicales deſtructiones. *Teychmeri In-
ſtitutiones Chemiæ*, pag. 11, 12.

' nature

' nature of the thing, is a *destructive* element, and
' has a tendency to *consume,* and *force asunder,* the
' bodies that are cast into it, surely that single
' circumstance would determine the considerate
' reader against the notion of *incorruption,* as being
' a sense of the *metaphor* which agrees not with
' the *nature* of the *thing:* How much more, when
' both the *nature* of the *thing,* and the *scripture-*
' *account* are agreed ; and both, in conjunction,
' oblige us to infer, not that the wicked shall be
' *preserved compact,* and *incorruptible,* by the *fire* ;
' but be *consumed,* and *burnt up,* in it ?

   ' I shall only add, that should it be imagined,
' that this *incorruptibility* by *fire* is favoured by that
' reference which our Saviour makes to the *Jewish*
' *sacrifices* under the law, in that clause, " And
" every sacrifice shall be salted with salt ;" I an-
' swer, that this clause relates to quite another
' thing : For the *sacrifices* under the law were not
' *salted* in order to *preserve* them from being *con-*
' *sumed* upon the altar, or to render them *incorrup-*
' *tible* in *fire,* but to represent that *moral purity,* or
' freedom from *moral corruption,* which should be-
' long to those, who, like to so many *sacrifices,* are
' devoted and consecrated to God. And, accord-
' ingly, our Saviour, considering the *metaphor* in
' this point of view, subjoins, " Salt is good, but
" if the salt have lost its saltness, wherewith will
" you season it ? Have salt in yourselves, and have
" peace one with another."

   It is added, upon the whole, which closes the
objection

objection we have been confidering—In what more
clear, ftrong, and decifive language, could the
endlefs never-ceafing mifery of the wicked have been
revealed? No words could have been chofen, the
fcriptures fcarce afford any words, that are more
obvioufly and certainly expreffive of this idea.

The anfwer is eafy, and I fhall give it in the
words of the foregoing author, rather than my
own, becaufe they are ready at hand, and appear
to me to be ftrongly convincing. He fays, ' I do
' much wonder to find, that one who has read the
' fcriptures, and underftands the *original* languages,
' fhould affirm, that thefe languages do hardly af-
' ford *more full* and *more certain* words than thofe that
' are ufed, whereby to exprefs a *duration* that has
' *no end*, when it is confeffed, on all fides, that the
' word, which we render *everlafting*, is frequently
' applied to things that are well known to have *an*
' *end*, and, confequently, of itfelf, is not *full* and
' *certain*: And, if the languages in which the
' fcriptures were written do hardly afford *more full*
' and *more certain* words, whereby to exprefs a
' *duration without end*, how come we to find, in
' *fcripture*, fuch words as INCORRUPTIBLE, IM-
' MORTAL, INDISSOLUBLE? [See the *original* of
' Heb. vii. 16. What we render, *endlefs life*, is,
' in the *original*, ακαταλευτου ζωης, that is, INDIS-
' SOLUBLE LIFE] And, in fo many words, it is af-
' firmed of the righteous, that *they cannot die any*
' *more*: Or, why are thefe terms conftantly *re-*
' *ftrained* to the *good* and *virtuous* part of mankind?
                                                    ' Why

' Why do we not read of the *wicked*, that they
' fhall be *incorruptible, immortal*, or *indiffoluble?* or,
' why is it not affirmed, that their *pain* or *torture*
' *endeth not?* Or will it be pretended, that the
' *languages*, in which the *fcriptures* were written, do
' hardly afford fuch terms as thefe ?'

Enough, I truft, has now been faid, to make it
fufficiently evident, that the doctrine of *univerfal
falvation* may be admitted as a *fcripture-truth*, notwithftanding the *objected phrafeologies*, in favour of
never-ceafing mifery, with refpect to *wicked* men, as
a contradiction thereto. Did the *fcripture* contain
nothing that might be thought to countenance the
opinion of *final univerfal happinefs*, there would be
good reafon, as we have feen, to think, that the
future torments would have an *end:* But it is much
more reafonable to believe this, while we take
into the argument the *above proof* of *this doctrine*;
becaufe, fo far as it carries with it any *real weight*,
it ought to be looked upon as a *good reafon*, why
we fhould underftand *thofe phrafes* in a *limited*, and
not an *endlefs*, fenfe, which are capable of either.

I fhall now finifh my reply to this *firft objection*,
with the following *general remarks*, which, perhaps,
may not be altogether unworthy of notice.

It does not appear to me, that it would be honourable to the infinitely righteous and benevolent
Governor of the world, to make wicked men *everlaftingly miferable.* For, in what point of light
foever we take a view of *fin*, it is certainly, in its
nature, a *finite evil.* It is the fault of a *finite
creature*,

creature, and the effect of *finite* principles, paffions, and appetites. To fay, therefore, that the finner is doomed to *infinite mifery* for the *finite* faults of a *finite* life, looks like a reflection on the *infinite juftice,* as well as goodnefs, of God. I know it has been often urged, that *fin* is an *infinite evil,* becaufe committed againft an *infinite object* ; for which reafon, an *infinite punifhment* is no more than its *due defert.* But this *metaphyfical nicety.* proves a great deal too much, if it proves any thing at all. For, according to this way of arguing, all finners muft fuffer *to the utmoft* in *degree,* as well as *duration* ; otherwife, they will not fuffer *fo much* as they *might* do, and as they *ought* to do : Which is plainly inconfiftent with that *difference* the fcripture often declares there fhall be in the punifhment of wicked men, according to the *difference* there has been in the *nature* and *number* of their evil deeds.

The *fmallnefs* of the *difference* between thofe, in this world, to whom the character of *wicked* belongs in the *loweft* fenfe, and thofe to whom the character of *good* is applicable in the *like* fenfe, renders it incredible, that fuch an *amazingly great difference* fhould be made between them in the *future* world. The *former differ* from the latter, by a difference, as to us, fo *imperceptible,* that it is, perhaps, impoffible we fhould be able fo much as to diftinguifh the *one* from the *other,* with any manner of certainty : And yet, the *difference* between them, in the other world, according to the common opinion, will be *doubly infinite* ; for the

good

good are fcreened from *infinite mifery*, and rewarded with *infinite happinefs*; whereas the *wicked* are excluded from *infinite happinefs*, and doomed to *infinite mifery*. For the *reward* and *punifhment*, being both *eternal*, however *fmall* they may be fuppofed to be in each finite portion of time, they muft at laft become infinite in magnitude. How to reconcile this with the abfolutely accurate *impartiality* of God, is, I confefs, beyond me.

A very great part of thofe, who will be miferable in the *other world*, were not, that we know of, INCURABLY finful in *this*. Multitudes are taken off before they have had opportunity to make themfelves *hardened abandoned* finners: And, fo far as we are able to judge, had they been continued in life, they might have been formed to a *virtuous temper* of mind by a fuitable mixture of *correction, inftruction*, and the like. And can it be fuppofed, with refpect to fuch, that an infinitely benevolent God, without *any other trial*, in order to effect their reformation, will confign them over to *endlefs* and *irreverfible torment*? Would this be to conduct himfelf towards them like a *Father?* Let the heart of a *father on earth* fpeak upon this occafion. Nay, it does not appear, that *any finners* are fo IN-CORRIGIBLE in wickednefs, as to be *beyond recovery* by ftill further methods within the reach of *infinite wifdom*: And if the infinitely wife God can, in any wife methods, recover them, even in *any other ftate of trial*, may we not argue, from his *infinite benevolence*, that he will? And is it not

Y   far

far more reaſonable to ſuppoſe, that the *miſeries* of the *other world* are a *proper diſcipline* in order to accompliſh this *end*, than that they ſhould be *final* and *vindiƈive* only ?

The *ſmallneſs* of the number of thoſe who ſhall be *ſaved*, in the *next ſtate*, ought, in all reaſon, to be eſteemed a weighty argument againſt interpreting any texts of ſcripture ſo as to mean *abſolutely eternal miſery*. It is a plain caſe, if the *next* ſtate is *final*, but very *few*, comparatively, of the ſons of Adam will be *ſaved*. Our Saviour himſelf has ſaid, Matt. vii. 14, " Strait is the gate, and nar-" row is the way which leadeth unto life, and few " there be that find it :" Nor will there be any room left to contrive ſhifts to elude the obvious natural ſenſe of theſe words, if we conſider the *neceſſary qualifications* in order to the *finding this life*, and then compare the *charaƈer* of mankind herewith. The *choſen*, and *faithful*, and *true*, though *in the world*, are not *of the world*, but a *peculiar* and *ſeparate* people. The *whole world lieth in wickedneſs*. It does ſo at *this day*; as we our-ſelves know, and cannot but know, if we do not ſhut our eyes againſt the light. So it has done in the *ages that are paſt*, if we may believe the in-ſpired writers of ſcripture. And ſo it will do in the *ages that are yet to come*, if the ſame ſacred pen-men may be depended on : For they aſſure us, that *the earth that now is*, with its inhabitants and works, *are kept in ſtore, and reſerved unto fire*, for the *ungodlineſs*, and *infidelity*, and *unrighteouſneſs*,

I   which,

which, in *future times*, fhall be *univerfally* prevalent. Now, if a *few* only of mankind, in the
final iffue of things, are to be *faved*, and the reft
damned, that is, fentenced to endure *never-ending
torments in hell*, what a ftrange idea muft we have
of the MERCY of the *Chriftian* difpenfation, which
is fo celebrated, in the New-Teftament writings, for
its *unfearchable riches* and *glory*? The *birth* of Jefus,
the Saviour, into the world is fpoken of as " glad
" tidings of great joy to all people," and an anthem
of praife was fung, on this account, by the heavenly hoft, to God, becaufe of the *good-will* hereby
difcovered towards mankind. But if the greater
part of mankind by far will *eternally perifh in hell*,
notwithftanding the incarnation of the Son of God,
and all that he has ever fuffered, or done, or will
do, for their relief, what occafion was there for
fuch *univerfal joy?* And with what propriety could
glory be given to God for his *good-will* towards
men? The *total ruin* of fuch multitudes of the
fons of Adam appears to me a moft palpable *inconfiftency* with the *grace of God* as exhibited in the
gofpel of Chrift. And it is indeed *incredible* in itfelf, that God fhould conftitute his *Son* the *Saviour*
of *men*, and the *bulk* of them be *finally* and *eternally*
damned. Nor can it be any other than a bafe and
grofs reflection on the *Saviour* of *men*, whofe proper bufinefs and office, as fuch, it is, to defeat the
defign of the *Devil*, and refcue mankind out of
his *deftroying* hands; I fay, it cannot but reflect
great difhonour on him to fuppofe, that the *Devil*,

not-

notwithſtanding his *mediatory interpoſition*, and all that he could do in oppoſition to him, ſhould *finally* get the better of him, by effecting the *everlaſting damnation* of the *greater part* of thoſe whom he came from heaven on purpoſe to *ſave.* To me, I own, the thought is ſhocking; nor can I ſee how it is poſſibly *reconcileable* with the *honour* that is due to *Chriſt*, in his character as the *Saviour* of *men.* The conſideration of *hell* as a *purging fire* * is that only which can make the matter ſit eaſy upon one's mind.

In fine, it ought to be particularly remembered and conſidered, the *proper tendency,* and *final cauſe,* of *evils* and *ſufferings,* in this *preſent ſtate,* are to do us *good,* in the *natural,* or *moral* ſenſe, or both. They are a ſuitably adapted *mean* to this *end*; and the all-wiſe merciful Governor of the world makes uſe of them as ſuch. This is the voice of *reaſon,* confirmed by obſervation and experience; and the *ſcripture* concurs herewith in ſpeaking of the *puniſhments, evils,* or *ſufferings,* which it pleaſes God

---

* Mr. Hartley, as I think, very juſtly obſerves, ' The ' doctrine of *purgatory,* as now taught by the *Papiſts,* ſeems ' to be a *corruption* of a *genuine doctrine,* held by the *ancient* ' *fathers,* concerning a *purifying fire.* It may, perhaps, be, ' that the *abſolute eternity* of puniſhment was not received, till ' after the introduction of metaphyſical ſubtleties, relating ' to *time, eternity,* &c. and the ways of expreſſing theſe; that ' is, not till after the *pagan philoſophy,* and *vain deceit,* had ' mixed itſelf with, and corrupted, *Chriſtianity.*' *Hartley's* *Obſervat. on Man,* vol. ii. pag. 429.

to bring upon the ſons of men, as a *proper diſci-*
pline in order to *humble, and prove, and do them good*
in their latter end. The texts to this purpoſe are
ſcattered all over the Bible. And we have ſuch
an obſervable paſſage as that, Pſal. lxxxix. 31,
32, 33, " If his children forſake my law, and
" walk not in my judgments ; if they break my
" ſtatutes, and keep not my commandments ; then
" will I viſit their tranſgreſſions with the rod, and
" their iniquity with ſtripes. Nevertheless,
" my loving-kindness will I not utterly
" take from them." Whether theſe words are
ſpoken of the *children of David,* or of the *children*
of Chriſt, of whom *David* was an illuſtrious *type,*
the *loving-kindneſs* of God is repreſented as *finally pre-*
vailing towards them. And his *viſiting their tranſ-*
greſſions with the rod, and *their iniquity with ſtripes,*
is ſpoken of as the *mean,* in a way of *diſcipline,*
correƈtion, or *chaſtiſement,* in order to promote this
end. And if *evil, puniſhment,* or *miſery,* in the
preſent life, is mercifully intended for the *good* of
the *patients themſelves,* why not in the next life?
Is the character of God, as the *Father of mercies,*
and God of *pity and grace,* limited to *this world*
only ? Why ſhould it not be ſuppoſed, that the infinitely benevolent Deity is the *ſame good being* in the
other world, that he is in *this* ? And that he has
the *ſame kind* and *good intention* in the *puniſhments*
of the *next* ſtate, that he has in this, namely, the
profit, or *advantage,* of the *ſufferers themſelves.* This
is certainly moſt agreeable to the *natural notions*

we entertain of the *only good* God : And it is moſt agreeable alſo to the ideas, which the ſcriptures give us of him. For they repreſent his *mercy* under the emblem of the tendereſt paſſion in men, that of a *father's pity towards his children* ; yea, they deſcribe it by ſpeaking of him, as *afflicted with us in our afflictions,* and as *grieved at the heart for the miſeries of Iſrael.* And why ſhould not theſe repreſentations of the *mercy* of God be extended to the *future* world ? Why ſhould he not be looked upon as *pitying* ſinners, and *puniſhing* them, in the *next* ſtate as well as this, in order to their *benefit ?* Surely a change in the *mode,* and *place,* of wicked men's exiſtence, will not infer a change in the *nature* of that God, who is " the ſame yeſterday, to-" day, and for ever," and muſt, in the *other* world as well as *this,* be diſpoſed to make it evident, that he is a being of *boundleſs* and *inexhauſtible goodneſs.*

It may be worthy of our ſpecial notice here, not only the language of mankind, in all ages, and in all places, as grounded on the moſt obvious reaſoning from the *whole courſe of nature,* but even the *revelations* of *ſcripture,* conſtantly ſpeak of God as the *univerſal Father,* as well as Governor, of men. And our Saviour, Jeſus Chriſt, has particularly taught us how to argue from *this relation* God ſtands in to us. The argument is, that (Matt. vii. 11) " If ye, being evil, know how to give " good gifts unto your children, how much more " ſhall your Father, which is in heaven, give good " things

" things to them that afk him ?" What now is the temper and conduct of *fathers on earth*, though they are *evil*, towards their *offspring?* They readily do them *good*, as they are able, while they behave fuitably; and as readily *chaftife* them for their *profit*, when they need *correction:* But they do not put off the bowels of parents, and *punifh* their children *without pity*, having no view to their *advantage.* We fhould entertain an opinion of thofe parents, as *degenerate* to the laft degree, who fhould inflict *mifery* on their own children, without any intention to promote their *welfare* thereby, in any fhape whatever. And fhall we fay *that* of *our Father in heaven*, (who, inftead of *being evil*, as all *earthly fathers* are more or lefs, is *infinitely good)* which we cannot fuppofe of *any father on earth*, till we have firft *divefted* him of the *heart* of a *father?* Can it reafonably be conceived, that *that* God, who calls *mankind* his *offspring* without exception, and *himfelf* their *father*, fhould *torment them eternally* without any *intention* to do them the leaft *imaginable good*, as muft be the cafe, if the doctrine of *never-ending mifery* is true? Will not God be as truly the *father* of wicked men in the *other* world, as he is in *this?* And, if he *punifhes* them *there*, muft it not be in the character of their *father*, who defires their *good*, and *corrects* them with a *kind intention* to promote it? No good reafon, I will venture to fay, can be affigned, why our *Saviour's* argument, founded on the nature of things, the *relation* that fubfifts between *God* and *men*; I fay, no good rea-

fon can be given, why our Saviour's argument,
" Much more will your Father in heaven give you
" good things," fhould be *confined* to the *prefent*, and not *extended* to the *future* world. And,
perhaps, the only thing that has led moft writers
to *confine* the *pity* of *our Father in heaven*, and
the *merciful intention* of his *punifhing* his *rebellious children*, to the *prefent* life, is, the notion they
have previoufly imbibed of *never-ceafing mifery*;
which, having no real foundation in the facred
books of *revelation*, as has, I would hope, been
abundantly proved, we are at liberty to conclude,
that the *defign* of *evil*, *punifhment*, or *mifery*, in
the FUTURE WORLD, as well as *this*, is to DISCI-
PLINE wicked men, and, in this way, to effect
their OWN PERSONAL, as well as the *general*, *good*.

OBJECTION II.

" The *woe*, which our Saviour denounced againft
" *Judas*, by whom he was betrayed, in thofe words,
" Mark xiv. 21, *Good were it for that man if he
" had never been born*, is inconfiftent with the *final
" falvation of all men*; though it will not certainly
" prove a ftate of *endlefs* mifery."

I anfwer—This paffage of fcripture muft be interpreted, according to the ftricteft rigour of the
letter, in order to make it contradict the above
doctrine of *final happinefs*. But what neceffity of
fuch a rigorous interpretation? The fpeech may
be

be *proverbial**; and *proverbial* sayings, we know, are never to be understood with rigour: Or, should this be rejected as a mere vain conjecture, it is obvious to remark, that the words are certainly well adapted to give, in the general, a *concise*, and yet *strong* and *lively*, representation of the *greatness* of Judas's *sin*, and the *aggravated punishment* he should suffer for it. And as this seems to have been the only intention of our Saviour, it is sufficient to absolve the meaning of his words, without going into a more particular interpretation of them. To be sure, it is not *necessary*, that we should understand them in any other sense. They are fairly capable of this, and might be thus taken, had the scripture no where said a word about the *final salvation of all men :* But, as so *many texts* have been produced, in proof of this point, it is highly reasonable, that *this text* should be construed in *consistency* with those ; especially as it is obviously capable of such a construction, and cannot, indeed, be construed otherwise, without taking the words in their *utmost literal rigour*, of which there is no real need.

Nay, should we suppose (to give the *objection* the greatest advantage) that the *strict literal* mean-

---

* It is spoken of by Mr. *Pool*, from *Lud. Capellus*, (Vid. Synops. Crit. in loc.) as *Locutio Rabbinica, et Talmudicis usitatissima.* And it was doubtless a saying intended *generally*, though *strongly*, to express the *unhappy condition of those* to whom it was applied : And this seems to have been its *only meaning.*

ing of these words, considering the *text simply in it-self*, is the most *reasonable*, and what any one would most naturally take them in ; yet, even upon this supposition, they could not be a *disproof* of the above doctrine ; because it is an allowed maxim, that the *strict literal* sense of words, not only *may*, but *ought* to be departed from, when *inconsistent* with *others* that speak of the same thing. It is therefore far more reasonable, as we have brought to view *so many* passages, which declare the *final salvation of all men*, to interpret *this* passage in *consistency* with *those*, though we should, by so doing, depart from its *strict literal* sense, than to adhere to its *strict literal* sense, and, by so doing, make the *scripture* at *variance* with itself. We do thus in an hundred other cases ; and it would be difficult to assign any good reason, why we should not do the like in the present case.

But, after all, it may be, interpreters have not hit upon our Saviour's *real meaning* in the words, καλον ην αυτω, ει ουκ εγεννηθη ο ανθρωπος εκεινος. It is remarked of *Judas*, in consequence of his having betrayed our Lord, that " he went, and hanged " himself," Matt. xxvii. 5. He was so *uneasy* in his mind, from a conviction of his *treachery* and *baseness*, that he preferred *death* to *life*, practically declaring, that he thought it *better not to have been born*, not to have had existence, than to hold it under the pressure of such *tormenting reflections* on himself for his folly. And why may not the passage under consideration be looked

upon

upon as a PROPHECY foretelling this event, in a way of warning, or caution? As if our Saviour had said, " Well may I pronounce a *woe* againſt the man that ſhall dare to betray me ; for, if he ventures upon this act of treachery, he ſhall, in a very little while, be weary of his life, and practically declare, by *hanging himſelf*, that TO HIM, in his apprehenſion, [ſo the pronoun, αυτω, I think, ought to be rendered, and not, *for him*, as in the common tranſlation] *it were good he had not been born*, had not been brought into being." This conſtruction evidently gives a ſtrong and very ſignificant meaning to the words, as, in this view of them, they contain a *prediction* intended by our Saviour, not only to ſet forth the *horrid nature* of this ſin, ᵢbut to be a *ſtanding proof* to all ages of the truth of his *divine miſſion*. And we may the rather be induced to underſtand *theſe words*, in *this ſenſe*, as our Lord, in this very *chapter*, took occaſion, from Peter's too great *confidence* in himſelf, to warn him in the *like prophetic* way, ſaying unto him, as in the 34th verſe, " This night, be- " fore the cock crow, thou ſhalt deny me thrice." The *newneſs* of this interpretation is no certain argument, that it is not the *true* one; and if, upon examination, it ſhould be found to be ſo, it is obvious, at firſt ſight, that the *objection*, grounded on this *text*, is wholly ſuperſeded.

OBJECTION

OBJECTION III.

" *Blafphemy againft the Holy Ghoft* is declared,
" by our Saviour himfelf, to be *unpardonable.* No
" lefs than three of the *evangelifts* have recorded
" his words to this purpofe ; and they are empha-
" tically expreffive of this thought.   In Matt. xii.
" 31, 32, the words are, *Wherefore I fay unto you,*
" *all manner of fin and blafphemy fhall be forgiven*
" *unto men*; *but the blafphemy againft the Holy*
" *Ghoft fhall not be forgiven unto men.*   *And who-*
" *foever fpeaketh a word againft the Son of man, it*
" *fhall be forgiven him* ; *but whofoever fpeaketh*
" *againft the Holy Ghoft, it fhall not be forgiven him,*
" *neither in this world, neither in the world to come.*
" —Mark expreffes the matter a little differently,
" but very ftrongly.   He fays, *chapter* iii. 28, 29,
" *Verily I fay unto you, all fins fhall be forgiven unto*
" *the fons of men, and blafphemies wherewith they*
" *fhall blafpheme* ; *but he that fhall blafpheme againft*
" *the Holy Ghoft hath never forgivenefs* ; *but is in*
" *danger of eternal damnation.* — Luke is more
" concife, but withal as peremptory as the other
" *evangelifts* ; for this is his language, *chapter*
" xii. 10, " *Whofoever fhall fpeak a word againft*
" *the Son of man, it fhall be forgiven him*; *but unto*
" *him that blafphemeth againft the Holy Ghoft, it*
" *fhall not be forgiven.*"

If

If the learned Grotius is right in his interpretation of *theſe texts*, the *difficulty objeɩted* from them
is entirely ſuperſeded. He ſuppoſes our Saviour's
meaning to be no more than this, " that *all other*
ſins and blaſphemies ſhall *ſooner* be forgiven, than
the *blaſphemy againſt the Holy Ghoſt* ;" looking upon
the words as an Hebraiſm, intended to ſignify,
not ſo much the *pardonableneſs* of ſome ſins, and
the *unpardonableneſs* of others, as the *greater difficulty* of obtaining pardon for *blaſphemy againſt
the Holy Ghoſt*, than for *any other blaſphemy*. His
reaſoning, in favour of this conſtruction, is to this
purpoſe :—" It could not be the deſign of our Saviour, in the *former* part of theſe ſentences, where
he ſpeaks of *other* ſins and blaſphemies, to affirm
abſolutely concerning them, that *they ſhall be forgiven* ; becauſe this is not true in fact, as there are
multitudes of *theſe ſins* that are *not forgiven :* And
therefore," ſays he, " we ought, in all reaſon, to
look upon theſe ſentences as *Hebrew forms* of
ſpeech, like that in the 5th chapter of Matthew,
where our Saviour declares, that " heaven and
" earth ſhall paſs away, but my words ſhall not
" paſs away." The meaning of which is explained by Luke, in the ſixteenth chapter of his
goſpel, where the words are, not that *heaven and
earth ſhall paſs away*, but that *it is eaſier for them
to paſs away*, than that *Chriſt's word ſhould fail*." —
This celebrated writer adds, " It was a common
way of ſpeaking among the Jews, *this thing ſhall
be, and that ſhall not be*, when it was not their intention

tention to affirm any thing *abſolutely* of *either*, but only to expreſs the *greater difficulty* of effecting the *latter* than the *former.*"—Upon which he concludes, that the only meaning of our Saviour, in theſe words, is, that it is *eaſier* to obtain the pardon of *any ſins*, and therefore of the *greateſt blaſphemies*, than the *blaſphemy againſt the Holy Ghoſt :* As if it was his deſign to be underſtood *comparatively*, ſignifying the *greater heinouſneſs* of the *blaſphemy againſt the Holy Ghoſt*, than *any other blaſphemy*, and that the pardon of it would be *more difficultly* obtained : Not that it is *ſtrictly* and *abſolutely unpardonable.* He refers us, as the final confirmation of this ſenſe of the words, to 1 Sam. ii. 25, where, he ſuppoſes, there is a like comparative mode of ſpeech with this of our Saviour, " If " one man ſin againſt another, the judge ſhall " judge him : But if a man ſin againſt the Lord, " who ſhall intreat for him ?"

Archbiſhop Sharp was fully ſatisfied with this interpretation of Grotius ; expreſſing his opinion of it (in his *Sermon* upon *this ſubject*) in theſe words, " I muſt confeſs, I think it the true one." And whoever goes about to prove, that there is no truth in it, will, perhaps, before he has done, find, that he has undertaken a very hard taſk.

But we ſhall ſuppoſe, that this great man has miſtaken the ſenſe of our Saviour ; and that his intention was, to repreſent the *blaſphemy againſt the Holy Ghoſt* as *abſolutely unpardonable.* And what will follow herefrom ? Not that which is pleaded

in

in the *objection*, namely, that mankind *universally* cannot be faved; as we fhall be foon convinced by afcertaining the *precife fenfe*, in which *this blafphemy* is here fpoken of as *unpardonable*. In order whereto it may be proper to make the following enquiry—

Wherein does the *pardonablenefs* of *all other* fins and blafphemies confift ? The true anfwer to this queftion will at once fettle the point in difpute. And the anfwer is,

The *pardonablenefs* of *all other* fins and blafphemies lies in this, it's being *poffible* for men to efcape the *torments of hell*, though they fhould have been guilty of *thofe fins.* The *gofpel-grace* is fuch, fo vaftly extenfive, as that, whatever *other* blafphemies men may unhappily commit, they may notwithftanding, if they do not commit the *blafphemy againft the Holy Ghoft*, be delivered from the *miferies of the coming world*; it is a *poffible* thing; thofe torments may be evaded by the *intervention* of a *pardon.* It is this, and this only, that diftinguifhes *all other* blafphemies from the *blafphemy againft the Holy Ghoft.*

Accordingly, the *unpardonablenefs* of the *blafphemy againft the Holy Ghoft* muft confift in the *reverfe* of the *pardonablenefs* of *all other* fins, that is to fay, in the *impoffibility* of their efcaping the *torments of hell,* who are chargeable with the guilt of *this fin.* Whoever *thus blafpheme* muft certainly go to the *place of future torment*, as being excluded from the *gofpel-privilege* of *forgivenefs.* And it is obfervable,
the

the evangelist Mark, having said, " He that shall
" blaspheme against the Holy Ghost hath never
" forgiveness," adds, in the words that immediately follow, by way of explanation, " but is in
" danger of eternal damnation," αλλ' ενοχος εστιν
αιωνιου κρισεως, *but is guilty of eternal judgment*, is
liable to the *judicial sentence*, which, at the great
day, will doom him, εις το πυρ το αιωνιον, *to eternal
fire.* So that *never to have forgiveness*, and to lie
exposed, without hope, or remedy, to the *doom of
the judgment-day*, mean precisely *one* and the *same*
thing. And, in truth, the *unpardonableness* of the
blasphemy against the Holy Ghost, in the sense even
of the *objectors* themselves, lies in *this*, and in this
solely, that, if men commit *this sin*, they must *unavoidably* go to the place of *future torment* ; having
no hope from the *gospel-promise* of *forgiveness*, because they are *excepted* persons.

This now being the *meaning* of the *unpardonableness* of *blasphemy against the Holy Ghost*, it is quite
easy to perceive, that even *these blasphemers*, notwithstanding the *unpardonableness* of the sin they have
committed, may *finally be saved*, if the torments of
hell are not *endless* ; as we have seen that they are
not. For, if they are not *saved*, till AFTER they
have passed through *these torments*, they have *never
been forgiven*, in the sense, in which our Saviour is
here speaking of *forgiveness*. The *divine law* has
taken its course ; nor has any *intervening pardon*
prevented the full execution of the *threatened penalty* on them. *Forgiveness*, *strictly* and *literally*
speaking,

speaking, *has not been granted to them.* Even their
salvation, as it is POSTERIOR to their having undergone the *torments of hell,* is not the *effect* of that
gospel-forgiveness our Saviour is treating about.
Their cafe is *essentially different* from the cafe of
others, who have not committed *this sin. Others,*
notwithstanding their commission of *all other sins,*
may be admitted to *mercy;* that is, by the *intervening privilege* of a *pardon,* they may be *saved
without first going through the torments of hell,* or,
as the *scripture* expresses it, *without being* " hurt of
" the second death:" Whereas, it is not *possible,* that
these should be *so saved.* They must *first suffer the
pains of hell,* because no *intervening pardon* can exempt them therefrom.

As to these words, in Matthew's gospel, " Who-
" soever speaketh against the Holy Ghost, it shall
" not be forgiven him, ουτε εν το νυν αιωνι, ουτε εν
" τω μελλοντι, neither in this world, neither in the
" world to come," it may be difficult to fix their
exact sense. Expositors greatly differ here. Some
suppose they are an allusion to the Jewish persuasion, that some sins which would not be forgiven upon their *sacrifices,* (whether their *daily* sacrifices, or that on the *great day* of *expiation)* and
so were *irremissible* in *that age,* might yet be remit-
ted in *that to come,* that is, the *age* of the *Messiah.*
Others suppose the words allude to the notion the
Jews entertained with reference to the *effect* of their
highest excommunication, the sentence whereof they
held to be reversible, *neither in this world, nor the*

Z   *other.*

other. Others refer the reason of this expression to that common, but vain, imagination of the Jews, as if there were *some sins*, that had not been forgiven here, which would be expiated by death, and forgiven after it. There are yet others, who think our Saviour refers to the two different times there are for *forgiveness*, the *one*, here upon earth to the believer and penitent sinner ; and the *other*, at the day of judgment, when the great Judge shall pronounce the sentence of absolution to all his faithful servants : As if he had said, " This *blasphemy against the Holy Ghost* shall neither obtain remission *now* in the sinner's conscience, nor at the great day of accounts."—But, to me, the most probable opinion is, that this *mode* of speech was *proverbial* in our Saviour's day. And that, when it was said, *a thing shall not be, neither in this world, neither in the world to come*, it was the same thing with saying, *it shall never be*. And, indeed, this is the very explanation that is given of this *idiomatical* phrase, by the evangelist Mark ; whose words are these, chap. iii. 29, " He that shall blaspheme against the " Holy Ghost, hath never forgiveness." And this, we have seen, is the *real truth*, with respect to such as *blaspheme against the Holy Ghost* ; notwithstanding which, as we have seen also, they *may be finally saved*.

I shall add here, Mr. Whiston supposes it is implied, in the *mode* of expression here used by our Saviour, that *some sins* may be forgiven in the *other world*, which were not forgiven in *this*. His

words

words are thefe, [*Hell Torments confidered*, pag. 37]
' That fome fins not forgiven in *this world* or
' *age*, will be forgiven in the *world* or *age to come*,
' feems very clear from this text [*viz.* Matt.
' xii. 32]: But what fins thefe are, will be con-
' fidered, when I come to the *Shepherd* of *Hermas*.'
When he comes there, he fays (pag. 59), ' Apof-
' tacy joined to *blafphemy* feems to be the *principal*
' fin *abfolutely irremiffible*, both in *this*, and the *fu-*
' *ture* world.' By this *future* world, or *age*, he
means *Hades*, the ftate between *death* and the *re-*
furrection; and accordingly fuppofes, that this is a
ftate, wherein *finners* (thofe excepted who have
been guilty of *blafphemy)* will have all poffible
means [fee pag. ibid.] ufed with them to bring
them to repentance and falvation. To this purpofe he interprets 1 Pet. iii. 18, 19. and iv. 16.
And he underftands thefe texts in this fenfe by a
text in Jeremiah, now loft, but produced by Juftin
Martyr, by another out of Thaddeus, another
out of Hermas, another out of Clement of
Alexandria, and another out of Origen; in all
which [fee pag. 44] this doctrine is contained.
But it does does not appear to me, I own, that it
was our Saviour's defign, in the expreffion he ufes,
with reference to the *blafphemy againft the Holy*
Ghoft, to fuggeft, that *any fins* might be forgiven
in the *coming world*, or *age*, which were not forgiven in *this :* Neither am I fatisfied, from the
two paffages in Peter's firft epiftle, that this apoftle
intended to infinuate, as though the *gofpel* was

preached

preached in *Hades*, in order to bring men to *repentance*; for which reason, I have silently passed over *those texts*, in the foregoing work. But should it be allowed, that our Saviour intended to declare, that *blasphemy against the Holy Ghost* was *unpardonable* in the *age to come*, as well as the *present age*; that is, in *Hades*, as well as on *earth*, it would be no difficulty in the way of our doctrine of *final happiness*, because *this kind* of sinners, being absolutely excluded from the privilege of *forgiveness*, must, as has been said, *suffer the torments of another world, before they can be saved.* Nay, should it be even supposed, that *these blasphemers* are so hardened in wickedness, as not to be subdued by the *pains* of the *next state*; they may, in a state *beyond that*, be wrought upon, and prepared for *final salvation.*

OBJECTION IV.

" It will greatly tend to *encourage* wicked men
" in their vicious courses, to be told, that the
" *future torments* will have an *end*; as must be the
" truth, if it is possible, that they should be *finally*
" *saved.* They are scarce kept under tolerable
" *restraints*, though they are taught to believe,
" that an *eternity of misery* will be the unhappy
" consequence of their habitually indulging to
" their lusts. To what *enormous lengths* then may
" it be expected they will soon run, in all manner
" of impiety and immorality, if, instead of receiv-
" ing

" ing this doƈtrine as the truth of ſcripture, they
" ſhould be made to think, that *hell torments* are
" of a *limited continuance*, and that they may *finally*
" *be happy?*"

It is eaſy to remark, in anſwer to this objeƈtion,
that it is deſigned, either as an *argument* to *diſ-*
prove a ſtate of *limited miſery only*, and together
with, it the *final ſalvation of all men*; or, to point
out the *dangerous tendency* of *publiſhing* ſuch tenets
as theſe.—I ſhall conſider the *objeƈtion* in both theſe
views.

If the thing meant by it is, to *diſprove* the notion of a *limited ſtate of miſery*, and, together herewith the *final ſalvation of all men*; it muſt be
plainly ſhown, that *theſe doƈtrines* do *naturally* and
direƈtly tend to *encourage* men in *vicious* praƈtice:
Otherwiſe it cannot, with the leaſt appearance of
reaſon, be pretended, that this *argument* carries in
it any real force. Wicked men may *pervert* the
tendency of any thing, and take occaſion, even from
that, which is *naturally* and *ſtrongly* adapted to *ſof-*
ten their hearts, and *effeƈt* their reformation, to *har-*
den themſelves in ſin. The " riches of God's good-
" neſs, and forbearance, and long-ſuffering," manifeſted towards ſinners, in the courſe of Providence,
are admirably ſuited to work upon their ingenuity,
melt them into grief and ſhame for their paſt
faults and follies, and *lead them to repentance:* And
this is the thing intended by a good God. But
they may *pervert* both the *deſign*, and *tendency*,

Z 3   of

of all this goodnefs, and take occafion, even from the *riches* of it, to encourage themfelves in an evil way. The fame may be faid in the prefent cafe. The doctrine of *final falvation,* as pleaded for, with refpect to wicked men, only in *confequence* of a *ftate of torment,* which will laft till their character, as *wicked,* is *deftroyed,* is *naturally* and *powerfully* adapted to *difcourage* them from going on in their finful courfes. But if, in oppo-fition to the *natural* and *genuine* tendency of this *doctrine,* they will *encourage* themfelves in *wicked-nefs,* it is not the *doctrine* that gives this *encourage-ment,* but their *abufe* of it. And if this is a good reafon why the doctrine fhould not be true, no doctrine can be true; for there is not one but what may be *perverted,* and turned to an ill ufe. The *grace of the gofpel,* according to the common fcheme, not only may be, but actually has been, and now is, *perverted* and *abufed* by thoufands of the fons of men. But fhall their *abufe* of that which is *well defigned,* and *ftrongly adapted,* to pro-mote their good, be conftrued as an argument againft the difplay of *this grace* towards them? The *objectors* are fenfible of the *infufficiency* of the argument, as thus applied; and it is equally in-fufficient in the *cafe* we are confidering.

Had we attempted to introduce mankind uni-verfally into a ftate of *happinefs,* upon their leaving this world, whatever their *moral conduct* had been in it, the argument would then have held ftrong. But, as we have not only allowed, but even

proved,

proved, that *moral depravity* is inconfiftent with *rational happiness*, and that it is as *impoffible* men fhould be *happy*, in the *other* world, as in *this*, till they are reduced under a *willing fubjection* to the government of God; yea, that the *reafon* of their fuffering the *torments* of the *next ftate*, which are awfully *great* in *degree*, as well as *long* in *duration*, is, that they might be made the *willing people* of God, and that they fhall not be delivered from *thefe torments* till this has been effected: I fay, as we have proved all this, it cannot, with any fhadow of truth, be pretended, that a *doctrine*, thus *circumftanced*, fhould, from its *natural tendency*, give *encouragement* to *vice*. It is, on the contrary, very *powerfully fuited* to check men's lufts, and difengage them from their fins; and if it hath not *actually* this effect, it is becaufe they will not hearken to the dictates of *reafon*, and act up to their character as *intelligent agents.*

It muft certainly argue *folly*, and to an high degree too, for men, rather than not proceed in their vicious ways, to *chufe* to undergo UNUTTERABLE PAINS FOR A LONG DURATION, God only knows how long, when they might, by approving themfelves *faithful fubjects* in the kingdom of Jefus Chrift, pafs, without fuffering thefe pains, into the JOYS OF THE RESURRECTION WORLD: And this folly will rather deferve the name of *downright madnefs*, if it be remembered, that they *muft ceafe from being wicked, before they can poffibly be fixed in final happinefs.* There is no room for debate here. Thofe men muft act in contradiction

to *all prudence*, and in defiance of *common sense*,
who will venture, for the sake of the *pleasures
of sin*, to expose themselves to that FIRE OF HELL,
which will effect their DEATH A SECOND TIME,
under all the circumstances of LINGERING HOR-
ROR, AND TORMENTING AGONY; especially if it
be considered, that they may, if they will but
renounce their sins, avoid this *miserable death*, and,
instead of it, be admitted to a GLORIOUS IMMOR-
TALITY IN HEAVEN. The plain truth is, if men
will *encourage* themselves in *wickedness* from the
above *doctrine*, it must be by laying aside their
reason, and acting a *distracted part*; for it is impossible they should take *encouragement* herefrom
in any other way.

But it will, perhaps, be said, the *discouragement
to sin* is *much greater* upon the scheme of *never-
ending torments*, than *this* that is pleaded for. We
shall, for the present, suppose it to be so. And
what is the consequence herefrom? Surely, not
that sin *must* be *thus discouraged*, and that any *lower
method* of discouraging it *cannot* be the *truth* of
revelation. For God is not obliged to make the
discouragements to vicious practice the *greatest*, it is
possible his *power* should make them. This would
not consist with his *wisdom*, which must consider
men as *free agents*, and adjust his *conduct* towards
them as *such*. He could, doubtless, in point of
power, represent *Hell* to the view of sinners in such
a striking light, even supposing the *torments* of it
were not *endless*, as that they should be *irresistibly*
stopped

stopped in their wicked pursuits : But *such* a method of dealing with men would not comport with their *free agency*. No room, in this case, would be left for the *trial* of their virtue. The *discouragement*, that sin would carry with it, would so overpower the mind, as to give no opportunity for *choice*. The *motive* could not be *withstood*.— The short of the matter is, God is a much better judge, than we are, what *motives* are the *wisest*, and *best*, to be used with his creatures : For which reason, it will not follow, that the *present doctrine* is not true, even upon the supposition, that it does not *discourage* sin so *strongly*, as it is *discouraged* on the *other* scheme.

It will not be thought, by any of these *objectors*, that our *Saviour* did not use the *wisest* and *most proper method* to convince the Jews, in his day, of his *Messiahship*, because he did not judge it fit to gratify that *humour* in them, which required *still further evidence* of this truth ; which evidence, in regard of *power*, he could easily have given them. He had done enough, by the *miracles*, and *wonders*, and *signs*, which he had wrought in the *midst of them*, to make it appear, to all *unprejudiced impartial* enquirers, that he was *a man approved of God* ; and he therefore justly calls them " an evil and " adulterous generation," attributing their *unbelief*, not to want of proper evidence, but to *perverseness* and *obstinacy* of temper, which would probably have made an ill use even of *stronger* evidence, if short of *irresistible*, had he laid it before them ; which therefore

therefore he wisely refused to do.—To apply this to the present case. God, no doubt, could have made the *discouragements* to vicious practice *much stronger* than he has done, had his *wisdom* judged it proper. And if any will not be satisfied with the *fitness* and *suitableness* of these *discouragements*, because they might, as they imagine, have been still *more powerful*, they would do well to consider, whether they do not discover a *disposition* very like to *that* of the Jews, in our Saviour's day, who would not believe in him, unless he would gratify their *humour*, by giving them *just that evidence*, in proof of his pretensions, that they desired. If the *motives* to discourage men from vice are, in their nature, *rationally* and *strongly* adapted to promote this design, it is highly absurd to *object* against their *divinity*, upon this consideration *merely*, that they are not *so powerfully* adapted to this purpose, as we may fondly conceit they might be.

But this *objection*, perhaps, is levelled, not so much against the *truth* of the foregoing scheme, as the *wisdom* of opening it to the world. It is feared, if the *restraint*, that is laid upon men, by their *faith* in the doctrine of *endless torments*, is taken off, by their being told, that they will sooner or later come to a *period*, when they shall be admitted to *happiness*, they would universally indulge to vice; insomuch that the *whole earth*, it might be expected, would quickly be overrun with *wickedness*, in all its various kinds.——To the *objection*, in this point

point of view, I would anſwer in the following particulars :

1. If men's *faith* in the doctrine of *never-ending torments* is founded, not on the *ſcripture itſelf*, but their *own wrong interpretation* of it, it would be very extraordinary, if the ſetting them right in this matter ſhould have the *bad tendency* that is *feared.* It ought not to be ſuppoſed, that men ſhould be made *worſe* by underſtanding the *ſcripture* in its *true* and *genuine* ſenſe. To ſuppoſe ſuch a thing, would carry with it a *baſe reflection* on the *revelations of God* contained in it. If *final univerſal happineſs* is a *ſcripture truth*, we need not *fear* its doing any *damage* to *men's morals*, ſhould they be told of it, and brought *univerſally* and *heartily* to believe it. And, indeed, to ſpeak plainly, all *fear*, upon this ſuppoſition, is ultimately founded on *man's wiſdom*, in oppoſition to the *wiſdom of God*; which ſtands in need of no *human craft*, but can without it guard mankind againſt wickedneſs, and make them *good* and *faithful ſubjects* in his kingdom of righteouſneſs and holineſs.

Some learned as well as good men, I am ſenſible, who had themſelves no faith in the doctrine of *never-ending torments*, have yet been under reſtraint in opening themſelves, upon this head, through *fear* of doing hurt, by leſſening the *received* and *credited* motive to diſcourage vice. Origen, one of the primitive and moſt celebrated Chriſtian fathers, having ſaid, ' He that deſpiſes ' the purifications of the word of God, and the
' doctrine

' doctrine of the goſpel, is reſerved for thoſe
' *dreadful* and *penal purifications* afterwards ; that
' ſo he may be purged by the *fire* and *torment* of
' *hell*, who would not receive purgation from the
' apoſtolical doctrine, and evangelical word, ac-
' cording to that which is written, of being *purified*
' *by fire.* But *how long* this purification, which is
' wrought out by *penal fire*, ſhall *endure*, or for
' *how many periods* or *ages* it ſhall *detain finful ſouls*
' *in torment*, he only knows to whom all judgment
' is committed by the Father :' I ſay, having
ſpoken thus, upon the ſame place and ſubject, he
adds, ' But we muſt ſtill remember, that the apoſ-
' tle would have this text accounted as a *myſtery*,
' ſo as that the *faithful* and *perfect ones* may keep
' its ſecret ſenſe *among themſelves*, and not *ordina-*
' *rily divulge it* to the *imperfect*, and *leſs capable of*
' *receiving it* *.' And Dr. Thomas Burnet, a writer in this preſent century, having largely, and
with a good deal of learning and judgment, oppoſed the common notion of the *eternity of hell*
torments, yet adds, upon the whole, in a marginal
note, ' that if any one ſhould tranſlate into the
' *vulgar language*, what he had written for the ſake
' of the *learned*, he ſhould think it was done with a
' *bad mind*, and a *finiſter view* †.'

---

* See the preface to Mr. *White's Reſtoration of all Things.*

† Hæc, quæ doctioribus inſcripta ſunt, fi quis in linguam
vulgarem tranſtulerit, id malo animo atque conſilio ſiniſtro
factum arbitrabor. *De Statu Mort. et Reſurg.* page 305.

But

But it appears to me an argument of evident *weakneſs*, taking riſe from the remains of *religious ſuperſtition*, for any to be *reſtrained* from ſpeaking what they eſteem a *real truth of God*, through *fear* of doing *hurt* thereby, provided they take care to ſpeak with *prudence.* For, as Mr. Whiſton well obſerves, [*Hell Torments conſidered*, pages 138,139]

'We have no warrant to *impoſe* upon Chriſtians,
'or upon mankind, in matters of religion. We
'have no authority from God, or his Chriſt, or
'Holy Spirit, to diſguiſe our Chriſtianity; to uſe
'frauds of either *prieſt-craft*, or *lay-craft:* But
'ought to lay the duties, the promiſes, and the
'threatenings, of the goſpel, *plainly* and *ſincerely*
'before men, without all *arts* or *tricks* whatſoever.
'I ſay further, I will not deny but that, during
'the times of *groſs ignorance*, ſuch as, in general,
'were the ſeveral ages, from the fifth to the ſix-
'teenth century of the goſpel, many *pious*, or
'rather *impious frauds*, with *falſe doctrines* in abun-
'dance, and, among the reſt, this abſurd doctrine,
'were univerſally believed: Which, how falſe ſo-
'ever in themſelves, did then do the leſs harm,
'becauſe few, or none, perceived them to be *falſe.*
'But the caſe is quite otherwiſe now. A *natural*
'curioſity of examining every thing, and a *ſceptical*
'curioſity of examining the books and doctrines
'of the *Bible*, and of *Chriſtianity*, in order to diſ-
'cover any flaws or impoſitions therein, does now
'greatly prevail; and makes it abſolutely neceſſary
'for all good men, and good ſcholars, eſpecially
'for

' for *Clergymen* and *Divines*, to difcard all *pious*
' *frauds*, and to lay the *naked truth* of every thing
' clearly before the world.   Nor indeed, does holy
' Job allow us to *fpeak wickedly for God*, nor to
' *talk deceitfully for him (a)* ; Nor St. Paul permit
' us to *tell lies to promote God's glory (b)* : nor, in
' general, *to do evil that good may come*, but pro-
' nounces *their damnation to be juft* that do fo.
' St. Peter alfo, in the *Recognition of Clement*, affures
' us, " that it was not lawful for him to lie ; nor
' ought he to deceive men, whether an unbeliever
' might be thereby faved, or not faved :" Which
' precepts, and example, therefore, ought to take
' place among Chriftians, before any *political max-*
' *ims* whatfoever.'

2. It ought to be confidered, that the *torments
of hell*, according to the fcheme we are pleading
for, are *fufficient* to difcourage any, that will act
under the influence of *reafon*, from going on in
a courfe of *fin* ; infomuch that, if they are not
wrought upon by this *motive*, it muft be, becaufe
they are *fhamefully inattentive*, nay, I might fay,
ftupidly thoughtlefs.   And to perfons, who will lay
afide their *reafon*, and live and act as though they
had none, what room is there to expect, that they
would be influenced by *diftant torments*, however
lengthened in *duration?* If they would *confider*, and
behave like *men*, it is *impoffible* they fhould go on
in a vicious courfe, under the profpect of being
condemned by the righteous judge of all the earth,

(a) Job. xiii. 7.   *(b)* Rom. iii. 7, 8.

not only to banifhment from the JOYS OF THE RE-
SURRECTION-STATE, but to POSITIVE TORMENTS,
which, though they will *end* in *death*, yet fhall be
AWFULLY GREAT IN DEGREE, and LONG IN CON-
TINUANCE, in proportion to the *number* and *greatnefs* of their crimes : But if they will not fuffer so
DREADFUL A PUNISHMENT as this to have any
influence upon them, by their *thoughtleffnefs* and
inconfiderction, there is certainly no good reafon to
fuppofe, was the punifhment made *greater* by the
increafe of its *duration*, but that the *fame thoughtleffnefs* and *ftupidity* would render it *ineffectual*. If
men will put off their character as *reafonable* creatures, no *diftant motives*, however increafed in
ftrength, will operate upon them. It is not indeed
poffible they fhould operate, but by making them
prefent to the *mind* by contemplation. And if
men would be *confiderate* and *attentive*, they would
be *fufficient*, without *heightening* them to the *utmoft*,
to have the defired effect : Whereas, if they will
be *thoughtlefs*, their being thus *heightened* will probably ferve to very little purpofe. Our Saviour
has faid, " If they hear not Mofes and the pro-
" phets, neither will they be perfuaded though
" one rofe from the dead ;" that is, it is not probable that they would. That very *perverfenefs* of
temper, which obftructs the influence of the *public
ftanding revelations of God*, would, in all likelihood,
prevent their being wrought upon by this propofed expedient. The fame may be faid, with
equal truth, in the *prefent cafe*. If men will go on

in

in vicious practice, notwithstanding the TERRORS
OF THAT DEATH, which shall be brought on with
PAINS AWFULLY CRUCIATING, and yet AWFULLY
PROTRACTED IN THEIR CONTINUANCE, it must be
because they are *stupidly inconsiderate*; and it is
highly probable, the *same stupidity* would prevent
their being disengaged from their mad pursuits,
if *those pains*, instead of *ending* in *death*, were to *last
always*. There is little reason to think otherwise.
But,

3. It may be well worth while to enquire, whether the *common doctrine* is *so likely* to restrain men
from sin, as *that* which has been explained in these
papers. It is seen, in *fact*, notwithstanding all that
has been said to make men believe, that the *torments* of the coming world shall *never have an end*,
that they *generally* " walk in the way of their own
" heart, and in the sight of their own eyes," and
will not be kept within due bounds. And, perhaps,
upon examination, it will be found, that one *principal reason* of this is, that *the terrors* proposed for
their persuasion *exceed their belief*. If they do not
openly speak of it as an *incredible thing*, that they
should be hereafter doomed to *never-ending torments*,
it may be questioned, whether they *inwardly* assent
to this as the *real truth*. The *natural* notions
they entertain of the *goodness* and *mercy* of God
rise up in opposition to it, and *strongly* operate,
though, it may be, *insensibly* many times, to *obstruct*
its *influence*, and *give* them *peace*. These *appre-
hensions* concerning their Creator, and Preserver,
and

and Father, have a *real existence* in their minds, and
in consequence hereof, their *inward secret hope* is,
that they *shall not suffer such dreadful torments.*
An infinitely *benevolent* God, they cannot well
help thinking, will not be *so severe* with his poor,
though sinful, creatures. It is, with me, past all
doubt, that the generality of wicked men, under
the gospel, whatever they may profess, or imagine
they believe, are not *really persuaded*, that *never-
ending misery* will be the *certain effect* of sin persisted
in. The conceptions they naturally, and as it
were insensibly, form of the *all-merciful* Being, are
a counterbalance to their *fear* from this quarter.
They recur in their thoughts, and cannot easily do
any other than recur, to the *infinite benevolence* of
the Deity, and ultimately place their dependence
here; and to this it is very much owing, I believe,
that the doctrine of *never-ending torments* has no
greater influence upon them. Whereas, upon the
foregoing scheme, there is nothing *incredible* in the
torments of *another world.* They are perfectly
analogous to what is experienced in the *present
state*; and there is no more reason to *object* against
them, than against the *present judicial* proceedings
of Heaven against *wicked* men. They are *equally
consistent* with men's *natural* notions of the *benevolence* of God. And, consequently, as proposed in
this scheme, their *influence* could not be at all ob-
structed from their *incredibility*; but they would
strike the mind with *full force,* and probably operate to much better purpose, restraining men more
effectually from their wicked courses.

A a

It

It may alfo be pertinently fuggefted here, the *public officers* of religion might be *more free*, and *full*, in urging upon men's confciences the doctrine of *future mifery*, in order to check their lufts and paffions, upon the *plan* exhibited in thefe papers, than upon the *common* one. And they would be likely to do a great deal more good. A very confiderable number of *Divines*, at this day, do not believe the *eternity* of *hell torments*; though they may not difclofe their minds to the *vulgar*, but, for political reafons, fuffer it to pafs among them, that they do believe it. And, as to fuch, they are evidently *reftrained* from making *that ufe* of the *terrors of the Lord*, for the warning of men, which they might otherwife do, and, it may be, to good effect, with refpect to many. And, in truth, as honeft Mr. Whifton, with his ufual frank-nefs, obferves, [*Hell Torments confidered*, pages 135, 136] ' Till this doctrine of the *equal* dura-
' tion of the *torments of hell* with the *joys of heaven*,
' and that they are to be *co-eternal with God*, be
' laid afide, Divines of real fagacity, and true judg-
' ment, dare hardly treat, in particular, of thefe
' *terrors of the Lord* *, in order to affrighten men
' from their wicked courfes, and to perfuade them
' to be religious; they dare hardly, in earneft, en-
' force our Saviour's folemn caution, to *fear him*
' *who is able to deftroy both body and foul in hell* †:
' Nor can they frequently, with an honeft heart,
' exhort them to cut off their darling lufts for *fear*

---

* 2 Cor. v. 11.　　　† Matt. x. 28.

' of

‘ of the worm that never dies, and the fire that never
‘ shall be quenched*, as our Saviour did : Nor can
‘ they fufficiently terrify the greateft finners, among
‘ Chriftians, as did the author to the Hebrews,
‘ with that *certain fearful looking for of judgment,*
‘ *and fiery indignation, which shall devour the adver-*
‘ *faries* †; with that *fore punishment that he shall be*
‘ *thought worthy of, that hath trodden under foot the*
‘ *Son of God, and hath counted the blood of the cove-*
‘ *nant, wherewith he had been fanctified, an unholy*
‘ *thing, and hath done defpite to the fpirit of grace;*
‘ fince *it is a fearful thing to fall into the hands of*
‘ *the living God* ‡ : Becaufe their own natural con-
‘ fciences would fly in their faces, and tell them,
‘ that what they affright their readers and hearers
‘ with, is unjuft in its own nature, cruel both in
‘ the threatening and in the execution, and what
‘ any one that believes and confiders the exact
‘ juftice, and infinite goodnefs of God, cannot pof-
‘ fibly believe at the fame time. We need not
‘ indeed much wonder, that a *weak enthufiaft,* or
‘ a *bigotted* [I would fay, *friend to topical orthodoxy,*
‘ rather than] *Athanafian,* may be in earneft in
‘ fuch a doctrine, and exhortation ; and that fuch
‘ as do not give themfelves leave to think, and
‘ examine, may follow their common interpreters,
‘ and may both believe, and preach up, and de-
‘ fend this *proper eternity* of *hell torments.* But if
‘ we come to fuch great and good men as arch-

* Mark ix. 43—48.　† Heb. x. 27.　‡ Ibid. ver. 29, 31.

A a 2　　　　　　　　‘ bifhop

' bifhop Tillotfon*, and Dr. Whitby †, who have
' both of them ventured to treat on that *eternity*,
' and this without either of them, or even Dr.
' Burnet himfelf, having made a thorough ex-
' amination into the foundation it ftands upon,
' we fhall find, that archbifhop Tillotfon was fo
' fully fenfible of its abfurdity, that he chofe rather
' to give up the *veracity* of God in thefe his
' *threatenings*, than to defend this *eternity*; and Dr.
' Whitby, who has been fo hardy as to defend it,
' is forced entirely to give up his *juftice* in fuch his
' *punifhments*: While much the greater part of
' Divines generally avoid the treating directly upon
' fo difagreeable and dangerous a fubject. Where-
' as, if they would enquire into the bottom of this
' matter, and go to the fountain-head of this
' common notion, they would find no more diffi-
' culty in treating upon this, than any other points
' of Chriftianity. If indeed the common doctrine
' were certainly true, the *juftice* of God muft in-
' evitably be given up, and much more his *mercy*:
' Which yet are the proper and only foundation of
' all filial fear, and rational reverence; of all juft
' honour, and truft, and hope, and love, and con-
' fidence in him, who has ever been efteemed as
' *optimus maximus*, the *beft*, as well as *greateft*, of be-
' ings; while this doctrine fuppofes him to delight
' in cruelty: And all his reafonable creatures, that

---

* Tillotfon's Sermons, vol. I. Serm. 86.

† Whitby's Appendix to the Comment on the Second to
the Theffalonians.

' dare

' dare think, muſt give themſelves up to deſpair
' and horror.—Such are the fatal conſequences
' of this amazing doctrine, ſo very unjuſtly, ſo
' very unjuſtly, I ſay it again, (bleſſed be the name
' of God, and his Chriſt, for ever!) fathered upon
' our holy religion.'

I ſhall only add—the *future torments*, conſidered
in the light we have ſet them, are *more ſuitably*
adapted, in the nature of the thing, to work upon
rational and *intelligent* agents, than in the *common*
point of view. The *end* propoſed by them perfectly coincides with *benevolence* ; for they are the
chaſtiſements of a *father*, as well as judge, and deſigned *principally* for the *reformation*, and conſequent good, of the *offenders themſelves*. And when
men are taught to think thus ; and that theſe
corrections ſhall be *heavy* in proportion to their *ſtub-
bornneſs* in ſin, and *continued* till they are *humbled*
and *ſubdued* ; and that they ſhall have no mercy till
this *end* is accompliſhed—what can be wanting,
in a motive *thus circumſtanced*, to operate, in a *moral*
way, upon *reaſonable* minds? It ſhould ſeem to be
as well calculated to the purpoſe, as it poſſibly can
be. And if men will not be wrought upon by it,
it muſt be becauſe they will not act *like men*. To
be ſure, if they ſhould be diſpoſed to take occaſion,
from ſuch a repreſentation of the *future torments*,
to give the reins to their luſts, they muſt act in
defiance of all *reaſon*, and *gratitude*, and *intereſt*,
and be looked upon as *abandoned ſtupid creatures*.

CON-

CONCLUSION,

I HAVE now offered what I had to fay in proof of the *final falvation of all men:* Nor am I. fenfible of any effential defect in the *evidence* upon which it has been fupported from the *revelations of God.* The more carefully I review it, the more clearly fatisfied I am it will ftand the fevereft trial, if it be an impartial one.

And as it is from the BIBLE, that we. are fur-nifhed with this *evidence ;* as it is in this *facred book,* that the infinitely benevolent God is reprefented as having fet on foot a *fcheme* for the *recovery* of the *whole race of Adam,* which fcheme he will go on profecuting by his *Son Jefus Chrift,* on whofe *blood* and *righteoufnefs* it was founded, till he has inftated them *all* in the poffeffion of *everlafting happinefs ;* — how *thankful* fhould we be for the *fcripture-revelation?* And how very imprudent are fuch as *voluntarily* put themfelves into the ftate of thofe who have *no hope,* but what they fetch by their own arguings from the *mere light of nature?* There are great numbers of this kind of perfons in the Chriftian world; and they feem to be upon the increafe. But why fhould any chufe to renounce the *hope of the gofpel* for one that is built upon
reafon

reason only? Is the profpect which *mere reason* gives
us of a *future world* to be compared with *that*,
which we may take of it by the help of *revelation?* By no means. The light of *reason*, it is
true, if duly attended to, may open to our view
a *state beyond the grave:* But does it difcover, with
clearnefs and *certainty*, what our *condition* will be
in *that state?* It may, if we have behaved *ill* in
this, excite our *fears*, and fill us with *anxiety*, when
we look into *that*; and it may also, if we have
endeavoured to act conformably to the rules of
virtue, encourage us to rely on the *divine goodnefs*
with fome degree of *hope:* But it cannot, upon
folid grounds, *affure* us of a *blessed immortality.*
' For who can fay, he hath performed a *virtue*,
' that, in the eftimate of his own *reason*, will entitle
' him to it ? Who can pretend to have fo behaved,
' as to deferve any one bleffing from God's hands?
' Is it not evident, that the beft virtue, any man
' performs, needs the relief of grace and mercy ?
' And where is that grace and mercy revealed, but
' in the gofpel ? The gofpel alone difcovers and
' enfures immortality ; or reveals the *grace* which
' exprefsly gives it, the *ground* upon which this
' grace ftands, the *end* for which it is given, and
' the *means* by which we may obtain it. And can
' the full perfuafion and view of immortal honour
' and glory be efteemed a trifle ?—The gofpel is
' good news from heaven ; pardon and eternal life
' promifed to a finful world. And can any be
' fo infatuated as to wifh its heavenly light and
A a 4 ' hopes

' hopes at once extinguifhed, and the darknefs
' of *Paganifm* reftored among the nations ? Doth
' not *nature* itfelf teach us to be thankful for
' fuperior bleffings, and to turn our eyes to the
' brighteft profpects of happinefs ? If the univerfal
' Father is pleafed to beftow upon us fingular fa-
' vours, is it not moft unnatural and wicked to
' defpife and reject them ? Such is the glory and
' excellence, fuch the delightful profpects of the
' gofpel, that, inftead of cavilling and oppofing,
' methinks the proper and only concern of every
' mind fhould be to feek out evidence, and all
' poffible means to eftablifh its truth.'   After
this manner Dr. Taylor reafons, excellently well,
in his dedication to his work on the Romans ;
though he had no notion of the *gofpel-plan of mercy*,
in that *extenfively benevolent fenfe* we have fet it
forth, in the foregoing pages : Upon which, the
reafoning is far more emphatically ftriking and
forcible.   The *Deifts* themfelves will not pretend
to fet up *reafon* in competition with *revelation*, if
the *happinefs* of the *whole human fpecies* is the
GREAT END of the fcheme of God there opened,
and an end that *fhall not fail of being accomplifhed*
in the iffue of its operation.   Suppofing this to
be the truth, nothing can be faid, upon the principles of *mere reafon*, that will reprefent the bleffed
God in fo amiable and endearing a light : Nor
could the human mind, in any way but this of
revelation, have been let into a *defign of mercy*, fo
wonderfully fitted to deliver mankind from that

                                        corruptible

corruptible miferable condition we know we are fubjected to, by preparing us for, and finally fixing
us in, the joys of a *glorious immortality. Reafon*
may perfectly acquiefce in this fcheme of *revelation,* not having a word to object againft it; but
it could not, of itfelf, have made the difcovery.
It might have put here and there a great genius
upon making *conjectures* refpecting *another world,*
and grounding *feeble hopes* upon them; but it
would not have enabled them to have made *fuch a
reprefentation* of it, and of the *way,* and *manner,* in
which *mankind univerfally,* fooner or later, in one
period of their exiftence or another, fhall be *made
happy* in it, as is given us in the *fcriptures :* A reprefentation eminently worthy of God, and of the
acceptance of every fon of Adam. Nor can I
fuppofe, that any foberly thoughtful *Deift* would
ever have recurred to *mere reafon,* in oppofition to
revelation, for the fupport of a *hope towards God,*
if he had entertained this idea of its *defign* and
tendency.

It is, I am verily perfuaded, very much owing
to the *falfe light* in which *revelation* has been
placed, and by its very good friends too, that fo
many have been led to *reject* it. And, in truth,
if the *fenfe* of revelation *really* was, what it has too
generally been reprefented to be, even by Chriftians themfelves, I fee not that blame could juftly
be reflected on them. It is impoffible *that* fhould
come from God, which is *unworthy of him ;* nor
would any *external evidence* be fufficient to juftify

a man

a man in believing him to be the author of *that*, which, in its own nature, is *unreasonable* and *absurd*. This, if I mistake not, is well worthy of the sober consideration of those, who profess a veneration for the BIBLE as a DIVINE BOOK. It is a fact too evident to be denied, that the *revelations of God*, as contained in the writings of the *Old* and *New Testament*, have been gradually and strangely *corrupted* by *false philosophy* and *vain deceit* ; and, perhaps, *as gross absurdities*, *as palpably wrong and dishonourable ideas of God*, have been received by *believers* for *sacred truths*, upon the foot of *revelation*, as were ever received by *infidels* upon the foot of *reason*, even in the darkest ages and places of *Paganism*. Yea, notwithstanding the *light* and *learning* of the present day, *horrible absurdities*, both in *doctrine* and *worship*, are still grounded on the writings even of the *apostles of Jesus Christ*, and by those too who profess a regard to them as wrote by inspiration of the Holy Ghost. Such are the *doctrines* taught in the church of *Rome*. More *enormous falsehoods* were never fathered upon the *God of truth*. They are indeed such an affront to the human understanding, such a defiance of common sense, as cannot but naturally and strongly tend to make men *infidels*. And such also, if not in so high a degree, are some of the doctrines which *Protestants* receive for *revealed truths*. Of this kind I may properly mention, upon this occasion, the doctrines of *election and reprobation* ; of *the eternity of hell torments* ; and of *the partial de-*

sign,

sign, and final effect, of *the mediatory interposition of Jesus Christ.* Mr. Whiston has declared it as his thought, " that the common opinion, concerning the *future torments,* if it were, for certain, a real part of Christianity, would be a more insuperable objection against it, than any or all the present objections of unbelievers put together." The same may be said, I think, with as much, if not more, truth of the doctrine of *absolute reprobation,* as it has been particularly explained, and warmly defended, by many *Christian Divines,* and of very considerable note. And the *mediatory undertaking of Jesus Christ,* as commonly understood, is perhaps incredible also. These, and such-like, representations of the *sense* of *scripture,* have, I doubt not, been " stones of stumbling, and rocks of offence." Many may have taken occasion herefrom to call that " foolishness," which in reality is " the wisdom of " God." And in vain shall we hope to silence the objections of *infidelity,* and put a stop to its growth, till we are able to exhibit an account of the *internal contents* of the sacred writings, that is *more honourable* to the *infinitely perfect Being,* and *more conducive* to the *real advantage* of mankind. Such an account, it appears to me, I have given, in the foregoing work, of the *revelations of scripture;* an account so far from being unreasonable and absurd, that it cannot but approve itself to the human mind, as that which reflects great glory on God, and his Son Jesus, in the *good* it *universally* brings to the sons of men: And it is the more to be re-

3   garded,

garded, as it is eminently fitted to promote true piety and real virtue in the world.

If, conformably to the account we have given from the *scriptures*, God has so loved us as to project a scheme, which, in the final result of its prosecution, will instate us *all* in *heavenly* and *immortal glory*; how powerfully are we herefrom excited to yield to him the intire homage of our hearts? Who but God, who in competition with God, should be the supreme object of our love, hope, confidence, joy, and delight? We may, with infinite reason, take to ourselves the words of the Psalmist, and say, " Whom have we in heaven " but thee? There is none on earth we desire be- " sides thee: Our flesh and our heart may fail us: " But God is the strength of our heart, and our " portion for ever."

If *Jesus Christ* is the glorious person *through whom* God has made the *promise of eternal life*, and *by whom*, as *prime minister* in the kingdom of his grace, he will prepare *mankind* for the *actual bestowment* of it; how right and fit is it, that, next to God, and in subordination to him, we should make *his Son*, whom he has authorized to be our king and Saviour, the beloved object of our faith and hope, our submission and obedience? And how constraining are the arguments, which urge us to a compliance with these *peculiar requirements* of the gospel? They naturally and necessarily grow out of the *relation* he sustains, as the *grand commissioned trustee* to carry into effect the benevolent plan, which

which God has laid with reference to the *whole
posterity of lapsed Adam.* And it is as reasonable,
upon suppofition of the truth of this plan, that we
" fhould honour the Son," as that we fhould " ho-
" nour the Father;" and the *motives* hereto are in-
vincibly ftrong : Nor can they be withftood, unlefs
by mifreprefentation, or non-attention.

If God is equally the *Father* of us all, if we
are all *joint-partners* in the fame hope of *eternal
life,* and fhall all *finally* make *one family,* and live
together as *brethren* in the *heavenly world* ; how
peculiarly proper is it that we fhould be *kindly af-
fectioned to each other,* and difcover that we are fo
by all Chriftian offices of good-will and benefi-
cence, as occafions are offered for them in providence ? Should any of our race make themfelves
vile, as is too commonly the cafe, we fhould not
be deftitute, upon this account of the fcripture
fcheme of mercy, of fufficient motives to embrace
them with the tendereft affection. We might
refent their folly, and in all fuitable ways teftify
againft it : But we fhould, at the fame time, if we
were ourfelves good Chriftians, pity them under
it, and do all in our power, within our proper
fphere, to reclaim them from it. And fhould
they, after all, appear to be " veffels of wrath
" fitted for deftruction," inftead of treating them
with rancour and ill-will, we fhould ftill view them
as *objects of the divine mercy,* and feel within ourfelves a fecret pleafure refulting from the thought,
that they will *finally* be recovered from the *fnare*

of

of the Devil, and partake, in common with ourfelves, of the *temper* and *inheritance* of God's
children.

In fine—If we fhall all, before the completion
of the fcheme of God, be *crowned with immortality
and honour* ; how fingularly forcible are the induce-
ments herefrom to meeknefs, patience, content-
ment, and refignation to the divine pleafure, under the various trials of this prefent vain, frail,
mortal life ? And how eafily reconcileable are *the
fufferings of the life to come*, with the wifdom, and
goodnefs, as well as juftice of God ? And how intirely are all complaints, upon this head, at once
filenced ? For if we are brought into being *expec-
tants* of a *bleffed immortality*, and upon a foundation that will not difappoint us, why fhould we
find fault with *that difcipline*, however *fevere*,
which may, in the reafon of things, be *morally*
connected with our coming to the *actual enjoyment* of it ? Ποθεν το κακον; *From whence came
evil ?* has been one of the grand puzzling quef-
tions in all ages of the world. We have here
the moft eafy fatisfactory anfwer to it. *Evils*
and *fufferings*, whether *prefent* or *future*, in *this
world* or *another*, are a *difciplinary mean* wifely
and powerfully adapted to promote the *good* of
the *patients themfelves*, as well as others ; they
ftand connected with *this end* in the plan of
God, and will, in the laft refult of its operation, certainly bring it into *fact*. Inftead therefore of being a *contradiction* to, they very obviously

viously coincide with, *wife* and *reasonable be-nevolence* : Yea, they are a wonderful illustra-tion of it, if it be true, as we have endeavour-ed to prove it to be, that they will *finally* issue, conformably to the original purpose of God, in an " exceeding and eternal weight of glory."

APPENDIX.

APPENDIX.

ANOTHER memorable paſſage, to the purpoſe of our preſent argument, we have in Rev. xx. 4, 5, 6, &c. which I ſhall have occaſion to inſert afterwards at large. It may perhaps be thought, the reaſoning here muſt be precarious and doubtful, becauſe the words upon which it is founded, together with the preceding and ſubſequent context, are of the *prophetic* ſort: And, as *all prophecy* is dark, *that* of the *Apocalypſe* is peculiarly ſo, and no branch of prophecy, even in the *Apocalypſe*, more juſtly falls under this character than the paſſage above referred to.——And it is readily acknowledged, *prophecy* in general is *hard to be underſtood*, and this is eminently true of *that* propoſed to be conſidered, with the context to which it is related. But though it may be difficult, it may not be impoſſible, to underſtand its meaning, and ſo to underſtand it too, as to argue from it to general ſatisfaction. I imagine, the ſenſe in which I take Rev. xx. 4, 5, 6, &c. and the *whole prophecy* contained in the three laſt chapters of this book, with which it is inſeparably connected, is ſo plain and natural, and ſo perfectly conſiſtent with the whole run of ſcripture, that I may reaſonably argue from it with reference to

B b

the

the great point in debate. But whether I judge right in the cafe muft be left with the reader to determine.

The interpretation I have to exhibit is *new*. To me, at leaft, it is fo. For which reafon I would introduce it with a few general remarks upon the *contents* of the three laft chapters in the *Apocalypfe*. The reader will then be prepared to underftand the *paraphrafe* that will follow, containing this interpretation, with the *notes*, which, as I think, do fufficiently juftify it.

Let it then be obferved, that *all the events* fpoken of in thefe *three chapters* belong to *one and the fame general period*, which period, under the adminiftrations of Jefus Chrift, takes in the general refurrection and judgment, and the refpective ftates of good and bad men univerfally in the world of retribution. The firft coming on of this period began with the *deftruction of Antichrift*, an account of which concluded the nineteenth chapter. The fucceeding order of events, as I fuppofe, is thus:—*Satan*, the grand tempter of men to wickednefs, is laid under a *divine reftraint*, Chap. xx. verfes 1, 2, 3. Upon having mentioned this, the apoftle John anticipates himfelf, by going into *fubfequent events*, that he might exhibit, in one view, all he had to fay relative to *Satan*'s being *bound*, and *loofened*, and the *ftate of things* that would refpectively follow thereupon; verfe 4th to the 11th. He now returns from this digreffion, and proceeds in his account of the *feries* of events.

events. Accordingly, the *next* event following upon the *restraint of Satan*, is the appearance of the Son of man, sitting upon a great and glorious throne; the passing away of the earth and heaven, as to their present form; the resurrection of all mankind from the dead; their standing before the throne of judgment; and their receiving their respective sentences according to their works; verses 11, 12, 13. The *next* event is the execution of the sentence passed upon the *wicked*, which is briefly represented in verses 14, 15, by their being cast into the *lake of fire:* See note *(n).* The *last* event is the happy condition of the *saints*, in consequence of their having been approved by the Judge, at the general judgment. This begins with the twenty-first chapter; in which it is declared, that a *new heaven*, and a *new earth*, were formed for their reception; that God dwelt with them; that he wiped away all tears from their eyes, &c. &c. In a word, such things are said concerning the *state* they were in, as discovered it to be a proper reward for God to bestow, and an object worthy the pursuit of all rational creatures. And with *this state of things*, these *chapters* and the *Apocalypse* conclude.

N. B. The FIRST RESURRECTION, spoken of in the sixth and seventh verses of the twentieth chapter, or, what means the same thing, the *living* and *reigning* of the saints for a THOUSAND YEARS with Christ, that is, for this space of time, without any attempt being made to molest them, (see note *(d)*) is to be brought forward, and referred to their *life* in the *paradiſaic earth* after the *judgment*. The attempt alſo of *Gog* and *Magog* to diſturb their quiet, is in like manner to be brought forward, and placed a *thouſand years* from the beginning of the judgment, and the happy reign of the ſaints in conſequence of it, in the *new heaven* and *earth* ; afterwards, they are to reign *for ages of ages*, (chapter xxii. ver. 5) without any further attempt againſt them.

A large treatiſe by itſelf might be requiſite in order to juſtify minutely and particularly this *ſeries of events*, and point out its *conſiſtency* with the *whole ſcheme of prophecy*. But my ſituation forbidding the attempt, I ſhall reſt the proof of this *general ſenſe* of the *chapters* upon the *notes*, which are intended to ſupport the following *paraphraſe* of ſo much of them as is neceſſary, in purſuance of the deſign I have in view.

TEXT.	PARAPHRASE.
Rev. xx. 4. *And I ſaw thrones, and they ſat upon them, and judgment was given to them ; and I ſaw the ſouls of them that were beheaded for the witneſs of Jeſus, and for the word of God, and*	And I ſaw thrones, and them that ſat upon them (*a*), and judicial power was given to them. And [to let you know who ſat on theſe thrones with this judicial power, I go on, and would ſay more particularly] I ſaw the ſouls of thoſe who were beheaded (*b*) for the teſtimony

TEXT.

and which had not worſhipped the beaſt, neither his image, neither had received his mark upon their foreheads, or in their hands; and they lived and reigned with Chriſt a thouſand years.

5. But the reſt of the dead lived not again until the thouſand years were finiſhed. This is the FIRST RESURRECTION.

6. Bleſſed and holy is he that hath part in the FIRST RESUR-

PARAPHRASE.

mony of Jeſus, and for the word of God; and I ſaw alſo the ſouls of them who had not worſhipped the beaſt, nor his image, nor had received his mark upon their foreheads, or in their hands; and they all, whether *martyrs,* or other righteous perſons, lived in their reſpective bodies *(c),* and reigned with Chriſt a THOUSAND YEARS, without any attempt from *Satan,* or *wicked men* under his influence, to diſturb their peace and quiet *(d).* But the reſt of the dead *(e),* the *wicked dead,* I mean, did not *thus* live and reign with Chriſt, though delivered from the power of the grave, till after the expiration of this period of a THOUSAND YEARS. This reigning of the ſaints with Chriſt in life, you muſt particularly note, is the FIRST RESURRECTION of this ſort *(f).* And bleſſed, and ſeparated, or diſtinguiſhed from the reſt of mankind *(g),* is

TEXT.	PARAPHRASE.

RESURRECTION: *On fuch the fecond death hath no power; but they fhall be priefts of God, and of Chrift, and fhall reign with him* A THOUSAND YEARS.

7. *And when the thoufand years are expired, Satan fhall be loofed out of his prifon;*

8. *And fhall go out to deceive the nations, which are in the four quarters of the earth,* GOG *and* MAGOG, *to gather them together to battle, the number of whom is as the fand of the fea.*

9. *And they went upon the breadth of the earth, and compaffed the camp of the faints about, and the beloved city: and fire*

he who is a partner in the FIRST RESURRECTION : And I may well fay fo, for over fuch the SECOND DEATH hath no power, and they fhall be priefts of God, and of Chrift, and they fhall reign with him a THOUSAND YEARS, as obferved before. And when thefe THOUSAND YEARS fhall be completed, the reftraint that had been laid upon *Satan* fhall be taken off; upon which he fhall go out into the four quarters of the earth, and delude the nations of it, who, like GOG and MAGOG (*h*), in the prophecy of Eze-kiel, fhall affemble in vaft numbers, in order to engage in battle againft the faints. And fo great a multitude were they, that, as they went up from their feveral coun-tries, they overfpread the very furface of the earth; and they encompaffed the camp of the faints, and fur-rounded even the beloved city, the new Jerufalem itfelf. But

TEXT.

PARAPHRASE.

fire came down from God, out of heaven, and devoured them.

But this attempt was perfectly fruitlefs; for God, in a fudden and extraordinary manner, defeated and deftroyed them by fire from heaven, as he did the *Gog* and *Magog* mentioned by the prophet Ezekiel, chapters xxxviii. 22.—xxxix. 6. And

10. *And the Devil, that deceived them, was caft into the lake of fire and brimftone, where the beaft and falfe prophet are, and fhall be tormented day and night, for ever and ever.*

the *Devil*, the chief fomenter of this enmity againft the faints, and rebellion againft the government of Chrift, was caft into a lake of fire and brimftone, where the beaft and the falfe prophet are, and fhall be tormented (*i*) day and night for ages of ages.

To be yet more particular (*k*) in the account of my vifion, that you may not miftake the *order* and *connexion* of events by what I have hitherto reprefented. At the fame time that I faw *Satan* laid under reftraint, [the mentioning of which led me to interrupt the *feries* of events, that I might place the whole

B b 4

of

TEXT.

PARAPHRASE.

11. *And I saw a great white throne, and him that sat on it, from whose face the earth and the heavens fled away, and there was found no place for them.*

12. *And I saw the dead, small and great, stand before God; and the books were opened: and another book was opened, which is the book of life: and the dead were judged out of those things which were written in the books, according to their works.*

13. *And the sea gave up the dead that were in it, and death and hell delivered up the dead that were in them, and*

of what I had to say upon that affair in one view] I saw also a magnificent and bright throne, and a glorious personage sitting on it, upon whose appearance, the *form* of the earth and heaven was quite changed from what it is at present (*l*), and was no more. —I then beheld in my vision the dead raised, both high and low, young and old, and they stood before the throne of God, and were judged in a most fair and equal manner (*m*), according to their works, whether they had been good or evil. And, that this retribution might be *absolutely universal*, taking in the whole race of men, the dead, without distinction or limitation, were raised again to life, whether they died and were buried in the sea, or whether they died on the land and were buried in a grave; all in the invisible state of the dead were brought to life, and judged according to their works.

TEXT.

and they were judged every man according to their works.

14. And death and hell were cast into the lake of fire. This is the SECOND DEATH.

15. And whoso-ever was not found written in the book of life, was cast into the lake of fire.

Chap. xxi. 1. *And I saw a new heaven and a new earth; for the first heaven and the first earth were passed away. And there was no more sea.*

PARAPHRASE.

works. And, in consequence of this judgment, death and the grave might, in a sense, be said to be cast into the lake of fire, such numbers were actually cast into it (*n*). This fire is that which will effect the *second death:* And do not wonder that I say such multitudes will be cast into it, for if any man's name is not then found written in the Lamb's book of life, he shall be cast into this lake of fire.

This is what I saw in con-sequence of the judgment, as it respects mankind. On the other hand, with respect to the righteous (*o*), and in or-der to their being suitably rewarded, I saw a new hea-ven and a new earth brought into existence by the wisdom and power of God; for the present heaven and earth (as I related before, ver. 11) were passed away; as to their *exterior form* and *fashion*; and there was, in this new earth, no more sea. And [to pro-

3   ceed

TEXT.	PARAPHRASE.
	ceed now to a particular re-prefentation of the happy and glorious ftate of the faints]
2. *And I John faw the holy city, the New Jerufalem, coming down from God out of heaven, prepared as a bride adorned for her hufband.*	I faw the holy city, the New Jerufalem, defcending from God out of heaven, and it appeared in fplendor, like to that which is ufed at marriage folemnities.

NOTES *juftifying the foregoing* PARAPHRASE.

(a) *And them that fat upon them*, &c.] The original words, και εκαθισαν επ᾽ αυτους, και κριμα εδοθη αυτοις, are tranflated by fome, *and they, to whom judgment was given, fat upon them.* But the και before κριμα, according to this conftruction, will, as it appears to me, be fuperfluous and need-lefs : Whereas, it will retain its proper ufe and force as a *copulative*, if the fentence is rendered, *and they fat upon them, and judgment was given to them*; and thus tranflated, it will run quite fmooth and eafy, with the *fupply* in the *paraphrafe*; which kind of fupply is often neceffary, and often re-paired to, in all parts of the New Teftament.

(b) *The fouls of thofe who were beheaded.*] The literal tranflation of των πεπελεκισμενων is, *fecuri percufforum*, the *fmitten with the ax*; but the verfion

fion in our Bibles is more elegant, *the beheaded.*
Though it ought to be obferved here, the apoftle
John undoubtedly intended to include all who
had undergone *death* for the fake of Chrift, and
his religion, in what way foever it was brought
upon them. And it is for this reafon that the
generality of them, who underftand the *life* fpoken
of in the latter claufe of this verfe, in the *literal
fenfe*, confine it to the *martyrs*; imagining that
they will be diftinguifhed from all other good
men, by being raifed from the dead a *thoufand
years* before them. But there does not appear to
me a juft foundation for fuch an opinion from any
thing here related. The *grammatical* order and
conftruction of the fourth verfe, upon which this
opinion is built, is plainly thus. The apoftle
firft declares in *general*, that he faw thrones, and
that he faw thofe that fat upon them, with judicial
power given to them, without faying *particularly*
who they were. He then goes on to a *more
particular* reprefentation of the matter. *I faw,*
fays he, *the martyrs for the fake of Chrift; and
I faw thofe who had not worfhipped the beaft*, &c.
The *martyrs for the fake of Chrift*, and thofe
who had not worfhipped the beaft, feem to me
plainly diftinguifhed from each other. The apoftle
faw not only the *martyrs*, but *thefe alfo*. But
who are thefe who *had not worfhipped the beaft ?*
Plainly, all thofe *whofe names were written in the
book of life*, Chap. xiii. 8. And *thefe* take
in the *whole number* of thofe who *fhall not be
caft*

caſt into the lake of fire, Chap. xx. 15, that is, the *ſaints univerſally.* Beſides, one of the *characteriſtics* of thoſe whom the apoſtle John ſaw *living* and *reigning* with Chriſt is, that the *ſecond death ſhall have no power over them,* ver. 6; which is a privilege *common* to the *ſaints,* and not peculiar to the *martyrs.* Further, it is ſaid of the perſons, who ſhall live in this *millennium* ſtate, that they ſhall be " prieſts of God and of " Chriſt, and ſhall reign with him," ver. 6; which is another privilege not confined to *martyrs,* but extended to *all the ſaints.* Hence that ſong, Rev. i. 5, 6, and v. 9, 10. Moreover, it ought to be remembered, the general viſion, in the firſt clauſe of this verſe, *of thrones, and them that ſat upon them, having judicial power,* is ſo far from being an honour *appropriated* to *martyrs,* that it is *common* to the *ſaints,* according to the current ſtrain of ſcripture, which every where repreſents the happineſs of *good men,* in the coming world, under the emblem of a *crown, a crown of glory, a crown of righteouſneſs, an incorruptible crown.* And when our Saviour would deſcribe the *happineſs* of the *ſaints,* in the future ſtate, he does it in theſe words, to the man in the parable, who had made a wiſe improvement of his talents, Matt. xxv. 21, " Well done, good and " faithful ſervant, thou haſt been faithful over " a few things, I will make thee RULER over " many things : Enter thou into the joy of thy " Lord ;" which words, upon a like occaſion,

are

are repeated in the twenty-third verſe. So in this book of Revelation, chap. iii. 21, the promiſe to *him that overcometh* is, " to him I will grant to ſit " with me on my throne, even as I alſo overcame, " and am ſet down with my Father in his throne." Or, perhaps the apoſtle John may here have in view more *particularly*, the *honour* which will be done, not the *martyrs* only, but the *ſaints in general*, in their being, in ſome ſenſe, *aſſeſſors with Chriſt*, in the judgment of the world. And if this was his thought, it may be explained by 1 Cor. vi. 2, 3, " Do ye not know that the ſaints ſhall judge the " world?—Know ye not, that we ſhall judge " angels ?" It is obſervable, our Saviour, looking forward to the *reviviſcence* of the ſaints, ſays to his apoſtles, Matt. xix. 28, " Ye which have " followed me, even ye, in the REGENERATION," or time of the ſaints reigning in happy life, " ſhall " ſit upon twelve thrones, judging the twelve " tribes of Iſrael." By the foregoing text, it ſhould ſeem as though all the ſaints would, in like manner, but in a lower degree, ſit upon thrones, judging the world.—Upon the whole, there is no reaſon to think, but that the *ſaints in general*, and not the *martyrs in particular*, are the *perſons* who ſhall live and reign with Chriſt theſe thouſand years.

(*c*) *And they lived in their reſpective bodies.*] Dr. Whitby, Mr. Lowman from him, and many others, underſtand the *life* here ſpoken of, in a *figurative* ſenſe, as meaning nothing more than a *ſpiritual reſurrection* of the church, *a general and glorious*

glorious revival of the true spirit of Christianity, to continue a *thousand years*. It would require more room than would be proper to take up in a *note*, to examine what has been said to justify this departure from the *letter* of the apostle's words. I shall only observe, at present, in opposition to the *figurative*, and in support of the *literal* sense of this *life* and *reign with Christ*, that it is twice expresly called, in this very passage, the FIRST RESURRECTION. Now, as this *life* and *reign*, according to these expositors, are *subsequent* to the *destruction of Antichrist*, and *immediately preceding* the *conflagration*, *general resurrection*, and *judgment*, there can be *no other revival* of religion, *no other spiritual resurrection of a spiritually dead church*. Why then is it called the FIRST RESURRECTION ? Can there be a *first* without a *second*? If there is a *spiritual life* and *reign*, it is the *last* that ever will take place in the *present earth*; and would, for this reason, have undoubtedly been styled the *last*, not the *first resurrection*. Besides, according to this scheme of interpretation, how shall we account for the rise of GOG and MAGOG ? The *prophecy* compares this *rabble-rout* of men to the *sand of the sea* for *multitude* ; and it brings in also the *extraordinary* power of God, to preserve the saints from being overrun by them. Upon which I would ask, whether it is likely there should be such a *formidable appearance* of wicked men in that period of time, in which, according to these very expositors, there is to be the *greatest* and *most extensive* revival

5

of

of religion that ever took place in the world? One would think, *a thousand years* continuance of the *true spirit of Christianity* among both Jews and Gentiles, and in *all parts* of the earth, would render it impossible, that INSTANTLY upon the expiration of this term, there should be found *such swarms* of abandoned wicked men, as to compose the GOG and MAGOG here described. It in truth exceeds all belief! Especially, if it be remembered here, that the *coming of the Son of man,* (which, according to these expositors, will be at the end of these *thousand years)* is compared, by our Saviour, to the *coming on of the flood* in the days of Noah, on account of the *wickedness* that would be *universally prevalent.* His words are these, Matt. xxiv. 37, 38, 39, " As the days of " Noah were, so shall also the coming of the Son " of man be. For as in the days that were be- " fore the flood, they were eating, and drinking, " marrying, and giving in marriage, until the " day that Noah entered into the ark, and knew " not, until the flood came, and took them all " away: So shall also the coming of the Son " of man be." In like manner, he says, describing the *character* of the *time* in which he should come, Luke xviii. 8, " Shall he find faith on the " earth?" And the apostle Paul, speaking of this same *advent* of Christ, declares, 2 Theff. i. 7, 8, 9, that he " shall then be revealed in " flaming fire, taking vengeance on them that " know not God, and obey not the gospel of our " Lord

" Lord Jefus Chrift, who fhall be deftroyed with
" everlafting deftruction."—It is evident, from
thefe texts, that the world will be *horribly wicked*
at the coming of Chrift, and that he will come to
deftroy it for its wickednefs. How then can this
millennium immediately precede this coming of
Chrift, and for this end? Can it reafonably be
fuppofed, that the *pureft* and *beft ftate* of the world,
and for a *thoufand years* continuance, fhould be
that ftate of the world, which fhould immediately
precede the *coming of Chrift* to *deftroy* it, for its
abounding wickednefs? To me, thefe are infuperable objections againft the *figurative* interpretation
of this *life* and *reign with Chrift.*

(d) *A thoufand years without any attempt, &c.*]
As *a thoufand years* are here particularly mentioned,
it has been generally thought, in former ages, as
well as more lately, that this is the *precife period* of
the happy ftate of the faints here fpoken of;
which feems to me an evident miftake; and it
may have been a means of hindering expofitors
from perceiving the true meaning of the *prophecy*
this *period* relates to. I fuppofe a *thoufand years*
are here mentioned, for no other reafon than this,
that *Satan* fhould be *fo long* confined and bound,
and *wicked* men *fo long* reftrained from making
any attempts at all to difturb the happinefs of the
righteous. For it is plain, as *this reign* of the
faints will be in the *paradifaic earth,* [See the
foregoing *order* and *connexion* of events] that it
fhall continue εις τους αιωνας των αιωνων, *for ages of*
ages,

ages, chap. xxii. 5 ; which will readily be allowed to mean a duration much longer than *a thousand years.*

(e) *The rest of the dead,* &c.] If the apostle John is speaking in the foregoing verse of *literal life,* as I imagine he is, (see note *(c)*) he must mean by the *dead* here, the *literally dead.* Dr. Burnet and others, who are in the scheme of a *literal* resurrection of *martyrs only* to reign with Christ *a thousand years,* suppose that, by *the rest of the dead,* we must understand *all the wicked,* and *those* among the *saints,* who were not called to lay down their lives for the sake of Christ. But it appears to me, the *wicked dead* are the only persons here meant; as also, that the *life,* it is said, they *lived not till the thousand years were expired,* is to be interpreted of *that sort of life* which had before been described, that is to say, of life connected with *a reign with Christ as kings and priests* ; the unavoidable implication of which is, that *wicked men,* AFTER the completion of this *thousand years,* though not *before,* MAY THUS LIVE WITH CHRIST. It may be worthy of special observation here, the supposition that *wicked men may live* BEFORE the expiration of this *period,* is not at all inconsistent with the affirmation, which here says, *they lived not till after it* ; provided the term *life* is understood *differently* in the *supposition* from what it is in the *affirmation.* My meaning is, there is no *contradiction,* not the shadow of an *inconsistency,* between this *affirmation,* namely, *the*

C c   *wicked*

wicked lived not till thefe thoufand years were com-
pleted, meaning hereby, they *lived not a life of*
happinefs as kings and priefts with Chrift ; and this
fuppofition, namely, *the wicked may live before thefe*
thoufand years are expired, meaning hereby, not a
happy life with Chrift, but *a life of mifery with evil*
angels. Thefe two forts of life fo obvioufly and
effentially *differ* from each other, that they may
refpectively be *affirmed* and *denied,* in the fame propofition, at the fame time, and of the fame perfons. Accordingly, it is here faid, that the *righte-*
ous only among the dead, *lived* and *reigned with*
Chrift, within the *thoufand years,* and that the *reft*
of the dead, that is, the *wicked dead,* did not any of
them THUS LIVE AND REIGN WITH CHRIST, TILL
AFTER THE COMPLETION OF THIS PERIOD. Nor
does it from hence follow, that the *wicked* may not,
at the beginning of this *period,* (as is the truth of
the cafe) be delivered from the *firft death,* fo as to
be put under circumftances of dying the *fecond*
death. There is no inconfiftency in this, with
their *not living as the righteous live* in happinefs
with Chrift, till the *thoufand years* are finifhed.
This fcheme of interpretation I take to be the
only one that will make *this paffage confiftent*
with the other parts of the *fame prophecy.* It will
accordingly be further explained, and enlarged
upon, and fupported, under the following note,
which the reader is defired carefully to compare
with this.

(*f*) *This is the firft refurrection of this fort.*] The
great

great queſtion to be decided here is, What is the true ground or reaſon of the epithet FIRST, applied to the word *reſurrection* ? And if I may ſpeak my mind freely, I cannot but think, the *true reaſon* has not been perceived by expoſitors, or any Chriſtian writers, ſo far as I have been able to conſult them. And to this it may be owing that they are ſo inconſiſtent with each other, and with themſelves alſo. But, without multiplying words, or enlarging upon what others have ſaid about this matter, I would briefly propoſe my own ſentiments.

And *firſt*—I would ſay *negatively*, this *reſurrection* of the ſaints is not diſtinguiſhed by the epithet FIRST, to inſinuate, as though the *wicked* ſhould not be raiſed from the dead within this period of a *thouſand years.* For it is evident, from the current ſtrain of the New-Teſtament books, that the *puniſhment of the wicked*, and the *reward of the righteous*, will commence *at one and the ſame time*, namely, at the end of the world, or the finiſhing of the preſent diſpenſation of the kingdom of God. The texts to this purpoſe are *numerous*, and ſo *explicit* as to admit of no diſpute.—Matt. iii. 12.
" Whoſe fan is in his hand, and he will through-
" ly purge his floor, and gather his wheat into
" the garner, but he will burn up the chaff with
" unquenchable fire." It is here evidently ſuppoſed, that the viſible church conſiſts both of *ſaints* and *ſinners* at preſent; but that the time is coming, when Chriſt ſhall make a ſeparation

C c 2   between

between them, and that when he does this, he will *punish the wicked, while he rewards the righteous.* This is more fully and particularly expressed in the parable of the *wheat* and the *tares,* Matt. xiii. from the 24th to the 31st verse, the conclusion of which parable is in these emphatical words; " Let both grow together until the harvest ; " and in the time of the harvest, I will say to the " reapers, Gather ye together first the tares, and " bind them in bundles to burn them : But ga- " ther the wheat into my barn." And, that we might be at no loss about the meaning of these words, the explanation of them, as given by our Saviour, is this ;——" The *good seed* are the *chil-* " *dren of the kingdom* ; the *tares* are the *children* " *of the wicked one* ; the *harvest* is the *end of the* " *world* ; the *reapers* are the *angels* : As therefore " the tares are gathered and burnt in the fire, so " shall it be in the end of the world : The Son " of Man shall send forth his angels, and they " shall gather all things that offend, and shall " cast them into a furnace of fire ; there shall " be wailing and gnashing of teeth. THEN shall " the righteous shine forth as the sun, in the king- " dom of their Father." And the explanation of the parable of the *Net,* contained in the 47th and 48th verses of this chapter, is this ;—" So shall " it be at the end of the world ; the angels shall " come forth, and sever the wicked from among " the just, and shall cast them into a furnace of " fire." ver. 49, 50. The same truth is obvi-

ously

oufly fuggefted in the parable of the *Virgins,*
chap. xxv. from the 1ft to the 13th verfe; and
in the parable of the man travelling into a far
country, the conclufion of which is, "The Lord
" faid to him that had improved his talents, Well
" done, good and faithful fervant, enter thou into
" the joy of thy Lord." ver. 23. And to him
that had made no improvement of his talent,
" Caft ye the unprofitable fervant into outer dark-
" nefs." ver. 30. And it is, in the moft exprefs
language, declared by our Saviour himfelf, that
when he comes in the glory of his Father, with the
holy angels, he will fay to the righteous, " Come,
" ye bleffed," &c. ver. 34; and to the wicked,
" Depart, ye curfed," &c. ver. 41: And accordingly, both thefe fentences are put directly in execution, " and thefe fhall go away into everlafting
" punifhment; but the righteous into life eter-
" nal." ver. 46. And the apoftle Paul, in fo many
words, declares, that when *Chrift* fhall be revealed
from heaven, at the great day of judgment, it fhall
be to " take vengeance on the wicked, and to be
" glorified in his faints," 2 Theff. i. 8, 10. And,
to put it out of all doubt, that *the punifhment of
the wicked,* and *the reward of the faints,* fhall commence at the fame period, he introduces the words
by faying, as in the 6th and 7th verfes, " It is
" a righteous thing with God to recompenfe tri-
" bulation to them that trouble you, and to them
" who are troubled, reft."—But it would be endlefs to tranfcribe all the paffages of the New

Teftament,

Teſtament, which directly lead us to think, that
the *wicked* ſhall be *puniſhed* at the SAME TIME that
the *virtuous* are *rewarded.* Now, this being an evident ſcripture truth, the obvious certain conſequence is, that *they* muſt at the *ſame time* alſo, be
delivered *from the power of the grave.* For it
is impoſſible their *puniſhment* ſhould commence
with the reward of the righteous, if their reſurrection is poſtponed a *thouſand years.* Accordingly,
our Saviour ſeems to have put this matter out of
all reaſonable doubt; for, as he connects the *ſalvation* of the *righteous* with the *damnation* of the
wicked, in point of time, ſo does he their *reſurrection*, in that obſervable paſſage, John v. 28, 29,
" The hour is coming, in the which all that are in
" their graves ſhall hear his voice, and ſhall come
" forth: They that have done good, to the reſur-
" rection of life, and they that have done evil, to
" the reſurrection of damnation." It appears then,
upon the whole, that, at the end of the world, or
the ſecond coming of Chriſt, the *wicked*, as well as
the *righteous*, ſhall be *raiſed from the dead.* The
reſurrection of the *ſaints* therefore, ſpoken of by
the apoſtle John, is not called the FIRST *reſurrection* MERELY on account of their *deliverance* from
the *power of death.* For the *wicked*, in this
ſenſe, will be *raiſed to life* as well as the *righteous*, within the term of theſe *thouſand years*: And
thus we are led to conceive of the matter in this
very *prophecy* itſelf; ſee the foregoing account of
the *order of events* in theſe chapters,

Secondly,—

Secondly,—But to speak more particularly, and *positively.* The resurrection of the saints is called the FIRST resurrection, because it is the *first general resurrection* of men that will secure them from *dying any more*; instate them in *immortality*, and make them happy in a *glorious reign with Christ*, in the *new heaven and earth.* Accordingly, this seems to be the explanation of its meaning in the following verse. For the *partners* in *this resurrection* are pronounced *blessed.* And why? Not because their deliverance from death, considered simply in itself, precedes that of the wicked; [for the *wicked* also, as we have seen, shall, in this sense, be delivered from death,] but because the *second death shall have no power over them,* as it will over the *wicked*; and because they shall be *kings and priests, and reign with Christ a thousand years,* without an attempt, from any quarter, to disturb their happiness; and after that *for ages of ages,* chap. xxii. 5. It seems plain to me, that the apostle Paul had this *first resurrection,* which the apostle John is here speaking of, in view, when he wrote the fifteenth chapter of his First Epistle to the Corinthians. But this we have considered already.

As to a *second resurrection,* it is true, John hath said nothing about it, in plain language. But, by speaking of a *first,* he has, in the *general,* given us reason to hope for the SECOND, the *manner, time,* and *circumstances* of which, though hid from us now, may hereafter be revealed. Upon the whole,

by

by the FIRST *refurreƈtion*, the apoſtle John could
not mean *fimple deliverance from death*, that death,
which all men are fubjeƈted to in confequence of
the lapfe, becaufe *mankind univerfally*, *bad* as well
as *good*, will be *thus raifed* at *Chriſt's fecond coming :*
Whereas, the *righteous*, they who are made fo in
this prefent world, and they only, are the FIRST
among mankind, who ſhall be so RAISED to life,
as to *reign with Chriſt in glory* and honour.   And
their refurreƈtion, THUS to reign with him, is called
the FIRST RESURRECTION, becaufe the FIRST OF
THIS KIND : Obvioufly and naturally implying,
that there will be a SECOND RESURRECTION of
the SAME SORT, that is to fay, that the *wicked*,
after the fecond death, being previoufly fitted for
it, ſhall be *raifed alfo to reign in glorious life*, in
fome ſtill future difpenfation of God.

(*g*) *And feparated or diſtinguiſhed.*] Perfons, as
well as things, are called *holy* in the fcriptures, on
account of their being *feparated from a common*,
and fet apart for, *and devoted to*, *a fpiritual ufe* and
fervice.   It would be a mifpending of labour to
point out inſtances to this purpofe, they are fo frequently to be met with.   And this feems to be
the fenfe of the word *holy*, αγιος, in this place.
They are reprefented not only as *happy*, but *feparated*, and *diſtinguiſhed* from the reſt of mankind,
being partakers of the *firſt refurreƈtion*.   And with
good reafon, for, as it follows, the *fecond death
hath no power over them*.

(*h*) *Gog and Magog*.] Expofitors have found it
vaſtly

vaftly difficult to point out the perfons here defcribed under the character of *Gog and Magog.*
And, upon every fcheme of interpretation I have
met with, infuperable objections attend their *rife*
and *numbers.* We have already feen (note *(c)*) the
impoffibility of ever getting together fuch a body
of wicked men, upon *their* plan, who give into a
figurative fenfe of the *firft refurrection.* And the
impoffibility is as great, if not greater, upon the
fcheme of Dr. Burnet, who begins the *millennium*
AFTER the *conflagration,* but BEFORE the *refurrection*
of the *wicked.* He can, upon his fcheme, no better
account for the *origin* of GOG and MAGOG *than
from the flime of the ground, and the heat of the fun,*
as *brute creatures,* he fays, *were generated at firft :*
An account too romantic to deferve a ferious confutation. It evidently carries with it the marks
of an *invented hypothefis* to ferve a prefent turn.
Though I wonder he fhould fix on one that was
rather *fhocking* than *plaufible,* upon the bare propofal of it.

Perhaps, the true reafon of the *difficulty* of ac-
counting for the rife of *Gog* and *Magog* is owing
to the miftake learned men have fallen into with
refpect to the *time* of their appearance. They all
of them place their appearance BEFORE the *general
refurrection and judgment.* Whereas, if they gave
it a date POSTERIOR to thefe events, and did not
look for them on this fide the grave, all difficulties
would at once vanifh, and an eafy, intelligible
account might be given both of their *rife, numbers,*

and

and *spirit*, fitting them to engage in the attempt here described. For let it be observed, the *multitudes* that make up the collective body, signified by *Gog* and *Magog*, perfectly fall in with the scripture representation of the *numbers* who, in consequence of the general judgment, will be obliged to live in misery. And where should they live but on *this earth*? It is at least as reasonable to think, that *this earth* will be the place where they will live in torment, as any other place that can be conceived. This earth, it is true, in some *other form*, will be the place where the *righteous* are to *reign in happy life*. But there is no difficulty in supposing, that the *conflagration*, under the all-wise and powerful government of God, may operate very differently upon *the earth*, making it, in one part, a *hell* for the *wicked*, and in another, a *heaven* for the *righteous*. And upon this supposition, which has nothing harsh or hard in it, there will, at the end of the *thousand years* here pointed out, be a *sufficient number* of men upon the earth, and with *dispositions* exactly fitted for the *attempt*, they, through the influence of the Devil, engage in. What then should hinder us from thinking, that *these wicked men* are the *Gog* and *Magog* here spoken of? Especially if it be remembered, that the *time* of their assembling to invade the saints is *posterior* to the general resurrection and judgment; as may be collected from the preceding notes, and further evidenced by succeeding ones.

(*i*) *Shall be tormented.*] See note pages 294, 295.

(*k*) *To*

(k) To be yet more particular.] The critical reader
will eafily perceive, by the manner in which I have
introduced the *vifion* in the 11th verfe, and onwards, that I look upon it as a *continuation* of the
vifion which was begun in the three firft verfes,
but interrupted for a while, that the apoftle might
exhibit, in one view, all he had to fay upon the
head of *Satan's* being *bound* and *loofened.* What
he has offered upon this head begins with the
4th, and ends with the 10th verfe ; and is intended
to give an account of the *events themfelves* relating
to the fubject he is upon, not the *order of them.*
This feems to be rather left with the reader to
adjuft, upon having carefully looked over the
whole prophetic vifion, as here reprefented. Expofitors have ftrangely taken it for granted, that it
was the defign of the *apoftle*, in thefe verfes, to
point out not only the *events themfelves* here fpoken
of, but the order in which they fhould take place ;
giving us to underftand, that the *thoufand years*
reign of the faints, the rife of *Gog* and *Magog*, and
their deftruction, would precede, in point of time,
the appearing of the Son of Man, the general refurrection and judgment, and future ftate of retribution : Whereas, it fhould feem plain, that *thefe
verfes* were brought in for no other reafon, than to
comprehend in one view, the whole of what be-
longed to one fubject. Upon which fuppofition,
the *order* of events could not, in the nature of
things, but be neglected, or rather anticipated to
make the account compleat. And in this view

of

of *thefe verfes*, which is quite eafy and natural, the *whole feries* of events in the *vifion*, which is continued to the end of the *Apocalypfe*, runs fmooth ; while, upon any other fuppofition, it will be perplexed, and the events rendered incapable of a reconciliation with each other. If the *thoufand years* reign of the faints, and the rife of *Gog* and *Magog*, precede the *general refurrection*, all the *difficulties* that have been mentioned, as accompanying either Dr. Burnet's fcheme, or the *figurative* one of others, will take place. Whereas thefe difficulties are entirely avoided by the plan of interpretation here propofed. Befides, the *life* and *reign* of the faints, fpoken of in *thefe verfes*, is the *fame life* and *reign* with that in the *paradifaic* earth defcribed chapters xxi. xxii. which, if it be true (as we fhall fee that it is, note *(o)*) makes it certain, that the *events themfelves* in thefe verfes, not the *order* of them, are what the apoftle had in view ; and what we are principally to regard, as has been faid.

(l) The form of the earth and heaven.] This we may reafonably take to be the meaning of the *heaven and earth's paffing away, to be no more* ; for according to the apoftle Peter, who has particularly treated of this matter, in his *fecond epiftle, third chapter,* the *form only* of the heaven and earth will be changed by the *conflagration.* Its *prefent form* fhall *be no more.* It fhall *pafs away*, that it may be fucceeded by one that is *quite new.*

(m) Were judged in a fair equal manner.] This feems to be the thought intended to be communicated

nicated by the *particular mode of diction* here ufed. See Lowman, as to the *reafon* why *books* are mentioned, and the *book of life* in particular.

(n) Death and the grave.] If the *paraphrafe* of this 14th verfe does not give its true fenfe, it is, I confefs, beyond me to underftand its meaning. The common interpretation is, *Death* and *Hades* were entirely deftroyed. They *were caft into the lake of fire*, that is, they were brought abfolutely to an end. *Death* fhall be no more ; there fhall be *no more fuch a place as Hades.* But two things feem to me infuperable objections to this interpretation. 1. It is not true in fact: For the wicked, after they are raifed from the dead, *fhall die again*, as we have repeatedly fhewn. And 2dly, if the *total deftruction* of *Death* and *Hades* is the thing meant, when they are faid to be caft into the *lake of fire* ; how comes it to pafs, that *total deftruction* is not the thing meant, when the wicked are faid, in the fame words, to *be caft into the lake of fire?* We may make words fignify juft what we pleafe, if we may underftand them in *contradictory fenfes*, in one and the fame paragraph. And two fenfes cannot be more contradictory to each other than *annihilation, ceafing to be*, and *never-ceafing life, exifting without end.*—I fhall only add here, the fenfe given in the *paraphrafe* perfectly falls in with the thread of the apoftle's difcourfe, and makes out an eafy and pertinent connection. For having, in the preceding verfes, given an account of men's being judged according to their works ; what more na-

tural

tural than that he fhould proceed to fpeak of their *refpective ftates* in confequence of this judgment? And thus he is made to fpeak in the *paraphrafe*; beginning with the *wicked*, and afterwards going on with the righteous. And it is the truth of the *thing*, which makes it more likely to be the truth of this *place*, that *fuch numbers* of wicked men will be *caft into the lake of fire*, that *Death* and *Hades*, upon the refurrection and judgment, may, in a fenfe, be faid to be *caft into it*.

(o) *I faw on the other hand.*] It appears to me evident, beyond all reafonable difpute, that this 21ft chapter is connected with the 20th in the manner pointed out in the *paraphrafe*. And, if the *ftate* here defcribed is confequent upon, and the refult of the *general judgment*, as it concerns *good men*, it is eafy to fee, that their *happy exiftence*, after the refurrection, will be upon *this earth*. ' It ' feems to me (to ufe the words of Mr. Hallett) ' that the reward of good men, in the future ftate, ' will be a reducing them to that happy ftate ' which *Adam* loft by his fall, together with the ' addition of fome other glorious circumftances of ' blifs. While good men are afcended up in the ' clouds to meet their Lord in the air, and the ' tranfactions of the laft judgment are carrying ' on, *this earth*, by the power of God, fhall be ' brought back to the fame ftate it was in before ' the fall; and will be a *paradife all over*. [*I* ' fhould fay, fo far as is neceffary to make it a ' proper feat for the faints to live happily]. As

I   ' in

' in the *old paradise* there was a *tree of life*, of
' which, if our firſt parents had always eaten, they
' would have *lived for ever*, Gen. iii. 22, 23; ſo
' on the *new earth*, there ſhall be a *tree of life*,
' and *waters of life*, Rev. xxii. 1, 2. And what-
' ever eaſe, peace and ſecurity, and happineſs, man
' enjoyed in *paradiſe*, the ſame ſhall good men
' partake of in the *New Jeruſalem:* Nay, in ſome
' reſpects, it will *exceed* the old paradiſe. There
' was *night* in *paradiſe*, Gen. i. 31. *The evening*
' *and the morning were the ſixth day.* But in the
' *New Jeruſalem*, there ſhall be *no night*, Rev.
' xxi. 25. *The city ſhall have no need of the ſun, and*
' *of the moon, that they ſhould ſhine into it* ; *for the*
' *glory of God*, the *Shechinah*, a bright cloud of
' light repreſenting the peculiar preſence of God,
' ſhall hang over it, and *enlighten it, and the*
' *Lamb ſhall be the light of it*, ver. 23. — This
' account of the *place* where good men ſhall dwell
' *for ever* [I would ſay for *ages of ages*], after
' the reſurrection, is of great uſe to give men an
' idea of the future ſtate. I own, I take St.
' John's account of the *new earth* to be, in moſt
' particulars, a *literal* deſcription, which is to be
' underſtood in a *literal ſenſe.* And then, it is
' poſſible for us to have a notion of a *future ſtate.*
' But what notion can we have of it, according
' to the common way of men's talking about it ?
' Where can the heaven be of which they ſpeak ?
' In the boundleſs ſpace that ſurrounds us ? We
' know of nothing there but *ſun, moon, fixed ſtars,*
' *earth,*

' *earth*, and *comets*. Neither of thefe, except the
' *earth*, can be thought fit to be the habitation of
' good men in the future ftate. In fuch a place,
' in the *new earth*, St. John and St. Peter fay,
' good men fhall dwell. Why then fhould we
' feek for another *unknown place*, of which the
' fcripture never fpeaks?—This is a very eafy
' and agreeable notion of the ftate of good men
' in the world to come. We may now form fome
' idea of it, by comparing it with the prefent ftate.
' We may conceive of good men as living in bo-
' dies, but become fpiritual, glorious, and immor-
' tal, upon a new earth, where they will feel no
' more heat or cold, pain or uneafinefs, where
' they will meet with no enemies, ftorms, or dan-
' gers, and where they fhall fpend all their dura-
' tion in love and happinefs." *Notes on particular
texts*, &c. Pages 201, 202, 203.

But what I would *principally* obferve with reference to this *paradifaic ftate* of good men, in confequence of the *general judgment*, is, that it is the
fame life with *that* fpoken of in the fourth and
fixth verfes of the twentieth chapter. Some things
have been faid in the foregoing notes, in juftification of this thought. I would here add fome further hints to the like purpofe. Let it be obferved
then, the OVERCOMERS, in thefe *three firft* chapters
of the *Apocalypfe*, are certainly to be ranked among
thofe that were *beheaded for the witnefs of Jefus*, or
thofe who *had not worfhipped the beaft*, concerning
whom it is faid, chap. xx. 4. " they lived and
" reigned

" reigned with Chrift." Now, moft of the fpecial promifes made to thofe OVERCOMERS, are made in thofe very words which are the *grand characteriftic* of the *paradifaic ftate,* defcribed in the twenty-firft and twenty-fecond chapters. The *promife* to him that *overcometh* is, in chap. ii. ver. 7, " that " he fhall eat of the tree of life, which is in the " midft of the paradife of God." And one of the defcriptions of the *New Jerufalem* on the *new earth* is, that " in the midft of the ftreet of it, " there was the tree of life," chap. xxii. 2. Agreeably to which defcription, it is declared in the fourteenth verfe, " Bleffed are they that do his " commandments, that they may have a right to " the tree of life." The *promife* to him that *overcometh,* in chap. ii. ver. 11, is, that " he fhall " not be hurt of the fecond death;" the very thing wherein *their* bleffednefs is made to confift, who are partakers of the *firft refurrection,* or *happy life,* fpoken of chap. xx. 4, 6. And this *fame bleffednefs* is one of the glorious *characteriftics* of the *paradifaic ftate* defcribed in the twenty-firft and twenty-fecond chapters; for it is faid, chap. xxi. ver. 4, " there fhall be no more death." The promife, chap. iii. 12, to him that *overcometh,* is, " I will " write upon him the name of my God, and the " name of the city of my God, which is the New " Jerufalem, which cometh down out of heaven, " from my God;" and it is faid of thofe, who are to live on the *paradifaic earth,* chap. xxii. 4, that " the name of God fhall be on their fore-
D d
" heads."

" heads." And the grand difcriminating privilege of this earth is, that the " New Jerufalem fhall " defcend down from God out of heaven upon it," chap. xxi. 2. and 10.——The promife to him that *overcometh*, chap. iii. 21, is, " to him I will grant " to fit with me on my throne, even as I alfo over- " came, and am fet down with my Father in " his throne :" and one of the defcriptive marks of the *New Jerufalem ftate* is, " the throne of God " and the Lamb fhall be in it," chap. xxii. 3.

Two things have led expofitors to think, that the *happy life* of the faints fpoken of chap. xx. ver. 4, 6, is *different* from, and *previous* to, *that* defcribed in the twenty-firft and twenty-fecond chapters. One is, that the *former* of thefe lives is diftinguifhed from the *latter* by a number of *intervening events.* But there is no need of fuppof-ing this, as may be feen, *note (k).* The other is, that the life, fpoken of in chap. xx. ver. 4, 6, is connected with the period of a *thoufand years*, whereas the *life* defcribed in the twenty-firft and twenty fecond chapters, is faid to be εις τους αιωνας των αιωνων, for *ages of ages.* This alfo has been accounted for, note *(a)* ; to which I would here further add, that *a thoufand years* might be parti-cularly fpecified, chap. xx. ver. 4, not only for the reafon before affigned, but becaufe this was the *period* that muft run out, before *the reft of the dead*, that is; the *wicked dead*, could any of them live as *kings and priefts with Chrift* ; plainly infinuating, that, at the expiration of *this term*, the *wicked* might

might thus *reign in happy life.* And this is a good and fufficient reafon, why this period of a *thoufand years* fhould be particularly mentioned. And, if it was mentioned for *this reafon,* not to infinuate that the faints fhould reign no longer than a *thoufand years,* but that they fhould reign this period without any attempt to moleft them, and before any of the *wicked* fhould be admitted to reign with them, there is not the leaft inconfiftency between their *reigning a thoufand years,* according to the *prophecy,* and their going on to reign εις τους αιωνας των αιωνων, for *ages of ages.* This fame *long period,* it is obfervable, is the very *fpace of duration,* that terminates the *utmoft length* of the *longeft punifhment,* which any of the fons of Adam fhall be obliged to fuffer. And as the *duration* of the *happy ftate* of the *faints* thus coincides with the *utmoft length* of the *future mifery,* with refpect to many of the *wicked,* I fuppofe, it contains the *period,* in which all enemies fhall be fubdued, and the way prepared, under the mediatory government of Chrift, for the coming on of that ftill *more glorious period,* when " God fhall be all in all," conformably to what has been faid upon 1 Cor. xv. 24—28 verfes, which the reader is defired to turn to, and compare with the difcourfe in this place.

The

The Application of the above PARAPHRASE *and* NOTES *to the present* ARGUMENT.

A few words only will be neceſſary to ſhew the pertinency and force of what has been offered above, in ſupport of the general argument now under conſideration. For, if we have given the true meaning of the phraſe, " the reſt of the dead " lived not till the thouſand years were expired," it is plain, that upon the completion of this period, the *wicked dead* MAY, ſo many of them as ſhall be prepared for it, be admitted into the *New Jeruſalem*, to *reign in life as kings and prieſts with Chriſt.* And, if we have given the juſt import of the word FIRST, applied to the reſurrection of the ſaints, it is plain alſo, that there will be a SECOND RESURRECTION, that is to ſay, a reſurrection from the the *ſecond death*, a reſurrection from the death that is effected by the *torments of hell*, to a *happy reign with Chriſt in life.* And perhaps there may be *other reſurrections* ſtill. Wicked men may not be ſubdued, till they have have again and again, in this and the other form of exiſtence, ſuffered torments that ſhall end in DEATH: The reſult of which ſhall finally be, their *reſurrection to reign in life for ever.* An aſtoniſhing thought this! We may well break forth in words of admiration, and ſay, " O " the depth of the wiſdom and knowledge of

I   " God!

" God! How unfearchable are his judgments,
" and his ways paſt finding out!"

Mr. Whiſton having ſaid, concerning Origen's
hopes of the delivery of all ſinners from the *torments* of *hell*; nay, of their admiſſion at laſt into
heaven, ' It would be a moſt acceptable piece of
' news to me to find ſome juſt and ſure founda-
' tion for ſuch hopes in the ſacred writings; as
' being very deſirous of the ſalvation of all God's
' rational creatures,' [*Eternity of Hell Torments
conſidered,* page 131]; I ſay, having obſerved this,
he further remarks, page 133, ' All I can ſee any
' hope for is *future to the world to come,* and to
' the *next age,* after the deſtruction of the bodies
' of the wicked in *Gehenna,* at the general reſur-
' rection. I mean, as the *Prophet Eſdras* ſeems
' to hint, that there may be, in the utmoſt bowels
' of compaſſion of the Almighty, *another reſurrec-
' tion,* and *another time of trial allotted,* to thoſe
' miſerable creatures ſomewhere, in which many
' or all of them may poſſibly be recovered, and
' ſaved at laſt by the infinite indulgence and love
' of their Creator.' Mr. Whiſton does not appear, from any of his writings, that I have ſeen,
to have perceived that the ſcripture any where
gave a hint of *ſuch a reſurrection,* and *ſuch a time
of trial.* But if we have juſtly interpreted this
paſſage in the *Apocalypſe,* what that gentleman
has conjectured as a *thing poſſible,* we may pronounce a *doctrine* of *revelation.* And I am the rather inclined to think, the interpretation we have

given

given of the above scripture is just, because it so perfectly coincides with the *general doctrines* illustrated in these papers. And so far was it from any previous bias, that I fell into these sentiments, that I entered upon the study of the *Apocalypse*, strongly prepossessed in favour of another sense of *this prophecy*. And I was gradually and insensibly brought off from it, and settled in this, by finding it impossible to make out a consistent meaning, according to any other scheme of interpretation.

F I N I S.

DAT

GAYLORD